Blockchain Technology and Computational Excellence for Society 5.0

Shahnawaz Khan
University College of Bahrain, Bahrain

Mohammad Haider Syed
Saudi Electronic University, Saudi Arabia

Rawad Hammad
University of East London, UK

Aisha Fouad Bushager
University of Bahrain, Bahrain

A volume in the Advances
in Computer and Electrical
Engineering (ACEE) Book Series

Published in the United States of America by
    IGI Global
    Engineering Science Reference (an imprint of IGI Global)
    701 E. Chocolate Avenue
    Hershey PA, USA 17033
    Tel: 717-533-8845
    Fax: 717-533-8661
    E-mail: cust@igi-global.com
    Web site: http://www.igi-global.com

Library of Congress Cataloging-in-Publication Data

Names: Khan, Shahnawaz, editor. | Syed, Mohammad Haider, 1976- editor. | Hammad,
   Rawad, 1981- editor. | Bushager, Aisha Fouad, 1985- editor.
Title: Blockchain technology and computational excellence for society 5.0 /
   Shahnawaz Khan, Mohammad Haider Syed, Rawad Hammad, and Aisha Fouad Bushager,
   editors.
Description: Hershey, PA : Engineering Science Reference, an imprint of IGI
   Global, [2022] | Includes bibliographical references and index. |
   Summary: "This book primarily focuses on the advent of Blockchain
   technology and how it essentially helps the reader to understand the
   concept as to how it can be useful in various walks of life like
   finance, insurance, voting, etc"-- Provided by publisher.
Identifiers: LCCN 2021031895 (print) | LCCN 2021031896 (ebook) | ISBN
   9781799883821 (h/c) | ISBN 9781799883838 (s/c) | ISBN 9781799883845
   (ebook)
Subjects: LCSH: Blockchains (Databases)--Social aspects. | Society 5.0.
Classification: LCC QA76.9.B56 B5635 2022 (print) | LCC QA76.9.B56
   (ebook) | DDC 005.74--dc23
LC record available at https://lccn.loc.gov/2021031895
LC ebook record available at https://lccn.loc.gov/2021031896

This book is published in the IGI Global book series Advances in Computer and Electrical Engineering (ACEE) (ISSN: 2327-039X; eISSN: 2327-0403)

British Cataloguing in Publication Data
A Cataloguing in Publication record for this book is available from the British Library.

All work contributed to this book is new, previously-unpublished material.
The views expressed in this book are those of the authors, but not necessarily of the publisher.

For electronic access to this publication, please contact: eresources@igi-global.com.

Advances in Computer and Electrical Engineering (ACEE) Book Series

Srikanta Patnaik
SOA University, India

ISSN:2327-039X
EISSN:2327-0403

MISSION

The fields of computer engineering and electrical engineering encompass a broad range of interdisciplinary topics allowing for expansive research developments across multiple fields. Research in these areas continues to develop and become increasingly important as computer and electrical systems have become an integral part of everyday life.

The **Advances in Computer and Electrical Engineering (ACEE) Book Series** aims to publish research on diverse topics pertaining to computer engineering and electrical engineering. **ACEE** encourages scholarly discourse on the latest applications, tools, and methodologies being implemented in the field for the design and development of computer and electrical systems.

COVERAGE

- Computer Science
- Microprocessor Design
- Applied Electromagnetics
- Electrical Power Conversion
- VLSI Design
- Power Electronics
- Qualitative Methods
- VLSI Fabrication
- Optical Electronics
- Algorithms

IGI Global is currently accepting manuscripts for publication within this series. To submit a proposal for a volume in this series, please contact our Acquisition Editors at Acquisitions@igi-global.com or visit: http://www.igi-global.com/publish/.

Titles in this Series

For a list of additional titles in this series, please visit: http://www.igi-global.com/book-series/

Handbook of Research on Advances and Applications of Fuzzy Sets and Logic
Said Broumi (Faculty of Science Ben M'Sik, University Hassan II, Morocco)
Engineering Science Reference • © 2022 • 450pp • H/C (ISBN: 9781799879794) • US $395.00

Handbook of Research on 5G Networks and Advancements in Computing, Electronics, and Electrical Engineering
Augustine O. Nwajana (University of Greenwich, UK) and Isibor Kennedy Ihianle (Nottingham Trent University, UK)
Engineering Science Reference • © 2021 • 522pp • H/C (ISBN: 9781799869924) • US $295.00

Emerging Nanotechnology Applications in Electrical Engineering
Ahmed Thabet Mohamed (Aswan University, Egypt)
Engineering Science Reference • © 2021 • 318pp • H/C (ISBN: 9781799885368) • US $225.00

Modeling and Applications of Solar Photovoltaic Thermal Technology
Chandra Shekhar Malvi (Madhav Institute of Technology & Science, India) and Siddhartha Kosti (Rajkiya Engineering College, India)
Engineering Science Reference • © 2021 • 315pp • H/C (ISBN: 9781799879169) • US $225.00

Hydrogen Fuel Cell Technology for Stationary Applications
Gheorghe Badea (Technical University of Cluj-Napoca, Romania) Raluca-Andreea Felseghi (Ștefan cel Mare University of Suceava, Romania) and Ioan Așchilean (Technical University of Cluj-Napoca, Romania)
Engineering Science Reference • © 2021 • 332pp • H/C (ISBN: 9781799849452) • US $215.00

IGI Global
PUBLISHER of TIMELY KNOWLEDGE

701 East Chocolate Avenue, Hershey, PA 17033, USA
Tel: 717-533-8845 x100 • Fax: 717-533-8661
E-Mail: cust@igi-global.com • www.igi-global.com

Table of Contents

Foreword xiv

Preface xvi

Section 1
Blockchain Fundamentals

Chapter 1
Blockchain Technology in Ecosystems 1
 Sidhu Sharma, Sri Venkateshwara University, Gajraulla, India
 Mohammad Haider Syed, Saudi Electronic University, Saudi Arabia
 Shahnawaz Khan, Torocs Consultancy Services, India

Chapter 2
Blockchain Technology: Principles and Algorithms 16
 Mohammad Khalid Imam Rahmani, Saudi Electronic University, Saudi
  Arabia

Chapter 3
Blockchain Primer: Introduction to Blockchain Foundations and
Implementation 28
 Mohammad Amin Kuhail, Zayed University, UAE
 Sujith S. Mathew, Zayed University, UAE
 Rawad Hammad, East London University, UK
 Mohamed Bahja, University of Birmingham, UK

Chapter 4
Blockchain: A Disruptive Technology...48
 Arish Sidiqqui, University of East London, UK
 Kazi Jubaer Tansen, University of East London, UK

Section 2
Blockchain and Computational Excellence

Chapter 5
Elaborative Investigation of Blockchain Technology in Intelligent Networks 60
    Dhaya R., King Khalid University, Saudi Arabia
    Kanthavel R., King Khalid University, Saudi Arabia

Chapter 6
Blockchain-Integrated Internet-of-Things Architecture in Privacy Preserving
for Large-Scale Healthcare Supply Chain Data 80
    Kamalendu Pal, City, University of London, UK

Chapter 7
Blockchain and Copyright: Challenges and Opportunities...............................125
    Pedro Pina, Polytechnic of Coimbra, Portugal

Chapter 8
Internet of Things in Cyber Security Scope...146
    Mazoon Hashil Alrubaiei, Modern College of Business and Science, Oman
    Maiya Hamood Al-Saadi, Modern College of Business and Science, Oman
    Hothefa Shaker, Modern College of Business and Science, Oman
    Bara Sharef, Ahlia University, Bahrain
    Shahnawaz Khan, University College of Bahrain, Bahrain

Section 3
Blockchain Emerging Trends and Applications

Chapter 9
Blockchain: Emerging Trends, Applications, and Challenges...........................189
    Taskeen Zaidi, Jain University (Deemed), India

Chapter 10
Digital Economy: The New Engine of Growth for Society 5.0 204
    Bilyaminu Auwal Romo, University of East London, UK

Chapter 11
Applications of Blockchain Technology in the Finance and Banking Industry
Beyond Digital Currencies..216
    Sitara Karim, ILMA University, Pakistan
    Mustafa Raza Rabbani, University of Bahrain, Bahrain
    Hana Bawazir, University of Bahrain, Bahrain

Chapter 12
Application of Blockchain in E-Healthcare Systems...239
    Aman Ahmad Ansari, The LNM Institute of Information Technology, India
    Bharavi Mishra, The LNM Institute of Information Technology, India
    Poonam Gera, The LNM Institute of Information Technology, India

Compilation of References 261

About the Contributors 302

Index.. 308

Detailed Table of Contents

Foreword xiv

Preface xvi

Section 1
Blockchain Fundamentals

Chapter 1

Blockchain Technology in Ecosystems 1

    Sidhu Sharma, Sri Venkateshwara University, Gajraulla, India

    Mohammad Haider Syed, Saudi Electronic University, Saudi Arabia

    Shahnawaz Khan, Torocs Consultancy Services, India

The complex human society needs a robust technological ecosystem that may interoperate cordially among the systems. As the systems are components, these components offer a variety of services for humankind. Services evolve and interact in a different manner and cater to numerous capabilities. These activities have many issues that need to be taken care of with the most advanced and secure technology. Blockchain is one such approach among the many approaches available. This study of blockchain technology will discuss its categorization. Also, it will address how and where all this recent technology has contributed to the ecosystem.

Chapter 2

Blockchain Technology: Principles and Algorithms 16

    *Mohammad Khalid Imam Rahmani, Saudi Electronic University, Saudi
        Arabia*

Blockchain is a distributed decentralized peer-to-peer network aiming to facilitate the immutability and security of data. Towards the service orientation, blockchain is a collection of distributed blocks having unique hash codes without any point of failure. Each block is stored on distributed ledgers, and transactions with them are secure, transparent, immutable, and traceable. To create a new block and allow a transaction to complete, an agreement between all parties is required. To reach an agreement in a blockchain network, consensus algorithms are used. In this chapter, fundamental principles and algorithms of blockchain networks have been discussed, and a detailed review of the blockchain consensus algorithms PoW, PoS, DPoS, PoET, PoWeight, PoB, PoA, and PoC have been provided including the merits and demerits of consensus algorithms with analysis to provide a deep understanding of the current research trends and future challenges.

Chapter 3
Blockchain Primer: Introduction to Blockchain Foundations and
Implementation 28

Mohammad Amin Kuhail, Zayed University, UAE
Sujith S. Mathew, Zayed University, UAE
Rawad Hammad, East London University, UK
Mohamed Bahja, University of Birmingham, UK

Blockchain technology has the potential to revolutionize several industries including finance, supply chain and logistics, healthcare, and more. This primer introduces readers to basic development skills to blockchain foundations including blockchain cryptography, the consensus algorithm, and smart contracts. Further, this primer explains stepwise how to implement and deploy basic data stores using blockchain with Python. The primer serves as a succinct introductory guide to blockchain foundations by relying on a case study illustrated with visuals together with instructions on implementation. This primer is intended for educators, students, and technology enthusiasts with foundational computer science and Python development skills.

Chapter 4
Blockchain: A Disruptive Technology..48

Arish Sidiqqui, University of East London, UK
Kazi Jubaer Tansen, University of East London, UK

Blockchain is distributed ledger technology. Its advancement has been compared to the rise of the internet with debate about the technology's probability to disrupt multiple industries including healthcare, transportation, real estate, public domains, manufacturing, intellectual property, education, and financial services. It is predicted that the blockchain will have a major impact on many trust-based environments due to its nature of recording any digital transaction that is secure, efficient, transparent, auditable, and resistant to the outage, thereby providing the much-needed security in the transfer of assets in cyberspace. This chapter will highlight some of the business processes that can be disrupted by blockchain technology.

Section 2
Blockchain and Computational Excellence

Chapter 5

Elaborative Investigation of Blockchain Technology in Intelligent Networks 60
Dhaya R., King Khalid University, Saudi Arabia
Kanthavel R., King Khalid University, Saudi Arabia

The fifth generation (5G) network advancements focus to help mixed upright applications by associating heterogeneous gadgets and machines with extreme upgrades regarding high quality of administration, extended organization limit, and improved framework throughput regardless of significant difficulties like decentralization, straightforwardness, dangers of information interoperability, network protection, and security weaknesses. The challenges and limitations of other intelligent 5G intelligent internet of networks (5G IoTs) are also to be met by using blockchain technology with the integration of cloud computing and edge computing technologies. In this chapter, the authors render an elaborated analytics of the empowering of blockchain technology in intelligent networks that includes 5G networks and 5G-based IoT. The solutions for the spectrum management, data sharing, security, and privacy in 5G networks will also be analyzed. It is believed that the chapter would be useful for researchers in the field of blockchain in intelligent networks.

Chapter 6

Blockchain-Integrated Internet-of-Things Architecture in Privacy Preserving for Large-Scale Healthcare Supply Chain Data 80
Kamalendu Pal, City, University of London, UK

The supply chain forms the backbone of healthcare industry operations. The design and development of healthcare information systems (HIS) help different types of decision-making at various levels of business operations. Business process management decision-making is a complex task requiring real-time data collection from different operational sources. Hence, information technology (IT) infrastructure for data acquisition and sharing affects the operational effectiveness of the healthcare industry. The internet of things (IoT) applications have drawn significant research interest in the service of the healthcare industry. IoT technology aims to simplify the distributed data collection in healthcare practice, sharing, and processing of information and knowledge across many collaborating partners using suitable enterprise information systems. However, implementing blockchain technology in IoT-based data communication networks demands extra research initiatives. This chapter presents a review of security-related issues in the context of a HIS consisting of IoT-based blockchain technology.

Chapter 7

Blockchain and Copyright: Challenges and Opportunities............................125
Pedro Pina, Polytechnic of Coimbra, Portugal

Advances in the field of digital technology are constantly introducing new levels of controversy into copyright policy. Blockchain is the most recent technology with significant impact in digital copyright. Combined with smart contracts, blockchain enables new efficient forms of distribution of copyrighted works and also a new model of private ordering regarding the control of uses of works on the Internet. The chapter aims to examine the relationship and the most relevant intersections between blockchain, digital exploitation of copyrighted works, copyright law, and privacy law.

Chapter 8

Internet of Things in Cyber Security Scope............................146
Mazoon Hashil Alrubaiei, Modern College of Business and Science, Oman
Maiya Hamood Al-Saadi, Modern College of Business and Science, Oman
Hothefa Shaker, Modern College of Business and Science, Oman
Bara Sharef, Ahlia University, Bahrain
Shahnawaz Khan, University College of Bahrain, Bahrain

IoT represents a technologically bright future where heterogeneously connected devices will be connected to the internet and make intelligent collaborations with other objects to extend the borders of the world with physical entities and virtual components. Despite rapid evolution, this environment is still facing new challenges and security issues that need to be addressed. This chapter will give a comprehensive view of IoT technologies. It will discuss the IoT security scope in detail. Furthermore, a deep analysis of the most recent proposed mechanisms is classified. This study will be a guide for future studies, which direct to three primary leading technologies—machine learning (ML), blockchain, and artificial intelligence (AI)—as intelligent solutions and future directions for IoT security issues.

Section 3
Blockchain Emerging Trends and Applications

Chapter 9

Blockchain: Emerging Trends, Applications, and Challenges............................189
Taskeen Zaidi, Jain University (Deemed), India

A blockchain is a specific database stored in an electronic form. The databases stored in a block are put in a chain. When new data is added, it will be put in a new block. The blockchain may be created for storing different kind of information in which the most popular use of blockchain is ledger for transactions. Anything of value can be put in a blockchain, and this will reduce risk factors and cost. The blockchain is a chain of blocks used to store public databases. The blockchain can be a powerful tool in business applications for sharing and updating data. The blockchain may be used for the business process for handling transaction-related problems in an effective manner. The blockchain is also helpful in developing an ecosystem between various stakeholders. The policies, benefits, and cost are serious risk factors.

Chapter 10

Digital Economy: The New Engine of Growth for Society 5.0 204
Bilyaminu Auwal Romo, University of East London, UK

Digital technology-enabled business processes are integrated into the digital economy. Such technologies also enable the internet to conduct digital commerce in a trustless network and decentralized environment. This chapter also draws attention to the new form of economy, which focuses on the development and functions of the digital economy as a new growth engine for Society 5.0 and sheds light on emerging technologies and how the disruptive element of blockchain technology challenges the status quo of the old economy and the underpinning digital disruption imposed by decentralize platformisation. The core components of the digital economy, including digital technologies that serve as the new engine of growth for Society 5.0, were identified. The chapter concluded by highlighting the implications of digital technologies, and how standardisation, upgrading curriculum, legislative frameworks, and policies remedy the impediment of growing the digital economy for Society 5.0.

Chapter 11

Applications of Blockchain Technology in the Finance and Banking Industry
Beyond Digital Currencies 216
Sitara Karim, ILMA University, Pakistan
Mustafa Raza Rabbani, University of Bahrain, Bahrain
Hana Bawazir, University of Bahrain, Bahrain

Blockchain and cryptocurrency have almost become synonymous. Cryptocurrency is arguably one of the most sensational financial innovations of the 21st century. The current study claims that blockchain technology is not limited to the application of digital currencies in finance and banking; there are wide applications of blockchain technology in the given field. Blockchain uses the unique properties enabling decentralized, secured, transparent, and temper-proof financial transactions that have the potential to revolutionize the financial services industry. Given such a stance, the chapter outlines the application of blockchain technology in the finance arena beyond the digital currency. In this chapter, the authors provide the 10 applications of blockchain technology in the financial services industry implementing the blockchain technology and revolutionizing the finance and banking industry. The chapter also highlights the hurdles to application of blockchain technology in the finance and banking industry.

Chapter 12

Application of Blockchain in E-Healthcare Systems..239

Aman Ahmad Ansari, The LNM Institute of Information Technology, India
Bharavi Mishra, The LNM Institute of Information Technology, India
Poonam Gera, The LNM Institute of Information Technology, India

The e-healthcare system maintains sensitive and private information about patients. In any e-healthcare system, exchanging health information is often required, making privacy and security a primary concern for e-healthcare systems. Another major issue is that existing e-healthcare systems use centralized servers. These centralized servers require high infrastructure and maintenance costs for day-to-day services. Along with that, server failure may affect the working of e-healthcare systems drastically and may create life-threatening situations for patients. Blockchain technology is a very useful way to provide decentralized, secure storage for healthcare information. A blockchain is a time-stamped series of immutable records of data that is managed by a cluster of computers not owned by any single entity. These blocks create a chain of immutable, tamper-proof blocks in a ledger. This chapter will discuss the different aspects of blockchain and its application in different fields of the e-healthcare system.

Compilation of References 261

About the Contributors 302

Index.. 308

Foreword

Blockchain has received a lot of attention in recent years and it has been seen as the biggest invention since the advent of the internet. Blockchain is a collection of distributed blocks connected through cryptographic hash code on a peer to peer network having no single point of failure. Blocks stores on a distributed ledger on a peer to peer network that makes it reliable to sustain and function. Blockchain transactions are secure, transparent, traceable, and immutable. It provides the ability to be used in a variety of businesses in numerous works of life such as insurance, healthcare, payments, land registration, internet of things, asset management, supply chain, cryptocurrencies, and many more. Cryptocurrency is one of the widely used applications of Blockchain that includes Bitcoin, Ethereum, Ripple, etc.

Blockchain technology essentially stores the transactional data in the distributed network. This data is validated by the majority of the stakeholders in the transaction set. On transaction is made it can never be non-repudiated. This makes it very secure as data once entered can never be erased.

Several publications have been published in the last few years about how blockchain works, its applications and overall benefits. However, this fascinating book targets to be the single point of reference for Blockchain technology for computing excellence. It will clearly explain the core theories, concepts, systems, and practical applications. The book will comprise a variety of real-life applications of Blockchain technology such as digital financial transactions, insurance, medical history management, voting, etc. with the help of visual examples as an integrated part of society 5.0. It will also explore certain aspects of the Blockchain technology from research, scientific and business perspective for secure, cryptographic, and transparent applications in the fields of industry 4.0/5.0, sustainability, healthcare, digital currency, and other related computing areas.

This book primarily focuses on the advent of Blockchain technology. It essentially helps the reader to understand the concept as to how it can be useful in various walks of life like finance, insurance, voting, etc. Technology is distributed so no central governing body and thus it makes it collaborative. The focus of the book will be on two major areas namely understanding the concept and its wide application areas. It will help the researchers, and learners to welcome the deep and engaging conversations with the peers working in Blockchain technology for computational excellence by using real-life applications, case studies, and examples from the book.

This timely book illustrates how this revolutionary technology can be used to transform businesses across many sectors such as, financial trading, insurance, healthcare, internet of things, asset management, supply chain management, Cryptocurrencies, etc.

The book will cater from beginners to intermediate readers and researchers. It illustrates from fundamentals theories to practical and sophisticated applications of Blockchain; and provides insight into various platforms, techniques, and tools used in Blockchain. This will develop the reader's understanding of proof-of-work, consensus algorithms, and smart contracts and their applications.

The book provides in-depth knowledge about Blockchain technology with supportive real-life problems and closes the gap in the literature by providing a selection of chapters that not only shapes the research domain but also presents pragmatic solutions. This book is for anyone who wants to understand blockchain in more depth. It can also be used as a textbook for courses related to computer science, disruptive technology and blockchain technology.

- Provides practical guidance for blockchain Technology which is one of the most talked-about technology currently.
- It will be beneficial for the academicians, researchers, post-graduates, graduates, and other technology enthusiasts
- Creating awareness and interest among learners and researcher
- Social media can be used to advertise and to build a relationship
- The book consists of a variety of examples, case studies, and practical applications of the Blockchain technology.

Reading through this well-crafted book, you will have gained a deep understanding of the theory and applications of blockchain real-world scenarios.

Hassan Abdalla
University of East London, UK

Preface

In the past couple of decades many technologies have been brought to the fore, however Blockchain remains of these key technologies. Blockchain, as an emerging technology, received a very considerable attention worldwide and continued to disrupt the business models in various ways. Bitcoin, which is known as a digital or cryptocurrency and uses peer to peer technology, is one of the key Blockchain applications in FinTech domain (Su et al, 2020). In a nutshell, Blockchain is a collection of distributed blocks connected through cryptographic hash code on a peer-to-peer network that have no single point of failure (Tandon et al, 2021). As Blockchain depends on cryptographic hashing functions in addition to consensus protocols and decentralised storage, it provides traceability, transparency and auditability (Ahmad et al, 2021). Hence, all blockchain transactions are secure, transparent, traceable, and immutable.

Blockchain paves the ground for businesses and organisations across many domains to opt for a new business model to provide reliable services to their customers. Such domains include Education, Finance, Healthcare, Insurance, Supply chain, Cryptocurrency, Internet of Things (IoT), to mention but a few (Durach et al, 2021). Just as an example, recalling the number of people using cryptocurrency at the moment allows us to imagine why this technology is, and will continue to be, so influential and significant. Blockchain essentially stores the transactional data in the distributed network. The data are validated by the majority of the stakeholder in the transaction set. Once transaction is made it can never be non-repudiated. This makes it very secure as data once entered can never be erased (Helo, and Shamsuzzoha, 2020). For the above-mentioned reasons, Blockchain is considered as a revolutionary technology and has the potential to transform businesses and economics to new dimensions.

However, successful adoption of Blockchain technology is quite challenging as it requires careful planning and implementation strategy. For instance, talking to businesses about Blockchain had led to huge interest but talking to business professionals had led to one key conclusion, which is many professionals lack accurate and detailed-enough understanding for this new technology. Consequently, they cannot provide compelling case studies for how such technology can be adopted/ adapted to benefit their businesses (Bao et al, 2020). On the top of that, leadership and management concerns, which include long and short-term impact, change resistance, budget restrictions, market analysis, legal and ethical aspects, to mention but a few, remains valid and unanswered in the majority of current businesses (Mohanta, 2018).

Developing a compelling case study can be less challenging in certain domains. For instance, Blockchain helps to detect the frauds with ease, and it is impossible, to a very large extent, to modify previous transactions. Double spending is one of the most haunting concerns in digital finance, which has been solved using blockchain (Hewa, Ylianttila & Liyanage, 2021). Moreover, smart contracts can be used in financial transactions and in place of conventional contracts to regulate and monitor the process with reliability and more security (Kuhail, Bhaja & Hammad, 2022). Despite the fact that Blockchain can reduce the cost of financial services to very large extent, it is still open to various number of challenges. For instance, in 2017 one of the Ethereum multi-signature wallet Parity lost approximately $30 million due some security vulnerabilities (Liu & Liu, 2019). Such vulnerabilities range from contract vulnerabilities such as: transaction-ordering dependence and timestamp dependence, to privacy and legal issues such as: contract data privacy and trusted data feed privacy. Hence, Destefanis et al (2018) argue that a rigor blockchain-specific software engineering approach is needed to handle the above-presented vulnerabilities and other challenges including: (i) readability, i.e., creation stage, (ii) dynamic control flow, i.e., deployment, (iii) execution efficiency, i.e., execution, and (iv) scamming, i.e., completion stage (Zheng, 2020). Recommended software engineering approaches should be aligned very well with Software Development Life Cycle for Ultra Large-Scale Software Systems, which ensure a thorough risk assessment and mitigation strategy to be in place (Barger et al, 2020).

This book provides broad coverage of Blockchain technology in finance, cloud computing, security, cryptocurrency, industrial internet of things, and healthcare, etc. It provides insights into blockchain features, business use cases, smart contracts, and its utility, mining, consensus, public and enterprise blockchains and cryptocurrency essentials. Furthermore, this book targets to be the single point of reference for Blockchain technology for computing excellence. It will clearly explain the core theories, concepts, systems, and practical applications. It will comprise a variety of real-life applications of Blockchain technology in different domains with the help of visual examples as an integrated part of society 5.0. It will also explore certain aspects of the Blockchain technology from research, scientific and business perspective for secure, cryptographic, and transparent applications in the fields of industry 4.0, sustainability, healthcare, digital currency, and other related computing areas.

This book should help the reader to understand Blockchain concepts, theories, models and best practices as to how they can be useful in various walks of life including: finance, insurance and voting. Additionally, it will address the distributed notion of this technology as no central governing body should be in place, and thus collaborative approach needs to be followed.

Three key areas will be discussed in the book as follows. First, blockchain fundamentals will be introduced. This includes: (i) Blockchain technology in ecosystem, (ii) Blockchain major principles and algorithms, (iii) Blockchain primer: foundations and implementation, and finally (iv) Blockchain as a disruptive technology and its potential to build an innovative decentralised system. Second, Blockchain and computational excellence will be discussed in relation to real life contexts. This includes: (i) elaborative investigation of Blockchain technology in intelligent networks, (ii) Blockchain integrated Internet of Things architecture in privacy-preserving for large scale healthcare supply chain, (iii) Blockchain and copyright: challenges and opportunities and (iv) Internet of Things in cyber security scope. Third, reflections on Blockchain Emerging Trends and Applications will be presented to conclude the progress made in this discipline. This section introduces the following: (i) Blockchain emerging trends, applications and challenges: Blockchain applications, (ii) digital economy: the new engine of growth for society 5.0, (iii) the applications of Blockchain technology in finance and banking industry beyond digital currencies and (iv) the application of Blockchain in e-healthcare system.

ORGANISATION OF THE BOOK

The book is organised into 12 chapters. A brief description of each of the chapters follows:

Chapter 1 presents the complex human society need for a robust technological ecosystem that may interoperate cordially among the systems. It also reflects on how the systems and its components offer variety of services for humankind in a reliable manner. This is linked very well with Blockchain services that evolve and interact in different manner and cater to numerous capabilities. Blockchain is one of such approaches among the many approaches available to provide reliable services. This chapter addresses how and where Blockchain technology has contributed to the ecosystem.

Chapter 2 explains the distributed decentralized peer-to-peer network of Blockchain that facilitates the immutability and security of data. From a service perspective, it presents: (i) how distributed blocks work together based on unique hash codes without any point of failure, and (ii) how each block is stored on distributed ledgers that keep transactions secure, transparent, immutable, and traceable. It also reflects on the process of creating a new block and allowing a transaction to complete, and why the agreement between all parties is essential in this context. In the chapter, fundamental principles and algorithms of Blockchain networks have been discussed. A detailed review of the Blockchain consensus algorithms including PoW, PoS, DPoS, PoET, PoWeight, PoB, PoA, and PoC have been provided in addition to the merits and demerits of consensus algorithms with their analysis so that the readers are acquainted with the current research trends and future application challenges.

Chapter 3 presents the potential of Blockchain technology to revolutionise several industries including finance, supply chain and logistics, healthcare, and more. This primer introduces readers with basic development skills to Blockchain foundations including Blockchain cryptography, the consensus algorithm, and smart contracts. Further, this primer explains stepwise how to implement and deploy basic data stores using Blockchain with Python. The primer serves as a succinct introductory guide to Blockchain foundations by relying on a case study illustrated with visuals together with instructions on implementation. This primer is intended for educators, students, and technology enthusiasts with foundational computer science and Python development skills.

Chapter 4 discusses the Blockchain advancement and its potential to disrupt multiple industries including healthcare, transportation, real estate, public domains, manufacturing, intellectual property, education and financial services. It discusses how Blockchain will have a major impact on many trust-based environments due to its nature of recording any digital transaction in a secure, efficient, transparent, auditable and immutable way. This chapter also reflects on the much-needed security in the transfer of assets in the Cyber-Space. In addition, this chapter will highlight some of the business processes that can be disrupted by Blockchain technology. This chapter concludes the first part of the book and paves the ground to the second part of the book which addresses the Blockchain and computational excellence.

Chapter 5 marks the beginning of the second section of the book and presents the connection between Blockchain and the fifth generation (5G) networks advancements. Such links explicates the applications of advance technologies supported by heterogeneous gadgets and machines with extreme upgrades regarding high quality of administration, extended organization limit and improved framework throughput. The challenges and limitations of other intelligent 5G intelligent Internet of Networks (5G IoTs) are also presented in this chapter to be met by Blockchain technology with the integration of cloud computing and Edge computing technologies. Moreover, the author renders elaborated analytics of Blockchain technology in intelligent networks that includes 5G networks and 5G based IoT. It alludes to the solutions for the spectrum management, data sharing, security and privacy in 5G networks.

Chapter 6 reflects on the importance of supply chain for healthcare industry and highlights the needs to design and develop innovative healthcare information systems (HIS) to help different types of decision-making at various levels of business operation. Business process management decision-making is a complex task requiring real-time data collection from different operational sources. Hence, information technology (IT) infrastructure for data acquisition and sharing affects the operational effectiveness of the healthcare industry which necessitates Blockchain adoption. The Internet of Things (IoT) applications have drawn significant research interest in the service of the healthcare industry. IoT technology aims to simplify the distributed data collection in healthcare practice, sharing and processing information and knowledge across many collaborating partners using suitable enterprise information systems. Therefore, implementing blockchain technology in IoT-based data communication networks demand extra research initiatives. This chapter presents also reviews security-related issues in the context of a HIS consists of IoT-based blockchain technology.

Chapter 7 summarises the challenges and opportunities of Blockchain in the context of copyrights. The continuously evolving advancements in the field of digital technology are constantly introducing new levels of controversy into copyright policy. This chapter identifies how Blockchain, the most recent technology with significant impact in digital copyright, can be beneficial to address copyright challenges. Combined with smart contracts, blockchain enables new efficient forms of distribution of copyrighted works and a new model of private ordering regarding the control of uses of works on the Internet. Finally, this chapter aims to examine the relationship and the most relevant intersections between blockchain, digital exploitation of copyrighted works, copyright law and privacy law.

Chapter 8 introduces the IoT as a vehicle for connecting heterogeneous set of devices to the internet to facilitate intelligent collaborations with other objects and to extend the borders of the world with physical entities and virtual component. Despite the rapid technological evolution, this chapter identifies few challenges and security issues that need to be addressed. It gives a comprehensive view of IoT technologies, along with security concerns. Furthermore, a deep analysis of the most recent proposed mechanisms is classified. Also, this chapter guides the readers to future directions that will impact this area of research. These areas are Machine Learning (ML), Blockchain, and Artificial Intelligent (AI) which will significantly impact the future direction for IoT security issues. The chapter concludes the second section of the book.

Chapter 9 summarises Blockchain emerging trends, applications, and challenges. It explains how Blockchain can be used for storing different kind of information in which most popular use of blockchain is ledger for transactions. Anything of value can be put in a blockchain which will be reducing risk factors as well as the cost. This chapter reflects as well on how Blockchain can be a powerful tool in business applications for sharing and updating data. It also highlights the use of Blockchain in business process for handling transactions related problems in an effective manner. The chapter concludes the role of Blockchain in developing an ecosystem between various stakeholders but somehow with various challenges, policies, cost, and risk.

Chapter 10 discusses the digital economy as the engine of growth for society 5.0. It highlights how digital technologies, including Blockchain, enable business processes to be integrated into the digital economy. Such technologies also enable the Internet to conduct digital commerce in a trustless network and decentralised environment. This chapter also draws attention to the new form of economy, which focuses on the development and functions of the digital economy as a new growth engine for society 5.0. As well as shed a light on emerging technologies and how the disruptive element of blockchain technology challenges the status of the old economy and the underpinning digital disruption imposed by decentralise platformisation. The core components of the digital economy, including digital technologies, were identified, as well as concluded by highlighting the implications of digital technologies, and how standardisation, upgrading curriculum, legislative frameworks and policies remedy the impediment of growing the digital economy for society 5.0.

Chapter 11 presents one of the most powerful applications of Blockchain, which is Cryptocurrency. Cryptocurrency is arguably one of the most sensational financial innovations of the twenty first century powered by the blockchain technology. This chapter claims that blockchain technology is not limited to the application of digital currencies in finance and banking, but there are wide applications of blockchain technology in the given field. Blockchain uses the unique properties enabling decentralized, secured, transparent and temper-proof financial transaction that has the potential to revolutionize the financial services industry. Given such stance, this chapter outlines the application of Blockchain technology in finance arena beyond the digital currency. It provides the ten applications of blockchain technology in the financial services industry implementing the blockchain technology and revolutionising the finance and banking industry. Finally, it shed lights on the hurdles to application of Blockchain technology in finance and banking industry.

Chapter 12 concludes the book by presenting the applications of Blockchain in e-healthcare systems that maintain sensitive and private information about patients. The chapter focuses on the need for Blockchain application in healthcare to ensure secure exchange for health information, to meet privacy and security concerns. In addition, this chapter presents a view where Blockchain allows healthcare to move away from centralised infrastructure as these centralised servers and infrastructure require high maintenance costs. Besides, it discusses how healthcare servers failure affect the working of e-healthcare systems drastically and may create life-threatening situations for patients. In this context, Blockchain technology can be very useful to provide decentralised, secure storage for health care information. The chapter explains how this blockchain technology is a time-stamped series of immutable records of data that is managed by a cluster of computers not owned by any single entity. At the end, this chapter concludes with different future applications for Blockchain in different fields of E-healthcare system.

To summarise, the book provides in-depth knowledge about Blockchain technology with supportive real-life problems and closes the gap in the literature by providing a selection of chapters that not only shapes the research domain but also presents pragmatic solutions and futuristic vision on how Blockchain can be applied across many disciplines.

Shahnawaz Khan
University College of Bahrain, Bahrain

Mohammad Haider Syed
Saudi Electronic University, Saudi Arabia

Rawad Hammad
University of East London, UK

Aisha Fouad Bushager
University of Bahrain, Bahrain

REFERENCES

Ahmad, R. W., Hasan, H., Jayaraman, R., Salah, K., & Omar, M. (2021). Blockchain applications and architectures for port operations and logistics management. *Research in Transportation Business & Management*. doi:10.1016/j.rtbm.2021.100620

Bao, J., He, D., Luo, M., & Choo, K. K. R. (2020). A survey of blockchain applications in the energy sector. *IEEE Systems Journal*.

Durach, C. F., Blesik, T., von Düring, M., & Bick, M. (2021). Blockchain applications in supply chain transactions. *Journal of Business Logistics*, *42*(1), 7–24. doi:10.1111/jbl.12238

Helo, P., & Shamsuzzoha, A. H. M. (2020). Real-time supply chain—A blockchain architecture for project deliveries. *Robotics and Computer-integrated Manufacturing*, *63*, 101909. doi:10.1016/j.rcim.2019.101909

Hewa, T., Ylianttila, M., & Liyanage, M. (2021). Survey on blockchain based smart contracts: Applications, opportunities and challenges. *Journal of Network and Computer Applications*, *177*, 102857. doi:10.1016/j.jnca.2020.102857

Kuhail, M., Mathew, S., Hammad, R., & Bahja, M. (2022). Blockchain Primer: Introduction to Blockchain Foundations and Implementation. Blockchain Technology and Computational Excellence for Society 5.0.

Liu, J., & Liu, Z. (2019). A survey on security verification of blockchain smart contracts. *IEEE Access: Practical Innovations, Open Solutions*, *7*(7), 77894–77904. doi:10.1109/ACCESS.2019.2921624

Su, C. W., Qin, M., Tao, R., Shao, X. F., Albu, L. L., & Umar, M. (2020). Can Bitcoin hedge the risks of geopolitical events? *Technological Forecasting and Social Change*, *159*, 120182. doi:10.1016/j.techfore.2020.120182

Tandon, A., Kaur, P., Mäntymäki, M., & Dhir, A. (2021). Blockchain applications in management: A bibliometric analysis and literature review. *Technological Forecasting and Social Change*, *166*, 120649. doi:10.1016/j.techfore.2021.120649

Mohanta, B., Panda, S., & Debasish, J. (2018). An Overview of Smart Contract and Use Cases in Blockchain Technology. *International Conference on Computing Communication and Networking Technologies*. 10.1109/ICCCNT.2018.8494045

Destefanis, M., & Ortu, T., Bracciali, & Hierons. (2018). Smart contracts vulnerabilities: A call for blockchain software engineering? In *2018 International Workshop on Blockchain Oriented Software Engineering (IWBOSE)* (pp. 19-25). IEEE.

Zheng, Xie, Dai, Chen, & Chen, Weng, & Imran. (2020). An overview on smart contracts: Challenges, advances and platforms. *Future Generation Computer Systems*, *105*, 475–491.

Barger, A., Manevich, Y., Meir, H., & Tock, Y. (2021). A Byzantine Fault-Tolerant Consensus Library for Hyperledger Fabric. In *2021 IEEE International Conference on Blockchain and Cryptocurrency (ICBC)* (pp. 1-9). IEEE.

Section 1
Blockchain Fundamentals

Chapter 1
Blockchain Technology in Ecosystems

Sidhu Sharma
Sri Venkateshwara University, Gajraulla, India

Mohammad Haider Syed
(iD) https://orcid.org/0000-0003-0838-0119
Saudi Electronic University, Saudi Arabia

Shahnawaz Khan
Torocs Consultancy Services, India

ABSTRACT

The complex human society needs a robust technological ecosystem that may interoperate cordially among the systems. As the systems are components, these components offer a variety of services for humankind. Services evolve and interact in a different manner and cater to numerous capabilities. These activities have many issues that need to be taken care of with the most advanced and secure technology. Blockchain is one such approach among the many approaches available. This study of blockchain technology will discuss its categorization. Also, it will address how and where all this recent technology has contributed to the ecosystem.

INTRODUCTION

Since the human evolution data has been of utmost importance from counting to barter system and other related activities. These data with human wisdom have meaningful information. Data in early history was inscribed on stone and then on paper with the invention of paper (Hunter, 1978). Years ago, in the ancient Mesopotamians

DOI: 10.4018/978-1-7998-8382-1.ch001

civilization started to record quantities on tablet of clay. The tablet consists of rows and columns. Data in those fields are stored as symbolically with number of dots to indicates the quantities. Thus, making it a kind of ledger. Later in the fourteenth century a new technique has been proposed and it gave a logical relationship to the entries. In this approach has been referred as double entry system. As this system maintain two entries one as debit and other as credit. Primal intention of humans is to accumulate wealth and in the form of intangible form rather than tangible form. Birth of internet and its security protocol developed in the 1998 allowed and encouraged to carry out financial transactions online. Most of the initial transaction were business to business. The technology got popularity among the people and transaction also covered the retails segment of the commerce in many folds. Thus, electronic commerce covered all aspect of the business i.e., business to business, business to consumers, consumers to consumers, etc. This growth of the electronic commerce has certain challenges that need to be addressed. Most important among the many challenges are cybersecurity, competition and order fulfillment.

Cybersecurity is the most challenging issue that is to be addressed for all the online transaction and appropriate policy and procedure need to formulate to safeguard the interest of the parties involved in the transaction. In order to safeguard the interest of the parties involved and avoid fraud etc. (Nakamoto, 2008a) (Nakamoto & Bitcoin, 2008) An anonymous person called "Satoshi Nakamoto" introduced the concept of "Bitcoin: A peer-to-peer Electronic Cash System". This is a distributed ledger, and this new approach was referred as "Blockchain". Core idea of the blockchain was to run over de-centralized peer-to-peer network. All the participant in the network must have agreement on the entries in the ledger. This is a public decentralized ledger not owned tool by any person, group, or government. Thus, blockchain can be simple be seen as a new way to create ledgers.

The proposed technique enables users in community to record transaction in a peer-to-peer ledger such that under normal situation alteration in the transaction cannot be done by individuals once it is published. Thus, it is a digital transaction that has been once executed, shared among all the entities participating into it. As all the events are public and the transactions are verified by all the participating entities and consensus of all the parties are mandatory for transaction the be recorded. A transaction once agreed and recorded cannot be deleted from the chain. Bitcoin is the most controversial entity since its inception as it has bypassed many governmental regulatory bodies.

Technology itself is well established and accepted by the scientific community to work without any glitch. This approach has been successfully applied to both non-financial and financial real-world problem. Current scenario of technology is all about the trustworthiness and reliability this blockchain technology has gain trust on both the areas. As an example, if Instagram post shared with the trusted participant it ensures that it does not get shared by any non-trusted participant or user. This digital era has phenomenally change/affected our life, so does security, privacy and trustworthiness are equally concern. None of the third-party resources can be fully trusted, that they cannot be hacked or compromised and thus data breach can be avoided.

Blockchain has overcome these issues by invoking the concept of distributed consensus along with the anonymity. The technology has all the historical repository of transaction, and these can be verified at any point in time when required. This can be achieved without violating or concerning the issues of privacy of the parties involved.

The blockchain technology has overcome many governmental regulations and challenges. Section II of the paper focuses on Blockchain technology, in section III discuss the penetration of blockchain the existing market. Section IV discuss the application of technology in financial and non-financial sectors and section V shows data about the trends and user growth in adapting the technology followed by conclusion in section VI.

BLOCKCHAIN TECHNOLOGY

Blockchain technology has now achieved a crucial role in the ever-growing digital economy as the use of the internet is inevitable in almost all walks of life. The proposer of the concept Bitcoin wanted to remain anonymous and hence no one knows Satoshi Nakamoto, but a few month latter in the January 2009 an open-source program implementing the protocol was released with the genesis block of 50 coins. Later in on January 9 in the year 2009, first version of bitcoin was released, on January the 12th, 2009 first historical transaction of bitcoin was executed. Since then, its growth has increased exponentially. As in any conventional financial transaction institution engaged in the transaction paly the role of preserving, validating, and safeguarding the transaction.

Cryptographic (Guegan, 2017; Liu & Xu, 2018) proof is used in bitcoin, instead of engaging third party to execute the transaction over the internet. Transaction executed over the internet is secured by using digital signature. The cryptographic concept used in the bitcoin is based on asymmetric cryptographic technique (Abreu, Aparicio, & Costa, 2018; Kube, 2018; Niranjanamurthy, Nithya, & Jagannatha, 2019). Where it has set of public and private key. An information once encrypted by public key can only be deciphered by private key and vice-versa. In case of any transaction owner has to prove the ownership of the private key he/she holds. Any transaction executed is broadcasted to all the participating entities or nodes in the bitcoin network, the transaction will be recorded in the public ledger only if it is verified and accepted by the participating nodes. Each transaction recorded in the public ledger in the network need to be first verified and validated. Verification of the transaction is the two-step process, first it will verify the ownership of the cryptocurrency followed by the sufficient availability of the transacted fund.

Figure 1. Transaction in blockchain technology

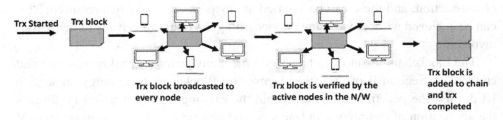

In some cases, order of transaction may create problem, if multiple transactions are executed together in the blockchain network.

Challenges of Multiple Transaction in Blockchain

If multiple transactions are initiated in the network (Cachin, 2016; Kan et al., 2018; Zheng, Xie, Dai, Chen, & Wang, 2018), then maintaining the order of transaction will be a matter of concerns as all the initiated transaction will be broadcasted in the blockchain network. As it is very likely that the transaction will not come in an ordered manner as they are generated in the network. Thus, a system needs to be ensured that there should be no duplicate transaction occur or recorded. As transactions propagate node to node in the network, thus ensuring that the order the nodes are received is same as the order they are generated in the network is a challenge.

Thus, a system needs to be developed such that the order of transaction (Cachin & Vukolić, 2017; Gramoli, 2020) executed in the network can be agreed by all the participating nodes. This daunting issue of distributed system to maintain the order of the transaction was addressed by blockchain technology. The transactions are ordered and placed in the form of block and linking then in the form of chain what is referred to blockchain. It is assumed that the all the transaction in a block happened together. These blocks are linked to the chain of the previous block along with the hash code of the previous block,

Still spurious block can be generated by any node in the network and broadcast it to the other connected entities in the network, deceiving it to the next block in the chain. Also, there could be multiple blocks generated in the network at the same time by the different node. These generated blocks may arrive in random order at the different node in the network.

All the blocks will be accepted provided the answer to the "special mathematical quiz", this will ascertain that the block has exhausted certain amount of computing resource to solve the mathematical quiz. In order to avoid replay, attach in the network, node needs to be generated the "nonce" (Hazari & Mahmoud, 2019; Rogaway, 2004). "Nonce" are a ciphered number to protect communication. A node in the network may be required to find a "nonce" to protect the privacy of the communicating node.

Likelihood of generating more than one block in the system at a given point in time is very less. The mathematical puzzle is complex in nature, so this will stabilize the blockchain. Also, the longest blockchain is considered to be more secure and is well accepted in the network. This property of the blockchain discourage the attackers as it has to race against the accepted good node in the network because it has to generate all subsequent blocks in same order so as to be accepted as legitimate transaction and block is/are valid.

Also, there are myth that with growing transaction and block of chain, technology need huge amount of space to keep the transaction record. (Nakamoto, 2008b; Nakamoto & Bitcoin, 2008) In the paper shown to reclaim the disk space. Once the transaction are very old and get buried under enough number of blocks, without breaking the hash chain transaction are hashed in a Markle tree (Jakobsson, Leighton, Micali, & Szydlo, 2003; Szydlo, 2004). In the tree old blocks can be stubbed off the branches of the tree and only the block hash is kept and there is no need to store the interior hash. This would reduce the reduce the storage space substantially.

For example: Let a block with only header and no transaction would be 80 bytes. Al let us assume that a block is generated every 5 minutes. In a year, the total disk space required will be 80 bytes x 12 x 24 x 365 = 8409600 bytes, which is equal to 8.4 MB. Thus, storage will not be a problem for long block chain.

PENETRATION OF BLOCKCHAIN THE EXISTING MARKET

The technology has gain popularity and since then it started penetration in both kinds of application i.e., financial, and non-financial application areas that traditionally relied on third party for validate and safeguard the transactions.

(Szabo, 1994, 1997) Paper proposed an application as "Smart Contract" (Bhargavan et al., 2016; Christidis & Devetsikiotis, 2016), the motive behind the proposed approach is the executed the contract automatically between the parties. This approach got realized with the invention of blockchain technology. The technologies namely smart contract and blockchain together can materialized an agreement of contract when initiated. The contracts are executed automatically using computer protocol and also made it easier to register and verify the contracts. (Atzei, Bartoletti, & Cimoli, 2017; Bhargavan et al., 2016; Luu, Chu, Olickel, Saxena, & Hobor, 2016) Ethereum and Codius (Cieplak & Leefatt, 2017; Cohn, West, & Parker, 2017) are pioneer in in the field. Next section discusses some of the interesting application of the blockchain technology in the financial and non-financial sector of the ecosystem.

APPLICATION OF TECHNOLOGY IN NON-FINANCIAL AND FINANCIAL ECOSYSTEM

Non-Financial Ecosystem

Traditional transactions have many parties involved to ascertain the security, authenticity, and privacy of the transaction but in blockchain ecosystem no central or administrative authority is involved for any transaction. There is no one entity that controls the network or blockchain. This has several benefits over the traditional transaction system. This system of transaction is cost effective, and the accepted transaction is recorded and available to all the parties of the network. This makes it safe and secure and temper resistant, a transaction can only be reversed with another transaction and both the transaction will be available in the network. Figure 2 shows business perspective of traditional and blockchain business network.

Figure 2. Conventional and blockchain based business model

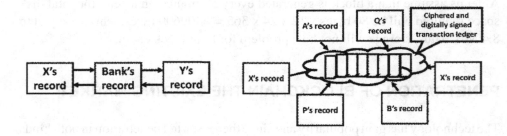

Blockchain network model has following characteristic, consensus of transaction among all parties in the network, participants know the origin of the transaction and its new ownership, transactions cannot be tempered once it has been recorded in the ledger. Improved visibility of blockchain technology has affected the ecosystem phenomenally.

Blockchain in Supply Chain Management

Blockchain technology has offered security, visibility, and reliability to the participating parties. This make it a potential tool in the supply chain management to improve the process of business modelling in the logistics and supply chain management. (Hackius & Petersen, 2017; Kersten, Seiter, Von See, Hackius, & Maurer, 2017) paper proposed the potential use of the blockchain technology in the supply chain management. Example proposed in the paper represents four major ideas. First idea is easing the tedious paperwork, as container transport has long trail of paperwork. This lots of paperwork incurs cost in term of time and money. Paper based documents are more prone of tempering, fraud or loss (Popper & Lohr, 2017). (Groenfeldt, 2017; Popper & Lohr, 2017) reported that cost of paper processing work cost half of the total cost of physical transport. In 2015 IBM and Maersk came out with a solution based on blockchain to connect the vast networks of carriers, ports and customs. The pilot project got materialized in the year 2017 enabling every participating to have visibility of the documents (Allison, 2017).

Blockchain in Identifying Counterfeit Products

Often a times high worth items are more prone to counterfeit, as these items are dependent on paper certificates which are again has high likelihood of being tempered or lost. To curtail such malpractices blockchain has emerged as one of the best alternatives. Using the public records available in the blockchain network authenticity of the product can be verified and the credential of the seller as well. One such system is implemented by the company Everledger to curb the malpractices and make available the authentic product to the end user.

Similarly in the health sector counterfeit drugs is serious concern and has taken many lives. Using the blockchain technology the supply chain could be monitored end to end i.e., from manufacturer to the patient (Biswas, Muthukkumarasamy, & Tan, 2017; Kumar & Tripathi, 2019; Toyoda, Mathiopoulos, Sasase, & Ohtsuki, 2017).

Blockchain in Healthcare

Healthcare has always been on the top of the concern to all, and it needs a robust system to maintain the medical records, payments, and insurance claim etc. As, most of such records are maintained by data centers this limits its access to only few. Such centralization of data record storage attracts breach in privacy and security which can be an expensive to the participating organizations. With Blockchain (Ekblaw, Azaria, Halamka, & Lippman, 2016; Hölbl, Kompara, Kamišalić, & Nemec Zlatolas, 2018; McGhin, Choo, Liu, & He, 2019) complete medical history of the patient can stored along with different level of granularity of control to all the involved parties. Thus, the information of the patient can be secured and maintained in comprehensive manner with fine level of visible granularity to all. This makes it temper resistant also the settlement of the insurance claim becomes more efficient. Patient data history, stored in the blockchain facilitates physician to access the condition of the patients and prescribed the right medicine.

Financial Application

Trade Finance

Finance is backbone of industry and blockchain technology revolutionized has many financial services like insurance, trade finance (Chang, Luo, & Chen, 2020), commercial financing (Osmani, El-Haddadeh, Hindi, Janssen, & Weerakkody, 2020) etc. With the invent of the technology trade has crossed many geographical boundaries. To streamline the business approval from many legal entities like transportation, port authority, customs for trading of good and services across border. The potential of the technology can be harnessed to ensure all legal formalities along keeping the parties about the update of approvals and its status. Thus, it has benefited by simplifying the complex processes into single window system as all accessing the same ledger. This will also improve the long assessment time, errors, and disputes along with increase in the capital access.

Insurance

Insurance as a financial intermediary is a commercial enterprise and is a major part of financial service industry. Industry needs an efficient way to verify and settle the claim along with the provenance of the incident. Automizing the insurance processing and claim, policy terms and condition can be recorder inn the smart contract (Alharby & Van Moorsel, 2017; Hewa, Hu, Liyanage, Kanhare, & Ylianttila, 2021) recorded on the blockchain, and data is made available to public over the internet. In case of any insurance claimant the incident is recorder or reported by trusted entity, claim policy is triggered automatically and claim is settled as per the laid guidelines or conditions. This will not only facilitate to minimize the cost of insurance claim processing but also substantially reduce the fraud and overall provide greater customer satisfaction.

TRENDS IN THE TECHNOLOGY

Blockchain has gain many folds popularity in the last decade and specially in the financial ecosystem. Figure 3 shows the google search trend of the term blockchain, bitcoin and smart contract world in the last five years.

Figure 3. Five-year google trend for bitcoin, blockchain, smart contract

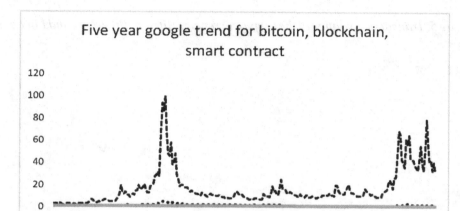

Figure 4. Cryptocurrency trend in the last five years

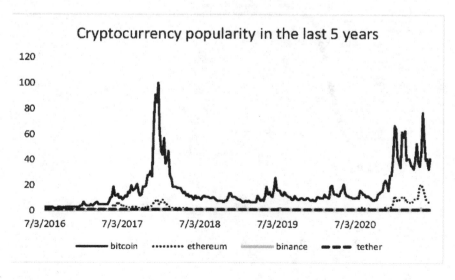

Cryptocurrency has gained much acclaimed popularity in the recent time as shown in the figure 4 as per the google search trend. Of the four most popular cryptocurrency shown in the figure 4 Bitcoin has outnumbered to all the other popular cryptocurrency.

As shown in the figure 5 the volume of transaction in the last ten (10) year for the cryptocurrencies Bitcoin, Ethereum, and Litecoin. Form the figure it is apparent that the volume of transaction has increased phenomenally.

Figure 5. Transaction volume of the cryptocurrencies Bitcoin, Ethereum and Litecoin

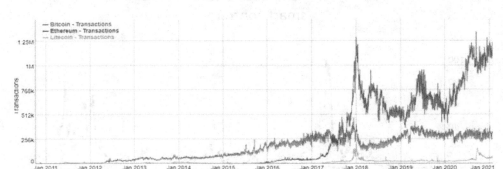

Figure 6. Hype Cycle for Blockchain Technologies-2019
Source: Gartner (October 2019)

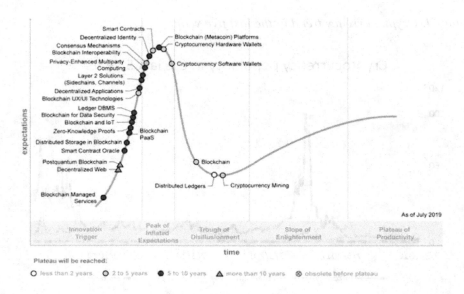

Figure 6 shows the prediction of blockchain as proposed by Gartner in the October 2019, as per the report it has pragmatic use and continues to grow and adapted by the industry. As project, it is still has to cover long path may be ten years to harness its full potential across the business ecosystem. As per the report of the bitcoin. com the user n the age group has accepted the technology and has seen substantial growth in the transaction volume of user group of eighteen to twenty-four year of age as shown in the figure 7. Continent-wise growth of used aged between 18 to 24 years is shown in the figure 7.

Figure 7. Continents with the most user growth in the age group 18 to 24
Source news.bitcoin.com

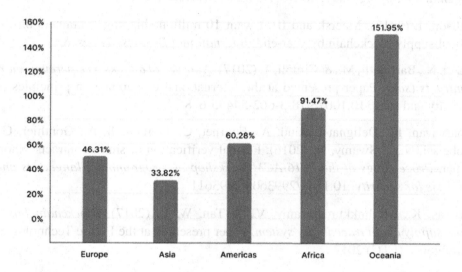

CONCLUSION

Blockchain is useful to understand not only in context of financial transaction such a Bitcoin, but as a robust and secure public ledger systems to execute transaction of different kind in the business ecosystem. The concept of peer-to-peer networking to record the transaction of both financial and non-financial ecosystem and making is hard to spoof or temper. Also, the requirement to store historical date does not squeeze the disk storage much, thus the history of transaction can be verified on demand. Technology reviewers are still not sure of it's legitimates use as cryptocurrency based technology is through of disillusionment. Interest in the technology has attracted many at the same time it is facing strong opposition by many. To conclude blockchain technology will go through slack adoption because of the risk associated. As reported by Gartner we would be seeing significant adoption of the technology.

REFERENCES

Abreu, P. W., Aparicio, M., & Costa, C. J. (2018). *Blockchain technology in the auditing environment.* Paper presented at the 2018 13th Iberian Conference on Information Systems and Technologies (CISTI). 10.23919/CISTI.2018.8399460

Alharby, M., & Van Moorsel, A. (2017). *Blockchain-based smart contracts: A systematic mapping study.* doi:10.5121/csit.2017.71011

Allison, I. (2017). Maersk and IBM want 10 million shipping containers on the global supply blockchain by year-end. *International Business Times, 8.*

Atzei, N., Bartoletti, M., & Cimoli, T. (2017). *A survey of attacks on ethereum smart contracts (sok).* Paper presented at the International conference on principles of security and trust. 10.1007/978-3-662-54455-6_8

Bhargavan, K., Delignat-Lavaud, A., Fournet, C., Gollamudi, A., Gonthier, G., Kobeissi, N., ... Swamy, N. (2016). Formal verification of smart contracts: Short paper. *Proceedings of the 2016 ACM workshop on programming languages and analysis for security.* 10.1145/2993600.2993611

Biswas, K., Muthukkumarasamy, V., & Tan, W. L. (2017). *Blockchain based wine supply chain traceability system.* Paper presented at the Future Technologies Conference (FTC) 2017.

Cachin, C. (2016). *Architecture of the hyperledger blockchain fabric.* Paper presented at the Workshop on distributed cryptocurrencies and consensus ledgers.

Cachin, C., & Vukolić, M. (2017). *Blockchain consensus protocols in the wild.* arXiv preprint arXiv:1707.01873.

Chang, S. E., Luo, H. L., & Chen, Y. (2020). Blockchain-enabled trade finance innovation: A potential paradigm shift on using letter of credit. *Sustainability, 12*(1), 188. doi:10.3390u12010188

Christidis, K., & Devetsikiotis, M. (2016). Blockchains and smart contracts for the internet of things. *IEEE Access: Practical Innovations, Open Solutions, 4,* 2292–2303. doi:10.1109/ACCESS.2016.2566339

Cieplak, J., & Leefatt, S. (2017). Smart contracts: A smart way to automate performance. *Georgetown Law Technology Review*, *1*(2), 417–427.

Cohn, A., West, T., & Parker, C. (2017). Smart after all: Blockchain, smart contracts, parametric insurance, and smart energy grids. *Georgetown Law Technology Review*, *1*(2), 273–304.

Ekblaw, A., Azaria, A., Halamka, J. D., & Lippman, A. (2016). A Case Study for Blockchain in Healthcare: "MedRec" prototype for electronic health records and medical research data. *Proceedings of IEEE open & big data conference.*

Gramoli, V. (2020). From blockchain consensus back to Byzantine consensus. *Future Generation Computer Systems*, *107*, 760–769. doi:10.1016/j.future.2017.09.023

Groenfeldt, T. (2017). *IBM and Maersk apply blockchain to container shipping.* https://www. forbes. com/sites/tomgroenfeldt/2017/03/05/ibm-and-maersk-apply-blockchain-to-container-shipping

Guegan, D. (2017). *Public blockchain versus private blockchain.* Academic Press.

Hackius, N., & Petersen, M. (2017). Blockchain in logistics and supply chain: trick or treat? *Proceedings of the Hamburg International Conference of Logistics (HICL)*, 23.

Hazari, S. S., & Mahmoud, Q. H. (2019). *A parallel proof of work to improve transaction speed and scalability in blockchain systems.* Paper presented at the 2019 IEEE 9th Annual Computing and Communication Workshop and Conference (CCWC). 10.1109/CCWC.2019.8666535

Hewa, T. M., Hu, Y., Liyanage, M., Kanhare, S., & Ylianttila, M. (2021). Survey on blockchain based smart contracts: Technical aspects and future research. *IEEE Access: Practical Innovations, Open Solutions*, *9*, 87643–87662. doi:10.1109/ACCESS.2021.3068178

Hölbl, M., Kompara, M., Kamišalić, A., & Nemec Zlatolas, L. (2018). A systematic review of the use of blockchain in healthcare. *Symmetry*, *10*(10), 470. doi:10.3390ym10100470

Hunter, D. (1978). *Papermaking: The history and technique of an ancient craft.* Courier Corporation.

Jakobsson, M., Leighton, T., Micali, S., & Szydlo, M. (2003). *Fractal Merkle tree representation and traversal.* Paper presented at the Cryptographers' Track at the RSA Conference. 10.1007/3-540-36563-X_21

Kan, L., Wei, Y., Muhammad, A. H., Siyuan, W., Linchao, G., & Kai, H. (2018). *A multiple blockchains architecture on inter-blockchain communication*. Paper presented at the 2018 IEEE International Conference on Software Quality, Reliability and Security Companion (QRS-C). 10.1109/QRS-C.2018.00037

Kersten, W., Seiter, M., Von See, B., Hackius, N., & Maurer, T. (2017). Trends and strategies in logistics and supply chain management. In Digital Transformation Opportunities. DVV Media Group GmbH.

Kube, N. (2018). *Daniel Drescher: Blockchain basics: a non-technical introduction in 25 steps*. Springer. doi:10.100711408-018-0315-6

Kumar, R., & Tripathi, R. (2019). *Traceability of counterfeit medicine supply chain through Blockchain*. Paper presented at the 2019 11th International Conference on Communication Systems & Networks (COMSNETS). 10.1109/COMSNETS.2019.8711418

Liu, L., & Xu, B. (2018). *Research on information security technology based on blockchain*. Paper presented at the 2018 IEEE 3rd international conference on cloud computing and big data analysis (ICCBDA). 10.1109/ICCCBDA.2018.8386546

Luu, L., Chu, D.-H., Olickel, H., Saxena, P., & Hobor, A. (2016). Making smart contracts smarter. *Proceedings of the 2016 ACM SIGSAC conference on computer and communications security*. 10.1145/2976749.2978309

McGhin, T., Choo, K.-K. R., Liu, C. Z., & He, D. (2019). Blockchain in healthcare applications: Research challenges and opportunities. *Journal of Network and Computer Applications*, *135*, 62–75. doi:10.1016/j.jnca.2019.02.027

Nakamoto, S. (2008a). *Bitcoin whitepaper*. https://bitcoin. org/bitcoin. pdf

Nakamoto, S. (2008b). Bitcoin: A peer-to-peer electronic cash system. *Decentralized Business Review*.

Nakamoto, S., & Bitcoin, A. (2008). *A peer-to-peer electronic cash system*. Bitcoin. https://bitcoin. org/bitcoin. pdf

Niranjanamurthy, M., Nithya, B., & Jagannatha, S. (2019). Analysis of Blockchain technology: Pros, cons and SWOT. *Cluster Computing*, *22*(6), 14743–14757. doi:10.100710586-018-2387-5

Osmani, M., El-Haddadeh, R., Hindi, N., Janssen, M., & Weerakkody, V. (2020). Blockchain for next generation services in banking and finance: Cost, benefit, risk and opportunity analysis. *Journal of Enterprise Information Management*.

Popper, N., & Lohr, S. (2017). Blockchain: A better way to track pork chops, bonds, bad peanut butter. *New York Times, 4*, 4.

Rogaway, P. (2004). *Nonce-based symmetric encryption.* Paper presented at the International workshop on fast software encryption. 10.1007/978-3-540-25937-4_22

Szabo, N. (1994). *Smart contracts.* Unpublished manuscript.

Szabo, N. (1997). Formalizing and securing relationships on public networks. *First Monday, 2*(9). Advance online publication. doi:10.5210/fm.v2i9.548

Szydlo, M. (2004). *Merkle tree traversal in log space and time.* Paper presented at the International Conference on the Theory and Applications of Cryptographic Techniques. 10.1007/978-3-540-24676-3_32

Toyoda, K., Mathiopoulos, P. T., Sasase, I., & Ohtsuki, T. (2017). A novel blockchain-based product ownership management system (POMS) for anti-counterfeits in the post supply chain. *IEEE Access: Practical Innovations, Open Solutions, 5*, 17465–17477. doi:10.1109/ACCESS.2017.2720760

Zheng, Z., Xie, S., Dai, H.-N., Chen, X., & Wang, H. (2018). Blockchain challenges and opportunities: A survey. *International Journal of Web and Grid Services, 14*(4), 352–375. doi:10.1504/IJWGS.2018.095647

Chapter 2
Blockchain Technology:
Principles and Algorithms

Mohammad Khalid Imam Rahmani
ⓘD https://orcid.org/0000-0002-1937-7145
Saudi Electronic University, Saudi Arabia

ABSTRACT

Blockchain is a distributed decentralized peer-to-peer network aiming to facilitate the immutability and security of data. Towards the service orientation, blockchain is a collection of distributed blocks having unique hash codes without any point of failure. Each block is stored on distributed ledgers, and transactions with them are secure, transparent, immutable, and traceable. To create a new block and allow a transaction to complete, an agreement between all parties is required. To reach an agreement in a blockchain network, consensus algorithms are used. In this chapter, fundamental principles and algorithms of blockchain networks have been discussed, and a detailed review of the blockchain consensus algorithms PoW, PoS, DPoS, PoET, PoWeight, PoB, PoA, and PoC have been provided including the merits and demerits of consensus algorithms with analysis to provide a deep understanding of the current research trends and future challenges.

INTRODUCTION

Blockchain is a distributed decentralized peer-to-peer network to facilitate transactions between participants that are not only secure but also transparent, immutable, and traceable (Ali et al., 2020). Blocks are stored on distributed ledgers having unique hash codes without any point of failure. The consensus algorithms and the underlying protocols are the backbones of Blockchain technology. The main objective of

DOI: 10.4018/978-1-7998-8382-1.ch002

blockchain technology is to make the concept of personal online valet a widespread reality in the entire world without fear of loss, cheat, or theft because there is no control of the government, banks, or any third party (Niranjanamurthy et al., 2019).

To create a new block and allow a transaction, a mutual agreement between all parties is required. Therefore, in a Blockchain network, various consensus algorithms are used for reaching that agreement. In the rapidly growing blockchain network initiatives in Government as well private departments, the security of the blockchain or cryptocurrencies is a major issue. The security assurance of the blocks and their transactions is a key to winning the trust of users for the safety and secrecy of the digital valet being spent by different parties over a network channel. The economical and widespread requirement of good quality consensus algorithms has created great opportunities for exploring more trustworthy and acceptable consensus techniques for first acquiring the blocks and then securing the transactions in a more efficient way (Jamil et al., 2021).

In this paper, first I have discussed some fundamental principles of Blockchain technology and then have given a detailed account of the Blockchain consensus algorithms as given by Alsunaidi et al. (2019), Gramoli (2020), Zheng et al. (2017), Pahlajani et al. (2019), and Bamakan et al. (2020) such as Proof of Work (PoW), Proof of Stake (PoS), Delegated Proof of Stake (DPoS), Proof of Elapsed Time (PoET), Practical Byzantine Fault Tolerance (PBFT), Delegated Byzantine Fault Tolerance (DBFT), Proof of Weight (PoWeight), Proof of Burn (PoB), Proof of Capacity (PoC), Proof of Importance (PoI), and Proof of Activity (PoA) including their merits and demerits to acquaint the researchers with the current research trends and future application challenges of Blockchain technology.

BACKGROUND

Blockchain can be dated back to 1982 when David Chaum proposed a similar protocol (Sherman et al., 2019; Chaum et al., 1998). Satoshi Nakamoto implemented the first digital currency Bitcoin using a Blockchain network and sent ten Bitcoins to Hal Finney (Buterin, 2014). Similar to the Internet there is no owner of the blockchain technology but people can have their blockchains.

WORKING PROCEDURE

Ledgers are used to record all transactions of a company through bookkeeping. There are two conventional bookkeeping methods: Single-entry and Double-entry methods. Single-entry ledgers are not transparent so their accountability is questionable. Similarly, one party cannot easily verify another party's records from a double-entry ledger. Moreover, traditional ledgers can easily be edited by adding, removing, or changing records. Parties would not trust such a system. Public Blockchain technology solves these issues by further enhancing the traditional bookkeeping method to a Triple-entry method wherein, every transaction in a blockchain network is cryptographically sealed by the third entry. This third entry is verified by a distributed consensus algorithm and stored in a secured block of the network. These consensus algorithms also decide how to create a new block in blockchain (Matthew, 2021).

THE MINING PROCESS IN BITCOIN

For sending a Bitcoin a small fee is paid in Bitcoin for the network computers to validate the transaction. A bundle of many transactions is put in a queue for adding to a new block. The nodes in the network try to solve a complex mathematical puzzle to validate the list of transactions in the block. When the puzzle is solved a 64-bit hexadecimal hash is generated and the block is added to the blockchain network (Matthew, 2021). The fee paid becomes the reward of the miner.

There are four types of Blockchains being described below:

1.   Public Blockchains

These are decentralized networks of nodes open to people for requesting or validating a transaction. PoW and PoS are two consensus algorithms used in this type of blockchain. Examples are Bitcoin and Ethereum.

2.   Private Blockchains

For these blockchains, access is restricted because they are centralized. For joining the network permission from the System Admin is required. Hyperledger and Quorum are private blockchains.

3.   Hybrid Blockchains

These are a combination of both public and private blockchains to combine the benefits of both but to minimize the disadvantages. R3 Corda comes under this type.

Figure 1. The basic model of blockchain technology
Source: ResearchGate, 2021

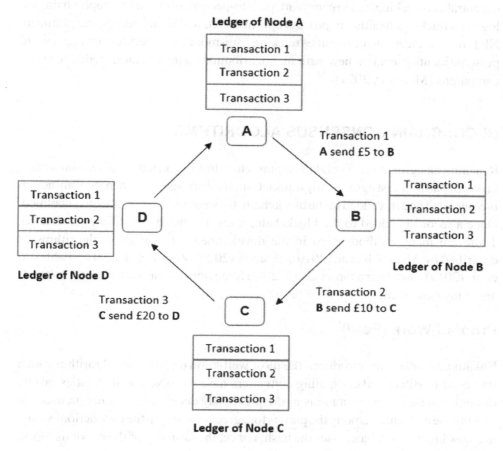

4.   Sidechains

Sidechains are used to improve scalability and efficiency while moving assets between two different blockchains. Liquid Network is a sidechain.

Some benefits of Blockchain are trustless, unstoppable, immutable, decentralized, lower-cost, Peer-to-Peer, transparent, universal banking, etc.

Some of the disadvantages of Blockchain are its environmental impact, the responsibility of the owner, and growing frustration due to the lack of scalability (Matthew, 2021). Bitcoin consumes more electricity than a small to the medium-sized country in Europe. If you forget the seed phrases used to recover your wallets, your money is gone. Bitcoin can process a maximum of seven transactions compared to Visa's 24,000.

Some great applications of Blockchain are cryptocurrencies, smart contracts, decentralized banking, video games/art, peer-to-peer energy trading, supply chain, and logistics tracking, healthcare process optimization, real estate processing platform, NFT marketplaces, music royalties tracking, anti-money laundering tracking system, personal identity security, new insurance distribution methods, automated advertising campaigns (Matthew, 2021).

BLOCKCHAIN CONSENSUS ALGORITHMS

Reaching an agreement to validate a transaction in a blockchain is a very important task. All parties must agree to any transaction. If all are agreeing then the transaction is completed and it is added to the blockchain. Otherwise, the transaction is declined. Once a record is added to the blockchain, it can neither be modified nor deleted. There are many methods used in the development of consensus algorithms as described by Alsunaidi et al. (2019), Gramoli (2020), Zheng et al. (2017), Pahlajani et al. (2019), and Bamakan et al. (2020). Here some of the widely used methods are being described.

Proof of Work (PoW)

Nakamoto (2008) has introduced the most well-known consensus algorithm which was used in Bitcoin. Participating computers have to solve a mathematics puzzle through a series of computations to the previously decided hash function used for making the consensus among the parties for agreeing to stamp the transactions stored in a new block. Each block uses the hash, nonce, the hash key of the previous block, and the list of its completed transactions. A miner has to locate a specific value called a nonce so that the hash key satisfies a predefined condition. It can be made more flexible and scalable by accommodating more pre-defined conditions. Every node in the network has to calculate a hash key of the block header. For accepting a consensus agreement, miners need to compute the hash key that is smaller or equal to a certain given value. After getting such a value, the node broadcasts the new block to the network for getting the proof of the hash value from the rest of the nodes. Then the block is validated for getting it appended into the respective chain of each user.

The strengths are its decentralized structure, high security, and workable scalability whereas its weaknesses are less throughput, energy inefficiency, high time for the creation of blocks, hardware dependency, more cost, and more bandwidth. It is not suitable for scalability in large networks.

Proof of Stake (PoS)

The idea of Proof of Stack was introduced in the year 2011 for Peercoin cryptocurrency (Barhanpure et al., 2018). The basis of the selection of the creator for the next block is many combinations of random selections, stake supply, and age with an orientation of good scalability. Who will create the new block, which will be determined by a quasi-random process? The selection will depend on the value of assets available in the user wallet. Low computing power is needed for validating the transactions. So, the miners get receive only transaction fees. It tends to depend on higher stake value shifting towards favoring the blockchain to a centralized one. If a node has "nothing at stake", it may misbehave because of no penalty or fear for losing anything to prevent him from misbehaving.

The strengths of these algorithms are that they can create a block faster, have better throughput, are energy-efficient, and are scalability. Orientation to centralization and low care for misbehaving in blockchain networks are the weaknesses.

Delegated Proof of Stake (DPoS)

Larimer (2017) has introduced this algorithm (Sun et al., 2021). For validating a new block, a process of voting is used to select representatives whose number is kept within a limit to organize the network effectively. The selection of limited representatives leads to a centralized structure. Its features include scalability, more energy-efficient, and low-cost transactions. Due to its centralized mechanism, it is used in private blockchains.

Proof of Elapsed Time (PoET)

Intel Corporation developed this algorithm that is similar to the PoW (Bowman et al., 2021). Each miner has to solve a problem. Approvers of each block are selected according to the shortest time taken to solve the problem. For this, a reliable function is used through block creation. This process selects the miner in the network randomly. The network provides a trusted environment for the security of the electoral process. Special Intel hardware is for the trusted execution environment. Its dependency on Intel increases decentralization that is against blockchain technology.

Practical Byzantine Fault Tolerance (PBFT)

Barbara Liskov and Miguel Castro introduced this algorithm. Byzantine Fault Tolerance is a phenomenon of distributed networks to reach consensus even if some minority number of the nodes are not responding or responding with wrong information. The objective is to safeguard the transaction failures through collective decision-making by reducing the faulty nodes influence. Malicious attacks on the industry and government's online services are serious issues that lead to very harmful consequences. The software for online services is very complex. As a result, software errors have been increased. These issues can be due to some misbehavior of any faulty node (Li et al., 2019). All nodes take part in voting for adding a new block to the network. But even if some minority number of nodes fail to respond, the transaction will be allowed to be completed. Therefore, the condition for consensus is to have a positive opinion by more than the two-thirds of nodes. The consensus is economical and reaches quickly as compared to PoW and there is no need for any minimum amount in the stake.

Delegated Byzantine Fault Tolerance (DBFT)

This method is similar to PBFT, but all nodes do not participate in the voting process for adding a new block (Zhan et al., 2021). The method is like a country's governance system where apart from the citizens, some delegates are selected by the citizens to run the country (network) through voting and a speaker is randomly selected from the delegates to create a new block. Citizens are the ordinary nodes. Some professional nodes fulfilling some minimum requirements are selected as the delegates through a voting process to validate transactions for all nodes. A speaker among the delegates is randomly picked up. The delegates listen to the citizen's demands and keep a vigil on all transactions and record them on the ledger. For verifying a new block, the speaker will propose the block and send it to all delegates. If at least the two-thirds of delegates agree, the block is accepted and added to the network. Otherwise, a new speaker is picked up to repeat the process.

Proof of Weight (PoWeight)

MIT Computer Science & Artificial Intelligence Laboratory created the cryptocurrency, Algorand based on this protocol. PoWeight combines different consensus algorithm. A Byzantine protocol is used to scale up users with different weights (Sharma et al., 2019). A weight is assigned to each user. These factors are determined by the amount of money in the accounts of users. Two-third or more users should behave honestly for the security of the transactions. Such networks safeguard against double-spend attacks. Proof of Reputation, Proof of Space, and Proof of Time are some variants. It is customizable, scalable, quicker in completing transactions but profitless for the participants. Cryptocurrencies like Chia and Filecoin are currently using PoWeight.

Proof of Burn (PoB)

In this algorithm, participants have to spend their cryptocurrencies to a specific address called an eater address to get rewards (Karantias et al., 2020). Such cryptocurrency spent can never be claimed nor re-spent because it goes out of circulation. So, the name is Proof of Burn. It consumes no resources and energy. A short-term loss is tolerated for a long-term reward. One currency is burned for getting another currency. It is similar to PoS in which stockholders with more stacks have more chances to get more rewards.

Proof of Capacity (PoC)

Dziembowski started Proof of Capacity (PoC), in 2015 (Azbeg et al., 2021). Miners utilize the available free spaces of their hard disk to mine free coins. Burstcoin used this algorithm in 2014 (https://www.burst-coin.org/features/proof-of-capacity/).

The algorithm first uses the plotting of hard disks in which miners create nonces by using a Shabal hash that is very slow. These nonces are similar to lottery tickets. Shabal hashes are kept precalculated in the hard disk to ensure faster mining. The condition for starting mining is that a miner should first fill all of his specified free space in a hard disk with nonces. A miner wins a block if a hash in a nonce is the nearest one to the recent puzzle in the blockchain. Another name for this algorithm is Proof of Space (PoSpace).

Burstcoin's slogan is "No more energy waste." PoC is greener than PoW. Bitcoin uses hardware like CPU, GPU, and ASIC for mining. PoC uses only HDD. So, it is fair enough for every miner because any miner cannot take advantage of special hardware. It is decentralized.

Proof of Importance (PoI)

To avoid issues in the Proof of Stake algorithm, Proof of Importance was introduced by the NEM project (Bach et al., 2018). In PoS, the criteria for getting any reward are to increase the score by holding back more amount of currency. But in PoI, each participant receives a score called importance score as a small reward for transactions completed in the network. Factors that determine a score of participants are as below:

Vesting: The number of vested coins will increase the score. But the coins should attain a minimum age to be considered for adding into the score.

Number of Transactions: More number transactions with other NEM accounts will further improve the score.

Amount in Transactions: Transactions above a threshold value will also increase the score.

Calculating the final score, a participant can add a new block to the network if she gets a chance. This method is more decentralized. It makes a good balance between locking the currencies in accounts and spreading them. No special hardware is required for mining.

Proof of Activity (PoA)

Bentov et al. (Bentov et al., 2014) presented this algorithm by combining PoW and PoS. It works as a guard to the serious problems in Bitcoin called the tragedy of the commons in which the miners think of their self-interests and attacks like DoS attack.

It requires more energy and resources. It is prone to double-spending. PoA is implemented in Decred and Espers.

ISSUES IN BLOCKCHAIN CONSENSUS ALGORITHMS

Due to the specific structure of blockchain, its speed and capacity are limited. The network has to be synchronized and validate all transactions through mutual agreement, transactions cannot be added to the distributed ledger at once. Transactions are updated at a regular interval. Target block rate is a typical parameter, e.g., for Bitcoin, it is 10 minutes (Bamakan et al., 2020). This is not practical in business. Even the slowest card payment is possible in a minute or two. Blocks are of fixed size with maximum value for safeguarding the network against DoS attacks. One solution to the capacity limit is the creation of sidechains used for offloading some of the transactions to them.

FUTURE RESEARCH DIRECTIONS

Future works in the field need to be explored for some more comprehensive consensus algorithm that can enhance the security of blocks, scalability of transactions, and efficiency of the network. These are the primary issues related to the consensus algorithms that should be addressed.

A more comprehensive permissionless hybrid consensus protocol can be explored that will combine the advantages in most of the consensus protocols and limit their disadvantages.

CONCLUSION

Consensus algorithms play an important role in the wider acceptability of Blockchain technology. All the participants must grow to a consensus before they agree to stamp the transaction into the new block and finally attach the new block into the blockchain. For blockchain technology to spread in all kinds of business transactions, the security of the blocks must be ensured. In this chapter, a brief description of the basic concepts of Blockchain technology is provided. A detailed description of consensus algorithms is given. In the end, some applications of Blockchain technology are provided including the advantages and disadvantages of the technology.

REFERENCES

Ali, M. S., Vecchio, M., Putra, G. D., Kanhere, S. S., & Antonelli, F. (2020). A Decentralized Peer-to-Peer Remote Health Monitoring System. *Sensors (Basel)*, *20*(6), 1656. doi:10.339020061656 PMID:32188135

Alsunaidi, S. J., & Alhaidari, F. A. (2019). A Survey of Consensus Algorithms for Blockchain Technology. *International Conference on Computer and Information Sciences (ICCIS)*, 1-6. 10.1109/ICCISci.2019.8716424

Azbeg, K., Ouchetto, O., Andaloussi, S. J., & Fetjah, L. (2021). An Overview of Blockchain Consensus Algorithms: Comparison, Challenges and Future Directions. *Advances on Smart and Soft Computing*, 357-369.

Bach, L. M., Mihaljevic, B., & Zagar, M. (2018, May). Comparative analysis of blockchain consensus algorithms. In *2018 41st International Convention on Information and Communication Technology, Electronics and Microelectronics (MIPRO)* (pp. 1545-1550). IEEE.

Baggetta. (n.d.). *Blockchain For Beginners: What Is Blockchain Technology? A Step-by-Step Guide*. Accessed on 4 July 2021 https://blockgeeks.com/guides/what-is-blockchain-technology

Bamakan, S. M. H., Motavali, A., & Bondarti, A. B. (2020). A survey of blockchain consensus algorithms performance evaluation criteria. *Expert Systems with Applications*, *154*, 113385. doi:10.1016/j.eswa.2020.113385

Barhanpure, A., Belandor, P., & Das, B. (2018, September). Proof of stack consensus for blockchain networks. In *International Symposium on Security in Computing and Communication* (pp. 104-116). Springer.

Bentov, I., Lee, C., Mizrahi, A., & Rosenfeld, M. (2014). Proof of activity: Extending bitcoin's proof of work via proof of stake [extended abstract]. *Performance Evaluation Review, 42*(3), 34–37.

Bowman, M., Das, D., Mandal, A., & Montgomery, H. (2021). *On Elapsed Time Consensus Protocols.* IACR Cryptol. ePrint Arch., 2021, 86.

Buterin, V. (2014). A next-generation smart contract and decentralized application platform. *White Paper, 3*(37).

Chaum, D., Rivest, R. L., & Sherman, A. T. (1998). *CRYPTO '82. In Advances in Cryptology 1981–1997.* Springer.

Gramoli, V. (2020). From blockchain consensus back to Byzantine consensus. *Future Generation Computer Systems, 107*, 760–769. doi:10.1016/j.future.2017.09.023

Jamil, F., Iqbal, N., Imran, Ahmad, S., & Kim, D. (2021). Imran, Ahmad, S., and Kim, D. "Peer-to-Peer Energy Trading Mechanism Based on Blockchain and Machine Learning for Sustainable Electrical Power Supply in Smart Grid. *IEEE Access: Practical Innovations, Open Solutions, 9*, 39193–39217. doi:10.1109/ ACCESS.2021.3060457

Karantias, K., Kiayias, A., & Zindros, D. (2020, February). *Proof-of-burn. In International Conference on Financial Cryptography and Data Security* (pp. 523-540). Springer.

Larimer, D. (2017). *Delegated Proof-of-Stake (DPOS) 2014.* Academic Press.

Li, J., Jing, X., & Yang, H. (2019). Blockchain electronic counting scheme based on practical Byzantine fault tolerance algorithm. *Jisuanji Yingyong, 40*(4), 954–960.

Nakamoto, S. (2008). Bitcoin: A peer-to-peer electronic cash system. *Decentralized Business Review*.

Niranjanamurthy, M., Nithya, B. N., & Jagannatha, S. (2019). Analysis of Blockchain technology: Pros, cons and SWOT. *Cluster Computing, 22*(S6), 14743–14757. doi:10.100710586-018-2387-5

Pahlajani, S., Kshirsagar, A., & Pachghare, V. (2019). Survey on private blockchain consensus algorithms. *2019 1st International Conference on Innovations in Information and Communication Technology (ICIICT),* 1-6. 10.1109/ ICIICT1.2019.8741353

Sharma, K., & Jain, D. (2019, July). Consensus algorithms in blockchain technology: A survey. In *2019 10th International Conference on Computing, Communication and Networking Technologies (ICCCNT)* (pp. 1-7). IEEE.

Sherman, A. T., Javani, F., Zhang, H., & Golaszewski, E. (2019). On the origins and variations of blockchain technologies. *IEEE Security and Privacy*, *17*(1), 72–77. doi:10.1109/MSEC.2019.2893730

Sun, Y., Yan, B., Yao, Y., & Yu, J. (2021). DT-DPoS: A Delegated Proof of Stake Consensus Algorithm with Dynamic Trust. *Procedia Computer Science*, *187*, 371–376. doi:10.1016/j.procs.2021.04.113

Why Proof-of-Capacity is the future. (n.d.). https://www.burst-coin.org/features/proof-of-capacity/

Zhan, Y., Wang, B., Lu, R., & Yu, Y. (2021). DRBFT: Delegated randomization Byzantine fault tolerance consensus protocol for blockchains. *Information Sciences*, *559*, 8–21.

Zheng, Z., Xie, S., Dai, H., Chen, X., & Wang, H. (2017). An overview of blockchain technology: Architecture, consensus, and future trends. 2017 IEEE international congress on big data (BigData congress), 557-564.

Chapter 3
Blockchain Primer:
Introduction to Blockchain Foundations and Implementation

Mohammad Amin Kuhail
Zayed University, UAE

Sujith S. Mathew
Zayed University, UAE

Rawad Hammad
https://orcid.org/0000-0002-7900-8640
East London University, UK

Mohamed Bahja
University of Birmingham, UK

ABSTRACT

Blockchain technology has the potential to revolutionize several industries including finance, supply chain and logistics, healthcare, and more. This primer introduces readers to basic development skills to blockchain foundations including blockchain cryptography, the consensus algorithm, and smart contracts. Further, this primer explains stepwise how to implement and deploy basic data stores using blockchain with Python. The primer serves as a succinct introductory guide to blockchain foundations by relying on a case study illustrated with visuals together with instructions on implementation. This primer is intended for educators, students, and technology enthusiasts with foundational computer science and Python development skills.

DOI: 10.4018/978-1-7998-8382-1.ch003

INTRODUCTION

Blockchain technology has rapidly become a disruptive technology for a host of industries including finance, healthcare, real estate, and more, thanks to its ability to assure data privacy, ownership protection, and manage huge volumes of data.

The first realization of blockchain began in 2009 with cryptocurrencies, particularly, the Bitcoin blockchain, a secure, peer-to-peer digital monetary system (Wallac, 2011). Since then, numerous other manifestations of blockchain technology have emerged ranging from securely transferring medical data (Burstiq, 2021) to automating and securing real estate transaction (Propy, 2021) and to identity and credential management (Evernym, 2021).

Simply put, a blockchain is a distributed growing network of data records, called blocks (Narayanan et al., 2016). Figure 1 shows a simplified version of a chain of blocks. Each block consists of the stored data as well as the data and time the data was stored (timestamp). Further, a block is uniquely identified by a hash code. Moreover, a block refers to the previous block using the previous hash code. The first block, also called the Genesis block, has no predecessor, and thus, it does not contain a previous hash attribute.

Figure 1. An illustration of a chain of blocks

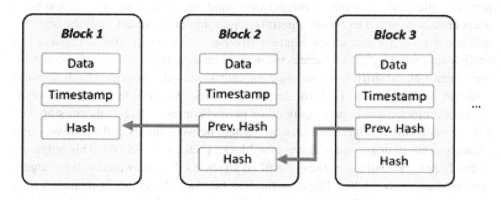

The purpose of this chapter is to introduce the reader to the foundations of the blockchain technology by answering the following research questions (RQ) using the literature:

1. RQ1: What type of cryptography does the blockchain technology use to protect data?
2. RQ2: How does the blockchain technology manage and tamperproof distributed data?
3. RQ3: How does the blockchain technology facilitate transactional contracts?
4. RQ4: How can we present a minimal case study that explains the implementation of a blockchain?

To answer the first question, we identified literature presenting foundational cryptography used by the blockchain technology. In short, blockchain uses an algorithm to calculate the hash codes. The value of the code depends on the data in the block (timestamp, data, etc.). As such, the generated code varies from block to block. Blockchain uses this mechanism to prevent data tampering (Al-Kuwari et al., 2011). For instance, assuming an attacker could change the data in Block 2. Accordingly, the hash of the block would also change. However, Block 3 would still refer to the old hash code of Block 2. As a result, this would make Block 3, and all succeeding blocks invalid since they do not contain the correct hash of the previous block. This concept is discussed in more detail in the section titled as "Cryptography in Blockchain".

To answer the second research question, we identified literature on how blockchain keeps track of distributed data and prevents data tampering. Some blockchains are permissionless whereas others are permissioned. In a permissionless blockchain, users are not required to obtain a permission to join and interact with the network making it ideal for use cases where a diverse set of the public is expected to participate (Stifter, 2021), whereas users can join a permissioned blockchain after their identities are sufficiently verified. In such a network, users may be designated different permissions to perform certain activities. Nevertheless, irrespective of whether a blockchain is permissioned or permissionless, its records are stored in a distributed and decentralized network, where network nodes collaboratively and securely communicate and validate new blocks (Nakamoto, 2008). This helps the technology to be resilient in the event of an attack, as the data would still be largely operational (BEIS, 2020). The coordination between the nodes is managed by a consensus algorithm, which is presented in the section titled "Consensus Algorithm". The section briefly explains some of the widely used algorithms that allow the data on the chain to be distributed and tamper-proof.

To answer the third research question, we identified literature on facilitating transactional contracts with blockchain. Another layer of security that Blockchain could use is smart contracts. Such contracts are programs run when certain conditions are fulfilled (Tapscott, 2018). Blockchain uses smart contracts to automate the agreement between participants of a transaction without any broker's involvement.

Smart contracts are discussed in detail in the section titled "Smart Contracts". The section presents how the technology allows for transactions between several parties to be seamlessly organized.

Finally, in the "Case Study" section, we attempt to answer the fourth research question by discussing the implementation of a program that uses blockchain to store medical records of patients. We used Python to implement the program as it is one of the most popular programming languages.

CRYPTOGRAPHY IN BLOCKCHAIN

Cryptography is the practice of developing techniques and protocols preventing third parties from accessing private data (Rivest, 1990). Cryptography draws its knowledge from several disciplines including mathematics, computer science, physics, engineering, and more.

The term "cryptography" is composed of two Greek terms: "Kryptos", meaning hidden, and "graphein", meaning to write (Marriam-Webster, 2021). The term "Kryptos" is related to a Greek term *"kryptein"* (meaning to hide), which is a root word shared by several English words, including "encrypt". *Encryption* is the process of converting normal text (plaintext) into unrecognizable random sequences of bits (ciphertext), while *decryption* is the inverse process of encryption, i.e., to convert ciphertext to plaintext (Kessler, 1998).

Public-Key Cryptography

Public-key cryptography uses a pair of keys: a public key and a private key. The public key may be freely distributed, whereas the private key is designed to be known only by the owner. For example, if John wants to send a message (i.e., "Hello") to Ann securely. He uses Ann's public key to encrypt it. Only Ann can decrypt the message using her private key (Figure 2).

In the context of blockchain, each transaction must be digitally signed. For instance, assuming someone wants to send a friend digital money on the blockchain. First, the transaction is encrypted using the public key of the receiver. Next, the transaction is signed using the private key of the receiver which proves that the transaction has not been altered (Brito & Castillo, 2013). The digital signature is generated through combining the private key with the data being sent in the transaction. Further, some algorithms incorporate a timestamp for the digital signature, so that even if the private key is exposed, the signature remains valid (Fang et al., 2020). Finally, the transaction can be verified as authentic using the accompanying public key.

Figure 2. Public-private cryptography

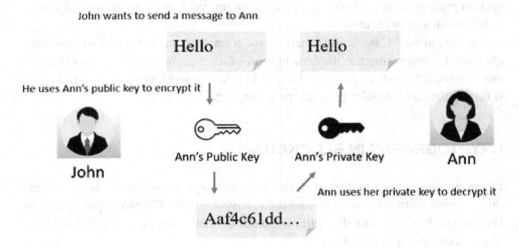

John wants to send a message to Ann

Hello

Hello

He uses Ann's public key to encrypt it

Ann's Public Key

Ann's Private Key

John

Ann

Ann uses her private key to decrypt it

Aaf4c61dd...

Once the involved parties receive the signed transaction, they validate the transaction and spread it throughout the network. All the peers who are involved in the transactions mutually validate the transaction to meet a consensus agreement (more about this in the consensus algorithm section). Once a consensus is reached, a special element, named as *miners*, incorporates the validated transaction into a block with a timestamp. Then, the block is broadcast into the network. The block is appended into the blockchain after hash-matching it with the previous block on the chain (Ferrag et al., 2019).

Cryptographic Hashing

Cryptographic hashing uses a function that converts plaintext into a unique string of letters and numbers. The output is deterministic and will always be the same for the same input (Lyubashevsky et al., 2008). Unlike encrypted data, it is not possible to reconstitute your original data from the output it produces. There are several examples of hashing functions such as SHA-256 (Khovratovich et al., 2011) and Blake2 (Aumasson, 2021; BLAKE2, 2021). Such functions are complex and based on advanced mathematics and can generate unique hash functions in a relatively short time.

A cryptographic hash function has these key features: (1) The same input always results in the same hash code, (2) It is relatively efficient to compute the hash code for a given piece of data, (3) It is not possible to reverse a hash code to the original data, (4) it is almost impossible to generate the same hash code for two different input data, and (5) the hash code relies on the input content. As such, even a small change to the message alters the hash code.

In the context of blockchain, when a new block is added to the chain, a hash code is generated to uniquely identify the block and the network reaches a consensus to validate the data contained in the block. We discuss how a consensus is reached in the following section.

CONSENSUS ALGORITHM

Consensus is achieved when the majority of the blockchain network nodes decide on a single state. However, there are problems to tackle before reaching a consensus. In general, the problems stem from a dilemma in the distributed computing space called the Byzantine fault. A *Byzantine fault* is described with an allegorical situation where generals of the Byzantine empire are camped with their troops on different sides of a large city that they plan to attack. The generals communicate with each other through messengers. The messages could be delayed, lost, destroyed, or malicious. To add to the dilemma, one or more of the generals are traitors and they may send out conflicting messages. The goal is to find an algorithm for a mutual plan among the loyal generals (Lamport et al., 1982). This problem is solvable if and only if two-thirds of the generals are not traitors. Consequently, there must be at least three generals to avoid a Byzantine fault.

Byzantine faults are difficult to handle and therefore Byzantine fault tolerance has been a mandatory requirement for many multi-nodal network-based real-time systems. Blockchains are distributed, peer-to-peer networks without a central curator and without ensuring Byzantine fault tolerance, peers in the network could effectively nullify the blockchain's reliability. Therefore, it becomes mandatory to ensure Byzantine fault tolerance and bring consensus among the nodes in a blockchain. Another well-known problem, that is specific to cryptocurrencies that use blockchain is called double spending. For instance, with physical currency, if some apples were purchased for $1 then that dollar cannot be used by the same person again, but with the digital currency, it would be possible if the system did not ensure Byzantine fault tolerance and judiciously validate transactions.

So, why is a consensus algorithm required? Firstly, a consensus algorithm is required to ensure Byzantine fault tolerance, and this is because blockchain-based systems are decentralized peer-to-peer networks and decision making is a critical process to ensure the stability of the system. Next, to ensure efficiency and fairness in the network the consensus algorithm is used for a reward and punishment mechanism based on participant behavior and this is typically exercised using an incentive scheme that involves cryptocurrencies. Finally, a consensus algorithm is used to decide which of the nodes can modify the blockchain i.e., to add a new block and verify the transactions. There are different algorithms to ensure consensus, here we discuss some of the popular implementations. A well-known consensus algorithm is Proof of Work which is employed in cryptocurrencies like Bitcoin, as described in the white paper by Satoshi Nakamoto (Nakamoto, 2008).

Proof of Work

This Proof of Work (PoW) algorithm is based on the computational power a network node would deploy to prove its demand to modify the blockchain. The power deployed, or the proof-of-work is to solve a puzzle that involves the determining of a value that when hashed, the hash has a certain number of leading zero bits called the nonce. The average computational power required is exponential to the nonce required and is verified by executing a single hash. Nodes in the network compete to solve the puzzle and the competing nodes are generally called validators or in the case of Bitcoin, they are called miners. Therefore, PoW requires the validators to guess the source of a given hash value with a specific number of leading zeros. The probability of arriving at the hash value is very low (Wang et al., 2018). The first node to solve the puzzle gets to modify the blockchain and is rewarded, while the other validators verify the solution. The incentivization scheme for the successful validator (usually with cryptocurrency) motivates the validators to continue competing. An issue with PoW is that it is resource-intensive and consumes a lot of electric energy. However, this expensive effort which includes hardware, software, and energy is also what deters attacks on the blockchain network.

Proof of Stake

With the Proof of Stake (PoS) consensus, the validators must prove their stake i.e. they have to invest an amount of currency in the blockchain. The higher the stake of a validator, the higher will be the possibility of being selected to modify the blockchain. In this case, it is less likely to have fraudulent transactions approved as it would adversely affect the validators themselves. The process requires the validators to verify all the transactions in a block and then to sign the block using a cryptographic hash function so that the block can be added to the blockchain. The validator node is incentivized for successfully completing this task and therefore the validators are motivated to continue investing in the blockchain. Successful implementation of PoS is seen in Ethereum Eth2 update (Buterin et al., 2020), BlackCoin (Li et al., 2017), and Algorand (Chen & Micali, 2019). PoS is a more energy-efficient option than PoW. An evolution of the PoS algorithm is the Delegated Proof of Stace (DPoS) algorithm. Here, the stakeholders elect delegates to validate the next block. In some applications of DPoS the delegates must stake an amount of cryptocurrency and in other applications like Ethereum 2.0 the stakeholders vote on delegates by pooling cryptocurrency into a staking pool and linking their stake to a delegate. Elected delegates receive a transaction fee for validating or including a block, and that reward is then shared with stakeholders who pooled their cryptocurrency towards the successful delegate's pool. It is also the responsibility of the stakeholders to vote against delegates that performed wrong transactions (Lee, 2015). Unlike PoW and PoS, the DPoS adapts a more democratic process for choosing the next validator, allowing more diversity of participation based on earned reputation and not just overall wealth.

Proof of Authority

The Proof of Authority (PoA) consensus requires the validators to leverage their reputation for an opportunity to modify the blockchain (De Angelis et al., 2018). In this case, the validators stake their real identities and therefore their reputation to get approved by network participants as delegates to modify the blockchain. These trustworthy delegates would also have invested currency into the blockchain. This process allows the elimination of validators with malicious intent while incentivizing continuing commitment. This approach would be favorable for permissioned blockchains within enterprises (Helliar et al., 2020). However, the same standard consensus algorithm must be used to select validators to ensure that all participants are given equal opportunities. The limitation of PoA is that the real identities of the validators are exposed, raising privacy concerns and the possibility of malicious manipulation of validators. PoA implementations are seen in VeChain (Liu, 2019) and Ethereum Express.

Practical Byzantine Fault Tolerance

The Practical Byzantine Fault Tolerance (pBFT) consensus algorithm assumes failures and malicious activities to occur and therefore as the name suggests plans to tolerate the failure or maliciousness of one-third (1/3) of the nodes. In general, pBFT algorithm has a group of validators predefined to receive a transaction and reach a consensus on the required tasks. The validators are ordered in a sequence where one of them gets to be a leader and the rest are backup validators. To reach a consensus, the validators communicate heavily with each other to verify the source and also to verify that data has not been tampered with during the communication. The first step in the process is that the leader receives the request to modify the blockchain from a client. Next, the leader broadcasts the request to the backup validators. Next, each backup node verifies the transaction and informs the client. The client can confirm its transaction if the number of responses is greater than the failures that the pBFT allows. The leader may be replaced if the majority of the validators decide that the leader is malicious or after a duration of time. Zilliqa (Hazari & Mahmoud, 2019) uses the pBFT implementation for consensus. The pBFT consensus algorithm allows the blockchain to operate with high performance, reduced energy consumption, and require no endorsements to finalize transactions. However, because of heavy communication pBFT is best suited for a small number of validators, but this makes it prone to Sybil attacks where a single node can manipulate many nodes in the network, thus compromising the consensus algorithm (Sukhwani et al., 2017). Also, since there is the notion of a centralized leader node, this is most suited in private or permissioned blockchains.

Hyperledger Consensus

Hyperledger is an open-source standard platform for distributed ledgers under the Linux Foundation. Hyperledger Fabric is an implementation of the Hyperledger project which is a Byzantine Fault-Tolerant Consensus library for operating permissioned blockchains (Cachin, 2017; Barger et al., 2021). Consensus is a multi-step process and applications that request modification of blockchain are notified of ledger updates when all operations are completed. There are three main operations in the process i.e. endorsement, ordering, and validation (Androulaki et al., 2018). The endorsement process starts with an application proposing a blockchain modification and defining which of the nodes must endorse a transaction. Endorsers verify if a given transaction will be successful or not, signs the transaction, and returns it to the application. Next, the ordering process starts with the Orderers receiving endorsed transaction proposals from many applications. They are responsible for a consistent ledger state by collecting proposed transaction updates, ordering them, packaging them into blocks, and delivering them to all the nodes. Finally, the distribution and subsequent validation of blocks, followed by the transactions committed to the ledger. In Hyperledger, this entire workflow is required to achieve consensus because all nodes have reached a consensus on the order and content of transactions as mediated by Orderers.

SMART CONTRACTS

Smart Contracts are essential to blockchain technology as it facilitates its decentralization concept. Smart Contracts, as a term, was first coined in 1996 by Nick Szabo, a well-known cryptographer, to describe a set of promises, specified in digital form, including protocols within which the parties perform on these promises

(Szabo, 1996). The overall aim of smart contract is to execute, automatically, the agreement terms whenever the early-specified conditions are met or achieved (Buterin, 2015). To do so, such smart contracts have executable code that can be developed and deployed on certain blockchain platforms. Despite the relatively long history of smart contracts, their development and adoption remained dormant due to many technological and legal challenges in the last couple of decades. Such challenges did not allow secure and reliable implementation for smart contracts in various industries. For instance, secure and reliable smart contracts should have the following two qualities, which are inherited from software engineering discipline. First, Smart Contract Quality, which describes the correctness of the program. Second, Smart Contract Quality-in-Use, which describes the security issues that may occur during the execution of these smart contracts in certain contexts. The former can be considered as a static concern, while the latter is more dynamic (Hammad et al., 2015).

The substantive recent developments in Blockchain technology coupled with technical disciplines such as Artificial Intelligence and non-technical disciplines such as internet law allow great progress in smart contracts implementation (Liu & Liu, 2019). Such progress includes the rapid increase of the emerging Blockchain platforms that facilitate the development and deployment of smart contracts to meet innumerable business demands in financial transactions, prediction markets, Internet of Things, to name a few. For instance, in a few years many platforms appear, and many are still under continuous development till now. Examples of stable platforms include: Ethereum, Bitcoin, Stellar, Hyperledger Fabric, to mention but a few. Each platform has its own qualities. However, recent research evidence, e.g., (Hammad et al., 2015), reveals that Ethereum is the most common deployment platform for smart contracts. Delineating all the differences between these platforms is beyond the purpose of this chapter, yet further information can be found in (Zheng et al., 2020).

Nonetheless, it is centric to highlight how effective adoption of any of these platforms can impact the life cycle of smart contracts. Briefly, the life cycle of smart contracts consists of the following four stages (Zheng et al., 2020). *First*, creation of smart contracts, where involved parties negotiate the obligations, rights, and prohibitions on contracts. Once agreement reached, after many iterations, parties representatives write it in natural language so software engineers can convert to a computational format. *Second*, deployment of smart contracts, where the early-validated smart contracts deployed to certain platforms on the top of blockchains. Consequently, deployed smart contracts can be accessed by all parties but cannot be modified due to blockchain immutability. *Third*, execution of smart contracts, where the contractual conditions/clauses of the early-deployed smart contracts have been under continuous monitoring and evaluation. Once these conditions are met, the contractual procedures, i.e., functions, will be automatically executed, which entails validating all transactions by miners in the blockchain (Koulu, 2016). Finally, *Fourth*, completion of smart contracts, where new states of the involved parties need to be amended and stored in the blockchain. In addition, digital assets need to be transferred from one party to another as per request.

It is crucial mentioning that throughout the above-mentioned stages, full software development life cycle for Ultra Large-Scale Software Systems occurs. Hence, a very thorough assessment for risks is needed to avoid any vulnerabilities. For example, in 2017, one of the Ethereum multi-signature wallet Parity lost approximately $30 million due some security vulnerabilities (Liu & Liu, 2019). Such vulnerabilities range from contract vulnerabilities such as: transaction-ordering dependence and timestamp dependence, to privacy and legal issues such as: contract data privacy and trusted data feed privacy. Hence, Destefanis et al. (2018) argue that a rigor blockchain-specific software engineering approach is needed to handle the above-presented vulnerabilities and other challenges including: (i) readability, i.e., creation stage, (ii) dynamic control flow, i.e., deployment, (iii) execution efficiency, i.e., execution, and (iv) scamming, i.e., completion stage (Zheng et al., 2020).

CASE STUDY

Blockchain technology and related applications are still emerging. Various case studies have been recently presented in the literature in the areas of higher education (Mikroyannidis et al., 2020), supply chain (Casado-Vara et al., 2018; Lu et al. 2017), business model (Oh et al., 2017), and digital security (Dorri et al., 2017; Ye et al., 2018). Case studies focused on the healthcare services have also been discussed in the literature (Jadhav et al., 2020; Heston, 2017).

While most of the case studies focus on the feasibility of integrating blockchain in the respective application domain, our case study focuses on the development of the technology using Python programming language. We explain a minimum viable Python-based version of Blockchain that stores medical information. The information includes names of patients as well as the medications they ordered, the quantity of each medication, and the number of refills. Figure 3 shows a visualization of three blocks: the first block is the genesis block, and the other two contain medical orders of several patients (Sam, Neil, Adam, Jose, and John). Each block has an index, date and time, proof of work, hash code, and previous hash.

To create the blockchain, we create a class named "BlockChain" that keeps track of the blocks in a list named "chain". The chain initially creates the genesis block, the first block on the chain. Further, the "Blockchain" class also keeps track of pending data named "temp_data". This data will be stored on the blockchain when a proof of work is presented.

Figure 3. Medication orders stored on the blockchain

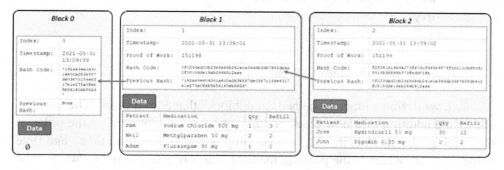

```python
class BlockChain ():
    def __init__(self):
        self.chain = [self.create_genesis_block()]
        self.temp_data = []
```

The function "create_genesis_block" defines the first block on the chain. The block index is 0 (Line 7) and is timestamped based on the current date and time (Line 8). The block does not contain data (Line 9). Since it's the first block on the chain, it does not have a previous hash code (Line 10).

```python
def create_genesis_block(self):
    return {
        'index': 0,
        'timestamp': time (),
        'data': None,
    'prev_hash': None
    }
```

Next, we define a function named "new_data" that adds a medical order to the current block. The medical order contains the patient's name (patient), the prescribed medication (medication), the medication quantity (qty), and the refill number (refill). We used a dictionary to store the patient information (Lines 13-18). Thereafter, the data is added to the list of pending data (temp_data) (Line 19). temp_data will be stored permanently when a new block is verified and added finally on the chain.

```python
def new_data (self, patient, medication, qty, refill):
    data = {
        'patient': patient,
```

```
        'medication': medication,
        'qty':qty,
    'refill':refill
    }
    self.temp_data.append(data)
```

Next, we define a function named "add_block" that adds a block. The function allows the addition of a new block containing an index representing the order of the block in the chain (Line 22), a timestamp which is the current date and time (Line 23), data which is the pending medical orders of patients (Line 24), and the hash code of the previous block (Line 25). The previous hash code is calculated by calling the hash_code function and passing the latest block on the chain to it. When a new block is added, the proof of work is presented, and thus, the temporary data is now permanently added on the block (Line 28).

```
def add_block (self, proof_of_work):
    block = {
        'index': len(self.chain) + 1,
        'timestamp': time (),
        'data': self.temp_data,
        'prev_hash': self.hash_code(self.chain[-1]),
    }
    self.temp_data = []
    self.chain.append(block)

    return block
```

The last piece in the puzzle is the hash_code function which simply calculates a hash code for a block based on its data and other attributes. The first step is to create a string representing the block using json.dumps (Line 32). To calculate a hash code based on the block data, the data must be first encoded (Line 33), then the hash code is computed using the "sha256" function (Line 34). The function calculates a unique number representing the data in the block. Thereafter, we convert the number into a hexadecimal number using the hexdigest() function (Line 35).

```
def hash_code (self, block):
    str_obj = json.dumps(block, sort_keys=True)
    str = str_obj.encode()
    hash_number = hashlib.sha256(str)
```

```
    hexadeimal_hash = hash_number.hexdigest()
    return hexadeimal_hash
```

Now that the Blockchain class is ready, we can start using it. First, we create an instance of the Blockchain class (Line 37). Then, we create three medical records for three patients, Sam, Neil, and Adam (Lines 38-40). Thereafter, in Line 41, we add the records to a block with a simulation of proof of work being presented: 151198.

Similarly, we add another block of medical orders in lines 42,43 for patients Jose and John. Finally, we show the blockchain data in the console (Line 45). The data is shown visually in Figure 3.

```
block_chain = BlockChain ()
d000 = block_chain.new_data ("Sam", "Sodium Chloride 800 mg",1,
3)
d001 = block_chain.new_data ("Neil", "Methylparaben 50 mg",2,
2)
d002 = block_chain.new_data ("Adam", "Flurazepam 30 mg",1, 1)
block_chain.add_block (151198)
d003 = block_chain.new_data ("Jose", "Hydrodiuril 50 mg",30,
12)
d004 = block_chain.new_data ("John", "Digoxin 0.25 mg",30, 12)
block_chain.add_block (151199)
print ("Block Chain: ", block_chain.chain)
```

CONCLUSION

This chapter presented blockchain, which is a revolutionary technology that allows for storing large amounts of data on a decentralized peer-to-peer network. The chapter answered the research questions (RQ) presented in the introduction:

- RQ1: *What type of cryptography does the blockchain technology use to protect data?* Blockchain technology uses public key as well as hashing cryptography, making the data immutable and reliable. Further details can be found in the "Cryptography in Blockchain" section.
- RQ2: *How does the blockchain technology manage and tamperproof distributed data?* Blockchain is decentralized, which means a centralized authority to manage the network is not needed. The peers on a network manage and validate the transactions using a consensus algorithm. Further details can be found in the "Consensus Algorithm" section.

- RQ3: *How does the blockchain technology facilitate transactional contracts?* Blockchain can potentially use smart contracts to monitor transactions between several parties based on an agreement. In essence, a smart contract is a self-executing protocol which is controlled by its explicit terms and conditions, which stores and carries out contractual clauses. Further details can be found in the "Smart Contracts" section.
- RQ4: *How can we present a minimal case study that explains the implementation of a blockchain?* The chapter presented a simplified case study explaining how blockchain can be used to store patient's medical information (medication prescriptions). The case study briefly explained how blocks are connected, the hashing mechanism, and the validation of the blocks.

The popularity of blockchain increased with cryptocurrencies such as Bitcoin, which is essentially a digital ledger capable of recording and verifying a high volume of transactions. Now the technology is spreading to many other sectors such as healthcare, agriculture, real estate, and more. Many blockchain enthusiasts believe that we are only scratching the surface when it comes to developing compelling Blockchain use cases. In the future, the authors will present a study that discusses the applicability of blockchain in several fields together with a detailed case study on implementation and deployment.

REFERENCES

Al-Kuwari, S., Davenport, J. H., & Bradford, R. J. (2011). Cryptographic Hash Functions: Recent Design Trends and Security Notions. Short Paper Proceedings of Inscrypt '10.

Androulaki, E. (2018). Hyperledger Fabric: A Distributed Operating System for Permissioned Blockchains. *Proceedings of the 13th EuroSys Conference.* 10.1145/3190508.3190538

Aumasson, J. P. (2021). *Crypto Dictionary: 500 Tasty Tidbits for the Curious Cryptographer.* No Starch Press.

Barger, A., Manevich, Y., Meir, H., & Tock, Y. (2021). A Byzantine Fault-Tolerant Consensus Library for Hyperledger Fabric. In *2021 IEEE International Conference on Blockchain and Cryptocurrency (ICBC)* (pp. 1-9). IEEE. 10.1109/ICBC51069.2021.9461099

BEIS. (2020). *The use of distributed ledgers to verify the provenance of goods.* Final Report Department for Business, Energy & Industrial Strategy, Research Paper Number 2020/036.

BLAKE2. (2021). *Fast Secure Hashing.* https://www.blake2.net/

Brito, J., & Castillo, A. (2013). Bitcoin: A Primer for Policymakers (PDF). Fairfax, VA: Mercatus Center, George Mason University.

Burstiq. (2021). *Blockchain based healthcare data solutions.* https://www.burstiq.com/

Buterin, V. (2015). *A next-generation smart contract and decentralized application platform.* Available: https://github.com/ethereum/wiki/wiki/White-Paper/

Buterin, V. (2020). *Combining GHOST and Casper.* Available: https://arxiv.org/abs/2003.03052

Cachin, C., (2017). Architecture of the Hyperledger Blockchain Fabric. *Leibniz Int. Proc. Informatics*, *70*, 24.1-24.16.

Casado-Vara, R., Prieto, J., De la Prieta, F., & Corchado, J. M. (2018). How blockchain improves the supply chain: Case study alimentary supply chain. *Procedia Computer Science*, *134*, 393–398. doi:10.1016/j.procs.2018.07.193

Chen, J., & Micali, S. (2019). Algorand: A secure and efficient distributed ledger. *Theoretical Computer Science*, *777*, 155–183. doi:10.1016/j.tcs.2019.02.001

De Angelis, S., Aniello, L., Baldoni, R., Lombardi, F., Margheri, A., & Sassone, V. (2018). PBFT vs proof-of-authority: Applying the CAP theorem to permissioned blockchain. *CEUR Workshop Proceedings*, *2058*. https://eprints.soton.ac.uk/415083

Destefanis, G., Marchesi, M., Ortu, M., Tonelli, R., Bracciali, A., & Hierons, R. (2018). Smart contracts vulnerabilities: a call for blockchain software engineering? In *2018 International Workshop on Blockchain Oriented Software Engineering (IWBOSE)* (pp. 19-25). IEEE. 10.1109/IWBOSE.2018.8327567

Dorri, A., Kanhere, S. S., Jurdak, R., & Gauravaram, P. (2017). *Blockchain for IoT security and privacy: The case study of a smart home. In 2017 IEEE international conference on pervasive computing and communications workshops (PerCom workshops).* IEEE.

Evernym. (2021). *The Self-Sovereign Identity Company.* Available: https://www.evernym.com/

Fang, W., Chen, W., Zhang, W., Pei, J., Gao, W., & Wang, G. (2020). Digital signature scheme for information non-repudiation in blockchain: A state of the art review. *J Wireless Com Network*, *56*(1), 56. Advance online publication. doi:10.118613638-020-01665-w

Ferrag, M. A., Derdour, M., Mukherjee, M., Derhab, A., Maglaras, L., & Janicke, H. (2019, April). Blockchain Technologies for the Internet of Things: Research Issues and Challenges. *IEEE Internet of Things Journal*, *6*(2), 2188–2204. doi:10.1109/JIOT.2018.2882794

Hammad, R., Odeh, M., & Khan, Z. (2015). Towards a model-based approach to evaluate the effectiveness of e-learning. *Proceeding of the 9th European Conference on IS Management and Evaluation ECIME*, 111-119.

Hazari, S. S., & Mahmoud, Q. H. (2019). Comparative evaluation of consensus mechanisms in cryptocurrencies. *Internet Technol. Lett.*, *2*(3), e100. doi:10.1002/itl2.100

Helliar, C. V., Crawford, L., Rocca, L., Teodori, C., & Veneziani, M. (2020, October). Permissionless and permissioned blockchain diffusion. *International Journal of Information Management*, *54*, 102136. doi:10.1016/j.ijinfomgt.2020.102136

Heston, T. (2017). *A case study in blockchain healthcare innovation*. Academic Press.

Jadhav, V. D., & Moosafintavida, D. S. (2020). Blockchain in Healthcare Industry and Its Application and Impact on Covid 19 Digital Technology Transformation. *Mukt Shabd Journal*, *9*, 479.

Kessler, G. C. (1998). *An Overview of Cryptography*. Available at: https://www.garykessler.net/library/crypto.html

Khovratovich, D., Rechberger, C., & Savelieva, A. (2011). Bicliques for Preimages: Attacks on Skein-512 and the SHA-2 family. *IACR Cryptology Archive.*, *2011*, 286.

Koulu, R. (2016). Blockchains and online dispute resolution: Smart contracts as an alternative to enforcement. *Script-ed*, *13*(1), 40–69. doi:10.2966crip.130116.40

Lamport, L., Shostak, R., & Pease, M. (1982, July). The Byzantine Generals Problem. *ACM Transactions on Programming Languages and Systems*, *4*(3), 382–401. doi:10.1145/357172.357176

Lee, L. (2015). New Kids on the Blockchain: How Bitcoin's Technology Could Reinvent the Stock Market. SSRN *Electron. J.*, *12*. doi:10.2139/ssrn.2656501

Li, W., Andreina, S., Bohli, J. M., & Karame, G. (2017). Securing proof-of-stake blockchain protocols. In *Lecture Notes in Computer Science, 2017* (Vol. 10436, pp. 297–315). LNCS. doi:10.1007/978-3-319-67816-0_17

Liu, X. (2019). MDP-based quantitative analysis framework for proof of authority. *Proceedings - 2019 International Conference on Cyber-Enabled Distributed Computing and Knowledge Discovery*, 227–236. 10.1109/CyberC.2019.00046

Liu, J., & Liu, Z. (2019, June 7). A survey on security verification of blockchain smart contracts. *IEEE Access: Practical Innovations, Open Solutions*, 7, 77894–77904. doi:10.1109/ACCESS.2019.2921624

Lu, Q., & Xu, X. (2017). Adaptable blockchain-based systems: A case study for product traceability. *IEEE Software, 34*(6), 21–27. doi:10.1109/MS.2017.4121227

Lyubashevsky, V., Micciancio, D., Peikert, C., & Rosen, A. (2008). SWIFFT: A Modest Proposal for FFT Hashing. Fast Software Encryption. *Lecture Notes in Computer Science, 5086*, 54–72. doi:10.1007/978-3-540-71039-4_4

Marriam-Webster. (2021). *Definition of Cryptography.* Available: https://www.merriam-webster.com/dictionary/cryptography

Mikroyannidis, A., Third, A., Chowdhury, N., Bachler, M., & Domingue, J. (2020). Supporting Lifelong Learning with Smart Blockchain Badges. *International Journal On Advances in Intelligent Systems, 13*(3 & 4), 163–176.

Nakamoto, S. (2008). *Bitcoin: A Peer-to-Peer Electronic Cash System.* Available: https://bitcoin.org/bitcoin.pdf

Narayanan, A., Bonneau, J., Felten, E., Miller, A., & Goldfeder, S. (2016). *Bitcoin and cryptocurrency technologies: a comprehensive introduction.* Princeton University Press.

Oh, J., & Shong, I. (2017). *A case study on business model innovations using Blockchain: focusing on financial institutions. Asia Pacific Journal of Innovation and Entrepreneurship.*

Propy. (2021). *Automating Real Estate Transactions.* Available: https://propy.com/

Rivest, R. L. (1990). Cryptography. In J. Van Leeuwen (Ed.), *Handbook of Theoretical Computer Science* (Vol. 1). Elsevier.

Stifter, N. (2021). What is Meant by Permissionless Blockchains? Cryptology ePrint Archive, Report 2021/023.

Sukhwani, H., Martínez, J. M., Chang, X., Trivedi, K. S., & Rindos, A. (2017). Performance modeling of PBFT consensus process for permissioned blockchain network (hyperledger fabric). *Proceedings of the IEEE Symposium on Reliable Distributed Systems*, 253–255. 10.1109/SRDS.2017.36

Szabo, N. (1996). *Smart Contracts: Building Blocks for Digital Markets*. https://www.fon.hum.uva.nl/rob/Courses/InformationInSpeech/CDROM/Literature/LOTwinterschool2006/szabo.best.vwh.net/smart_contracts_2.html

Tapscott, D., & Tapscott, A. (2018). The Blockchain Revolution: How the Technology Behind Bitcoin is Changing Money, Business, and the World. Academic Press.

Wang, H., Zheng, Z., Xie, S., Dai, H. N., & Chen, X. (2018). Blockchain challenges and opportunities: A survey. *International Journal of Web and Grid Services*, *14*(4), 352. doi:10.1504/IJWGS.2018.10016848

Wallac, B. (2011). *The Rise and Fall of Bitcoin*. https://www.wired.com/2011/11/mf-bitcoin/

Ye, C., Li, G., Cai, H., Gu, Y., & Fukuda, A. (2018, September). Analysis of security in blockchain: Case study in 51%-attack detecting. In *2018 5th International Conference on Dependable Systems and Their Applications (DSA)* (pp. 15-24). IEEE.

Zheng, Z., Xie, S., Dai, H. N., Chen, W., Chen, X., Weng, J., & Imran, M. (2020). An overview on smart contracts: Challenges, advances and platforms. *Future Generation Computer Systems*, *105*, 475–491. doi:10.1016/j.future.2019.12.019

ADDITIONAL READING

Narayanan, A., Bonneau, J., Felten, E., Miller, A., & Goldfeder, S. (2016). *Bitcoin and cryptocurrency technologies: a comprehensive introduction*. Princeton University Press.

KEY TERMS AND DEFINITIONS

Blockchain: A distributed growing network of data records which are connected using cryptography.

Consensus Algorithm: A procedure used to reach agreement on a single data value among distributed systems or processes.

Cryptography: The practice of developing techniques and protocols preventing third parties from accessing private data.

Decryption: The inverse process of encryption, i.e., to convert ciphertext to plaintext.

Encryption: The process of converting normal text (plaintext) into unrecognizable random sequences of bit (ciphertext).

Hashing: The process of converting plaintext into a unique string of letters and numbers. It is not possible to reconstitute your original data from the output it produces.

Proof of Work: A mechanism that requires nodes of a network to solve an arbitrary mathematical puzzle to prevent anybody from gaming the system.

Smart Contract: A self-executing program or protocol which is controlled by explicit terms and conditions, which stores and carries out contractual clauses.

Chapter 4
Blockchain:
A Disruptive Technology

Arish Sidiqqui
University of East London, UK

Kazi Jubaer Tansen
iD https://orcid.org/0000-0003-4667-2868
University of East London, UK

ABSTRACT

Blockchain is distributed ledger technology. Its advancement has been compared to the rise of the internet with debate about the technology's probability to disrupt multiple industries including healthcare, transportation, real estate, public domains, manufacturing, intellectual property, education, and financial services. It is predicted that the blockchain will have a major impact on many trust-based environments due to its nature of recording any digital transaction that is secure, efficient, transparent, auditable, and resistant to the outage, thereby providing the much-needed security in the transfer of assets in cyberspace. This chapter will highlight some of the business processes that can be disrupted by blockchain technology.

INTRODUCTION

In recent years, the implementation of Blockchain technology has materialised rapidly with the potential to revolutionise not only the financial domain but also various spheres globally. This technology gained vast attention all over the world after the cryptocurrency known as Bitcoin was introduced by the pseudonym '*Satoshi Nakamoto*', an unknown entity (Baki, 2019). This technology is receiving significant

DOI: 10.4018/978-1-7998-8382-1.ch004

attention because of its usability and faultlessness. The decentralised architecture of Blockchain technology empowers a distributed consensus where transactions are verifiable and data is immutable. Therefore, advantages of transparency, security, efficiency, cost-effectiveness, adaptability and many more can be achieved perfectly through proper utilisation of Blockchain. It preserves data integrity and quality by enabling decentralised defence (Zheng et al., 2017). The decentralised concept makes the Blockchain a distributed database where all node contains the entire copy of records. Distributed nodes are used in this Peer-to-Peer network to access, verify and transmit data that cannot be fabricated (Iansiti & Lakhani, 2017). In order to appreciate the true disruptive potential of this technology, five core principles of Blockchain, such as Distributed Database, Transparency, P2P Transmission, Computational Logic and Immutable Records are required to be considered.

TECHNOLOGY

A Blockchain is a form of distributed ledger that records the transaction in 'Blocks'. A set of transactions are stored in the Block which contains a link to the previous Block, consequently, a chain of sequentially ordered Blocks is formed (Mayes, Jayasinghe & Markantonakis, 2014). A distributed ledger is the core of Blockchain through which data can be inserted and amended using the nodes' Consensus mechanism in the network. Every collaborating node in a Blockchain contains a copy of the entire records in a sequence of the interconnected system (Valduriez & Ozsu, 2011). In a Blockchain, the cryptographic hash function is used to link sequential Blocks together in such a way that, any modification of transaction data in a Block would alter the hash value of the following Block and consequently this alteration process goes on for the rest of the subsequent Blocks in the chain. This mechanism introduces easily noticeable discrepancies in the event of any slightest alteration to the Blockchain (Ferretti, D'Angelo & Marzolla, 2018). In order to provide a reasonable level of anonymity, Blockchain utilises digital pseudonyms which are hashed public keys. This pseudonym can be used to trace the actions of an individual. However, correlating a pseudonym to an exact individual is resource-intensive (Zhu et al., 2016).

The fundamental properties of Blockchain technology are Decentralisation, Transparency and Immutability. Decentralisation refers to the process that enables the function of dispersing and restraining control from centralised authority or location. It contains the potential to facilitate the transaction of data in a transparent manner without the requirement of a trusted third party. The structure of a decentralised system ensures that one single entity does not store the information, but every single entity contains it. Since decentralisation empowers multiple participants for managing the network, it resolves the trust issue (Wright & De Filippi, 2015). In the context of Blockchain, Accessibility is offered by facilitating encrypted access to the information. As distributed architecture stores information at multiple nodes in the network, information is constantly available and accessible. In terms of Usability, standardisation and frameworks are utilised during the development. The processing power of Blockchain serves the aptitude of operation and performance to validate the transaction in nodes at different networks (Deshpande et al., 2017). In regard to the feature of Instructiveness, Blockchain provides the comprehensive information stored in Blocks permanently, where any attempt of modification generates a new block with a reference to the original information of the previous Block. Moreover, Blockchain offers Comprehensibility through storing relevant information of transactions and smart contracts enclosed in the Blocks including essential data for upcoming validation (Lin & Liao, 2017). It also ensures Auditability through an algorithm that verifies the conditions and requirements before accumulating new Blocks. In a Blockchain environment, Immutability refers to the capability of the Blockchain to remain unchanged and indelible (Ølnes & Jansen, 2017). The property of immutability is the outcome of the Blocks that are cryptographically linked making the Blockchain a prime contender to bring disruption in many areas such as government, public, health, education and transport which all form part of the future *'Smart Cities'*.

EXPECTED DISRUPTIONS

The intersection between the social, economic and technological domains can be defined as disruption. In an article titled "Disruptive Technologies: Catching the wave", Clayton Christensen introduced the term Disruptive Technology (Bower & Christensen, 1995). By definition, Disruptive Technology refers to such a technology that is proficient in transfiguring the typical approach of operating consumers, businesses, industries, even the global economy. An innovation that enters in a conventional domain and radically changes the way of operation can be categorised as a disruptive technology. It offers ground-breaking benefits that are remarkably higher than the current technologies and capable of replacing its precursors (Manyika et al., 2013). In recent years, disruptive technologies have become progressively ubiquitous. Therefore, society and the global economy are observing technological innovation at an exceptional speed. Blockchain is a technology that contains the aptitude to cause disruptions in various sectors.

Figure 1. Blockchain applications across different sectors

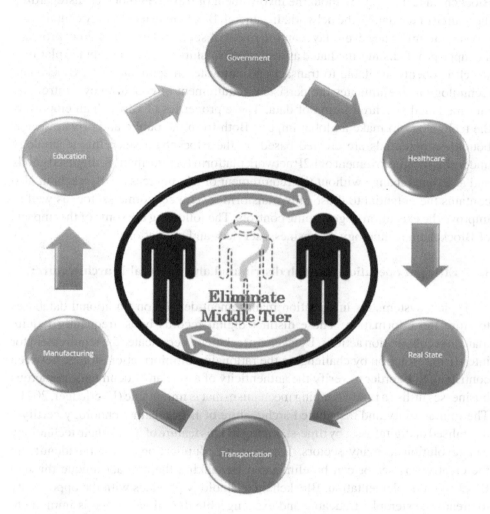

Generally, in the sphere of digital networks, data transmission occurs through replication from source to destination. Verification of the data authenticity in this context is one of the fundamental concerns. Although this issue can be confronted by assigning trust to someone. However, the assurance of a trustworthy entity in terms of data authenticity is not always flawless. In addition, consigning an intercessor persistently can be expensive. Blockchain technology contains the capability to address the authenticity issue without the intervention of any trusted intercessor which is one of the prominent aptitudes of this technology to be measured as disruptive. Data authenticity can be verified effortlessly and autonomously by

Blockchain technology without the involvement of trusted authorities disregarding the source of the data in the network. In general, Blockchain technology contains the potential to influence every layer and segment of society. This technology provides a tamper-proof, disintermediated as well as censorship-resilient distributed platform which is openly available to transact and innovate on spontaneously. Blockchain technology also eliminates the persistent requirement of concurrency control and intermediated synchronisation of data. These properties of Blockchain empowers the technology to make a global impact. Both from the public and private sector, boundless potentials are erected based on the Blockchain since this technology underpins the improvement of P2P network platform for information, digitised goods and asset interchange without the requirement of any intercessor. Blockchain also contains the potential to drastically transform several economic sectors as well as improve the execution of governing controls. The following are some of the impacts of Blockchain technology on business, services and regulations:

1. **Efficient operation through distributed and immutable architecture:**

Typical systems for information management depend on traditional databases to store the information. These distinct digital records book frequently require manual reconciliation actions. Blockchain technology eradicates the requirement for inter-firm resolution by challenging the rationality of information storage between contributors. In order to verify the authenticity of assets and documents, numerous businesses utilise a time-stamping mechanism that is immutable (Everledger, 2021). The immutability and distributed architecture of Blockchain technology certify a digitalised or digital asset by time-stamping it. This feature of Blockchain technology can revolutionise many sectors. For example, duplication of digital identity in the creative art sector can be eliminated by making the artefact unique through Blockchain implementation. Blockchain technology provides with the opportunity to create transferable, tradeable and exchangeable digital value that is immune to forged and illegal duplication.

2. **Symmetric and transparent information:**

Generally, symmetric information influences negotiations and trades amongst economic agents which introduces complications such as confrontational selection, moral hazard and so on. These complications are eliminated by central authorities. However, this increases the governing inaccuracy because of the absence of transparency and traceability. In this scenario, Blockchain technology can eliminate the information discrepancy between representatives. It provides access to verifiable, auditable, immutable and time-stamped data which also ensures a transparent environment where rules are possible to enforce, adapt and implement. Hence, Blockchain implementation in the government and private sector has great potentials (FCA, 2016).

3. Decentralised Establishments:

The socio-economic populations and their activities are administered by the centralised structure of our society and institutional chain of command. However, Blockchain as a disruptive technology can enable unique business models or unique work process where the limit between non-territorial and hierarchical organisations are removed. The Decentralised Autonomous Organisations (DAO) enable unique non-hierarchical model-based governance, where a business can be run under a set of rules that is incorruptible and completely autonomous. *The DAO* is a group of smart contracts which handles the decision-making process autonomously and without the intervention of any intermediaries. Smart Contract contains a set of rules which enables, validates and implements a transaction or agreement. This can be described as a transaction protocol for executing the term of the contract. Containing the properties of tamper-resistance, self-verification and self-execution, Smart Contracts allow code execution without the intervention of any third party (Mohanta, Panda & Debasish, 2018). Such Decentralised Autonomous Organisations known as *The DAO* was deployed on a prominent Blockchain network called Ethereum that does not follow an orthodox management structure. Instead, it operates business projects by open community members' votes and is capable of scattering funds autonomously (Ethereum, 2021).

The possible disruptions can be classified under the following categories that form an integral part of Smart Cities:

- Smart Governance
- Procurement
- Land Records
- Public Records
- Health Records
- Transport infrastructure
- Tradeable funds
- Birth and Death Registration
- Education
- Certifications
- Intellectual property (IP Protection)

APPLICABLE PLATFORMS

In recent years, the distribution of digital information is being stimulated by Blockchain technology. However, the full potential of this disruptive technology is yet to be unleashed although the landscape of the financial domain has been transmuted significantly through Blockchain implementation (Aitken, 2018). The efficacy and prospects of Blockchain in the financial sphere have been established by the colossal attention of Cryptocurrency, even though this transparent, decentralised and artifice-resistant technology is capable of transforming various domains such as healthcare, voting, banking, charity, real estate, education, retail, insurance, supply chain, critical infrastructure security and so on (CBInsights, 2021). International Data Corporation has predicted that amongst two thousand international companies, 25% are going to be utilising Blockchain-based resources by the end of the year 2021. It is also anticipated that Blockchain-related global spending will surpass $11 billion by the end of the year 2022 (I-Scoop, 2021). The following are some examples of the industries that are being disrupted by Blockchain technology:

1. **Finance:** One of the most prominent applications of Blockchain technology in the financial domain is Cryptocurrency. Bitcoin is one such cryptocurrency powered by Blockchain technology, which is the combination of a verifiable ledger of transactions and decentralised architecture with distributed network security. This allows people to obtain complete control of their digital currency without any banks or centralised authority. Implementation of Smart Contracts in the cryptocurrency field was also ground-breaking. Since any terms of the contract can be executed automatically by utilising Smart Contract, it is also possible to set any constraints in the transaction. For example, a payment or transaction can be processed after a certain date or only when the beneficiary satisfies the specific condition.

2. **Voting:** One of the vital support of a democratic system is an election which provides the public with the authority to express their opinion through the voting process. The implication of this process to public life is very perceptible and decisive. On account of this, it is crucial for a voting process to be fair and accountable. The integrity of the voting industry is a global concern. The legitimacy of the process cannot be subject to any distrust. A publicly accessible distributed ledger in conjunction with transparent and immutable features of Blockchain technology can recover the accountability and impartiality of the voting system (Syeed, 2018).

3. **Healthcare:** Secure data sharing is prominent incompetence of the healthcare sector. As a consequence of several data breach incidents that occurred during the year 2009 to 2017, approximately 176 million patient records were exposed

(Daley, 2021). Accurate diagnoses, affordable care and effective treatment can also be hindered due to the lack of enhanced data collaboration amongst the providers. Implementation of Blockchain technology can augment the network access sharing among healthcare providers, patients and any third parties without conceding integrity and security of data.

4. **Real Estate:** Lack of transparency makes the real estate domain vulnerable to bureaucratic interruptions and deception. Massive inaccuracies are also observed in public records (Bernhard, 2018). The immutability and transparent structure of Blockchain technology can intensify the swiftness of real estate transfers and sales as well as promote honesty in record keeping. Ownership verification and tracking process can also be immensely enhanced through Blockchain implementation (Zilbert, 2018).

5. **Insurance:** Blockchain technology is being experimented with for developing the operational efficacy of the insurance industry. Increasing market promptness, reducing costs, enhancing customer experience are some of the objectives of these experimentations. Blockchain is proficient to reduce costs and processing time significantly by establishing a single source of truth amongst contributors. Additionally, the features of version control and immutability of Blockchain empowers the insurance industry with cross-border transactions functionality (Daley, 2019).

6. **Charity:** Blockchain contains the potential to revolutionise the charity and humanitarian aid area. Numerous incidents of misuse all over the world have caused reputational damage to this noble sector resulting in the decline in charity donations (Koksal, 2019). Being a transparent, immutable, decentralised and autonomous technology, Blockchain can reinstate the lost trust in the charity sector by providing accountability through evident and traceable donations. Blockchain provides a transparent picture of donors' funds which strengthen the trust among donors, beneficiaries and other contributors. This also develops the efficacy of the system in order to assure that the generous donations are making a positive difference to the world. This disruptive technology is not only a game-changer in charity and humanitarian aid activities but also capable of providing novel solutions to various enduring problems in this domain.

From the application and creative technological design, Blockchain is a disruptive technology that leads to the standard from centralised to decentralised mechanism. The P2P nature, transparent and decentralised structure made the Blockchain highly valued. It has proven its potentials for transfiguring concepts of various traditional industries with the core physiognomies of transparency, decentralisation, immutability and anonymity. The disruptive power of Blockchain technology is also recognised to generate positive influence in global economic operations and contains limitless possibilities to disrupt a variety of industries (Spatz, 2018). To become a vital part of the socio-economic system, Blockchain is being researched, developed and optimised. This progression may be time-consuming but certainly feasible.

CONCLUSION

It is perfectly reasonable for people to have doubts about any emerging technology. The evolution and future of the Internet were also raised questions to many people worldwide. It was first assumed that very specific and a handful of industries will be benefited from Blockchain technology. However, the reality is very different and more encouraging for this disruptive technology as it contains the potential to revolutionise almost any industry by generating a more dynamic ecosystem that enables the participation of stakeholders for crafting a proactive value. In the intervening years, it was ascertained that Blockchain technology is more comprehensive in many ways and its expediency is not limited to the cryptocurrency domain only. The introduction and application of this technology in an assorted set of industries are believed to be the new epoch after the Internet that is transforming the digital sphere globally. With the potential to elucidate concerns corresponding to deception, inadequate mutual trust and soaring transaction cost, Blockchain is being argued to be amongst the most disruptive technologies of the current age. This technology inspires opening up the information silos for constructive effect in many industries by establishing decentralised control, refining trust, easing information sharing and swifter transactions on the network. The influence of this emerging technology on global economic operation also speaks for its disruptive power. As the potentials of this technology are being unleashed through vigorous research and experimentation worldwide, the implementation of Blockchain in the diverse field is also being observed. Blockchain technology is here to reign indeed as global interest is mounting persistently over its disruptive power.

REFERENCES

Aitken, R. (2018). *Bitcoin & Beyond: Can Blockchain bring in "The Masses" to realize its full potential?* https://www.forbes.com/sites/rogeraitken/2018/06/30/bitcoin-beyond-can-blockchain-bring-in-the-masses-to-realize-its-full-potential

Baki, M. (2019). Auctioning Using Blockchain Advantage Analysis. *International Journal of New Technology and Research, 5*.

Bernhard, K. (2018). *How Blockchain Technology could alter the real estate business.* https://www.bizjournals.com/houston/news/2018/08/15/how-blockchain-technology-could-alter-the-real.html

Bower, J., & Christensen, C. (1995). *Disruptive technologies: Catching the wave.* Academic Press.

CBInsights. (2021). *Banking Is Only The Beginning: 58 Big Industries Blockchain Could Transform.* https://www.cbinsights.com/research/industries-disrupted-blockchain

Daley, S. (2019). *9 Companies using Blockchain in Insurance to revolutionize possibilities.* https://builtin.com/blockchain/blockchain-insurance-companies

Daley, S. (2021). *How using Blockchain in healthcare is reviving the industry's capabilities.* https://builtin.com/blockchain/blockchain-healthcare-applications-companies

Deshpande, A., Stewart, K., Lepetit, L., & Gunashekar, S. (2017). Distributed Ledger Technologies/Blockchain: Challenges, opportunities and the prospects for standards. *Overview Report of BSI.*

Ethereum. (2021). *What is Ethereum? The foundation for our digital future.* https://ethereum.org/en/what-is-ethereum

Everledger. (2021). *The Everledger Platform.* https://everledger.io/

FCA. (2016). *Business Plan 2016/17.* https://www.fca.org.uk/publication/corporate/business-plan-2016-17.pdf

Ferretti, S., D'Angelo, G., & Marzolla, M. (2018). *A Blockchain-based flight data.* Academic Press.

I-Scoop. (2021). *The future of Blockchain in organizations and business ecosystems.* https://www.i-scoop.eu/blockchain-distributed-ledger-technology/business-ecosystems-future-blockchain

Iansiti, M., & Lakhani, K. (2017). The truth about Blockchain. *Harvard Business Review, 95*(1), 118–127.

Koksal, I. (2019). *How Blockchain Technology can re-invent charity.* https://www.forbes.com/sites/ilkerkoksal/2019/07/12/how-blockchain-technology-can-re-invent-charity

Lin, I., & Liao, T. (2017). A Survey of Blockchain Security Issues and Challenges. *International Journal of Network Security, 19*(5), 653–659.

Manyika, J., Chui, M., Bughin, J., Dobbs, R., Bisson, P., & Mars, A. (2013). *Disruptive Technologies: Advances that will transform life, business and the global economy.* McKinsey Global Institute.

Mayes, K., Jayasinghe, D., & Markantonakis, K. (2014). Optimistic Fair-Exchange with Anonymity for Bitcoin Users. *IEEE Computer Society, 11*, 44–51.

Mohanta, B., Panda, S., & Debasish, J. (2018). An Overview of Smart Contract and Use Cases in Blockchain Technology. *International Conference on Computing Communication and Networking Technologies.* 10.1109/ICCCNT.2018.8494045

Ølnes, S., & Jansen, A. (2017). Blockchain Technology as s Support Infrastructure in e-Government. *International Conference on Electronic Government*, 215-227. 10.1007/978-3-319-64677-0_18

Spatz, K. (2018). *Eight ways Blockchain will impact the world beyond Cryptocurrency.* https://www.forbes.com/sites/theyec/2018/03/09/eight-ways-blockchain-will-impact-the-world-beyond-cryptocurrency

Syeed, N. (2018). *Is Blockchain Technology the Future of Voting?* https://www.bloomberg.com/news/articles/2018-08-10/is-blockchain-technology-the-future-of-voting

Valduriez, P., & Ozsu, M. (2011). *Principles of distributed database systems.* Springer Science & Business Media.

Wright A. De Filippi P. (2015). *Decentralized Blockchain technology and the rise of Lex Cryptographia.* doi:10.2139/ssrn.2580664

Zheng, Z., Xie, S., Dai, H., Chen, X., & Wang, H. (2017). An Overview of Blockchain Technology: Architecture, Consensus, and Future Trends. *IEEE International Congress on Big Data.* 10.1109/BigDataCongress.2017.85

Zhu, Y., Guo, R., Gan, G., & Tsai, W. (2016). Interactive incontestable signature for transactions confirmation in Bitcoin Blockchain. *COMPSAC - IEEE 40th Annual, 1*, 443–44.

Zilbert, M. (2018). *The Blockchain for Real Estate.* https://www.forbes.com/sites/forbesrealestatecouncil/2018/04/23/the-blockchain-for-real-estate-explained

Section 2
Blockchain and Computational Excellence

Chapter 5
Elaborative Investigation of Blockchain Technology in Intelligent Networks

Dhaya R.
King Khalid University, Saudi Arabia

Kanthavel R.
King Khalid University, Saudi Arabia

ABSTRACT

The fifth generation (5G) network advancements focus to help mixed upright applications by associating heterogeneous gadgets and machines with extreme upgrades regarding high quality of administration, extended organization limit, and improved framework throughput regardless of significant difficulties like decentralization, straightforwardness, dangers of information interoperability, network protection, and security weaknesses. The challenges and limitations of other intelligent 5G intelligent internet of networks (5G IoTs) are also to be met by using blockchain technology with the integration of cloud computing and edge computing technologies. In this chapter, the authors render an elaborated analytics of the empowering of blockchain technology in intelligent networks that includes 5G networks and 5G-based IoT. The solutions for the spectrum management, data sharing, security, and privacy in 5G networks will also be analyzed. It is believed that the chapter would be useful for researchers in the field of blockchain in intelligent networks.

DOI: 10.4018/978-1-7998-8382-1.ch005

INTRODUCTION

Blockchain has been actually made and viably used first for Bitcoin computerized capital. Blockchain gives security, mystery, and data decency with no untouchable relationship in the control of the trades, and likewise, it makes entrancing assessment locales, especially from the perspective of particular troubles and hindrances (Kaushik et al., 2017). Most of the expounding on this advancement fixates on uncovering and improving the obstructions of blockchain from insurance and security perspectives.

Man-made awareness (AI) and AI (ML) figuring's may be the enhancement that blockchain models ought to be used in more applications, for instance, Industry 4.0, Internet of things, domestic structures, Secures, crypto chips, and so forth Blockchain is a conveyed data base course of action that keeps a continually creating summary of data records that are insisted by the centers checking out it. The data is recorded in an openly available report, including the information of each trade ever wrapped up. It is a decentralized game plan where AI and ML estimations may expect different parts to confirmation security in a beneficial manner (Dinh & Thai, 2018). In spite of the way that blockchain is apparently a fitting response for driving trades using computerized types of cash, it has some specific incites that ought to be tended to. High uprightness of trades and security of centers are required to prevent attacks, and AI may offer a response, especially when it is used in distant sensors. Far off crypto chips may be a response for some coordination issues, and ML counts may be used on them also. Blockchain gives off an impression of being tangled, and it surely can be, yet its focal thought is in reality extremely clear. A blockchain is a sort of data base. To have the choice to grasp blockchain, it serves to at first understand what a data base truly is. An informational index in the form of variety of data can be taken care of digitally on a PC system and informational indexes is characteristically coordinated by chart association in the direction of considering more straightforward looking and filtering for unequivocal information (Aste et al., 2017).

The differentiation between someone using an accounting page to store information instead of a data base has been given as follows: Spreadsheets are proposed for one individual, or a bit of social occasion of group, to accumulate and right to use restricted proportions of data. On the other hand, an informational index is proposed to house generally greater proportions of data with the intention to be cleaned, and controlled rapidly to convince users. Colossal data bases accomplish this by accommodating information on laborers which are completed of historic PCs (Litke et al., 2019). The laborers at a time are created by means of voluminous number of PCs to encompass the processing command and limit significant intended for certain customers to get into the data base concurrently. At the same time as an accounting page or data base possibly will be available to many individuals, it be regularly controlled through a industry and directed via an assigned person who have full oversight above to see the statistics inside of it. One key differentiation between a blockchain and normal data base is the manner wherein the information is coordinated. A BC assembles message within social events, in any case considered squares so as to grasp setting of data. Squares contain assured limit limits and, once packed, have been secured against the as of late crammed square, outline a sequence of information identified by "blockchain."

Every innovative data which pursues with the intention of recently further obstruct is requested keen on an as of late outlined square so as to similarly be included. Data base constructions embed in to its information into bench however a blockchain, similar to its title proposes arrangement interested in irregularities to facilitate jointly. This constructs it with the objective to every BC have been data bases yet not every informational collection has been BCs and this structure in like manner intrinsically creates an irrevocable plan of figures after the completion in a distributed environment. Exactly as soon as a square is crammed it is unchangeable in order to transform into spitted schedule. Every square in the sequence is known an accurate instance stamp once the chain is included. This chapter presents the Elaborative investigation of Blockchain Technology in intelligent networks in three main sections namely Features, advantages, disadvantages and need of Blockchain for Intelligent Networks, Integration of 5G networks with Blockchain along with Potential of 5G network using Black chain technology and finally the Role of Blockchain in 5G- IoT.

NEED OF BLOCKCHAIN FOR INTELLIGENT NETWORKS

Coming up next are the highlights of the Blockchain innovation. BC is a specific kind of data collection.

- BC supplies data in open area which have been then attached jointly.
- As novel data approaches in it is moved out to be keen on another square. At the point when the square is stacked up in the midst of information joined on the preceding square that builds the information integrated inside consecutive request (Alkadi et al., 2020).
- Dissimilar sorts of data are being taken care of BC yet the broadly perceived employ so far-off is while a record intended for trades.
- For Bitcoin's purpose, BC as a form of distributed manner and no individual or social event have managed relatively, every customer aggregately holds be in charge of.
- Decentralized BCs are constant, that infers the data noted is permanent.

Figure 1 shows the features of blockchain. These highlights will give us some significant properties of Blockchain.

Figure 1. Significant properties of blockchain

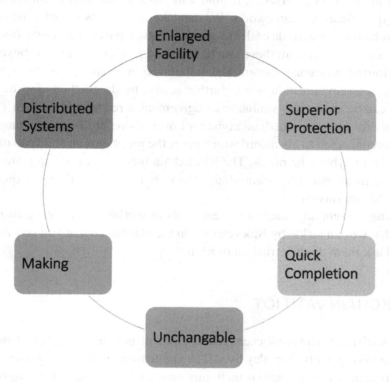

Enlarged Facility: This is the first and a significant element of Blockchain. The most exceptional thing about this Blockchain innovation is that it expands the limit of the entire organization. On account of the explanation that there are a ton of PCs cooperating which in complete offers an extraordinary force then not many of the gadgets where the things are unified.

Superior Protection: Blockchain innovation has a superior security in light of the fact that there isn't so much as a solitary possibility of closing down of the framework. Indeed, even the most significant level of the monetary framework is liable to get hacked. Bitcoin in the second hand had never been hacked. the explanation is that the blockchain network is made sure about by various PCs called hubs and these hubs affirm the exchange on this organization

Unchangeable: Making unchanging records is one of the primary estimations of Blockchain. Any data set that is incorporated is exposed to get hacked and they require trust in the outsider to keep the data set secure. Blockchain like Bitcoin keeps its records in an endless **condition of sending force.**

Quick Completion: Customary financial frameworks can be moderate, as they require a ton of settlement time which typically requires days to continue. This is one of the primary motivation behind why these financial foundations need to redesign their financial frameworks. We can take care of this issue by the methods for Blockchain as it can settle cash move at super quick paces. These eventually save a ton of time and cash from these foundations and give comfort to the buyer too.

Distributed Systems: Decentralized innovation enables you to store your resources in an organization which further access by the methods for the web, a resource can be in any way similar to an agreement, a record and so forth Through this proprietor has an immediate command over his record by the methods for a key that is connected to his record which gives the proprietor an ability to move his resources for anybody he needs. The Blockchain innovation ends up being a truly compelling instrument for decentralizing the web. It has the ability to acquire huge changes the enterprises

Making: Essentially, there are great deals of methods of printing an issue of control that we can tackle by Blockchain. On the off chance that you go toward the west and ask them do they trust innovation.

BLOCKCHAIN WITH IOT

The quick advancement of blockchain development and the Internet of Things (IoT) are felt all during our time by day lives. The applications will agitate existing cycles across grouping of organizations including manufacturing, trading, transportation, the money related region and clinical administrations. Despite these movements security remains a top concern for the IoT climate as it uncovered various contraptions, monstrous proportions of data, store network associates and the neighborhood general to security infiltrates (Gupta et al., 2018). With IoT gadgets multiplying, these gadgets regularly come up short on the confirmation principles important to protect client information. Basic foundation will be harmed if programmers enter through the expansive scope of IoT gadgets. To guarantee trust, verification and normalization across all components of IoT are fundamental for far and wide selection. Here are a few different ways the circulated design of blockchain can help address large numbers of these security and trust difficulties: BC usefulness can be used to pursue the sensor information evaluation and delay repetition by way of any another wicked data. The figure 2 shows the benefit of Blockchain and IoT in combined together.

Figure 2. Benefit of blockchain and IoT in combined together

- The IoT Deployments of device are marvelous, and suitable evidence is appropriate to provide IoT tool ID, endorsement and dependable protected information move.
- Instead of encountering a recluse to develop confidence, the exchange data within IoT devices anyway a BC.
- A scattered record takes out a singular wellspring of disillusionment inside the organic framework, protecting an IOT device's data from changing.
- Blockchain engages device self-rule (sagacious agreement), particular character, and uprightness to support circulated correspondence by killing specific bottlenecks and weaknesses.
- The association and action costs of IoT can be reduced through blockchain since there is no agent.
- IoT devices are clearly addressable with blockchain, giving a foundation set apart by related contraptions for researching purposes.
- BC-based IOT measures have been suitable to disentangle trade measures, humanizing user knowledge and bring about enormous expenses.

BLOCKCHAIN CHARACTERISTICS, ADVANTAGES AND DISADVANTAGES

For the entirety of its multifaceted nature, BC probable as a distributed sort unbounded information. As of more vital customer insurance and expanded security to cut down handling charges and fewer blunders, blockchain innovation might just see applications past those illustrated previously (Gochhayat et al., 2020). In any case, there are likewise a few inconveniences.

Pros

- Improved precision by taking out human commitment in the affirmation
- Cost diminishes by clearing out outcast check
- Distribution formulates it difficult to adjust
- Communication have been protected, confidential, and capable

- See-through development
- Provide a monetary other decision and scheme to deal with ensuring singular in order for inhabitants of states by means of uncertain.

Cons

- Noteworthy development charge identified by taking out bitcoin
- Short trades each moment
- The past of usage in unlawful behavior
- Directives
- Favorable conditions of Blockchain
- The exactness of the Chain

BC business system have been attested through an organization by hundreds ofs PCs. This disposes of essentially every individual consideration by check cycle, achieving the fewer individual missteps and a precise evidence of data. Whether or not a PC of any organization was in the direction of submitting a processing error, the bungle can simply be completed to the reproduction of the BC.

Impact of Blockchain

The impacts of Blockchain are debated in a detailed manner as follows:

- **Cost Reductions:** Regularly, a client disburses a depository to affirm a trade, a legitimate authority to symptom a manuscript, or a nun to play out matrimony. BC executes the necessity designed for outcast affirmation and, in the midst of it, their connected expenditure. Industry people cause a little charge at whatever point they recognize portions using Mastercards, for example, since banks and portion getting ready associations need to deal with those trades. Bitcoin, of course, doesn't comprise an essential force and has restricted trade charges (Zou et al., 2020).
- **Decentralization:** BC doesn't accumulate whichever data in a central region. Taking everything into account, the BC has been recreated and increased across an organization of PCs. At no matter what position an extra square is supplementary to the BC, each PC on the organization revives its BC to reproduce the modification. By distribution of that data from corner to corner an organization, relatively than taking care of it in single middle data base, BC ends up being harder to meddle by. If a reproduction of the BC cuts down heavily influenced by a developer, simply a lone reproduction of the data, to a certain extent than the complete organization point is done.

- **Productive communication:** Trades put from side to side an essential power that can require up to a certain day to resolve. When you try to store a watch out for a particular night, then you might not in fact perceive resources in your record in anticipation of the next morning. While money related associations work for the duration of business duration, 5 days out of each week, BC is operational by 24 hours consistently, 7 days of the week, and one year. Trades are done because possible be seen while secure after several hours because of significant intended for cross-line deal, that ordinarily obtain any more considering time-locale issues and the way that all social affairs ought to certify portion taking care of.

- **Private Transactions:** Various blockchain networks fill in as open data bases can see an overview of the organization's trade history. Despite the way that customers can get to experiences concerning trades, they can't get to perceiving data on the subject of the customers creating individuals who trades. It has been a regular wrong insight that BC networks similar to bitcoin have been secretive while without a doubt of its characterization. With the intention, where a user divulges trades, their exceptional code named a public key, has been documented on the BC, to a certain extent than their own data. In the event that someone has completed a Bitcoin buy on a trade which necessitates recognizable proof after that the individual's character is as yet connected to their blockchain address, yet an exchange, in any event, when attached to an individual's name, doesn't uncover any close to home data (Naz & Lee, 2020).

- **Secure Transactions:** At the point when a trade is recorded, its realness ought to be affirmed by means of the BC set-up. An enormous numbers of PCs competitions en route for attesting that the nuances to procure the ones which are correct. Subsequent to a PC has affirmed the trade to a new to the BC block. Every square on the blockchain contains it's possess stand-out hash, close by the exceptional hash of the square previous to it. Exactly when the information on a square is adjusted into several ways, so as to square's hash code modifications regardless to the hash-code on the square subsequent to it and this mistake composes it staggeringly hard for the sequence happening the BC to be altered exclusive of become aware of.

- **Straightforwardness:** The larger part BCs are out and out open foundation programming and this suggests that everyone could see its system to empower analysts to overview advanced types of cash like Bitcoin for security. This manner suggests, no veritable master in Bitcoin is able to adjust. Thus, anyone can prescribe switches or climbs to the scheme. But predominant organization customers have the same opinion that the novel type of the system with the renewal is good enough.

- **Banking the Unbanked:** The significant feature of blockchain and Bitcoin are the capacity, identity, sexual orientation and social foundation. As per the world bank, almost 2 billion grown-ups with the intention of not comprising financial balances or any methods for putting away their cash or wealth.5 Nearly these people live in non-industrial nations where the economy is at its outset and completely reliant on money. These individuals frequently bring in little cash that is paid in actual money. They at that point need to store this actual money in concealed areas in their residences or spaces of livelihood send-off the theme to theft or superfluous brutality (Peters et al., 2015). Inputs to a bitcoin folder can be put away on a bit of document, a modest PDA, or even retained if important. For the vast majority, almost certainly, these alternatives are more effectively covered up than a little heap of money under a sleeping cushion. Blockchain of things to come are additionally searching for answers for not exclusively be a unit of record for abundance stockpiling, yet additionally to stock up clinical reports, possessions datas, and an assortment of additional legitimate agreements.
- **Disservices of BC:** As there have been tremendous expected increases to the BC an immense confrontation in terms of allocation. The hindrances to the development of BC nowadays have not been particular. The certified troubles are authoritarian, for the the majority element in order to try also countless times of BC programming plan and back-end programming expected to organize BC to present industry organizations. At this point a segment of the dispute is disturbing the overall progression of broad blockchain choice.
- **Innovation rate:** In spite of the way that blockchain can get a decent arrangement on trade costs, development is distant as of at no cost. The "confirmation of employment" system that bitcoin is to make use to support trades, for example, putting away huge proportions of processing power. Disregarding the expenses of taking out bitcoin, customers carry on driving out of bed their force statement to affirm trades of BC. Since, at what time diggers append a square to the bitcoin BC, they have been repaid through adequate bitcoin to formulate their moment and power valuable. With respect to blockchain that don't use advanced cash, regardless, diggers ought to be paid or regardless, helped to favor trades. A couple of answers for the problems of BC are starting to happen and hence, bitcoin farmhouses are building to make use of solar power, bounty combustible chat as of profound earth boring districts, or power from wind ranches (Al-Jaroodi & Mohamed, 2019).
- **Speed ineffectiveness:** The ideal pertinent assessment of Bitcoin intended for the expected inadequacies of BC. Bitcoin's structure needs approximately certain proceedings to put in one more square. Next to that price, it has been

reviewed that the blockchain organization could basically supervise around seven do businesses intended for each second (TPS). Thus far other advanced monetary standards, for instance, Ethereum acts in a way that is in a way that is enhanced than bitcoin, they are up till now incomplete by BC.

- **Criminal behavior:** Despite the fact that grouping lying on the BC network shields customers commencing slashes and jam insurance, it similarly considers unlawful deal and action.

INTEGRATION OF 5G NETWORKS WITH BLOCKCHAIN

The Blockchain Provides high security for 5G organizations drew in with decentralized records. Blockchain ensures about the 5G organizations by outfitting disseminated trust models with high access approval, thusly empowering 5G frameworks to secure themselves and guarantee information protection. The ramifications of combining the two advancements can confront different difficulties (Klessig et al., 2016). To meet the complete 5G assumptions, there are a ton of primary and specialized angles that should be investigated. Clear administrative systems should be characterized and found for the usage of different arrangements like shrewd agreements. Likewise, in particular, the versatility of Blockchain should be improved to manage a high number of gadgets, as each gadget should have kind locations. Additionally, noxious gadgets can make confusion inside the network, hence confining the progression of development. The incorporation of Blockchain with 5G can give another definition to the creating society.

It is not just blockchain innovation that is exclusively changing the 5G networks. It wouldn't be reasonable on the off chance that we do exclude other arising innovations like distributed computing, NFV (Network Function Virtualization), D2D interchanges to give some examples. Yet, without a doubt, Blockchain opens the chance for putting away and overseeing information on 5G networks by means of its distributed record. Blockchain can be viewed as a key empowering agent guaranteeing security and network executives, and there is no denying the way that Blockchain will inspire the generally advanced portable administrations. In any case, a huge transformation in the versatile network society is yet to be predicted. With developing Blockchain, advance yourself as well. For moment refreshes about blockchain news and confirmations, look at Blockchain Council.

Characteristics and Challenges of Blockchain Technology Based Fifth Generation Networks

The outline for a critical attributes of BC innovation that are necessary to its latent capacity.

- Fraud discovery and anticipation
- No outsider contribution
- Operates trustless
- Decentralized stockpiling
- Making computerized cash secure
- Transparent yet made sure about
- Processing execution
- Trust in the trustless world

As 5G is headed to be conveyed across the world, interfacing all the heterogeneous gadgets and machines. The world is getting obsessed with its rapid, decreased inertness, and expanded network limit, and can hardly wait to profit of such extraordinary availability (Mafakheri et al., 2018).

In any case, there are a couple of moves that should be tended to and can't be disregarded.

- Excessive human traffic can cause clog and over-burden.
- Depending upon the quantity of passages, low throughput settlement takes place.

POTENTIAL OF 5G NETWORKS USING BLOCKCHAIN TECHNOLOGY

As Blockchain is unchanging and follows decentralized exchange records, it can offer monstrous correspondence without breaking security, hence keeping up dependability among associations and organizations. As we as a whole know about the attributes of blockchain innovation, it is straightforward how these highlights empower the turn of events and change of 5G networks (Mistry et al., 2020). The fifth-age 5G innovation is the following huge stage in the business of broadcast communications that will be presented soon. With regards to modern and completely fledged innovation, Blockchain and 5G are the most talked about and advertised advancements that are hitting the commercial center. The majority of the organizations and associations have just received this arising innovation while few are yet to take an action. It is intriguing to sort out how Blockchain can affect the media transmission industry and what are the difficulties that innovation will confront while changing.

- **Decentralized Approach:** Blockchain innovation doesn't include any outsider or supporters of play out the exchanges; along these lines, it is a decentralized framework that dispenses with the prerequisite of believed outer experts in the 5G networking. The decentralizing methodology further dispenses with bottleneck issues, in this way proficiently upgrading administration conveyance (Shafee, 2020).
- **Blockchain-An Immutability Feature:** Blockchain empowers unchanging nature for 5G network administrations which permit the shared information and asset exchanging to be recorded permanently importance there is no adjustment or change of information.
- **Permitting Localized Availability:** We know about the straightforwardness that blockchain offers and the joining of Blockchain into 5G permits specialist co-ops and customers with full access where an approved individual can follow and check the exchanges.
- **Cost-Saving Methodology:** Blockchain follows the shared strategy, and consequently it eliminates the outsider understanding prompting cost decreases while fabricating better coordination and trust levels among accomplices and furthermore saving time and clashes.
- **Security-The Prime Factor:** Blockchain utilizes cryptography that implies all the data is encoded and made sure about. The mix of Blockchain with the 5G can change security by giving distributed trust models, in this way making 5G fit for shielding themselves from security penetrating. Decentralized Blockchain utilizes helter kilter cryptography and different hash calculations which helps in securing the characters of the clients. Blockchain can empower the gadgets to be enrolled with their blockchain address; consequently, there is no doubt about personality misfortune (Global Mobile Suppliers Association, 2015).

How Blockchain will Solidify 5G Inspired Services

5G is the current wireless network standard that promises to deliver more than the customary increase in speed as with previous generation networks. Predicted to be at least 100 times faster than 4G and having a higher capacity to accommodate a myriad of connected devices, 5G will be radically different from other generations – something it has in common with modern blockchain tech. Yet, what truly distinguishes this highly anticipated light-speed mobile network is its significantly reduced latency in the transfer and sharing of huge datasets. Consequently, these characteristics of

5G will spur a rethinking of the IoT. A community of compact and low-powered devices can be easily connected via 5G. While data may flow in real-time, thanks to the heightened connectivity due to 5G, it needs to travel through secured means such as encryption or blockchain-powered solutions (Liyanage et al., 2018).

Blockchain, as an immutable, distributed ledger, has already outgrown the singular context of crypto-currencies. Various organizations have been making big strides on non-crypto applications of blockchain, which will be discussed below and will further support the materializing fifth-generation mobile network. Blockchain will bring security and standardization to various 5G applications, for example, the development of autonomous vehicles. Autonomous vehicles rely on massive heaps of data to be transmitted between the vehicle, a central operating system, and its surrounding environment during development. There are a plethora of devices, sensors, and gadgets embedded in the vehicles and across the environment; it's of paramount importance to ensure the data is kept safe from the hands of hackers. Besides the streams of data exchange bolstered by 5G's ultra-speed, tech giants such as IBM and digital-first automakers are recognizing the significance of blockchain in managing, storing, and transferring vital digital records for automobiles. Additionally, projects like the Mobility Open Blockchain Initiative (MOBI) indicate the major role blockchain will play in the autonomous vehicles sphere but also contribute to supporting 5G applications in the industry. With 5G on the rise, SMEs are eager to get a slice of this next-gen mobile network, and more processes will migrate to the cloud and online; hence, data security and verification are essential (Popovski et al., 2018). As an example, Boeing enlisted blockchain to power the sale of airplane parts, replacing its predominantly paper-based certificates. Essentially, the distributed ledger technology (DLT) will include all parties from the manufacturer, distributor, and seller in the sales of airplane parts, adding more transparency to the key details and transaction history. Researchers have consistently been exploring and analyzing the capabilities of blockchain to potentially empower 5G applications, from spectrum supervision, information sharing and organization virtualization, asset the executives to obstruction the board, unified learning, protection, and security arrangement.

BLOCKCHAIN ON EDGE AND CLOUD COMPUTING

Blockchain and edge processing have a fascinating reliant relationship. Edge computing is a distributed process that can give a framework to blockchain hubs to store and check exchanges. Then again, blockchain could empower a genuinely open distributed cloud commercial center. Then again, Blockchain is a morally sound online record of financial exchanges that can be customized distinctly through approval from each gathering included (Dhaya & Kanthavel, 2022). The information is overseen through a bunch of PCs that are not possessed by any single gathering, so the information submitted isn't corruptible. A cloud is something that we can access through the web. It is where we can get the information on the web. Then again, blockchain is an encoded framework that utilizes various styles of encryption and hash to store information in secured data sets. Edge figuring can serve to cut down IT foundation costs, for instance in facilitating. Not exclusively does information not need to go as far, there's less equipment required, which thus is additionally of gigantic advantage to the climate. Most sites are fabricated utilizing arrangements, for example, WordPress or Wix which thusly are facilitated on mists like Amazon AWS or Microsoft Azure. Very soon sites will be assembled utilizing programming arrangements that are facilitated tense networks, at a small amount of the expense of customary cloud-based administrations. The table 1 shows the difference between EC & CC.

Table 1. Differentiate EC and CC

Edge Computing(EC)	Cloud Computing(CC)
Edge Computing is viewed as ideal for tasks with outrageous dormancy concerns. In this manner, medium scale organizations that have spending constraints can utilize edge registering to save monetary assets.	CC more appropriate for manage activities and associations which manage huge information stockpiling
A few unique stages might be utilized for programming, all having distinctive runtimes.	Real writing computer programs is more qualified in mists as they are by and large made for one objective stage and uses one programming language.
Edge Computing requires a hearty security plan including progressed confirmation strategies and proactively handling assaults.	It requires to a lesser degree a powerful security plan.

In any case, quite possibly the most energizing territories where the innovation is required to have a genuine effect is encouraging the advancement of shrewd urban communities. Around the globe there are numerous urban communities that are now utilizing sensors to computerize things, for example, street lamps turning on and off to save power, stopping, squander the board, and in any event, shopping. In specific pieces of China, canister covers will just open on facial acknowledgment prompting more proficient waste administration. Before long you will have the option to stroll into a bistro, plunk down and have an espresso, and essentially leave with installment being consequently taken from your ledger. The quantity of the two urban areas and savvy advances are developing quickly and at such a speed that the cloud just won't have the option to adapt at the speed and figuring limit required. It isn't difficult to see the legitimacy of the forecasts of a huge number more associated gadgets turning into a reality and the dramatic measure of information that should be overseen. This IoT expansion will be served by a horde of innovations. We accept edge figuring will have a key impact in the manner information is prepared, overseen, and put away, and the manner in which we see this event rapidly is on the off chance that we can permit individuals to loan their extra processing ability to turn into a piece of the new cloud.

ROLE OF BLOCKCHAIN IN FIFTH GENERATION IOT

Development of Blockchain will be useful in after hundreds of Crores of related contraptions, allow the treatment of trades and harmonization among strategy; consider immense speculation assets to IoT industry makers. In an IoT organization, the blockchain can keep an absolute documentation of the verifiable background of adroit strategy. IoT and blockchain are cooperating as one to make the world a superior associated place. Instances of IoT and blockchain remember everything from record security for modern IoT gear to blockchain being utilized as a strategy to track-and-follow IoT-empowered steel trailers. Blockchain, which is generally natural for bitcoin and Ethereum, offers a fascinating answer for IoT security. The blockchain contains solid securities against information altering, locking admittance to the Internet of Things gadgets, and permitting bargained gadgets in an IoT network to be closed down.

IoT innovation permits unmistakable objects of ordinary use to have the option to associate with the web to communicate information by means of calculations and serve proprietors better. The world is as of now seeing a multiplication of savvy gadgets like TVs, furniture things, vacuum cleaners, etc. As of now, there are savvy homes, which are totally worked by in-constructed calculations. Assessments by the Fraunhofer Institute place possible keen home investment funds at 40% taking everything into account, an objective that applies to the business as much as property holders. Thoughts of savvy urban areas are not a long way from being acknowledged, by the same token. Savvy urban communities dream past the reducing of discharges and energy expenses, assessed by McKinsey to improve drive times by a potential 15-20% and crisis administration reaction times by 20-35% with the assistance of intelligent streets. As referenced before, 5G would give a road to these shrewd homes, keen urban areas, and a lot more savvy gadgets to understand their actual potential.

Once there is level ground for shrewd gadgets, particularly low-fueled ones to flourish, at that point IoT would get a gigantic lift. Since it would turn out to be more helpful to work these gadgets, there would be a lot a greater amount of them and even a lot more individuals to promptly receive it. The world is arriving at a level where it is hard to live as an individual without admittance to the web. Truth be told, the UN has since 2016 proclaimed admittance to the web as a basic liberty. Notwithstanding, while the marriage of 5G and IoT as of now vows to be a happy one, there are as yet authentic concerns particularly in the zones of security and protection. That is the place where blockchain comes in. Numerous individuals today are in any event mindful of virtual monetary forms today like Bitcoin, Ethereum, Swisscoin, Litecoin, etc. However, a couple truly has a grip of the innovation behind it: Blockchain. Blockchain is a shared, decentralized information base stage for putting away squares of exchange information connected together in chains – thus the name. The decentralized idea of blockchain implies it is impervious to most security issues. Its significant level encryption gives more noteworthy assurance from hacking than the customary customer worker framework. That is the thing that makes online exchanges and installments utilizing virtual monetary forms are so secure (Yang et al., 2019).

IoT and 5G together have incredible potential however which must be acknowledged by injecting the blockchain innovation. While 5G gives an availability cover to IoT gadgets and exchanges, blockchain handles security and guarantees the insurance of client and exchange information. Furthermore, truly, this trinity would be extremely solid as each part reinforces the other. The web of abilities would get an enormous lift with the presentation of blockchain. Recently, a Chinese specialist did the world's first 5G far off a medical procedure on the cerebrum of a patient who was a few miles away utilizing robots. A greater amount of this is relied upon to occur as we see significantly better medical care conveyance around the world. Security around there is, for evident reasons, fundamental and blockchain executed in medical care would make distant cycles considerably more secure (Stanciu, 2017) .

Moreover, the foreseen 5G-persuaded monstrous expansion in appropriation of brilliant gadgets implies that the blockchain would have within reach, unquestionably more information than previously. This information is an extraordinary push towards globalization in innovation.

SCOPE

Because it can monitor and trade nearly everything of value on a virtual platform, blockchain is the way of the future. Interestingly, blockchain eliminates the difficulties and expenses associated with such transactions in the past. Different ways could be used by businesses to create blockchain networks (Dhaya & Kanthavel, 2021). Users of 5G IoT networks can now connect and transact (save and retrieve data) with the assurance of data provenance, authenticity, accountability, immutability, and non-repudiation. Blockchain technology will make it possible to build secure mesh networks in which IoT devices may communicate securely while avoiding dangers like device spoofing and impersonation. Because blockchain can enhance IoT infrastructure in a variety of ways, it is acceptable and necessary to examine blockchain's use in smart city applications (Zheng et al., 2018). Because blockchain can enhance IoT infrastructure in a variety of ways, it is acceptable and necessary to examine blockchain's use in smart city applications. Both IoT and blockchain are still in their infancy, but they both hold the promise of making machine-to-machine communication a breeze. Companies are currently working to combine the two technological powerhouses. IoT and blockchain technology, when combined, will allow various businesses to prosper by allowing them to easily monitor, track, and secure data. The possibilities are unlimited after that, and you never know what will happen next! Financial services are predicted to be severely disrupted by blockchain systems (Dhaya & Kanthavel, 2020). Banks, for example, may employ blockchain technology to conduct payments at reduced prices and higher production, increasing transactional efficiency without compromising security. On top of existing financial goods (e.g., derivatives), blockchain will develop new types of financial products (e.g., derivatives) for better risk management.

CONCLUSION

This chapter presented the Elaborative investigation of Blockchain Technology in intelligent networks. By its content structure, at first Black chain features, characteristics, integration aspects with 5G and potential impact and challenges have been analyzed and secondly Potential of 5G network using Black chain technology was taken in to account for the interpretation. Finally, the Blockchain on Edge and Cloud Computing and Role of Blockchain in 5G-IoT also have been assessed and discussed in a detailed way by considering the points of the security aspects, decentralization and interoperability. From the studies it is inferred that as a conclusion, 5G, IoT and blockchain all need and effect each other to flourish in this globalized world. There is no halting 5G and IoT now, except to trust that architects and blockchain engineers will figure out how to address or go around the foreseen its adaptability issues so the three innovations can arrive at their brought together potential.

REFERENCES

Al-Jaroodi, J., & Mohamed, N. (2019). Blockchain in industries: A survey. *IEEE Access: Practical Innovations, Open Solutions, 7*, 36500–36515. doi:10.1109/ACCESS.2019.2903554

Alkadi, O., Moustafa, N., & Turnbull, B. (2020). A Review of Intrusion Detection and Blockchain Applications in the Cloud: Approaches Challenges and Solutions. *Access IEEE, 8*, 104893–104917. doi:10.1109/ACCESS.2020.2999715

Aste, T. D. M. T., Tasca, P., & Di Matteo, T. (2017). Blockchain Technologies: The Foreseeable Impact on Society and Industry. *Computer, 50*(9), 18–28. doi:10.1109/MC.2017.3571064

Dhaya & Kanthavel. (2020). A wireless collision detection on transmission poles through IoT technology. *Journal of Trends in Computer Science and Smart Technology, 2*(3), 165-172.

Dhaya & Kanthavel. (2021). Investigation on Industry Applications of Blockchain Technology. In *Blockchain Technology and Applications for Digital Marketing*. IGI Global.

Dhaya, R., & Kanthavel, R. (2022). *Elaborative Investigation of Blockchain Technology in Intelligent Networks: Advancing Smarter and More Secure Industrial Applications Using AI, IoT, and Blockchain Technology*. IGI Global Publisher.

Dinh, T. N., & Thai, M. T. (2018). AI and Blockchain: A Disruptive Integration. *Computer, 51*(September), 48–53. doi:10.1109/MC.2018.3620971

Global Mobile Suppliers Association. (2015). *The Road to 5G: Drivers, applications, requirements and Technical Development*. Global Mobile Suppliers Association.

Gochhayat, S. P., Shetty, S., Mukkamala, R., Foytik, P., Kamhoua, G. A., & Njilla, L. (2020). Measuring Decentrality in Blockchain Based Systems. *Access IEEE, 8*, 178372–178390. doi:10.1109/ACCESS.2020.3026577

Gupta, Y., Shorey, R., Kulkarni, D., & Tew, J. (2018). The Applicability of Blockchain in the Internet of Things. *10th International Conference on Communication Systems & Networks (COMSNETS)*. 10.1109/COMSNETS.2018.8328273

Kaushik, A., Choudhary, A., Ektare, C., Thomas, D., & Akram, S. (2017). Blockchain – Literature Survey. *2nd IEEE International Conference On Recent Trends in Electronics Information & Communication Technology (RTEICT)*. 10.1109/RTEICT.2017.8256979

Klessig, H., Ohmann, D., Reppas, A. I., Hatzikirou, H., Abedi, M., Simsek, M., & Fettweis, G. P. (2016). From immune cells to self-organizing ultra-dense small cell networks. *IEEE Journal on Selected Areas in Communications, 34*(4), 800–811. doi:10.1109/JSAC.2016.2544638

Litke, A., Anagnostopoulos, D., & Varvarigou, T. (2019, January). Blockchains for supply chain management: Architectural elements and challenges towards a global scale deployment. *Logistics*, *3*(1), 5. doi:10.3390/logistics3010005

Liyanage, M., Ahmad, I., Abro, A. B., Gurtov, A., & Ylianttila, M. (2018). *A Comprehensive Guide to 5G Security*. John Wiley & Sons. doi:10.1002/9781119293071

Mafakheri, B., Subramanya, T., Goratti, L., & Riggio, R. (2018). Blockchainbased Infrastructure Sharing in 5G Small Cell Networks. *14th International Conference on Network and Service Management (CNSM)*.

Mistry, I., Tanwar, S., Tyagi, S., & Kumar, N. (2020). Blockchain for 5G enabled IoT for Industrial Automation: A Systematic Review, Solutions, and Challenges. *Mechanical Systems and Signal Processing*, *135*, 106382. doi:10.1016/j.ymssp.2019.106382

Naz, S., & Lee, S. U.-J. (2020). Why the new consensus mechanism is needed in blockchain technology?. *Blockchain Computing and Applications (BCCA) 2020 Second International Conference on*, 92-99. 10.1109/BCCA50787.2020.9274461

Peters, G., Panayi, E., & Chapelle, A. (2015, November). Trends in cryptocurrencies and blockchain technologies: A monetary theory and regulation perspective. *J. Financial Perspect.*, *3*(3), 1–25.

Popovski, Trillingsgaard, Simeone, & Durisi. (2018). 5G Wireless Network Slicing for eMBB, URLLC, and mMTC: A communication- theoretic View. *IEEE Access*, *6*, 765–779.

Shafee, A. (2020). Botnets and their detection techniques. *Networks Computers and Communications (ISNCC) 2020 International Symposium on*, 1-6. 10.1109/ISNCC49221.2020.9297307

Stanciu, A. (2017). Blockchain based distributed control system for edge computing. In *2017 21st International Conference, on Control Systems and Computer Science (CSCS)* (pp. 667–671). IEEE. 10.1109/CSCS.2017.102

Yang, R., Yu, F. R., Si, P., Yang, Z., & Zhang, Y. (2019). Integrated blockchain and edge computing systems: A survey, some research issues and challenges. *IEEE Communications Surveys and Tutorials*, *21*(2), 1508–1532. doi:10.1109/COMST.2019.2894727

Zheng, Z., Xie, S., Dai, H.-N., Chen, X., & Wang, H. (2018). Blockchain challenges and opportunities: A survey. *International Journal of Web and Grid Services*, *14*(4), 352–375. doi:10.1504/IJWGS.2018.095647

Zou, Y., Meng, T., Zhang, P., Zhang, W., & Li, H. (2020). Focus on Blockchain: A Comprehensive Survey on Academic and Application. *Access IEEE*, 8, 187182–187201. doi:10.1109/ACCESS.2020.3030491

Chapter 6
Blockchain–Integrated Internet–of–Things Architecture in Privacy Preserving for Large–Scale Healthcare Supply Chain Data

Kamalendu Pal

iD https://orcid.org/0000-0001-7158-6481
City, University of London, UK

ABSTRACT

The supply chain forms the backbone of healthcare industry operations. The design and development of healthcare information systems (HIS) help different types of decision-making at various levels of business operations. Business process management decision-making is a complex task requiring real-time data collection from different operational sources. Hence, information technology (IT) infrastructure for data acquisition and sharing affects the operational effectiveness of the healthcare industry. The internet of things (IoT) applications have drawn significant research interest in the service of the healthcare industry. IoT technology aims to simplify the distributed data collection in healthcare practice, sharing, and processing of information and knowledge across many collaborating partners using suitable enterprise information systems. However, implementing blockchain technology in IoT-based data communication networks demands extra research initiatives. This chapter presents a review of security-related issues in the context of a HIS consisting of IoT-based blockchain technology.

DOI: 10.4018/978-1-7998-8382-1.ch006

INTRODUCTION

The coronavirus pandemic (simply known as COVID-19) is placing enormous strain on the global health care industry's workforce, infrastructure, supply chain and exposing social inequalities in healthcare. The current pandemic catalyzes change across the healthcare ecosystem and provokes private and public collaboration to quickly adapt and innovate service provision. Several foundational changes are emerging from and aggravated by coronavirus's spread around the world. Examples include patients' (or consumers') growing involvement in healthcare-related decision-making, quick endorsement of web-based healthcare services, and other forms of digital innovation practice.

Patients are steering and speeding up the pace of change in the healthcare industry. Their needs and aims are orchestrating innovation in healthcare-related products and services. Their preferences are guiding the development of seamless digitally enabled and on-demand connectivity of medics-patient communications. Their requirements guide the transition to patient-centric care delivery for different socio-economic groups in some parts of the world. Their expectations drive industry stakeholders to elevate a transactional patient healthcare encounter into a holistic human heath experience.

The long-held view that healthcare is "*sick care*" for the physical body includes patients' minds and spirits. Focus shifting from healthcare to health and well-being and providers should integrate this shift into the design of their service offering and delivery channels and locations. In addition, the patient will expect care to be available when and how it is most valuable and secure for them. It includes virtual care, at-home prescription and medicine delivery for elderly citizens, remote assessment (e.g., digital diagnostic and decision support), self-service educational applications, and social support.

Consequently, healthcare organizations started investing in replacing foundational structures, technologies, business process operational techniques. Digital transformation is helping individual healthcare organizations and the broader health ecosystem improve working methods, enhance access to service provisions, and deliver a more effective patient and clinician experience. Five important aspects of computing are playing increasingly pivotal roles around the globe – the Internet of Things (IoT), blockchain technology, service-oriented computing (or cloud computing), artificial intelligence (e.g., AI-based techniques), and virtual care delivery.

Along with technological advancement, healthcare service provision is changing rapidly. The IoT paradigm has revolutionized the healthcare industry. The IoT technology can help collect valuable patient and medication data, automate workflows, provide insights on disease symptoms and trends, and facilitate remote patient care.

Even though the health problems are rising, the world has not had enough medical professionals to tackle society's health problems.

However, academics and practitioners are spreading the goodwill message of Society 5.0. This vision of an emerging society is characterized as a "Creative Society" enabled by digital transformation. Digital transformation, especially with AI and robotics, provides augmented abilities to people, enabling them to pursue their dreams, big or small, which shall contribute to the global agenda, including sustainability and social inclusions, and another breakthrough to push humans for a better future. Society 5.0 is an initiative. First, mother earth is facing a massive tide of change against a backdrop of rapidly advancing innovation in digital technologies (e.g., AI, IoT, robotics, and blockchains), as well as biotechnologies. It will go beyond mere technological innovation to trigger revolutionary changes in industries and healthcare applications.

This way, having enough facilities to offer in-house treatment is currently under review from the healthcare society to remove the barriers of significant problems. It has gained the attention of researchers on IoT technology, and it is the most promising solution one can have because, with IoT, patients can manage their health problems and get help in emergency cases. On the other hand, doctors can manage and consult patients quickly. Over these years, several advanced IoT applications have been developed to support patients and healthcare staff. IoT technology-based healthcare improves existing features by supporting patient management, medical records management, medical emergency management, patient treatment management, and other functionalities, thus increasing healthcare information technology (IT) based applications.

Healthcare organizations are transitioning to health IT systems powered by cloud computing-based data storage, and analytics tools enable real-time innovative digital health service systems. These systems use interoperable data and platforms supported by deep learning capabilities, biosensors, and behavioural research to consider consumers (e.g., patient, medical staff) beliefs and actions. They are also applying virtual care, AI, and other technologies to personalize medicine, enable real-time care interventions, and provide behavioural nudges.

The new initiative of virtual medical services needs to have appropriate interactions among patients, medics, and clinicians. Training personnel (e.g., medic, nurse, clinician) to build virtual interpersonal relationships can significantly improve patients' virtual visit experience. Also, radical data interoperability is a required foundational capability to enable health care providers, insurers, and other stakeholders to deliver patient-centric programs and associated technologies. Implementing correct ways can help significantly improve care delivery and patient empowerment, and all these things are dependent on smooth data processing capability.

In recent decades, academics and practitioners (Pal, 2017) (Pal & Karakostas, 2018) are emphasizing the strategic importance of healthcare supply chain management (SCM) operations for better patient care. Also, researchers (McKone-Sweet et al., 2005) identified different barriers in implementing effecting SCM solutions for healthcare, including misaligned or conflicting incentives, the need for better data collection, and performance metrics. Further exacerbating the problems in the healthcare supply chain concerns the use of disparate information systems and software applications with limited interoperability. Consequently, the current inefficient, manual, and ad hoc practice for product tracking-traceability presents a compelling case to embrace automated technological solutions. A group of researchers (Landry & Beaulieu, 2013) discuss the challenges and complexities of the hospital's internal supply chain related business processes and their management issues. Also, a researcher (De Vries, 2011) mainly discusses multiple goals among stakeholders in the healthcare industry that strongly influence inventory-based decisions. Privett and fellow researchers (Privett & Gonsalvez, 2014) highlight and prioritize significant global pharmaceutical supply chain challenges (e.g., lack of business partner coordination, vulnerable warehouse inventory and order management system, missing product demand information, improper temperature control during product transport and storage). The same researchers also discuss the requirement for shipment visibility, inadequate tracking mechanism to avoid product shortage and expiration, and particular dependency regarding human resources to run the smooth functionality of the medical care supply chain.

In a typical healthcare supply chain, raw materials are purchased from suppliers and products (e.g., medicine, blood, human organs for transplant, instrument) are manufactured at one or more healthcare plants or collection points. Then they are transported to intermediate storage (e.g., warehouse, distribution centre) for packaging and shipping to retailers or customers. Depending on the products and destinations, the path from supplier to the customer can include several intermediaries such as wholesalers, warehouses, and retailers. In this way, supply chain management interconnectes to business processes such as inbound and outbound transportation, inventory control, and warehousing. Importantly, it also embodies the information systems necessary to monitor all these business activities. Figure 1 shows a simple diagrammatic representation of a pharmaceutical (or medical) supply chain, highlighting the main internal business activities.

Increased internalization of pharmaceutical industries is changing the operational practices of global pharmaceutical supply chains, and many pharmaceutical companies have adopted new models, either by outsourcing or by establishing business alliances in other countries. Globalization has also led to changes in operational practices, where products are manufactured in one part of the world and sold in another. The pharmaceutical supply chain has become more global in its geographical scope; the international market is getting more competitive and customer demand-oriented. Customers are looking for more variety as well as better quality assured products and services. Effective pharmaceutical supply chain management is thereby increasingly appreciated by businesses today (Pal, 2016).

Figure 1. A schematic diagram of a pharmaceutical supply chain

This global evolution of many healthcare supply chain networks means that their members work across different time zones and bring together many culturally diverse workforces. These teams are often quickly brought together and coordinated in nearly real-time to provide project deliverables within short periods and limited resources. In this way, collaboration and coordination among these teams play an essential role in delivering the ultimate customer experience; it is also more information intensive. Under these working environments, nearly real-time collaboration between mobile and geographically distributed healthcare supply chain members is challenging. It highlights the need for an efficient communications infrastructure that provides reliable on-demand access to support process information accurately. This way, the global healthcare industry has become diverse and recent information and communication technology (ICT) advancements have created new possibilities for managing the deluge of data generated by worldwide business operations of its supply chain. In this business, external data from supplier networks provide a massive influx to augment existing data. This is combined with data from sensors and intelligent machines, commonly known as the Internet of Things (IoT) data. In addition, the healthcare business networks use this IoT generated data to monitor the operational activities in a nearly real-time situation.

The digitalization of business activities attracts healthcare network management, improves communication, collaboration, and enhances trust within business partners due to real-time information sharing and better business process integration. However, the above new technologies come with different types of disruptions to operations and ultimate productivity. For example, some of the operational disruptions are malicious threats that hinder the safety of goods, services, and customers' trust to do business with the healthcare companies.

As a potential solution to tackle the security problems, practitioners and academics have reported some attractive research with IoT and blockchain-based information systems for maintaining transparency, data integrity, privacy, and security related issues. In a healthcare communication network context, the Internet of Things (IoT) system integrates different heterogeneous objects and sensors, which surround healthcare operations (Pal, 2019) and facilitates the information exchange within the business stakeholders (also known as nodes in networking terms). With the rapid enlargement of the data communication network scale and the intelligent evolution of hardware technologies, typical standalone IoT-based applications may no longer satisfy the advanced need for efficiency and security in the high degree of heterogeneity of hardware devices and complex data formats. Firstly, burdensome connectivity and maintenance costs brought by centralized architecture result in its low scalability. Secondly, centralized systems are more vulnerable to adversaries' targeted attacks under network expansion (Pal & Yasar, 2020).

Intuitively, a decentralized approach based on blockchain technology may solve the above problems in a typical centralized IoT-based information system. Mainly, the above justification is for three reasons. Firstly, an autonomous decentralized information system is feasible for trusted business partners to join the network, independently improving the business task-processing ability. Secondly, multiparty coordination enhances nodes' state consistency that information system crashes are avoidable due to a single-point failure. Thirdly, nodes could synchronize the whole information system state only by coping with the blockchain ledger to minimize the computation related activities and improve storage load. Besides, blockchain-based IoT architecture for healthcare information systems attracted researchers' attention (Pal, 2020).

Despite the potential of blockchain-based technology, severe security issues have been raised in its integration with IoT to form an architecture for healthcare business applications. This chapter presents different types of security-related problems for information system design purposes. Below, this chapter introduces first the basic idea of digitation of healthcare business process. Next, the chapter presents the use of blockchain technology in IoT for the healthcare industry. Then, it discusses the future research directions that include data security and industrial data breach-related issues. Finally, the chapter presents the concluding remarks and future research directions.

DIGITATION OF MEDICAL BUSINESS PROCESS

The pharmaceutical business's backbone is its supply chain networks and appropriate management of business functionalities. Supply chain business functionality consists of procuring and processing raw materials to produce semifinished or finished products at dedicated pharmaceutical plants. Afterwards, the intermediate or finished products are stored in warehouses or distribution centres. At last, the finished products are delivered to retail outlets or other customers (e.g., wholesalers, business alliance partners) (Pal, 2019).

Figure 2. A multi-layered view of the pharmaceutical industry

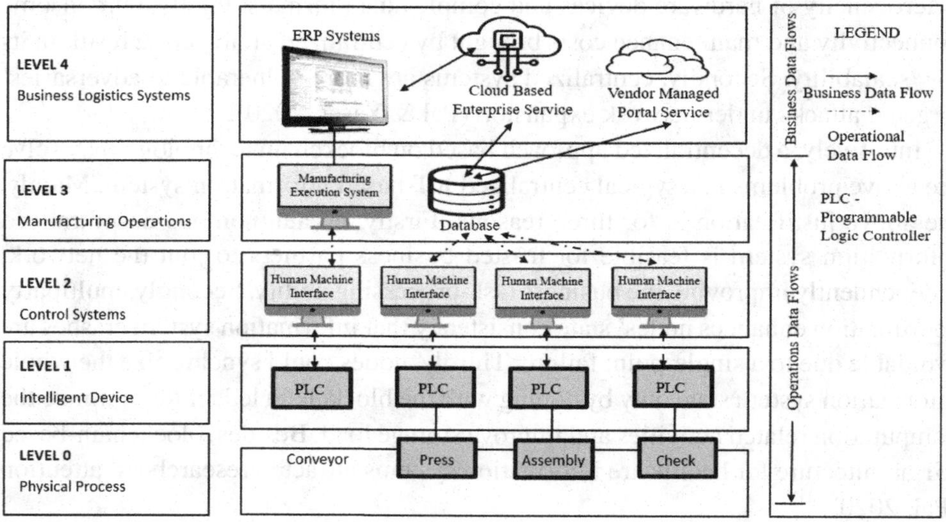

Consequently, intelligent pharmaceutical operations generally involve many silos within an organization, each with their automation and interconnected with other systems, including shop floor management, personnel scheduling, supplier relations, purchasing coordination, engineering design, product planning, sales forecasting and more. All these automated systems need interconnected information systems, and timely, reliable data exchange has become the lifeblood of efficient pharmaceutical operations. This way, a modern pharmaceutical system is generally supported by information technology (IT) and operational technology (OT), and there are challenges to interconnecting these technologies for the global pharmaceutical industry. Generally, OT consists of software and hardware (e.g., radio frequency identification (RFID) tags, sensors, actuators) used to manage pharmaceutical plants'

regular functionalities. The OT collects data from pharmaceutical machinery and equipment in real-time and sends it to the supervisory control unit and data acquisition (SCADA) systems. There are different constituent parts (e.g., Programmable Logic Controllers (PLC), Human Machine Interface (HMI), data communication network equipment – routers, gateways) in the supervisory systems.

The pharmaceutical machinery and equipment are connected over data communication networks, which facilitate business applications information management. Technically this connectivity of multiple healthcare-related objects (e.g., device, RFID tag attached pallets) is known as the Internet of Things (IoT). IoT is the network of associations between those connected objects that can exchange information using agreed methods (or protocols) and data schema. In this way, IoT technology-based pharmaceutical business processes automation is ushering a scope for OT devices to be interconnected to computer networks, and this facility provides the controlling ability for industrial applications ubiquitously. Modern IoT business applications can be extended to interconnect to enterprise-based information system operations, giving rise to a new way of using the IoT technology in industrial applications generally known as the Industrial Internet of Things (IIoT).

IIoT systems play a vital role in collaborating, coordinating and decision-making for globalized pharmaceutical businesses. Recent development in enterprise information systems (e.g., Enterprise Resource Planning (ERP), Material Requirement Planning (MRP), Customer Relation Management (CRM), Vendor Managed Inventory Systems (VMIS), Transportation Management Systems (TMS), Warehouse Management Systems (WMS), marketing and collaborative planning, forecasting and procurement) help to make global pharmaceutical more efficient. The modern enterprise information systems generate large volumes of pharmaceutical data by these systems has provided an impetus for global pharmaceutical networks to extract information from raw data to enhance business operations.

More and more business operations are digitized and computerized; new sources of information and machinery within global pharmaceutical networks bring new types of information. The amount of digital information about a specific pharmaceutical network fluctuates in real-time on different business topics (e.g., weight, price, packing dimension). Business practitioners get excited about '*Big Data*' – the du jour that describes the expanding universe of available data outside of that traditionally circulating in a pharmaceutical business's CRM, ERP, or MRP systems stored for analysis. These new data sources originate in the cyber-physical computing environments of global pharmaceutical networks. For example, with every online survey from customers, Global Positioning Systems (GPS) signals from pharmaceutical logistic tracks or trains, tweets from the heads of marketing, every RFID tagged package speeding off to the shrink-wrap station, manufacturers have more data than they know what to do with this. Pharmaceutical network operations are hotbeds of data inputs sought, captured, and reported. Some of this data produced within the global pharmaceutical network is unstructured and unwieldy – not suitable for applications based on standard relational database management systems (RDMS). There is, however, a massive amount of unwanted noise in generated data simply waiting to be released into the operational environment. Intelligent business analysis brings rigorous data manipulating techniques within special-purpose software – the business analytic platform – for the intelligent pharmaceutical industry's timely decision-making.

Today's modern pharmaceutical tries to achieve beyond automation of business processes and production plants. The focus is on data-driven innovations to accomplish high levels of optimization of pharmaceutical business activities. This way, the IoT infrastructure and big data collection facility help realize the connectivity of cyber-physical pharmaceutical business processes. This new connected infrastructure flourished through real-time data collection and processing, ultimately gaining value for business information and decision-making. Analytics in cyberspace use operational knowledge and information gathered, appropriate feedback actions (or control mechanisms) are sent to the physical world. Cyber-physical connectivity and communication are surmountable to achieving intelligent or smart healthcare. Additionally, the Internet has changed its face from hard-wired computer networks through wireless human connected networks to the modern era of intelligent and interconnected pharmaceutical networks. This new way of pharmaceuticals integrated with enhancement in service-oriented (or cloud) computing and big data analytics to usher a paradigm for intelligent healthcare.

In addition, digitization of pharmaceutical business processes provoke motivation from a pharmaceutical operation management perspective, enhance interaction, and improves trust within the business collaborators. However, the above technologies (e.g., IoT based collected data, cloud computing) come with problems that slow down the ultimate productivity of the business. For instance, many businesses activity-related disruptions are due to malicious threats that hinder the trust of the business partners in the manufacturer, safety of goods, and services.

There is massive use of IoT devices in the medical industry. However, most IoT devices are easy to attack, and industrial sabotage can be accomplished. Ideally, these IoT devices are limited in computational capability, network capacity, storage, and hence they are much more vulnerable to attacks than other endpoint devices such as smartphones, tablets, or computers. This chapter presents a survey of many security issues for IoT. The chapter reviews and categorizes popular security issues regarding the IoT layered architecture, in addition to protocols used for networking, communication, and management. It also outlines security requirements for IoT along with the existing attacks, threats, and state-of-the-art solutions. Besides, the chapter tabulates and map IoT security problems against existing solutions found in the academic literature. More importantly, the chapter discusses how blockchain technology can be a crucial enabler to solve many IoT security problems. The chapter also identifies open research problems and challenges for IoT security.

With the quickest increase of smart devices and high-speed data communication networks, IoT-based technology has gained massive popularity for automating medical business processes. This popularity is mainly due to (i) low power consumption in standard IoT devices and (ii) lossy data communication networks having constrained resources. It represents a network where "things" or embedded devices with sensors are interconnected through private or public data communication networks. The devices in IoT-based technology can be controlled remotely to perform the desired functionality. The information sharing among the devices then occurs through the network, which employs the standard communication protocols. The smart connected devices or "things" range from simple wearable accessories to large machines, each containing sensor chips. For example, the intelligent warehouse smart robots contain chips that support tracking and analyzing material management data. Similarly, electrical appliances, including machinery and inventory rack tracking robots, can be controlled remotely through IoT devices. The security cameras used for surveillance of a location can be monitored remotely anywhere in the world.

Apart from the industry-specific use, IoT serves the different business process automation needs as well. Different innovative electromechanical types of machinery (or devices) perform various business processes functionalities (e.g., detecting transport vehicles movement within medical plants, providing tracking and connectivity in industrial robots, measuring temperature and pressure in highly inhuman conditions). This way, an IoT-based system comprises "Things" (or IoT devices) that have remote sensing and actuating abilities and can exchange data with other connected devices and applications (e.g., directly or indirectly).

The data collected through these devices may be sent locally or to centralized servers or cloud-based applications to perform the real-time processing, monitoring, and improvement of the entire industrial, medical system. In recent years, an on-demand model of medicine that is leveraging IoT technologies is called Cloud-Based Medical (CBM) (Rosen et al., 2015) highlighted some of the leading technical themes. CBM provides a convenient, ubiquitous computing environment and on-demand network access to a shared pool of configurable medical resources quickly available for indented service.

The IoT application continues to proliferate due to the evolution of hardware-related issues (e.g., bandwidth improvement using cognitive radio-based networks) to address the underutilization of the frequency spectrum. In addition, the wireless sensor network (WSN) and machine-to-machine (M2M) or cyber-physical systems (CPS) have now evolved as integral parts of the broader concept of the technical term IoT. Consequently, the security-related problems to WSN, M2M, or CPS are lurking a threat for IoT-based medical applications, with the internet protocol (IP) being the central standard for connectivity. Hence, the industrial deployment architecture needs to be secured from attacks that may create problems for the services provided by IoT and may pose a threat to confidentiality, privacy, and integrity of data. Since the IoT technology-based applications deal with a collection of interconnected data communication networks and heterogeneous devices, it inherits the conventional security issues related to the computer networks. The constrained resources pose extra challenges to IoT security since the small devices or things containing sensors have limited power and memory. As a result, the security solutions need to be adapted to the constrained architectures.

Along with the rapid growth of IoT applications and devices in the medical industry, there has been an increasing number of research efforts highlighting security issues in the IoT environment. Some of these research target security issues at a specific layer, whereas other researchers aim at presenting end-to-end security for IoT applications. A research group presented an IoT applications survey and categorized security issues in the application, architecture, communication, and data (Alaba et al., 2017). This proposed categorization for IoT security is different from the conventional layered architecture. The threats on IoT applications are highlighted for the hardware layer, network layer, and application layers. In another survey, a research group (Granjal et al., 2015) highlighted security related issues for the IoT application protocols. The security analyses presented by other research groups (Roman et al., 2011) (Granjal et al., 2008) (Cirani et al., 2013) discuss and compare different critical management systems and algorithmic cryptographic techniques. Besides, other researchers (Butun et al., 2014) (Abduvaliyev et al., 2013) (Mitchell & Chen, 2014) presented a comparative evaluation of intrusion detection systems. The IoT applications in the *'fog computing environment'* were analyzed and presented by a few research groups (Yi et al., 2015) (Wang et al., 2015). A systematic survey by Sicari and colleagues (Sicari et al., 2015) provided different aspects of middleware related technical issues (e.g., confidentiality, security, access control, privacy). The authors highlighted trust management, privacy-related issues, authentication, network security, data security, and intrusion detection systems. For edge-computing based applications, including mobile cloud computing, mobile edge computing and computing, identity and authentication, access control systems, network security, trust management, fault tolerance and implementation of forensics are surveyed by a group of researchers (Roman et al., 2016).

Motivated by an increasing number of vulnerabilities, a researcher (Oleshchuk, 2009) presented a survey of privacy-preserving mechanisms for specific IoT applications. The author explained in the research paper the secure multiparty computations to preserve privacy for IoT-based application users. Zhou and collaborative researchers (Zhou et al., 2017) discussed various security threats and possible solutions for cloud-based IoT applications. The authors described identity and location privacy, node compromising, layer removing or adding, and critical management threats for IoT using the cloud. In another survey, Zhang and colleagues (Zhan et al., 2014) presented some crucial IoT security issues about unique identification of objects, privacy, authorization, authentication, and the requirement of lightweight cryptographic techniques, malware, and software vulnerabilities. The IoT-A project (IoT-A, 2013) described a reference architecture for IoT that compliance needs implementation for privacy, security, and trust. The used trust model provides data integrity and confidentiality while creating end-to-end data communication through an authentication technique. Besides, to eliminate improper data usage, the privacy model needs to define access policies and methods for encrypting and decrypting data. The security-related issues are included in a three-layers corresponding to the services, communication, and application. In the same way, the Open Web Application Security Project (OWASP) (OWASP, 2016) introduced ten vulnerabilities for the IoT architecture. Notably, these vulnerabilities include insecure interfaces of IoT architecture, inappropriate security configuration, physical security, and insecure firmware/software.

IOT ARCHITECTURE AND SECURITY CHALLENGES

IoT becomes the foundation for connecting things, sensors, actuators, and other smart technologies. IoT technology gives immediate access to physical objects and lends to innovative services with high efficiency and productivity. The characteristics of IoT include: (i) the pervasive sensing of objects; (ii) the hardware and software integration; and (iii) many nodes. In developing an IoT, objects must be capable of interacting with each other, reaching autonomously to the change of medical environment (e.g., temperature, pressure, humidity).

IoT Protocols and Standards

A typical IoT deployment in the medical industry contains heterogeneous devices with embedded sensors interconnected through a network, as shown in Figure 1. This architecture consists of physical devices and communication layers, network and transport layers, and application and messaging layers. Radio Frequency Identification (RFID) technology has received massive attention from the medical industry's daily operations as a critical component of the IoT world (IoT) world. In RFID-enabled medical chain automation, an EPC (Electronic Product Code) is allocated to an individual item of interest and is attached to an RFID tag for tracking and tracing purposes.

Figure 3. Common IoT standards and protocols

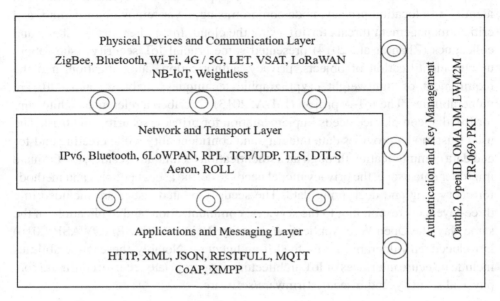

In addition, wireless sensor networks (WSNs) are used to provide computing services to enterprises. WSNs are the essential infrastructure for the implementation of IoT. Various hardware and software systems are available to WSNs: (i) Internet Protocol version 6 (IPv6) makes it possible to connect an unlimited number of devices, (ii) Wi-Fi and WiMAX provide high-speed and low-cost communication, (iii) Zigbee, Bluetooth, and RFID provide the communication in low-speed and local communication, and (iv) a mobile platform offers communications for any-time, anywhere and anything.

Figure 2 shows a layered architecture with the standard IoT protocols used for medical applications and messaging, and routing or forwarding, physical devices and those for key management and authentication. It shows the standards and protocols for the commonly used low-rate wireless personal area networks (LR-WPANs) (IEEE, 2012) and the recently evolved protocols for the low power vast area network (LPWAN) based protocols.

Again, LR-WPANs (i.e., IEEE standard 802.15.15.4) consist of two low-level layers: the Physical Layer and the Medium Access Control (MAC) layer. The physical layer specification is related to communication over wireless channels having diverse frequency bands and data rates. The MAC layer specification is related to mechanisms for channels access as well as for synchronization.

A simple IoT architecture composed of devices (e.g., machinery and equipment), networks, cloud-based storage, and information system applications are shown in Figure 1. This architecture consists of four layers, such as perception, network, processing, and application layer. The perception layer consists of electromechanical devices like different types of sensors, RFID tag readers, security surveillance cameras, geographical positioning system (GPS) modules, and so on. These devices may be accompanied by other industrial appliances like conveyor systems, automated guided vehicles (AGVs), and different industrial robots for a medical industry context. These devices' primary function is to capture sensory data, monitor environmental conditions and medical assembly areas, and transport materials (e.g., semifinished, finished products). These collected data needs transportation to the processing layer. The processing layer consists of dedicated servers and data processing software that ultimately produce management information, and operational managers can act based on the produced information. In this way, the application layer produces user-specific decision information. Few critical IoT based information system applications in the medical industry are smart factories, smart robotics, intelligent supply chain, smart warehouse management. Besides, the importance of WSNs to industrial control systems have been discussed by researchers (Araujo et al., 2014). In the research field of WSNs, most ongoing work focuses on energy-efficient routing, aggregation, and data management algorithms; other challenges include the large-scale deployment and semantic integration of massive data (Aberer et al., 2014) and security (Gandino et al., 2014).

Security Requirements for IoT

To secure IoT-based information systems applications in the medical industry, the following issues need to consider.

Data Privacy, Confidentiality, and Integrity: As IoT data moves in a data communication network, an appropriate encryption algorithm is needed to ensure the confidentiality of data. Due to a diverse integration of services, devices and data communication networks, the data stored on a device is vulnerable to privacy violation by compromising nodes in an IoT applications network. The IoT devices susceptible to attacks may cause an attacker to disturb the integrity of stored data by modifying the stored data for malicious intentions.

Authentication, Authorization, and Accounting: To secure communication in IoT, authentication is required between two parties communicating with each other. For privileged access to services, the devices must be authenticated. The diversity of authentication mechanisms for IoT exists mainly due to the diverse heterogeneous underlying architectures and environments that support IoT devices. These environments challenge defining a standard and global protocol for authentication in IoT devices and applications.

Access control systems face many problems, such as third-party, inefficiency, and lack of privacy. These problems can be addressed by blockchain, the technology that received significant attention in recent years, and many potentials. Jemel and other researchers (Jemel & Serhrouchni, 2017) report a couple of centralized access control systems problems. As there is a third party with access to the data, the risk of privacy leakage exists. Also, a major party is in charge to control the access, so the risk of a single point of failure also exists. This study presents an access control mechanism with a temporal dimension to solve these problems and adapts a blockchain-based solution for verifying access permissions. The attribute-based Encryption method (Sahai & Waters, 2005) also has some problems, such as privacy leakage from the private key generator (PKG) (Hur & Noh, 2011) and a single point of failure as mentioned before. Wang and colleagues (Wang et al.,2018) introduce a framework for data sharing and access control to address this problem by implementing decentralized storage.

IoT Devises Management: In IoT, devices management relates to security solutions for the physical devices, embedded software, and residing data. Internet of Things (IoT) comprises "Things" (or IoT devices) that have remote sensing and data collecting capabilities and can exchange data with other connected devices and applications (directly or indirectly). IoT devices can collect data and process it locally or send it to centralize servers or cloud-based application back-ends for processing. A recent on-demand model of medicine that is leveraging IoT technologies is called Cloud-Based Medical (CBM). It enables ubiquitous, convenient, on-demand network access to a shared pool of configurable medical business processes information collection and use it service provision.

However, attackers seek to exfiltrate IoT devices' data using malicious codes in malware, especially on the open-source Android platform. Gu et al. (Gu et al., 2018) reported a malware identification system in a blockchain-based system named CB-MDEE composed of detecting consortium chains by test members and public chain users. The CB-MDEE system uses a soft-computing-based comparison technique and more than one marking function to minimize the false-positive rate and improve malware variants' identification ability.

Availability of Services: The attacks on IoT devices may hinder services through the conventional denial-of-service attacks. Different strategies (e.g., jamming adversaries, sinkhole attacks, replay attacks) are used to deteriorate service quality (QoS) to IoT medical application users.

Single Points of Failure: A considerable growth of heterogeneous networks for the IoT-based global medical infrastructure may expose many '*single points of failure*' that may, in turn, deteriorate the services envisioned through IoT applications. Hence, it is essential to develop a tamper-proof ecosystem for many IoT devices and provide alternative mechanisms for implementing a fault-tolerant IoT applications network.

Categorization of Security Issues

With the development of ubiquitous computing (e.g., IoT based applications in medical, logistics, and smart grid), uses have become widely used globally (e.g., medical, digital healthcare, smart city). According to the statistics website Statista (TSP, 2021), the number of connected devices in the industry will drastically increase in the coming years. At the same time, with the vast growth of IoT applications and devices, security attacks pose a more serious threat for industries. For example, remote adversaries could compromise health services implantable medical devices (3), or smart cars (4), which will create massive economic losses to the world. IoT devices are widely used in industry, military, and other critical operational areas of society. Malicious attackers can jeopardize public and national security. For example, on 21 October 2016, multiple distributed denial of service (DDoS) (5) attacks took place by Domain Name System provider Dyn, which caused the inaccessibility of several websites (e.g., GitHub, Twitter). For example, Stuxnet (6), a malicious computer worm that targeted industrial computer systems were responsible for causing a substantial problem to Iran's nuclear program. The ransomware attack, WannaCry, was a worldwide cyberattack in May 2017, which targeted computer systems worldwide. A new variant of WannaCry forced Taiwan Semiconductor Medical Company (TSMC) to temporarily shut down several of its chip-fabrication factories in August 2018 (Wikipedia, 2021). The virus spread to 10,000 machines in TSMC's most advanced facilities.

Inspired by an increasing number of vulnerabilities, predatorial attacks and information leaks, IoT device manufacturers, service-oriented computing service providers, and researchers are working on designing systems to securely control the flow of information between devices, to find out new vulnerabilities, and to provide security and privacy within the context of users and the devices. For example, adversaries can exploit the envisioned design and verification limitations to compromise the system's security. The system becomes vulnerable to malicious attacks from cyberspace (Sturm et al., 2017). Some well-known attacks (e.g., Stuxnet, Shamoon, BlackEnergy, WannaCry, and TRITON) (Stouffer, 2020) created significant problems in recent decades.

The distributed medical industry's critical issues are coordinating and controlling secure business information and its operational network. Applying cybersecurity controls in the operating environment demands the most significant attention and effort to ensure that appropriate security and risk mitigation are achieved. For example, medical device spoofing and false authentication in information sharing (Kumar & Mallick, 2018) are significant problems for the industry.

However, disadvantages of the centralized IoT information system architecture issues have been reported by researchers (Ali et al., 2019). A central point of failure could easily paralyze the whole data communication network. Besides, it is easy to misuse user-sensitive data in a centralized system; users have limited or no control over personal data. Centralized data can be tampered with or deleted by an intruder, and therefore the centralized system has lacks guaranteed traceability and accountability.

The vast popularity of IoT based information systems in the medical industry also demands the appropriate protection of security and privacy-related issues to stop system vulnerabilities and threats. Also, traditional security protections are not always problem-free. Hence, it is worth classifying different security problems based on objects of attack relevant to IoT-based systems. This classification of security-related attacks would help industry-specific practitioners and researchers to understand which attacks are essential to their regular business operations. The additional layer-specific security-related research is shown in Table 1, Table 2, and Table 3.

Table 1. Perception layer attacks

Type of attack	Description
Tampering	Physical damage is caused to the device (e.g., RFID tag, Tag reader) or communication network (Andrea et al., 2015).
Malicious Code Injection	The attacker physically introduces malicious code onto an IoT system by compromising its operation. The attacker can control the IoT system and launch attacks (Ahemd et al., 2017).
Radio Frequency Signal Interference (Jamming)	The predator sends a particular type of radiofrequency signal to hinder communication in the IoT system, and it creates a denial of service (DoS) from the information system (Ahemd et al., 2017).
Fake Node Injection:	The intruder creates an artificial node and the IoT-based system network and illegally access the information from the network or control data flow (Ahemd et al., 2017).
Sleep Denial Attack	The attacker aims to keep the battery-powered devices awake by sending them with inappropriate inputs, which causes battery power exhaustion, leading to the shutting down of nodes (Ahemd et al., 2017).
Side-Channel Attack	In this attack, the intruder gets hold of the encryption keys by applying malicious techniques on the devices of the IoT-based information system (Andrea et al., 2015), and by using these keys, the attacker can encrypt or decrypt confidential information from the IoT network.
Permanent Denial of Service (PDoS)	In this attack, the attacker permanently damages the IoT system using hardware sabotage. The attack can be launched by damaging firmware or uploading an inappropriate BIOS using malware (Foundry, 2017).

Table 2. Network layer attacks

Type of attack	Description
Traffic Analysis Attack	The attacker sniffs confidential data flowing to and from the devices, even without going close to the network to get network traffic information and attacking purpose (Andrea et al., 2015).
RFID Spoofing	The intruder first spoofs an RFID signal to access the information imprinted on the RFID tag (Ahemd et al., 2017). The intruder can then send its manipulated data using the original tag ID, posing it as valid. In this way, the intruder can create a problem for the business operation.
RFID Unauthorized Access	An intruder can read, modify, or delete data present on RFID nodes because of the lack of proper authentication mechanisms (Andrea et al., 2015).
Routing Information Attacks	These are direct attacks where the attacker spoofs or alters routing information and makes a nuisance by creating routing loops and sending error messages (Andrea et al., 2015).
Selective Forwarding	In this attack, a malicious node may alter, drop, or selectively forward some messages to other nodes in the network (Varga et al., 2017). Therefore, the information that reaches the destination is incomplete.
Sinkhole Attack	In this attack, an attacker compromises a node closer to the sink (known as sinkhole node) and makes it look attractive to other nodes in the network, thereby luring network traffic towards it (Ahemd et al., 2017).
Wormhole Attack	An attacker maliciously prepares a low-latency link in a wormhole attack and then tunnels packets from one point to another through this link (Varga et al., 2017).
Sybil Attack	A single malicious node claims multiple identities (known as Sybil nodes) and locates itself at different places in the network (Andrea et al., 2015). It leads to colossal resource allocation unfairly. • Man in the Middle Attack (MiTM): Here, an attacker manages to eavesdrop or monitor the communication between two IoT devices and access their private data (Andrea et al., 2015).
Replay Attack	An attacker may capture a signed packet and resend the packet multiple times to the destination (Varga et al., 2017). It keeps the network busy, leading to a DoS attack.
Denial/Distributed Denial of Service (DoS/DDoS) Attacks	Unlike DoS attacks, multiple compromised nodes attack a specific target by flooding messages or connection requests to crash or slow down the system server/network resource (Rambus).

Table 3. Software layer attacks

Type of attack	Description
Virus, Worms, Trojan Horses, Spyware and Adware	Using this malicious software, an adversary can infect the system by tampering with data, stealing information, or even launching DoS (Andrea et al., 2015).
Malware	Data in IoT devices may be affected by malware, contaminating the cloud or data centres (Varga et al., 2017).

An attacker launches software attacks taking advantage of the associated software or security vulnerabilities presented by an IoT system, as shown in Table 3. This way, a malicious code can attack IoT-based infrastructure applications and create disruption (e.g., repeating a new connection request until the IoT system reaches maximum level) of an existing service for global connectivity.

Besides, the IoT based application system provides an innovative technology that has become a guiding technology behind the automation of the medical industry and smart computing. The IoT application produces countless digitized services and applications that provide several advantages over existing solutions. The applications and services share some standard features, which include: (i) sensing capabilities, (ii) connectivity, (iii) extensive scale network, (iv) dynamic system, (v) intelligence capabilities, (vi) Big Data processing using traditional data analytics methods, (vii) unique identity of the objects to connect over the computer network, (viii) autonomous contextual and real-time decision making, and (ix) heterogeneity – the IoT system allows different devices and objects to be addressable and communicate with each other over the Internet. These devices have heterogeneous characteristics, including platforms, operating systems, communication protocols, and other hardware and software components. Despite these heterogeneous characteristics, the IoT system allows all the devices to communicate efficiently and effectively in a medical environment.

The convergence of IoT with blockchain technology will have many advantages. The blockchain's decentralization model will have the ability to handle processing a vast number of transactions between IoT devices, significantly reducing the cost associated with installing and maintaining large, centralized data centres and distributing computation and storage needs across IoT devices networks. Working with blockchain technology will eliminate the single point of failure associated with the centralized IoT architecture. The convergence of Blockchain with IoT will allow the P2P messaging, file distribution, and autonomous coordination between IoT devices with no centralized computing model.

However, IoT-based applications' deployment results in an enlarged attack surface that requires end-to-end security mitigation. Blockchain technologies play a crucial role in securing many IoT-oriented applications by becoming security providing medical applications. Blockchain technology is based on a distributed database management system that keeps records of all business-related transactional information that have been executed and shared among participating business partners in the network. This distributed database system is known as distributed ledger technology (DLT). Individual business exchange information is stored in the distributed ledger and must be verified by most network members. All business-related transactions that have ever been made are contained in the block. Bitcoin, the decentralized peer-to-peer (P2P) digital currency, is the most famous example of blockchain technology (Nakamoto, 2008).

BACKGROUND OF BLOCKCHAIN TECHNOLOGY

Blockchain technology is based on a distributed database management system that keeps records of all business-related transactional information that have been executed and shared among participating business partners in the network. This distributed database system is known as a DLT. Individual business exchange information is stored in the distributed ledger and must be verified by most network members. All business-related transactions that have ever been made are contained in the block. Bitcoin, the decentralized peer-to-peer (P2P) digital currency, is the most famous example of blockchain technology (Nakamoto, 2008).

The blockchain technology infrastructure has motivated many innovative applications in the medical industry. This technology's ideal blockchain vision is tamper evident and tamper resistant ledgers implemented in a distributed fashion, without a central repository. The central ideas guiding blockchain technology emerged in the late 1980s and early 1990s. A research paper (Lamport, 1998) was published with the background knowledge of the Paxos protocol, which provided a consensus method for reaching an agreement resulting in a computer network. The central concepts of that research were combined and applied to the electronic cash-related research project by Satoshi Nakamoto (Nakamoto, 2008), leading to modern cryptocurrency or bitcoin-based systems.

Distributed Ledger Technology (DLT) Based Blockchain

The blockchain's initial basis is to institute trust in a P2P network bypassing any third managing parties' need. For example, Bitcoin started a P2P financial value exchange mechanism where no third party (e.g., bank) is needed to provide a value-transfer transaction with anyone else on the blockchain community. Such a community-based trust is the main characteristic of system verifiability using mathematical modelling techniques for evidence. The mechanism of this trust provision permits peers of a P2P network to transact with other community members without necessarily trusting each other. This behaviour is commonly known as the trustless behaviour of a blockchain system. The trustlessness also highlights that a blockchain network partner interested in transacting with another business entity on the blockchain does not necessarily need to know the real identity.

It permits users of a public blockchain system to be anonymous. A record of transactions among the peers is stored in a chain of a data structure known as blocks, the name blockchain's primary basis. Each block (or peer) of a blockchain network keeps a copy of this record. Moreover, a consensus, digital voting mechanism to use many network peers, is also decided on the blockchain that all network stores' nodes. Hence, blockchain is often designed as distributed ledger-based technology.

An instance of such a DLT is stored at each blockchain node (or peer) and gets updated simultaneously with no mechanism for retroactive changes in the records. In this way, blockchain transactions cannot be deleted or altered.

Intelligent Use of Hashing

Intelligent techniques are used in hashing the blocks encapsulating transaction records together, which makes such records immutable. In other words, blockchain's transactions achieve validity, trust, and finality based on cryptographic proofs and underlying mathematical computation between different trading-peers (or partners), known as a hashing function. Encryption algorithms are used to provide confidentiality for creating hash functions. These algorithmic solutions have the essential character that they are reversible in the sense that, with knowledge of the appropriate key, it must be possible to reconstruct the plaintext message from the cryptographic technique. This hashing mechanism of a piece of data can be used to preserve the blockchain system's integrity. For example, Secure Hash Algorithm 256 (SHA256) is a member of the SHA2 hash functions currently used by many blockchain-based systems such as Bitcoin.

Terminologies in Blockchain

Some private blockchains provide read restrictions on the data within the blocks. Consortium blockchains are operated and owned by a group of organizations or a private community. Blockchain users use asymmetric key cryptography to sign on transactions. The trust factor maintenance within a distributed ledger technology (DLT) can be attributed to the consensus algorithms and the key desirable properties achieved thenceforth. Wüst and Gervais (2018) give a good description of these properties. Some of them are Public Verifiability, Transparency, Integrity. The main terminologies in blockchain have discussed below.

Terminologies in Blockchain:

Blocks: The transactions that occur in a peer-to-peer network associated with a blockchain are picked up from a pool of transactions and grouped in a block. Once a transaction is validated, it is basically impossible to be reverted. Transactions are pseudonymous as they are linked only to the user's public key and not to the user's real identity. A block may contain several hundreds of transactions. The block size limits the number of transactions that can be included in a block. The diagrammatic structure of a blockchain is shown in Figure 4. A block consists of version no., a previous block's hash, the Merkle root tree to trace the block's transactions, the current block's hash, timestamp, and nonce value. A blockchain starts with a genesis block.

Mining is when the designated nodes in the blockchain network called miners collect transactions from a pool of unprocessed transactions and combine them in a block. In mining, each miner competes to solve an equally tricky computational problem of finding a valid hash value with a particular no. of zeroes below a specific target. In Bitcoin mining, the number of zeroes indicates the difficulty of the computation. Many nonce values are tried to arrive at the golden nonce that hashes to a valid hash with the current difficulty level. When a miner arrives at this nonce value, we can say that he has successfully mined a block. This block then gets updated to the chain.

Figure 4. An overview of blockchain architecture

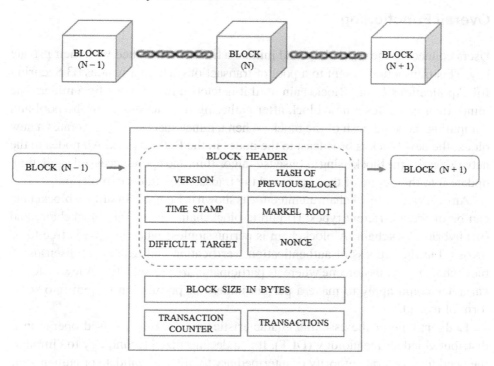

Consensus: The consensus mechanism serves two primary purposes, as given in Jesus et al. (2018): block validation and the most extensive chain selection. Proof-of-Work is the consensus algorithm used in Bitcoin Blockchain. The proof-of-stake algorithm is much faster than Proof-of-Work and demands less computational resources. The Ethereum blockchains use a pure proof-of-stake algorithm to ensure consensus. Besides Proof-of-Work, there are other consensus algorithms such as Proof of Byzantine Fault Tolerance (PBFT), proof- of activity, etc. Anwar (2018) presents a consolidated view of the different consensus algorithms. Proof-of-Work is a signature that indicates that the block has been mined after performing computation with the required difficulty level. The peers can easily verify this signature in the network to ensure a block's validity. The longest chain is always selected as the consistent one for appending the new block.

Smart Contracts: They are predefined rules deployed in the Blockchain network that two parties involved in a settlement must agree to priorly. Smart contracts were designed to avoid disagreement, denial, or violation of rules by the parties involved. They have triggered automatically in the blockchain on the occurrence of specific events mentioned in the rules.

Overall Functioning

Users connect to the blockchain and initiate a transaction signed with their private key. This transaction is sent to a pool of transactions where it resides 63 Securing IoT Applications Using Blockchain until it is fetched into a block by a miner. The miner then generates a new block after gathering transactions from the pool and computing the valid hash of the block. When a miner successfully generates a new block, the new block is broadcast to the nodes in the P2P network. All nodes in the network verify the block using a consensus algorithm, and upon successful validation, update it to their copy of the chain, and the transaction attains completion.

An overview of blockchain architecture is shown in Figure 2. In simple, blockchain can be of three different types: (i) public blockchain, (ii) private blockchain, and (iii) hybrid blockchain. A blockchain is permissionless when anyone is free to be involved in the process of authentication, verification and reaching consensus. A blockchain is permission one where its participants are pre-selected. A few different variables could apply to make a permissionless or permission system into some form of hybrid.

Ledger: One of the essential characteristics of blockchain-based operation is distributed ledger technology (DLT). It is a decentralized technology to eliminate the need for a central authority or intermediary to process, validate or authenticate transactions. Medical businesses use DLT to process, validate or authenticate transactions or other types of data exchanges.

Secure: Blockchain technology produces a structure of data with inherent security qualities. It is based on principles of cryptography, decentralization, and consensus, which ensure trust in transactions. Blockchain technology ensures that the data within the network of blocks has not been tampered with.

Shared: Blockchain data is shared amongst multiple users of this network of nodes. It gives transparency across the node users in the network.

Distributed: Blockchain technology can be geographically distributed. The decentralization helps to scale the number of blockchain network nodes to ensure it is more resilient to predators' attacks. A predator's capability to impact the blockchain network's consensus protocol is minimized by increasing the number of nodes.

Also, for blockchain-based system architectures that permit anyone to anonymously create accounts and participate (called *permissionless* blockchain networks), these capabilities produce a level of trust amongst collaborating business partners with no prior knowledge of one another. Blockchain technology provides decentralization with the collaborating partners across a distributed network. This decentralization means there is no single point of failure, and a single user cannot change the record of transactions.

Figure 5. represents the outline of how one can manipulate blockchain to ensure security. The figure helps understand the relationship [between offerings such as immutability, province, and so on. Moreover, which aspect is needed to satisfy the specific security requirements in user specifications.

Figure 5. Relationship between the offering of blockchain and security requirements

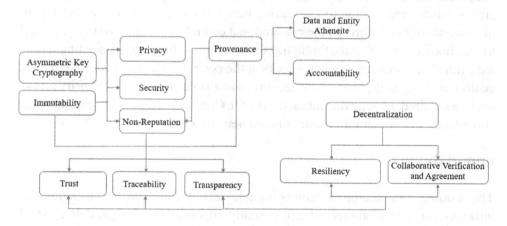

SECURING IOT APPLICATIONS USING BLOCKCHAIN

Blockchain technology uses a new way of managing trust in information systems and their transaction processing capabilities. A transaction processing system gathers and stores data regarding business activity (known as a transaction) and sometimes controls business decisions made as part of a transaction. The transaction is the activity that changes stored data. An individual transaction must succeed or fail as a complete unit; it can never be only partially complete. Since the introduction of the Bitcoin, blockchain technology has shown popularity in other business applications and attracted much attention from academia and industry. The blockchain's interest is its features that provide security, anonymity, and data integrity without third-party involvement in transaction control.

Primary Properties of Digital Blockchain

The information on the blockchain is digitized, getting rid of the requirement for manual documentation. Transactions are structured into blocks for information processing purposes, and standard data communication network protocol ensures that every node (i.e., business partner) receives every transaction in near real-time and uses the same rules. By design, blockchain is distributed and synchronized across the networks and ideal for a multi-organizational business network such as supply chain management.

Decentralization

All blockchain participants (nodes) copy all data in the system and have no central authorization organization (e.g., clearing bank). It ensures to have no single point of vulnerability or failure. In the conventional centralized transaction system, each transaction must be validated through a central authority (e.g., bank), needing service fees, time, and performance bottlenecks at the central servers. Besides, there is no central authority in the blockchain network, and no intermediary or authority service fees are required, making the transaction faster. Consensus algorithms maintain data consistency in a decentralized, distributed network (Zheng et al., 2017).

Immutability

The residing data on a blockchain is immutable. Once the participants agree on a business transaction and record it, it is nearly impossible to change, delete, or roll back transactions once they are included in the blockchain. If someone records another transaction about that asset to change its state, the participant cannot hide the original transaction. The provenance of assets deals with any asset; one can tell where it is, where it has been, and what has happened throughout its life (Pattison, 2017).

Consensus

There is a standard algorithm (or mechanism) used to make sure that all participants (or nodes) agree on the validity of transaction data in the system, replacing the requirement for a trusted third party (e.g., bank) for authorization purposes. There must be an agreement among all the participants that the transaction is valid before executing a transaction. The agreement process is known as "consensus", and it helps keep inaccurate or fraudulent transactions out of the blockchain. Blocks that include erroneous transactions could be revealed promptly.

Anonymity in Blockchain

Each participant can interact with the blockchain with a generated address, which does not reveal the user's real identity, but participants can see the transaction (Zheng et al., 2017). Arguably, the bitcoin blockchain cannot guarantee perfect privacy preservation due to its intrinsic constraints, but some other alternative blockchain protocols claim to provide a better privacy protection mechanism.

Traceability

The individual transaction included in a blockchain (i.e., public or private) is digitally signed and timestamped, which means that participants can trace- back to a specific time for an individual transaction and identify the appropriate party (through their public address) on the Blockchain (Swan, 2015). Therefore, every block is immutably and verifiably linked to the previous block. A complete history can always be reconstructed right back to the beginning (the genesis block).

RELATED RESEARCH ON IOT SECURITY AND PRIVACY USING BLOCKCHAIN

Leveraging the advantages of integrating blockchain in IoT, academics and practitioners have investigated how to handle critical issues, such as IoT device-level security, managing enormous volumes of data, maintaining user privacy, and keeping confidentiality and trust (Pal, 2020) (Dorri et al., 2019) (Shen et al., 2019). In research work, a group of researchers (Kim et al., 2017) have proposed a blockchain-based IoT system architecture to prevent IoT devices' hacking problems.

A group of researchers (Azzi et al., 2019) have introduced a blockchain integrated, IoT based information system for the supply chain management. It provides an example of a reliable, transparent, and secured system. Another group of researchers

(Mondal et al., 2019) has reported a blockchain-based food supply chain that uses a proof-of-object (PoO) based authentication method. In this research, RFID tags are attached to the individual food products that are used for tracking purposes throughout their lifecycle within the supply chain network. All the real-time tracking and monitoring data produced are stored in a blockchain-based information system, which monitors food quality.

Francesco Longo and colleagues (Longo et al., 2019) have proposed an information system consisting of blockchain technology for supply chain management. The system allows supply chain business partners to share their information with appropriate authentication and integrity among peers.

Practitioners and academics (Pal, 2020) advocated three primary aspects of modern medical: (i) integration of heterogeneous data along with the global operations, (ii) data collection, and (iii) analysis of collected data. Within heterogeneous data integration, service-oriented computing (SOC) plays a dominating role, given that intelligent perception and collection from the various computer networks of physical medical resources and abilities. At the same time, new innovative technologies have emerged. They have wide use in different medical applications, such as the IoT. The data collected by Radio Frequency Identification (RFID) tags and sensors for their underlying assets can help find the essential attributes (e.g., location, condition, availability) that form the essential ingredient for the modern medical system.

Standard IoT systems are built on a centralized computing environment, which requires all devices to be connected and authenticated through the central server. This framework would not be able to provide the needs to outspread the IoT system in globalized operation. Therefore, moving the IoT system into the decentralized path may be the right decision. One of the popular decentralization platforms is blockchain technology.

Blockchain technology provides an appropriate solution to the security mentioned above challenges posed by a distributed IoT ecosystem. Blockchain technology offers an approach to storing information, executing transactions, performing functions, and establishing trust in secure computing without centralized authority in a networked environment. A blockchain is a chain of timestamped blocks connected by special mathematical techniques (i.e., cryptographic hashes) and behaves like a distributed ledger whose data are shared among a network of users. This paper emphasizes how the convergence of blockchain technology with IoT can provide a better medical industry solution.

Blockchain in IoT

With the booming growth of IoT, the number of connected IoT devices and the data generated by them has become a massive bottleneck in meeting Quality-of-

Service (QoS) (Ferrag et al., 2019). In this way, blockchain comes into the picture by supporting a decentralized way of storing data and trustful and anonymous transactions. Blockchain technology can thereby be used for tracking and coordinating the billions of connected devices. It can also enable the processing of transactions to allow significant savings for IoT industry manufacturers. This decentralized approach would further eliminate single points of failure, creating a more resilient ecosystem for devices to run on (Ali et al., 2019). The blockchains cryptographic algorithms would also help make consumer data privacy more robust (Makhdoom et al., 2019).

A blockchain is a distributed immutable, verifiable ledger. A typical design of a blockchain consists of a series of transactions that are put into one block. These blocks are then linked so that if a transaction is altered in one block, it must be updated in all the subsequent blocks (Makhdoom et al., 2019). Since the ledger is maintained with many peers, it is challenging to alter a transaction (Ferrag et al., 2019). All the blockchain peers need to agree or validate each transaction to add to a block (Reyna et al., 2018). Once validated, the block gets updated in the blockchain.

This agreement is achieved with the help of consensus algorithms like Proof of Work (PoW), Proof of Stake (PoS), Delegated Proof-of-Stake (DPoS), Proof-of-Authority (PoA) etc. Blockchain technology is radically reshaping not only the modern IoT world but also the industries. Researchers of late have focused on integrating blockchain into the IoT ecosystem to include distributed architecture and security features. However, before this section discusses how blockchain is bringing about a significant paradigm shift in IoT, we explain the significant features of blockchain as follows (Ali et al., 2019):

- The decentralization offered by Blockchain technology enables two nodes to engage in transactions without a trusted third party. This eliminates the bottleneck of a single point of failure, thereby enhancing fault tolerance.
- All new entries made in the blockchain are agreed upon by nodes using a decentralized consensus algorithm. The design is such that all subsequent blocks in all the peers must be altered to modify an entry in a block. This ensures the immutability of blockchains.
- The audibility property of blockchains ensures transparency by allowing peers to look up and verify any transaction.
- The blockchain peers hold copies of identical replicas of ledger records. Blockchains, therefore, ensure fault tolerance. This property helps maintain data integrity and resiliency in the network.

The benefits of decentralizing IoT are numerous and notably superior to current centralized systems and are discussed below:

- Improved Trust and Security: The distributed and immutable nature of blockchain would eliminate the single point of entry/vulnerability for attackers/hackers. All transactions are cryptographically signed using unforgeable signatures, making them non-repudiable and resistant to attacks.

- More Robust: Decentralization will make IoT more accessible, and damage costs from hacks can be more easily prevented or avoided altogether. Intermediaries that operate for centralized IoT systems will be eliminated by decentralizing IoT, thereby reducing costs.

- Autonomy: Blockchains enable smart devices to act independently according to the pre-determined logic (using Smart Contracts). This would altogether remove intermediary players and central authority.

- More trustworthy: The use of efficient Smart Contracts for communication amongst IoT devices and the decentralization offered by blockchain makes the entire system more trustworthy.

- Data provenance: Since all transactions are recorded on the ledger and signed by the devices/entities generating data, data provenance can be achieved.

- Fairness: By using native cryptocurrency in blockchain, parties can be incentivized. This makes the IoT system fair.

Despite the advantages (discussed above) that the integration of blockchain into the IoT platform will bring, the traditional blockchains (like Ethereum and Bitcoin) suffer from the following drawbacks too (Popov, 2018):

- Scalability: As the number of IoT devices increases, the amount of data generated will be huge, leading to more storage space to keep the transactions updated in the ledger. This will further lead to high transaction and storage costs.

- Communication Overhead and Synchronization: Since each new transaction that is added to the blockchain needs to be broadcast to all the peers, it involves a lot of communication overhead. Further, all the blockchain peers need to synchronize and maintain the blockchain's duplicate copy, which further adds to the overhead.

- Efficiency: To approve a transaction, it needs to be verified by all other peers. Thus, the verification algorithm is run multiple times at each peer, which drastically reduces operational efficiency.

- Energy Wastage: Most popular blockchain technologies use Proof of Work (PoW) to achieve consensus and are inefficient. They need to perform many computations, thereby leading to energy wastage.

Due to the disadvantages of traditional blockchain technology, a challenging work direction is to design scalable, computable, and energy-efficient, secure blockchains for IoT applications. The IOTA Foundation has provided some examples of works in this direction (Popov, 2018).

The IOTA Foundation (As a distributed ledger technology, IOTA provides a trust layer for any devices connected to the global Internet) was specifically designed for the IoT. It differs from the existing blockchains as it does not use any traditional Blockchain at all. IOTA's main structure is the Tangle, a Directed Acyclic Graph (DAG) (Popov, 2018). The transactions (referred to as sites in Tangle) are stored in a graph format, where the nodes are entities that issue and validate transactions (Popov, 2018). Whenever a new transaction arrives, it is represented by directed edges and must be approved by two previous transactions.

For a node to validate a transaction, it must give Proof of Work, which is successfully executed registers the transaction. This functionality of Tangle allows us to eliminate the need for miners in the network as the node itself acts as a miner now, which further reduces the transaction costs to zero (Popov, 2018). To issue a transaction, users must work to approve other transactions. If a node realizes that a transaction conflicts with the Tangle history, the node will not approve the conflicting transaction, thereby ensuring network security (Popov, 2018). Despite all these, IOTA's Tangle has several advantages, as described below (Popov, 2018):

- Scalability: IOTA addresses this issue by not using a blockchain-based decentralized network instead of opting for its Tangle platform. With IOTA, as the transaction rate increases, scalability also increases, i.e., the more subscribers and transactions the system has, the faster it gets. More importantly, the latency, that is, the time between placing a transaction and validating it, also approaches zero as soon as a specific size is reached.
- Centralization of Control: For a transaction to occur in the Tangle, the previous two transactions must be validated by it. This makes the network faster with increasing use. Thus, IOTA allows each user who has initiated a transaction to act as a miner.
- Quantum Computing: IOTA uses 'exclusively quantum-resistant cryptographic algorithms, making it future-oriented and immune to brute force attacks. Moreover, Tangle holds the power to decrease quantum consensus attacks by almost a million times.
- Micro Payments: In traditional blockchain platforms, the concept of mining involves transaction fees (i.e., financial rewards set by the transaction's sender). As a result, even the most minor payment amounts result in high transaction fees. However, in IOTA's Tangle, each site does its PoW to get added to the network, so the concept of transaction fees is completely eliminated.

However, Tangle also has the following disadvantages for which Ethereum or Bitcoin is preferred over Tangle for commercial use in IoT (Popov, 2018):

- Smart Contracts do not exist for IOTA/Tangle and are a significant drawback while building a decentralized application. It is mathematically easier for a malicious node to attack Tangle.

FUTURE RESEARCH DIRECTIONS

The growth of IoT itself and its advancement in the industrial sector puts a strain on the computing resources needed to maintain the connectivity and data collection that IoT devices require (Chan, 2017). This is where service-oriented computing comes into the picture by acting as the backbone of everything IoT offers. Cloud computing, setting up virtual servers, launching a database instance, and creating data pipelines to help run IoT solutions become easier (Chan, 2017). Moreover, data security is an essential concern in an environment where the cloud can improve security by providing proper authentication mechanisms, firmware, and software update procedures. Besides, the central data attacks that are prevalent in the IoT world today: (i) data inconsistency, which helps an attack on data integrity, leading to data inconsistency in transit or data stored in a central database is referred to as Data Inconsistency (ii) unauthorized access control; and with unauthorized access, malicious users can gain data ownership or access sensitive data., and (iii) data breach or memory leakage refers to disclosing personal, sensitive, or confidential data in an unauthorized manner.

The data breach has posed severe threats to users' personal information in recent years. Researchers are highlighting different aspects of data breach-related issues. One such work (Gope & Sikdar, 2018) on preventing data breaches has proposed a lightweight privacy-preserving two-factor authentication scheme to secure communication between IoT devices. In future, this research will review other research in IoT technology and data breach-related issues.

CONCLUSION

The current healthcare industry operating environment has been extensively scrutinized to determine the primary needs of the enterprise information system's architecture purpose. It is encouraging that the emerging IoT infrastructure can support information systems of next-generation healthcare enterprises appropriately. Anywhere, anytime, and anything, data collection systems are more than appropriate for gathering and sharing data among healthcare supply chains resources. IoT technology-based information systems bring different opportunities to advance healthcare businesses to sustain good system performance in a distributed and globalized environment. However, the application of IoT in executive information systems is at its primitive age; more research is needed in the areas (e.g., modularization, semantic integration, standardization) of encouraging technologies for safe, effective, reliable communication operational decision making.

The global healthcare communication systems domain is well suited to a hybrid (i.e., IoT and blockchain) information system architecture approach because of its distributed nature and operating characteristics. Blockchain-based systems' most appealing traits are autonomy, collaboration, and reactivity from a smart healthcare management perspective. Blockchain-based systems can work without the direct intervention of humans or others. This feature helps to implement an automated information system in the global healthcare industry.

The modern healthcare industry is a paradigm-changing way to operate on the edge of emerging IT-based applications (e.g., IoT, blockchain, big data, SOC). A driver of industrial sustainability concerns the security and the safety of these technologies. The blockchain technology that has been used successfully for cryptocurrencies contributes to this industrial sustainability by providing security, immutability, trust, and a higher degree of automation through smart contracts.

REFERENCES

Abduvaliyev, A., Pathan, A. S. K., Zhou, J., Roman, R., & Wong, W. C. (2013). On the vital areas of intrusion detection systems in wireless sensor networks. *IEEE Communications Surveys and Tutorials*, *15*(3), 1223–1237. doi:10.1109/SURV.2012.121912.00006

Aberer, K., Hauswirth, H., & Salehi, A. (2006). *Middleware Support for the Internet of Things*. Available: www.manfredhauswirth.org/research/papers/WSN2006.pdf

Adat, V., & Gupta, B. B. (2017). A DDoS attack mitigation framework for Internet of things. *2017 International Conference on Communication and Signal Processing (ICCSP)*, 2036–2041. 10.1109/ICCSP.2017.8286761

Ahemd, M. M., Shah, M. A., & Wahid, A. (2017). IoT security: a layered approach for attacks and defenses. *2017 International Conference on Communication Technologies (ComTech)*, 104–110. 10.1109/COMTECH.2017.8065757

Airehrour, D., Gutierrez, J. A., & Ray, S. K. (2019). Sectrust-rpl: A secure trust-aware rpl routing protocol for the Internet of things. *Future Generation Computer Systems*, *93*, 860–876. doi:10.1016/j.future.2018.03.021

Al-Turjman, F., & Alturjman, S. (2018). Context-sensitive access in industrial Internet of things (iiot) healthcare applications. *IEEE Transactions on Industrial Informatics*, *14*(6), 2736–2744. doi:10.1109/TII.2018.2808190

Alaba, F. A., Othman, M., Hashem, I. A. T., & Alotaibi, F. (2017). Internet of things security: A survey. *Journal of Network and Computer Applications*, *88*, 10–28. doi:10.1016/j.jnca.2017.04.002

Alccer, V., & Cruz-Machado, V. (2019). Scanning the industry 4.0: A literature review on technologies for manufacturing systems, Engineering Science and Technology. *International Journal (Toronto, Ont.)*, *22*(3), 899–919.

Ali, M. S., Vecchio, M., Pincheira, M., Dolui, K., Antonelli, F., & Rehmani, M. H. (2019). *Applications of blockchains in the Internet of things: A comprehensive survey. IEEE Commun. Surv. Tutorials*.

All, I. F. (2017). *The 5 Worst Examples of IoT Hacking and Vulnerabilities in Recorded History*. Academic Press.

Aman, M. N., Chua, K. C., & Sikdar, B. (2017). A lightweight mutual authentication protocol for IoT systems. *GLOBECOM 2017 - 2017 IEEE Global Communications Conference*, 1–6.

Andoni, M., Robu, V., Flynn, D., Abram, S., Geach, D., Jenkins, D., McCallum, P., & Peacock, A. (2019). Blockchain technology in the energy sector: A systematic review of challenges and opportunities. *Renewable & Sustainable Energy Reviews*, *100*, 143–174. doi:10.1016/j.rser.2018.10.014

Andrea, I., Chrysostomou, C., & Hadjichristofi, G. (2015). Internet of things: security vulnerabilities and challenges. *2015 IEEE Symposium on Computers and Communication (ISCC)*, 180–187. 10.1109/ISCC.2015.7405513

Araujo, J., Mazo, M., Anta, A. Jr, Tabuada, P., & Johansson, K. H. (2014, February). System Architecture, Protocols, and Algorithms for Aperiodic wireless control systems. *IEEE Transactions on Industrial Informatics*, *10*(1), 175–184. doi:10.1109/TII.2013.2262281

Ashibani, Y., & Mahmoud, Q. H. (2017). An efficient and secure scheme for smart home communication using identity-based encryption. *2017 IEEE 36th International Performance Computing and Communications Conference (IPCCC)*, 1–7.

Atlam, H. F., Alenezi, A., Alassafi, M. O., & Wills, G. B. (2018). Blockchain with Internet of things: Benefits, challenges, and future directions. *Int. J. Intell. Syst. Appl.*, *10*(6), 40–48. doi:10.5815/ijisa.2018.06.05

Atlam, H. F., Azad, M. A., Alzahrani, A. G., & Wills, G. (2020). A Review of Blockchain in Internet of Things and AI. *Journal of Big Data and Cognitive Computing*, 1-27.

Azzi, R., Chamoun, R. K., & Sokhn, M. (2019). The power of a blockchain-based supply chain. *Computers & Industrial Engineering*, *135*, 582–592. doi:10.1016/j.cie.2019.06.042

Boyes, H., Hallaq, B., Cunningham, J., & Watson, T. (2018). The industrial Internet of things (iiot): An analysis framework. *Computers in Industry*, *101*, 1–12. doi:10.1016/j.compind.2018.04.015

Butun, I., Morgera, S. D., & Sankar, R. (2014). A survey of intrusion detection systems in wireless sensor networks. *IEEE Communications Surveys and Tutorials*, *16*(1), 266–282. doi:10.1109/SURV.2013.050113.00191

Cervantes, C., Poplade, D., Nogueira, M., & Santos, A. (2015). Detection of sinkhole attacks for supporting secure routing on 6lowpan for Internet of things. *2015 IFIP/IEEE International Symposium on Integrated Network Management (IM)*, 606–611. 10.1109/INM.2015.7140344

Cha, S., Chen, J., Su, C., & Yeh, K. (2018). A blockchain connected gateway for ble-based devices in the Internet of things. *IEEE Access: Practical Innovations, Open Solutions*, *6*, 24639–24649. doi:10.1109/ACCESS.2018.2799942

Chan, M. (2017). *Why Cloud Computing Is the Foundation of the Internet of Things*. Academic Press.

Chaudhary, R., Aujla, G. S., Garg, S., Kumar, N., & Rodrigues, J. J. P. C. (2018). Sdn-enabled multi-attribute-based secure communication for smart grid in riot environment. *IEEE Transactions on Industrial Informatics*, *14*(6), 2629–2640. doi:10.1109/TII.2018.2789442

Chen, G., & Ng, W. S. (2017). An efficient authorization framework for securing industrial Internet of things. *TENCON 2017 - 2017 IEEE Region 10 Conference*, 1219–1224.

Chen, L., Lee, W.-K., Chang, C.-C., Choo, K.-K. R., & Zhang, N. (2019). Blockchain-based searchable encryption for electronic health record sharing. *Future Generation Computer Systems*, *95*, 420–429. doi:10.1016/j.future.2019.01.018

Choi, J., & Kim, Y. (2016). An improved lea block encryption algorithm to prevent side-channel attack in the IoT system. *2016 Asia-Pacific Signal and Information Processing Association Annual Summit and Conference (APSIPA)*, 1–4.

Cirani, S., Ferrari, G., & Veltri, L. (2013). Enforcing security mechanisms in the IP-based Internet of things: An algorithmic overview. *Algorithms*, *6*(2), 197–226. doi:10.3390/a6020197

De, S. J., & Ruj, S. (2017). *Efficient decentralized attribute-based access control for mobile clouds*. IEEE Transactions on Cloud Computing.

Dorri, A., Kanhere, S. S., Jurdak, R., & Gauravaram, P. (2019). *LSB: A Lightweight Scalable Blockchain for IoT Security and Privacy*. Academic Press.

Esfahani, A., Mantas, G., Matischek, R., Saghezchi, F. B., Rodriguez, J., Bicaku, A., Maksuti, S., Tauber, M. G., Schmittner, C., & Bastos, J. (2019). A lightweight authentication mechanism for m2m communications in industrial IoT environment. *IEEE Internet of Things Journal*, *6*(1), 288–296. doi:10.1109/JIOT.2017.2737630

Fernndez-Carams, T. M., & Fraga-Lamas, P. (2018). A review on the use of blockchain for the Internet of things. *IEEE Access: Practical Innovations, Open Solutions*, *6*, 32979–33001. doi:10.1109/ACCESS.2018.2842685

Ferran, M. A., Derdour, M., Mukherjee, M., Dahab, A., Maglaras, L., & Janicke, H. (2019). Blockchain technologies for the Internet of things: Research issues and challenges. *IEEE Internet of Things Journal*.

Forbes. (2019). Blockchain in healthcare: How it Could Make Digital Healthcare Safer and More Innovative. *Forbes*.

Frustaci, M., Pace, P., Aloi, G., & Fortino, G. (2018). *Evaluating critical security issues of the IoT world: present and future challenges*. IEEE Internet Things.

Gai, J., Choo, K., Qiu, K. R., & Zhu, L. (2018). *Privacy-preserving content-oriented wireless*. Academic Press.

Gandino, F., Montrucchio, B., & Rebaudengo, M. (2014). *Key Management for Static Wireless Sensor Networks with Node Adding*. IEEE Transaction Industrial Informatics. doi:10.1109/TII.2013.2288063

Gibbon, J. (2018). *Introduction to Trusted Execution Environment: Arm's Trust zone*. Academic Press.

Glissa, G., Rachedi, A., & Meddeb, A. (2016). A secure routing protocol based on rpl for Internet of things. *IEEE Global Communications Conference (GLOBECOM)*, 1–7. 10.1109/GLOCOM.2016.7841543

Gomes, T., Salgado, F., Tavares, A., & Cabral, J. (2017). Cute mote, a customizable and trustable end-device for the Internet of things. *IEEE Sensors Journal, 17*(20), 6816–6824. doi:10.1109/JSEN.2017.2743460

Gope, P., & Sikdar, B. (2018). *Lightweight and privacy-preserving two-factor authentication scheme for IoT devices*. IEEE Internet Things.

Granja, J., Silva, R., Monteiro, E., Silva, J. S., & Boavida, F. (2008). Why is IPSec a viable option for wireless sensor networks. *2008 5th IEEE International Conference on Mobile Ad Hoc and Sensor Systems,* 802–807.

Granville, K. (2018). *Facebook and Cambridge Analytica: what You Need to Know as Fallout Widens*. Academic Press.

Griggs, K. N., Osipova, O., Kohlios, C. P., Baccarini, A. N., Howson, E. A., & Hayajneh, T. (2018). Healthcare blockchain system using smart contracts for secure automated remote patient monitoring. *Journal of Medical Systems, 42*(7), 1–7. doi:10.100710916-018-0982-x PMID:29876661

Guan, Z., Si, G., Zhang, X., Wu, L., Guizani, N., Du, X., & Ma, Y. (2018). Privacy-preserving and efficient aggregation based on blockchain for power grid communications in smart communities. *IEEE Communications Magazine, 56*(7), 82–88. doi:10.1109/MCOM.2018.1700401

Guin, U., Singh, A., Alam, M., Caedo, J., & Skjellum, A. (2018). A secure low-cost edge device authentication scheme for the Internet of things. *31st International Conference on VLSI Design and 17th International Conference on Embedded Systems (VLSID)*, 85–90. 10.1109/VLSID.2018.42

Hei, X., Du, X., Wu, J., & Hu, F. (2010). Defending resource depletion attacks on implantable medical devices. *2010 IEEE Global Telecommunications Conference GLOBECOM 2010*, 1–5. 10.1109/GLOCOM.2010.5685228

Huang, J., Kong, L., Chen, G., Wu, M., Liu, X., & Zeng, P. (2019b). Towards secure industrial IoT: blockchain system with credit-based consensus mechanism. IEEE Trans. Ind.

Huang, X., Zhang, Y., Li, D., & Han, L. (2019a). An optimal scheduling algorithm for hybrid EV charging scenario using consortium blockchains. *Future Generation Computer Systems, 91*, 555–562. doi:10.1016/j.future.2018.09.046

Huh, J.-H., & Seo, K. (2019). Blockchain-based mobile fingerprint verification and automatic log-in platform for future computing. *The Journal of Supercomputing, 75*(6), 3123–3139. doi:10.100711227-018-2496-1

Huh, S.-K., & Kim, J.-H. (2019). The blockchain consensus algorithm for viable management of new and renewable energies. *Sustainability, 11*(3184), 3184. doi:10.3390u11113184

IEEE. (2012). *IEEE Standard for Local and metropolitan networks–Part 15.4: LowRate Wireless Personal Area Networks (LR-WPANs)*. IEEE.

IoT-A. (2013). *Internet of Things–Architecture IoT-A Deliverable D1.5 –Final architectural reference model for the IoT v3.0.* https://iotforum.org/wpcontent/uploads/2014/09/D1.5-20130715-VERYFINAL.pdf

Islam, S. H., Khan, M. K., & Al-Khouri, A. M. (2015). Anonymous and provably secure certificateless multireceiver encryption without bilinear pairing. *Security and Communication Networks, 8*(13), 2214–2231. doi:10.1002ec.1165

Kang, J., Xiong, Z., Niyato, D., Ye, D., Kim, D. I., & Zhao, J. (2019a). Toward secure blockchain-enabled Internet of vehicles: Optimizing consensus management using reputation and contract theory. *IEEE Transactions on Vehicular Technology, 68*(3), 2906–2920. doi:10.1109/TVT.2019.2894944

Kang, J., Yu, R., Huang, X., Maharjan, S., Zhang, Y., & Hossain, E. (2017). Enabling localized peer-to-peer electricity trading among plug-in hybrid electric vehicles using consortium blockchains. *IEEE Transactions on Industrial Informatics, 13*(6), 3154–3164. doi:10.1109/TII.2017.2709784

Kang, J., Yu, R., Huang, X., Wu, M., Maharjan, S., Xie, S., & Zhang, Y. (2019b). Blockchain for secure and efficient data sharing in vehicular edge computing and networks. *IEEE Internet of Things Journal, 6*(3), 4660–4670. doi:10.1109/JIOT.2018.2875542

Karati, A., Islam, S. H., & Karuppiah, M. (2018). Provably secure and lightweight certificateless signature scheme for iiot environments. *IEEE Transactions on Industrial Informatics, 14*(8), 3701–3711. doi:10.1109/TII.2018.2794991

Khan, F. I., & Hameed, S. (2019). Understanding security requirements and challenges in the Internet of things (iots): A review. *Journal of Computer Networks and Communications*.

Khan, M. A., & Salah, K. (2018). IoT security: Review, blockchain solutions, and open challenges. *Future Generation Computer Systems, 82*, 395–411. doi:10.1016/j. future.2017.11.022

Kim, J.-H., & Huh, S.-K. (1973). A study on the improvement of smart grid security performance and blockchain smart grid perspective. *Energies*, 11.

Kim, S.-K., Kim, U.-M., & Huh, H. J. (2017). A study on improvement of blockchain application to overcome vulnerability of IoT multiplatform security. *Energies, 12*(402).

Konigsmark, S. T. C., Chen, D., & Wong, M. D. F. (2016). Information dispersion for trojan defense through high-level synthesis. *ACM/EDAC/IEEE Design Automation Conference (DAC)*, 1–6. 10.1145/2897937.2898034

Kouicem, D. E., Bouabdallah, A., & Lakhlef, H. (2018). Internet of things security: A top-down survey. *Computer Networks, 141*, 199–221. doi:10.1016/j. comnet.2018.03.012

Li, C., & Palanisamy, B. (2019). Privacy in Internet of things: From principles to technologies. *IEEE Internet of Things Journal, 6*(1), 488–505. doi:10.1109/ JIOT.2018.2864168

Li, R., Song, T., Mei, B., Li, H., Cheng, X., & Sun, L. (2019). Blockchain for large-scale Internet of things data storage and protection. *IEEE Transactions on Services Computing, 12*(5), 762–771. doi:10.1109/TSC.2018.2853167

Li, X., Niu, J., Bhuiyan, M. Z. A., Wu, F., Karuppiah, M., & Kumari, S. (2018a). A robust ECC-based provable secure authentication protocol with privacy-preserving for industrial Internet of things. *IEEE Transactions on Industrial Informatics, 14*(8), 3599–3609. doi:10.1109/TII.2017.2773666

Li, Z., Kang, J., Yu, R., Ye, D., Deng, Q., & Zhang, Y. (2018b). Consortium blockchain for secure energy trading in industrial Internet of things. *IEEE Transactions on Industrial Informatics, 14*(8), 3690–3700.

Lin, C., He, D., Huang, X., Choo, K.-K. R., & Vasilakos, A. V. (2018). Basin: A blockchain-based secure mutual authentication with fine-grained access control system for industry 4.0. *Journal of Network and Computer Applications, 116*, 42–52. doi:10.1016/j.jnca.2018.05.005

Ling, Z., Liu, K., Xu, Y., Jin, Y., & Fu, X. (2017). An end-to-end view of IoT security and privacy. *IEEE Global Communications Conference*, 1–7. 10.1109/ GLOCOM.2017.8254011

Liu, C., Cronin, P., & Yang, C. (2016). A mutual auditing framework to protect iot against hardware trojans. *2016 21st Asia and South Pacific Design Automation Conference (ASP-DAC)*, 69–74.

Liu, C. H., Lin, Q., & Wen, S. (2019b). *Blockchain-enabled data collection and sharing for industrial IoT with deep reinforcement learning*. IEEE Transaction Industrial Informatics. doi:10.1109/TII.2018.2890203

Liu, J., Zhang, C., & Fang, Y. (2018). Epic; A differential privacy framework to defend smart homes against internet traffic analysis. *IEEE Internet of Things Journal, 5*(2), 1206–1217. doi:10.1109/JIOT.2018.2799820

Liu, Y., Guo, W., Fan, C., Chang, L., & Cheng, C. (2019a). A practical privacy-preserving data aggregation (3pda) scheme for smart grid. *IEEE Transactions on Industrial Informatics, 15*(3), 1767–1774. doi:10.1109/TII.2018.2809672

Longo, F., Nicoletti, L., Padovano, A., d'Atri, G., & Forte, M. (2019). Blockchain-enabled supply chain: An experimental study. *Computers & Industrial Engineering, 136*, 57–69. doi:10.1016/j.cie.2019.07.026

Lu, Y., & Li, J. (2016). A pairing-free certificate-based proxy re-encryption scheme for secure data sharing in public clouds. *Future Generation Computer Systems, 62*, 140–147. doi:10.1016/j.future.2015.11.012

Lukac, D. (2015). The fourth ICT-based industrial revolution "Industry 4.0"??? HMI and the case of CAE/CAD innovation with EPLAN. *23rd Telecommunications Forum Telfor (TELFOR)*, 835-838.

Machado, C., & Frhlich, A. A. M. (2018). IoT data integrity verification for cyber-physical systems using blockchain. *2018 IEEE 21st International Symposium on Real-Time Distributed Computing (ISORC)*, 83–90.

Makhdoom, I., Abolhasan, M., Abbas, H., & Ni, W. (2019). Blockchain's adoption in iot: The challenges, and a way forward. *Journal of Network and Computer Applications, 125*, 251–279. doi:10.1016/j.jnca.2018.10.019

Manditereza, K. (2017). *4 Key Differences between Scada and Industrial IoT*. Academic Press.

Manzoor, A., Liyanage, M., Braeken, A., Kanhere, S. S., & Ylianttila, M. (2019). Blockchain-Based Proxy Re-encryption Scheme for Secure IoT Data Sharing. *Clinical Orthopaedics and Related Research*.

Minoli, D., & Occhiogross, B. (2018). Blockchain mechanism for IoT security. *International Journal of Internet of Things*, 1-13.

Mitchell, R., & Chen, I. R. (2014). Review: A survey of intrusion detection in wireless network applications. *Computer Communications*, *42*, 1–23. doi:10.1016/j.comcom.2014.01.012

Mondal, S., Wijewardena, K. P., Karuppuswami, S., Kriti, N., Kumar, D., & Chahal, P. (2019). Blockchain inspired RFID-based information architecture for food supply chain. *IEEE Internet of Things Journal*, *6*(3), 5803–5813. doi:10.1109/JIOT.2019.2907658

Mosenia, A., & Jha, N. K. (2017). A comprehensive study of security of internet-of-things. *IEEE Transactions on Emerging Topics in Computing*, *5*(4), 586–602. doi:10.1109/TETC.2016.2606384

Naeem, H., Guo, B., & Naeem, M. R. (2018). A lightweight malware static visual analysis for IoT infrastructure. *International Conference on Artificial Intelligence and Big Data (ICAIBD)*, 240–244.

Observe, I. T. (2018). *5 Examples of Insider Threat-Caused Breaches that Illustrate the Scope of the Problem*. Author.

Okorie, O., Turner, C., Charnley, F., Moreno, M., & Tiwari, A. (2017). A review of data-driven approaches for circular economy in manufacturing. *Proceedings of the 18th European Roundtable for Sustainable Consumption and Production*.

Oleshchuk, V. (2009). Internet of things and privacy-preserving technologies. *2009 1st International Conference on Wireless Communication, Vehicular Technology, Information Theory and Aerospace Electronic Systems Technology*, 336–340. 10.1109/WIRELESSVITAE.2009.5172470

Omar, A. A., Bhuiyan, M. Z. A., Basu, A., Kiyomoto, S., & Rahman, M. S. (2019). Privacy-friendly platform for healthcare data in cloud-based on blockchain environment. *Future Generation Computer Systems*, *95*, 511–521. doi:10.1016/j.future.2018.12.044

OWASP. (2016). *Top IoT Vulnerabilities*. https://www.owasp.org/index. php/Top_IoT_Vulnerabilities

Oztemel, E., & Gusev, S. (2018). Literature review of industry 4.0 and related technologies. *Journal of Intelligent Manufacturing*.

Pal, K. (2017). *Building High Quality Big Data-Based Applications in Supply Chains*. IGI Global Publication.

Pal, K. (2018). *Ontology-Based Web Service Architecture for Retail Supply Chain Management*. The 9th International Conference on Ambient Systems, Networks and Technologies, Porto, Portugal. 10.1016/j.procs.2018.04.101

Pal, K. (2019). Algorithmic Solutions for RFID Tag Anti-Collision Problem in Supply Chain Management. *Procedia Computer Science*, *151*, 929–934. doi:10.1016/j.procs.2019.04.129

Pal, K. (2020). Information sharing for manufacturing supply chain management based on blockchain technology. In I. Williams (Ed.), *Cross-Industry Use of Blockchain Technology and Opportunities for the Future* (pp. 1–17). IGI Global. doi:10.4018/978-1-7998-3632-2.ch001

Pal, K. (2021). Applications of Secured Blockchain Technology in Manufacturing Industry. In *Blockchain and AI Technology in the Industrial Internet of Things*. IGI Global Publication. doi:10.4018/978-1-7998-6694-7.ch010

Pal, K., & Yasar, A. (2020). Internet of Things and blockchain technology in apparel manufacturing supply chain data management. *Procedia Computer Science*, *170*, 450–457. doi:10.1016/j.procs.2020.03.088

Park, N., & Kang, N. (2015). Mutual authentication scheme insecure Internet of things technology for comfortable lifestyle. *Sensors (Basel)*, *16*(1), 20. doi:10.339016010020 PMID:26712759

Porambage, P., Schmitt, C., Kumar, P., Gurtov, A., & Ylianttila, M. (2014). Pauthkey: A pervasive authentication protocol and key establishment scheme for wireless sensor networks in distributed IoT applications. *International Journal of Distributed Sensor Networks*, *10*(7), 357430. doi:10.1155/2014/357430

Pu, C., & Hajjar, S. (2018). Mitigating forwarding misbehaviors in rpl-based low power and lossy networks. *2018 15th IEEE Annual Consumer Communications Networking Conference (CCNC)*, 1–6.

Rahulamathavan, Y., Phan, R. C., Rajarajan, M., Misra, S., & Kondoz, A. (2017). Privacy-preserving blockchain-based IoT ecosystem using attribute-based encryption. *IEEE International Conference on Advanced Networks and Telecommunications Systems (ANTS)*, 1–6. 10.1109/ANTS.2017.8384164

Rambus. (n.d.). *Industrial IoT: Threats and countermeasures*. https://www.rambus.com/iot/ industrial-IoT/

Reyna, A., Martn, C., Chen, J., Soler, E., & Daz, M. (2018). On blockchain and its integration with iot. challenges and opportunities. *Future Generation Computer Systems*, *88*, 173–190. doi:10.1016/j.future.2018.05.046

Roblek, V., Mesko, M., & Krapez, A. (2016). A complex view of Industry 4.0. *SAGE Open*, *6*(2). Advance online publication. doi:10.1177/2158244016653987

Roman, R., Lopez, J., & Mambo, M. (2016). Mobile edge computing, Fog et al.: A survey and analysis of security threats and challenges. *Future Gener. Comput. Syst.*

Sfar, A. R., Natalizio, E., Challal, Y., & Chtourou, Z. (2018). A roadmap for security challenges in the Internet of things. *Digital Communications and Networks.*, *4*(2), 118–137. doi:10.1016/j.dcan.2017.04.003

Shen, M., Tang, X., Zhu, L., Du, X., & Guizani, M. (2019). Privacy-preserving support vector machine training over blockchain-based encrypted IoT data in smart cities. *IEEE Internet of Things Journal*, *6*(5), 7702–7712. doi:10.1109/JIOT.2019.2901840

Shrestha, R., Bajracharya, R., Shrestha, A. P., & Nam, S. Y. (2019). *A new type of blockchain for secure message exchange in vanet*. Digital Communications and Networks.

Shukla, P. (2017). Ml-ids: A machine learning approach to detect wormhole attacks in the Internet of things. *Intelligent Systems Conference (IntelliSys)*, 234–240. 10.1109/IntelliSys.2017.8324298

Sicari, S., Rizzardi, A., Grieco, L., & Coen-Porisini, A. (2015). Security, privacy and trust in Internet of things: The road ahead. *Computer Networks*, *76*(Suppl. C), 146–164. doi:10.1016/j.comnet.2014.11.008

Sicari, S., Rizzardi, A., Miorandi, D., & Coen-Porisini, A. (2018). Reatoreacting to denial-of-service attacks in the Internet of things. *Computer Networks*, *137*, 37–48. doi:10.1016/j.comnet.2018.03.020

Singh, M., Rajan, M. A., Shivraj, V. L., & Balamuralidhar, P. (2015). Secure MQTT for the Internet of things (IoT). *5th International Conference on Communication Systems and Network Technologies*, 746–751. 10.1109/CSNT.2015.16

Song, T., Li, R., Mei, B., Yu, J., Xing, X., & Cheng, X. (2017). A privacy-preserving communication protocol for IoT applications in smart homes. *IEEE Internet of Things Journal*, *4*(6), 1844–1852. doi:10.1109/JIOT.2017.2707489

SOPHOS. (2015). *49 Busted in Europe for Man-In-The-Middle Bank Attacks*. https://nakedsecurity.sophos.com/2015/06/11/49-busted-in-europe-for-man-in-themiddle-bank-attacks/

Sreamr. (2017). *Streamr White Paper v2.0.* https://s3.amazonaws.com/streamr-public/streamr-datacoin-whitepaper-2017-07-25-v1_0.pdf

Srinivas, J., Das, A. K., Wazid, M., & Kumar, N. (2018). *Anonymous lightweight chaotic map-based authenticated key agreement protocol for industrial Internet of things. IEEE Trans. Dependable Secure Comput.*

Su, J., Vasconcellos, V. D., Prasad, S., Daniele, S., Feng, Y., & Sakurai, K. (2018). Lightweight classification of IoT malware based on image recognition. *IEEE 42nd Annual Computer Software and Applications Conference (COMPSAC), 2*, 664–669.

Varga, P., Plosz, S., Soos, G., & Hegedus, C. (2017). Security Threats and Issues in Automation IoT. *2017 IEEE 13th International Workshop on Factory Communication Systems (WFCS)*, 1–6.

Vechain Team. (2018). *Vechain White Paper.* https://cdn.vechain.com/vechain_ico_ideas_of_ development_en.pdf

Vogel-Heuser, B., & Hess, D. (2016). Guest editorial Industry 4.0 -prerequisites and vision. *IEEE Transactions on Automation Science and Engineering, 13*(2).

Waltonchain. (2021). *Waltonchain white paper v2.0.* https://www.waltonchain.org/en/ Waltonchain_White_Paper_2.0_EN.pdf

Wan, J., Li, J., Imran, M., Li, D., & e-Amin, F. (2019). A blockchain-based solution for enhancing security and privacy in smart factory. *IEEE Transaction.*

Wan, J., Tang, S., Shu, Z., Li, D., Wang, S., Imran, M., & Vasilakos, A. V. (2016). Software-defined industrial Internet of things in the context of industry 4.0. *IEEE Sensors Journal, 16*(20), 7373–7380.

Wang, Q., Zhu, X., Ni, Y., Gu, L., & Zhu, H. (2019b). *Blockchain for the IoT and industrial IoT: a review.* Internet Things.

Wang, X., Zha, X., Ni, W., Liu, R. P., Guo, Y. J., Niu, X., & Zheng, K. (2019a). Survey on blockchain for Internet of things. *Computer Communications, 136*, 10–29.

Wang, Y., Uehara, T., & Sasaki, R. (2015). Fog computing: Issues and challenges in security and forensics. *2015 IEEE 39th Annual Computer Software and Applications Conference, 3*, 53–59.

Wurm, J., Hoang, K., Arias, O., Sadeghi, A., & Jin, Y. (2016). Security analysis on consumer and industrial IoT devices. *21st Asia and South Pacific Design Automation Conference (ASP-DAC)*, 519–524.

Xiong, Z., Zhang, Y., Niyato, D., Wang, P., & Han, Z. (2018). When mobile blockchain meets edge computing. *IEEE Communications Magazine*, *56*(8), 33–39.

Xu, L. D., He, W., & Li, S. (2014). Internet of things in industries: A survey. *IEEE Transactions on Industrial Informatics*, *10*(4), 2233–2243.

Xu, L. D., Xu, E. L., & Li, L. (2018). Industry 4.0: State of the art and future trends. *International Journal of Production Research*, *56*(8), 2941–2962. doi:10.1080/00 207543.2018.1444806

Xu, Y., Ren, J., Wang, G., Zhang, C., Yang, J., & Zhang, Y. (2019). *A blockchain-based non-repudiation network computing service scheme for industrial IoT. IEEE Transaction Industrial Informatics.*

Yan, Q., Huang, W., Luo, X., Gong, Q., & Yu, F. R. (2018). A multi-level DDoS mitigation framework for the industrial Internet of things. *IEEE Communications Magazine*, *56*(2), 30–36.

Yang, W., Wang, S., Huang, X., & Mu, Y. (2019a). On the Security of an Efficient and Robust Certificateless Signature Scheme for IIoT Environments. *IEEE Access: Practical Innovations, Open Solutions*, *7*, 91074–91079.

Yang, Y., Wu, L., Yin, G., Li, L., & Zhao, H. (2017). A survey on security and privacy issues in internet-of-things. *IEEE Internet of Things Journal*, *4*(5), 1250–1258.

Yang, Z., Yang, K., Lei, L., Zheng, K., & Leung, V. C. M. (2019b). Blockchain-based decentralized trust management in vehicular networks. *IEEE Internet of Things Journal*, *6*(2), 1495–1505.

Yao, X., Kong, H., Liu, H., Qiu, T., & Ning, H. (2019). An attribute credential-based public-key scheme for fog computing in digital manufacturing. *IEEE Trans. Ind. Inf.*

Yi, S., Qin, Z., & Li, Q. (2015). Security and privacy issues of fog computing: A survey. *Wireless Algorithms, Systems, and Applications the 10th International Conference on*, 1–10.

Yin, D., Zhang, L., & Yang, K. (2018). A DDoS attack detection and mitigation with software-defined Internet of things framework. *IEEE Access: Practical Innovations, Open Solutions*, *6*, 24694–24705.

Zhang, H., Wang, J., & Ding, Y. (2019b). Blockchain-based decentralized and secure keyless signature scheme for smart grid. *Energy*, *180*, 955–967. doi:10.1016/j. energy.2019.05.127

Zhang, N., Mi, X., Feng, X., Wang, X., Tian, Y., & Qian, F. (2018). *Understanding and Mitigating the Security Risks of Voice-Controlled Third-Party Skills on Amazon Alexa and Google Home*. Academic Press.

Zhang, Y., Deng, R., Zheng, D., Li, J., Wu, P., & Cao, J. (2019a). *Efficient and Robust Certificateless Signature for Data Crowdsensing in Cloud-Assisted Industrial IoT*. IEEE Transaction Industry.

Zhang, Z. K., Cho, M. C. Y., Wang, C. W., Hsu, C. W., Chen, C. K., & Shieh, S. (2014). IoT security: Ongoing challenges and research opportunities. *2014 IEEE 7th International Conference on Service-Oriented Computer Applications*, 230–234.

Zheng, D., Wu, A., Zhang, Y., & Zhao, Q. (2018). Efficient and privacy-preserving medical data sharing in the Internet of things with limited computing power. *IEEE Access: Practical Innovations, Open Solutions, 6*, 28019–28027.

Zhou, J., Cao, Z., Dong, X., & Vasilakos, A. V. (2017). Security and privacy for cloud-based IoT: Challenges. *IEEE Communications Magazine, 55*(1), 26–33.

Zhou, R., Zhang, X., Du, X., Wang, X., Yang, G., & Guizani, M. (2018). File-centric multi-key aggregate keyword searchable encryption for industrial Internet of things. *IEEE Transactions on Industrial Informatics, 14*(8), 3648–3658.

Ziegeldorf, J. H., Morchon, O. G., & Wehrle, K. (2014). *Privacy in the Internet of Things: Threats and Challenges*. Academic Press.

Chapter 7
Blockchain and Copyright:
Challenges and Opportunities

Pedro Pina

ⓘD https://orcid.org/0000-0002-9597-3918
Polytechnic of Coimbra, Portugal

ABSTRACT

Advances in the field of digital technology are constantly introducing new levels of controversy into copyright policy. Blockchain is the most recent technology with significant impact in digital copyright. Combined with smart contracts, blockchain enables new efficient forms of distribution of copyrighted works and also a new model of private ordering regarding the control of uses of works on the Internet. The chapter aims to examine the relationship and the most relevant intersections between blockchain, digital exploitation of copyrighted works, copyright law, and privacy law.

INTRODUCTION

Throughout history, from the printing press to the Internet, emerging technologies have been raising novel questions and introducing new levels of controversy into copyright policy. The exteriorization (*corpus mechanicum*) of creative expression (*corpus mysticum*) is shaped according to the possibilities that constantly evolving technologies provide (*e.g.* through a book, a painting, a vinyl record, a CD, or software). Therefore, the way creative contents are revealed to the public depend on the existing and available technology. Moreover, technology is relevant for the copyright realm also because it enables new types of storage and distribution of copyright material. If, on the one hand, it facilitates innovative forms of economic

DOI: 10.4018/978-1-7998-8382-1.ch007

exploitation of creative content, especially in the digital world, on the other hand, it provides new ways of infringement (e.g., unauthorized sharing of digital copies through p2p platforms), which poses new challenges to the enforcement of rights granted by copyright law.

Blockchain is the most recent technology with significative impact on copyright law in the digital context, not only by allowing a new efficient and decentralized form of distribution of works but also by enabling smart contracting and a new model of private ordering regarding the control of works in the Internet.

After the seminal work of the unknown creator of the Bitcoin, commonly known under the pseudonym Sakamoto (2008), blockchain technology has been mainly associated to cryptocurrencies. Nevertheless, blockchain is a versatile technology with numerous other potential applications in diverse fields where a storage structure is required such as finance, banking, healthcare, land registration or intellectual property amongst several other industries.

The purpose of the present chapter is to analyze some of the most relevant copyright issues that may suffer direct influence from Blockchain technology such as the clarification of the legal status of a copyrighted work and the registration of copyrighted works; the use of digital rights management systems based on technological protection measures to control unauthorized uses of copyrighted works and to implement self-help or private ordering systems based on the use of smart contracts and, finally, the compliance of blockchain with copyright legal provisions foreseeing limitations and exceptions based on the public interest.

BACKGROUND

Blockchain technology constitutes a decentralized infrastructure for the storage of data and the management of software applications (De Filippi & Wright, 2018, p. 34). Blockchain may be described as a form of distributed ledger technology where transactions are grouped into blocks which are chained to the previous one, therefore enabling a transparent and tendentially immutable record of every transaction held on the platform. As Finck & Moscon (2019) state, each block assemblies multiple transactions, is then added to the existing chain of blocks and, after reaching a certain size, is chained to the existing ledger "through a hashing process (The ledger's blocks have different key components, including the hash of all transactions contained in the block (its 'fingerprint'), a timestamp, and a hash of the previous block (which creates the sequential chain of blocks)" (pp. 89-90).

One of the main features of blockchain technology is the non-absolute necessity of a third-party (e.g. public registers or banks) involvement for transactions and transfers of value, while providing the parties involved with absolute confidence in the validity and security of the transaction. According to Gürkaynak et al. (2018), whereas "a transaction needs to be verified by the central server in traditional databases, with blockchain technology, every node in the system has the ability to cryptographically check and verify any transaction. Instead of having to trust the central server (and the central authority maintaining such a server), peers using blockchain technology are able to create and maintain trust by relying on cryptographical proof in a consensus method" (p. 848).

Even though blockchain does not require a central register authority or other kinds of middlemen, that does not mean that it cannot be used by intermediaries. Blockchain technology can be used in an open manner but also in a private or proprietary way. The aforesaid is related to a basic distinction between public/permissionless and private/permissioned blockchain. In the first case, the data storage platform relies on open-source software, and anyone can join the ledger simply by downloading and running the relevant software without the need for prior permission or approval to operate (Finck & Moscon, 2019, p. 90). This way, every user can become a node and verify/reject transactions since every piece of data produced from the moment that the blockchain begins operating is shared amongst every node (Gürkaynak et al., 2018, p. 849).

More recently, private/permissioned blockchains, based in proprietary software, have been created. Such blockchains demand permission from the administrator to a new user to become a node in the verification system. Normally, such permissioned blockchains belong to a company or to the State with proprietary privileges that may change the nature of first generation blockchains as "the system generally shifts to a partially decentralized point, where transactions' creation and validation and/or block mining are orchestrated by a node oligarchy that is selected, e.g. by the network owner or the majority of the participants" (Charalampidis & Fragkiadakis, 2020, p. 3). That may happen for trust and security purposes related to public or private interests as the quality of a more reduced number of validators is given preference over the quantity of validations.

In addition to disintermediation, the decentralized new data storage security paradigm provided by blockchain – mainly by public blockchains - can also be characterized by its transparency, redundancy and immutability (Savelyev, 2017, p. 3).

Blockchain is transparent considering that all the data on blockchain is publicly available.

The technology is characterized by its redundancy since every user of the blockchain holds a copy of the data, diminishing the risk of being taken offline due to a system malfunction or malicious actions of third parties. Regarding this fact, there is a collective maintenance of the blockchain system as it also adopts a specific economic incentive mechanism to ensure that all nodes in the distributed system can participate in the verification process of the data block (Chen et al., 2020, p. 441).

The immutability of the data stored derives from the fact that Blockchain is an append-only data structure. It is extremely difficult to remove blocks and to change records in blockchain since it requires consensus of the majority of the blockchain users provided in accordance with the protocol, which ensures the integrity of records (Finck & Moscon, 2019, p. 90).

Moreover, blockchain has the ability to be combined with smart contracts which are basically self-executing small computer programs that can be run in blockchain nodes. In a disintermediated machine-to-machine communication context where human intervention is not required, smart contracts are "cryptographic 'boxes' that contain value and only unlock it if certain conditions are met" (Buterin, 2013) with the terms of the agreement between buyer and seller being directly written into lines of code (Gürkaynak et al., 2018, p. 849).

BLOCKCHAIN AND COPYRIGHT

Problems of Pre-Blockchain Era Digital Copyright from the Rightholders' Perspective

All the above-mentioned features of Blockchain turn this technology interesting and relevant for the digital copyright domain particularly on what is related to licensing online uses and preventing or controlling unauthorized uses that infringe rightholders exclusive right to explore the protected work.

According to article 27, § 2, of the Universal Declaration of Human Rights "[e]veryone has the right to the protection of the moral and material interests resulting from any scientific, literary or artistic production of which he is the author". At the international level, the Berne Convention for the Protection of Literary and Artistic Works and the Universal Copyright Convention, grant rightholders an exclusive right of economic exploitation of copyrighted works excluding others from it without proper authorization as an incentive to artistic or scientific creation. Rights such as the distribution right or the communication to the public right are comprised in the referred protection and recognized all around the world by national legislators.

Digital technology configured a major challenge to copyright law since it enabled online users to copy and to share creative works without a corporeal fixation on the Internet and, more recently, in peer-to-peer (p2p) and file-sharing platforms. Even before the Blockchain era, rightholders were facing a massive, global and almost uncontrolled flow of copyrighted content, potentially escaping their control. Digital technology enabled the establishment of parallel economies based on counterfeiting and unauthorized but economically significant non-commercial uses, such as the exchange of digital files through p2p networks which have grown to such an extent that they are now competing with the normal exploitation of works and challenging established commercial models (Geiger, 2010, p. 4). Digital technology has, in fact, facilitated several possible violations of exclusive patrimonial rights that copyright laws usually grant to rightholders, such as the right to display the work publicly, the right to perform works publicly, the right to publicly distribute copies of the copyrighted works or the right to reproduce the works in copies. The plurilocalized distribution of the infringers and the massive quantity of online infractions revealed how unprepared the international or national copyright legal systems were to enforce rights in the digital context, since courts usually act reactively besides being limited to the territory of their country.

For such reasons, for a rightholder to share a work in the Internet, it would mean to lose control over it.

The solution for rightholders seemed to be technological, through the implementation of digital rights management systems (DRM) based on technological protection measures (TPM) – such as steganography, cryptography or electronic agents like web crawlers or spy-bots –, and rights management information (RMI), which, combined with contractual arrangements, could maintain their control on the access to works, allowing them to prevent unauthorized copies and its distribution online. Digital technology seemed to have the effect of diminishing the importance of copyright in a digital environment in favour of a control-by-code based solution. The "answer to the machine is in the machine", affirmed Clark (1996, p. 139) and code gained the status of law in cyberspace (Lessig, 2006) "code is law" whereas technology is used to enforce existing rights and legal or contractual provisions.

Nevertheless, circumvention software and digital devices rapidly showed the insufficiency of electronic fences to prevent copyright infringement. As a consequence, DRM systems often fail to maintain control of the digital asset and are mostly vulnerable to hostile manipulations (Tresise et al., 2018, p. 7). For that reason, the copyright industry started lobbying to achieve a more robust, broader and harmonized intellectual property framework.

Legal documents at the international level were foreseen such as the Agreement on Trade Related Aspects of Intellectual Property Rights (TRIPS), the World Intellectual Property Organization (WIPO) Copyright Treaty and the WIPO Performances and Phonograms Treaty, or, at the regional or national levels, the Digital Millennium Copyright Act (DMCA), in the USA, or the Information Society Directive (InfoSoc Directive), in the European Union, recognizing the lawful right to use TPM and DRM and, therefore, the possibility of private ordering, private enforcement and self-help systems based on TPM and contracts. For instance, according to article 11 of the WIPO Copyright Treaty and article 18 of the WIPO Performances and Phonograms Treaty, contracting Parties shall provide adequate legal protection and effective legal remedies against the circumvention of effective technological measures that are used by authors, performers or producers of phonograms in connection with the exercise of their rights and that restrict acts, in respect of their works, which are not authorized by the authors concerned or permitted by law".

A similar obligation is foreseen in articles 12 of the WIPO Copyright Treaty and 19 of WIPO Performances and Phonograms Treaty now regarding rights management information, defined as information which identifies the work, the author of the work, the performer, the performance of the performer, the producer of the phonogram, the phonogram, the owner of any right in the work or in the performance or phonogram, or information about the terms and conditions of use of the work, and any numbers or codes that represent such information, when any of these items of information is attached to a copy of a work or appears in connection with the communication of a work to the public. According to the identified articles, contracting parties are obliged "to provide adequate legal protection and effective legal remedies against any person knowingly performing any of the following acts knowing, or with respect to civil remedies having reasonable grounds to know, that will induce, enable, facilitate or conceal an infringement of any right covered by this Treaty or the Berne Convention: (i) to remove or alter any electronic rights management information without authority; (ii) to distribute, import for distribution, broadcast or communicate to the public, without authority, works or copies of works knowing that electronic rights management information has been removed or altered without authority".

A consequence of such kind of provisions – later replicated by national legislators – is that law recognized three levels of cumulative protection by the combination of copyright, DRM/TPM and legal protection against circumvention of technological protection measures (Werra, 2001, p. 77). Considering the referred state of things, digital copyright legal provisions allow the combination of technology with contractual provisions where licensors can contractually predict which users' behaviours are lawful or not while having the means to digitally control them. Since this kind of provisions are substantially more related to copyright enforcement than to substantive regulation of the protection of creative expression, it is acceptable to distinguish it from primary substantive copyright calling it paracopyright (Jaszi, 1988) or übercopyright (Helberger & Hugenholtz, 2007).

The advent of Blockchain does not constitute the first clash between law and technology; however, it brings new features to the relationship between copyright law and technology particularly as a means to a strengthened and tendentially perfect enforcement system (from the rightholders' point of view). Blockchain technology may be "a powerful tool to give visual artists what they truly need and deserve—a maximum royalty payment for every resale of the physical embodiment of their artwork" (Zhao, 2021, p. 269).

In fact, in the digital context, different elements related to copyright, from the protected work itself to ownership and rights metadata or licensing terms and remuneration, may be translated into code and represented by cryptographic tokens (Bodó et al., 2018, p. 312), *i. e.,* "digitally scarce units of value the properties and circulation of which are prescribed via computer code" (Ferrari, 2020, p. 326). In this framework, copyright tokens can represent a copy of a protected work, a record of rights management information, namely the terms of use of the copyrighted content, or remuneration for the use of a work which can be encoded in cryptocurrencies or fiat currency equivalents (Buzu, 2020, p. 4).

Considering the above mentioned, Blockchain technology may act as a decentralized platform not only to build and maintain registries and transactions of works, but also to celebrate smart contracts with copyright license agreements.

Transparency of the Legal Status of Copyrighted Works

Unlike the protection granted by industrial property law, particularly by patent law, in most countries the protection of creative content by copyright does not require a previous and constitutive of rights registration in a public register. Even when such mechanism exists, it is merely voluntary and not constitutive of rights. As Savelyev (2017) points out, the "absence of any formal certification/approval requirements for copyright ownership leads to its invisibility to third parties. Although this problem is not created by the technology, it is substantially amplified by it" (p. 5).

It is not always an easy task to identify who the rightholder of works circulating in the Internet is. Without a mandatory previous registration, it is sometimes hard to find information on copyright ownership or authorship. Such situation impedes users who would like to act lawfully to obtain access to the copyrighted work and favors piracy and infringement in disadvantage of the rightholders who do not receive remuneration for the usage of their works.

As a decentralized data storage technology, blockchain may be a solution to the identified problem by establishing an accessible and consistent copyright database on specific works distributed online thus ensuring that copyrighted works, their authors, owners and other right holders, are known to potential users of the protected works (Kiemle, 2018, p. 2). Blockchains' characteristics provide an opportunity to conceive of a global registry for copyright and neighboring rights (Finck & Moscon, 2019, p. 94). The blockchain copyright database would promote the visibility of authorship and copyright information, as well as transactional data stored by means of trusted timestamps (Savelyev, 2017, p. 8). As said above, although copyright protection does not require a previous registration, in the blockchain context the solution follows a registration by design model and brings a simple, direct and public access to all the relevant data concerning the copyrighted work involved in the transaction. However, central public authorities or copyright enterprises may create permissioned blockchains to promote the registration of information over copyrighted works. For public interest purposes and authors protection, a permissionless blockchain-based registration system "to which any member of the public could upload rights management information as a time-stamped entry, would only be useful if an authoritative and trusted third party, such as an IP office or a Collective Management Organization was involved" (Rose, 2020). Enterprises, associations or foundations exploring digital copyrighted assets can also be interested in using blockchain to clarify its legal status and the proposed license agreements, whether granted in proprietary terms or not, as it happens in copyleft or free/open software licenses.

If in permissionless and public blockchains authors and performers can act directly in almost libertarian and self-regulated terms, it is also true that entities such as collective management organization or copyright industries may be interested in using and administrating permissioned blockchains to obtain accurate information on ownership and on transactions of works in order to control its usages. In fact, three of the largest collection societies (ASCAP, SACEM and PRS for Music) have already announced a groundbreaking partnership to prototype a new shared system of managing authoritative music copyright information using blockchain technology in order to confirm correct ownership information and conflicts particularly in cases of cross-border licensing.

Such information is vital for rightholders' interests since they can be used as proof in case of judicial procedures but also because its automated integration with smart contracts will generate immediate incomes.

The Rightholders' Dream of a Perfect DRM System

Based on a decentralized peer-to-peer network of nodes, blockchain technology has the potential to fulfill the rightholders' dream of a perfect control of the copies of copyrighted works on the Internet. In fact, blockchain technology enables a disintermediated framework which facilitates the distribution and the exploitation of copyrighted works by means of smart contracts with subsequent immediate revenue according to the conditions foreseen in the software code while giving rightsholders powers of surveillance and control of users or consumers' behaviors online and simultaneously keeping a record of all the related transactions.

One of the novelties brought by blockchain to this matter is the possibility of identification of each copy of the work with the record of its unique information about creation, ownership, licenses and circulation. When copying works, previous digital technology creates perfect replicas without information about its ulterior distribution, thus favoring piracy and infringement. But now, as Savelyev (2017) states, "Blockchain allows scope to individualize each digital copy of a copyrighted work" (p. 10) by means of hash function and timestamping used to self-issue new and unique identifiers for each copy. According to the mentioned author, the solution "may allow assignment of separate license terms to each copy, e.g. one copy can be provided with the modification rights, another – with limited public access rights via the Internet. Or, for example, it is possible to assign different types of open source licenses to each copy of computer code distributed via blockchain" (p. 10).

The referred possibilities increase the commodification of specific copies of copyrighted works in blockchain and its *de facto* and not only *de jure* appropriation by rightholders. Beyond the constant storage of continuous information, blockchain and smart contracts can be implemented as a means of providing fair and fast remuneration to individual copyright holders, by allowing them to directly license uses by third parties and to foresee if the user is entitled to experience the work, to re-use it, to remix it or to make derivative works. Different uses may generate different remunerations according to the license granted and blockchain combined with smart contracts potentiates dynamic control of pricing.

As soon as the purchase of the digital work is complete, transactional information is converted into a hash which will be immutably embedded on the blockchain and "the smart contract will be triggered immediately so that all other actions – e.g. payment of royalties to right holders – are automated" (Finck & Moscon, 2019, p. 95). Subsequently, "information about the copyright owner would be recorded in the same hash that recorded the information about the user, their purchase, and their use rights" ((Tresise et al., p. 7).

The described facts create an excellent private ordering system where rightholders are able to control the works from creation to the purchase by end users (and even the concrete uses made by these).

Furthermore, the direct and immediate payment of the user to the rightsholder will reduce the costs associated with collecting and managing statistics, maintaining databases and the distribution of royalty payment (Tresise et al., 2017, p. 7).

Nevertheless, history has showed that when a disruptive technology turns available, after the first unregulated times giving the feeling of total freedom of individuals, in a subsequent period, market and states adapt to the context using the new tools to pursue agents' specific public or private interest. It is expectable that intermediaries like collective management organizations develop permissioned blockchain based platforms and act as an alternative to individual or direct private licensing systems.

CHALLENGES TO THE IMPLEMENTATION OF BLOCKCHAIN-BASED COPYRIGHT MANAGEMENT PLATFORMS

Technical Problems

At the present time, the exploitation of copyrighted content in blockchain systems is still viewed in a potential perspective. Blockchain seems to be an open field for the development of exploitation platforms but we have not seen large-scale experiences yet. Probably because some relevant issues are yet to be clarified regarding technological and legal problems.

According to Pech (2020, p. 16) and Guadamuz (2019, p. 19), the first set of problems relies on the lack of scalability of blockchains when compared to traditional databases. Given blockchain architecture, the massive use of the structure is not yet prepared to compete with traditional and fastest databases. For instance, according to Croman et al. (2016) "[t]oday's representative blockchain such as Bitcoin takes 10 min or longer to confirm transactions, achieves 7 transactions/sec maximum throughput. In comparison, a mainstream payment processor such as Visa credit card confirms a transaction within seconds, and processes 2000 transactions/sec on average, with a peak rate of 56,000 transactions/sec" (p. 1). Moreover, blockchain networks is energy inefficient considering that is consumes a tremendous amount of energy (Orcutt, 2017) and there is currently no solution to the problem energy inefficiencies of blockchain, despite the fact that engineers are considering multiple ways to reduce blockchain energy consumption (Zhao, 2018). The problem is intensified when one has to consider the storage space required by the system. Since blockchain is an append-only database, the more information stored, the more storage space is needed. De Filippi & Wright (2018) note that if these requirements become too onerous, "fewer individuals or entities will be able to invest resources to maintain the shared database, weakening the security of the blockchain by making it easier for a small number of large mining pools to take over the network and potentially compromise its contents (p. 56).

Legal Concerns

Privacy Rights

One other sort of problems derives from legal provisions regarding the protection of other interests rather than those of copyrightholders.

A special concern is related to users' privacy. Market-oriented and blockchain-based copyright management systems will require the collecting of some users' personal data in order to award a contract and to clarify the terms of the granted licenses.

In the European Union (EU), for instance, several pieces of legislation foresee a broad protection of users' privacy. The right to privacy is not perceived only as "the right to be left alone" (Warren & Brandeis, 1890). Following a pivotal decision of the Germany Federal Constitutional Court (BVerfGE, 1983) ruling that in the context of modern data processing, the protection of the individual against unlimited collection, storage, use and disclosure of his/her personal data is encompassed by the general personal rights' constitutional provisions. This basic right warrants in this respect the capacity of the individual to determine in principle the disclosure and use of his/her personal data. The EU's conceptualization of the individual's right over personal data goes beyond a mere guarantee of the right to privacy to a true fundamental right with an independent meaning.

The right to communicational and informational self-determination is constituted by two inseparable but complementary dimensions. The first one, perceived as a negative right, has a defensive nature and protects the holder against interference by the State and by individuals or corporations who are responsible for collecting and processing digital or analogical data. The referred dimension is similar in its *raison d'être* to the guarantee for the secrecy of correspondence and of other means of private communication. The second dimension constitutes a positive right and a true fundamental freedom of the individual to dispose of his/her own personal information, granting him/her the power of controlling it and from which exercise he/she may at every moment determine what others know about his/her respect.

The two described dimensions are legally recognized in article 8 of the EU, where it is foreseen that

1. Everyone has the right to the protection of personal data concerning him or her.

2. Such data must be processed fairly for specified purposes and on the basis of the consent of the person concerned or some other legitimate basis laid down by law. Everyone has the right of access to data which has been collected concerning him or her, and the right to have it rectified.

On derivative law level, Directive 95/46/EC of the European Parliament and of the Council of 24 October 1995 on the protection of individuals with regard to the processing of personal data and on the free movement of such data and Directive 2002/58/EC of the European Parliament and of the Council of 12 July 2002 concerning the processing of personal data and the protection of privacy in the electronic communications sector (Directive on privacy and electronic communications) can be singled out. However, the main legal document on the matter is without a doubt the General Data Protection Regulation (Regulation (EU) 2016/679) (GDPR). According to current EU legislation, the activity of electronic collecting and computer processing of personal data must follow a data protection by design and by default solution and must embody the following principles: a) the principle of lawful collecting (according to which collecting and processing data constitute a restriction on holder's informational self-determination and, as so, shall be only permitted within the parameters of the law and, particularly, with the holder's knowledge and consent; b); the finality principle (meaning that the data collection and the data processing can only be made with a clear, specific and socially acceptable purpose that must be identifiable in every moment the data is treated); c) the principle of objective limitation, as the use of the collected data must be restricted to the purposes that were communicated to the holder in the moment of the collection, and also proportional, needed and adequate to the communicated finality; d) the principle of temporal limitation, meaning that data shall not be kept

by more than the time needed to achieve the justificative finality; e) the principle of data quality (according to which the collected data must be correct and up to date; f) the principle of the free access to data by its subject (for purposes not only of knowing the existence of the collection and the storage of his/her personal data but also to eventually rectify, erasure or block the information if incomplete and inaccurate; g) the security principle (under which the controller must implement appropriate technical and organizational measures to protect personal data against accidental or unlawful destruction or accidental loss, alteration, unauthorized disclosure or access, in particular where the processing involves the transmission of data over a network); h) the confidentiality principle (meaning that confidentiality of communications and the related traffic data by means of a public communications network and publicly available electronic communications services shall be ensured, as it is prohibited to listen, tap, store or other to perform other kinds of interception or surveillance of communications and the related traffic data by people other than users, without the consent of the users concerned, except when legally authorized to do so) (Pina, 2011, p. 247).

Beyond the principles, the GDPR imposes controllers very demanding procedural obligations Article 24 foresees that the controller shall implement appropriate technical and organisational measures to ensure and to be able to demonstrate that in any moment processing is performed in accordance with the regulation.

The controller is obliged to implement appropriate technical and organisational measures for ensuring that, by default, only personal data which are necessary for each specific purpose of the processing are processed and also that personal data is not made accessible without the individual's intervention to an indefinite number of natural persons (article 25 GDPR).

According to article 32, controllers and processors shall implement appropriate measures for the security of processing including, inter alia, as appropriate, the pseudonymisation and encryption of personal data; the ability to ensure the ongoing confidentiality, integrity, availability and resilience of processing systems and services; the ability to restore the availability and access to personal data in a timely manner in the event of a physical or technical incident; a process for regularly testing, assessing and evaluating the effectiveness of technical and organisational measures for ensuring the security of the processing.

Article 33 establishes an obligation of controllers and processors to notify personal data breaches to the supervisory authority, no later than 24 hours after having become aware of it. According to Article 34, when the personal data breach is likely to adversely affect the protection of the personal data or privacy of the data subject, the controller shall, after the notification referred to in Article 33, communicate the breach to the data subject without undue delay.

Article 39 introduces a mandatory data protection officer for the public sector, and, in the private sector, for enterprises where the core activities of the controller or processor consist of processing operations which require regular and systematic monitoring on a large scale. The data protection officer shall be entrusted at least with the following tasks: to inform and advise the controller or the processor of their obligations pursuant to the Regulation and to document this activity and the responses received; to monitor the implementation and application of the policies of the controller or processor in relation to the protection of personal data; to monitor the implementation and application of the Regulation, in particular as to the requirements related to data protection by design, data protection by default and data security and to the information of data subjects and their request in exercising their rights; to maintain documents of all processing operations under its responsibility; to monitor the documents, notifications, and communication of personal data breaches; to monitor the performance of the data protection impact assessment by the controller or processor and the application for prior authorization or prior consultation; to monitor the response to requests from the supervisory authority, and, within the sphere of the data protection officer's competence, co-operating with the supervisory authority at the latter's request or on the data protection officer's own initiative; to act as the contact point for the supervisory authority on issues related to the processing and consult with the supervisory authority.

Moreover, the GDPR sanctions noncompliance with extremely high potential administrative fines up to 20 000 000 EUR, or in the case of an undertaking, up to 4% of the total worldwide annual turnover of the preceding financial year, whichever is higher (Article 83).

The described data protection framework demanding centralized actions to collect titles to the treatment of personal data like the users' consent to collect data or meeting requirements for other legal titles like fulfillment of a contract or balancing of legitimate interests, to constantly provide documentation certifying the legality of data treatments, to give access to holders so that they can exercise their rights to rectify or to eliminate data or to data portability, to give notice of data breaches, etc, strongly challenges decentralized systems like blockchain considering peer-to-peer network distributed peer-to-peer network architecture. This disconnect – state Shah et al. (2019) – "can make it difficult to reconcile current data protection laws with blockchain's other core elements, such as the lack of centralized control, immutability, and perpetual data storage".

Nevertheless, according Giannopoulou (2020), "legal compliance can be the gateway for a lot of these projects to reach some level of recognition and usability but also it can be the tool that ensures that these projects deliver on their promise to redesign personal data exchanges" since "the GDPR is a malleable enough framework to convey both fundamental protections necessary to data protection but also to accommodate a decentralized network of actors that deploy technological architectures in order to achieve a high level of security and privacy" (p. 100).

In public permissionless blockchains, considering its main characteristics of complete disintermediation, redundancy, transparency and immutability, it will be extremely difficult or tendentially impossible to comply with strong duties like the ones imposed by GPDR. Permissioned blockchains are more fitted to comply with strong regulations related to privacy rights since they are more similar to traditional centrally administered databases. Savelyev (2017) introduces the concept of a superuser, restricted to permissioned blockchains, "which will have a right to modify the content of blockchain databases in accordance with a specified procedure" (p. 15). Such entity would have powers to rectify wrong data – challenging the tendential immutability of the blockchain – to remove it when unnecessary or after holders' request and to act in case of data breach. However, as said above, permissionless blockchains as known today will surely fail to comply with strong and broad data protection laws.

Limitations on Copyright

Copyright law works as a tool to stimulate the production and the dissemination of creative expression and knowledge by means of granting authors or other rightholders exclusive economic rights to explore their works, excluding others from using it without proper authorization and, if required, remuneration. However, experiencing previous intellectual works is essential to new creations. In a context of cumulative research and inputs, access to knowledge and to information are fundamental values to the production of new works. As so, copyright protection must not go beyond what is strictly needed to protect rightolders. A legislative framework that grants absolute proprietary and monopolistic powers on creative content would harm new authors interests in detriment of the public interest in more works and knowledge. For such reason, copyright law, beyond the rights and privileges granted to rightholders, has also internalized public interests' concerns and creation values through the prediction of a set of limitations on exclusive rights safeguarding users' fundamental individual rights or liberties as freedom of expression, the right to make quotations or the right to parody. The provision of limitations on exclusive rights by copyright law itself is the key for an internal balance between the interests and the rights of creators or other rightholders, on the one side, and the public interest or other individuals' interests – amongst them students or future authors, on the other.

In the USA, a general clause of fair use doctrine is predicted an open concept at 17 U.S.C. § 107 as a limitation on holders' rights for purposes such as criticism, comment, news reporting, teaching, scholarship, or research. To determine if a use is fair, some factors must be taken into account like the purpose and character of the use, including whether such use is of a commercial nature or is for nonprofit educational purposes; the nature of the copyrighted work; the amount and substantiality of the portion used in relation to the copyrighted work as a whole; and the effect of the use upon the potential market or the value of the copyrighted work.

The EU legislator opted for a different technic and to set an exhaustive list of limitations, instead of a general clause of free usages. Recent Directive (EU) 2019/790 of the European Parliament and of the Council of 17 April 2019 on copyright and related rights in the Digital Single Market (CDSMD) and Directive 2001/29/EC of the European Parliament and of the Council of 22 May 2001 on the harmonisation of certain aspects of copyright and related rights in the information society (Infosoc Directive), as amended by the former, while setting a high level of protection of copyright and related rights, recognize that "fair balance of rights and interests between the different categories of rightholders, as well as between the different categories of rightholders and users of protected subject-matter must be safeguarded" (Recital 31 of the InfoSoc Directive) and that it "should seek to promote learning and culture by protecting works and other subject-matter while permitting exceptions or limitations in the public interest for the purpose of education and teaching" (Recital 34 of the InfoSoc Directive). The CDSMD, although having the purpose of modernizing and adapting EU copyright regulation regarding the technological development – e.g. in the fields of text and data mining – has also recognized that "[i]n the fields of research, innovation, education and preservation of cultural heritage, digital technologies permit new types of uses that are not clearly covered by the existing Union rules on exceptions and limitations" (Recital 5). Moreover, the CDSMD, reaffirming that the "protection of technological measures established in Directive 2001/29/EC remains essential to ensure the protection and the effective exercise of the rights granted to authors and to other rightholders under Union law", clarifies that such "protection should be maintained while ensuring that the use of technological measures does not prevent the enjoyment of the exceptions and limitations provided for in this Directive" (Recital 7). In the specific case of text and data mining, the CDSMD provides a new limitation on copyright exclusive right in case of "reproductions and extractions made by research organisations and cultural heritage institutions in order to carry out, for the purposes of scientific research, text and data mining of works or other subject matter to which they have lawful access" (Article 3, (1).

Article 17, 7, of the CDSMS foresees that "Member States shall ensure that users in each Member State are able to rely on any of the following existing exceptions or limitations when uploading and making available content generated by users on online content-sharing services: (a) quotation, criticism, review; (b) use for the purpose of caricature, parody or pastiche reviewed" as long as article 5 (2) of the Infosoc Directive sets a list of exceptions to reproduction rights, to the right of communication to the public of works and to the right of making available to the public other subject-matter that are related to educational or scientific purposes. Furthermore, according to article 5 (3) Member States may provide for limitations on the reproduction right and on the make available right in case of use for the sole purpose of illustration for teaching or scientific research, as long as the source, including the author's name, is indicated, unless this turns out to be impossible and to the extent justified by the non-commercial purpose to be achieved.

Furthermore, blockchains constitute databases for the purposes of Directive 96/9/EC of the European Parliament and of the Council of 11 March 1996 on the legal protection of databases (Databases Directive). After granting the author of a database the exclusive right to carry out or to authorize acts of reproduction, translation, adaptation, arrangement and any other change, any form of distribution to the public of the database or of copies thereof, any communication, display or performance to the public (Article 5), the Databases Directive also predicts in its Article 6 that Member States shall have the option of providing for limitations on the rights set out in Article 5 in case of reproduction for private purposes of a non-electronic database; where there is use for the sole purpose of illustration for teaching or scientific research, as long as the source is indicated and to the extent justified by the non-commercial purpose to be achieved; where there is use for the purposes of public security or for the purposes of an administrative or judicial procedure; where other exceptions to copyright which are traditionally authorized under national law are involved.

The referred legal framework displays a clear challenge to blockchain since smart contracts may conflict with limitations and uses that were declared free by legislators in order to pursue public interests. In these cases, "a court could impose an appropriate remedy, such as allowing circumvention of DRM or the reduction of any payment due" (Bodó et al., 2018, p. 323). In fact, in order to respect and enforce copyright limitations and exceptions the only plausible solution shall include at a certain point human casuistic intervention since automated decisions are not reliable as means to safeguard the complex balance of interests that copyright law must safeguard. Which means that only permissioned blockchains seem to have the potential to act lawfully from a copyright limitations perspective.

CONCLUSION

When a disruptive technology like blockchain arises, the first perspectives regarding its application may be excessively optimistic. In the field of copyright, blockchain technology is appointed to serve as perfect tool for DRM since, exclusively from a technological point of view and when combined with smart contracts, it gives rightholders the opportunity to exploit their works under total control and with immediate revenues. Blockchain has the technical potential to serve as a private ordering system where rightholders can directly license their works with end-users without the intervention of intermediaries.

Nevertheless, blockchain faces several technical and legal problems regarding the safeguard of public interests that challenges the implementation of the potential to serve as technological replacement of traditional copyright management systems. It is not expectable that jurisdictions and courts peacefully accept that technological possibilities and private contracts override and replace copyright law as a delicate brunch of law promoting a fair balance of interests between rightholders and the public interest or users' legitimate interests. Bodo et al (2018) point out that "if there is a friction, it is not between a particular technology and copyright. Rather, the friction is between the social, economic, and political conditions that produced the blockchain technology ecosystem, on the one hand, and the social, economic, and political premises from which the current copyright system developed" (p. 336).

Blockchain technology created modern network topologies where the clash between pre-existing rights and political, economic, or social powers may now take place. Distributed networks are indeed "one element in a complex, interdependent framework of how we govern ourselves" and it does not seem likely that the future will be radically centralized (Bodó et al, 2021, p. 15).

At the moment, permissioned blockchains seem to be in an acceptable starting point to comply with copyright law (as whole) or privacy law provisions, leaving residual space for the development of permissionless blockchains based systems of DRM.

One must wait for future technological advances in order to evaluate if blockchain-based copyright platforms will flourish or not.

REFERENCES

Bodó, B., Brekke, J. K., & Hoepman, J.-H. (2021). Decentralisation: A multidisciplinary perspective. *Internet Policy Review*, *10*(2). Advance online publication. doi:10.14763/2021.2.1563

Bodó, B., Gervais, D., & Quintais, J. P. (2018). Blockchain and Smart Contracts: The missing link in copyright licensing? *International Journal of Law and Information Technology*, *26*(4), 311–336. doi:10.1093/ijlit/eay014

Buterin, V. (2013). *A Next Generation Smart Contract & Decentralized Application Platform*. https://ethereum.org/whitepaper/

BuzuI. (2020). Blockchain, Smart Contracts and Copyright Management Disruption. doi:10.2139/ssrn.3759260

BVerfGE. (1983). *1BVerfGE 65, 1 – Volkszählung Urteil des Ersten Senats vom 15. Dezember 1983 auf die mündliche Verhandlung vom 18. und 19. Oktober 1983 - 1 BvR 209, 269, 362, 420, 440, 484/83 in den Verfahren über die Verfassungsbeschwerden.* https://www.servat.unibe.ch/dfr/bv065001.html

Charalampidis, P., & Fragkiadakis, A. (2020). *When Distributed Ledger Technology meets Internet of Things - Benefits and Challenges*. https://arxiv.org/pdf/2008.12569.pdf

Chen, W., Zhou, K., Fang, W., Wang, K., & Bi, F. (2020). Review on blockchain technology and its application to the simple analysis of intellectual property protection. *International Journal on Computer Science and Engineering*, *22*(4), 437–444.

Clark, C. (1996). The answer to the machine is in the machine. In P. Bernt Hugenholtz (Ed.), *The future of copyright in a digital environment*. Kluwer Law International.

Croman, K., Decker, C., Eyal, I., Gencer, A. E., Juels, A., Kosba, A., Miller, A., Saxena, P., Shi, E., Sirer, E. G., Song, D., & Wattenhofer, R. (2016). *On Scaling Decentralized Blockchains (A Position Paper)*. https://www.comp.nus.edu.sg/~prateeks/papers/Bitcoin-scaling.pdf

De Filippi, P., & Wright, A. (2018). *Blockchain and the Law: The Rule of Code*. Harvard University Press. doi:10.2307/j.ctv2867sp

Ferrari, V. (2020). The regulation of crypto-assets in the EU – investment and payment tokens under the radar. *Maastricht Journal of European and Comparative Law, 27*(3), 325–342. doi:10.1177/1023263X20911538

Finck, M. & Moscon, V. (2019). Copyright Law on Blockchains: Between New Forms of Rights Administration and Digital Rights Management 2.0. *IIC International Review of Intellectual Property and Competition Law, 50*(1), 77-108.

Geiger, C. (2010). The future of copyright in Europe: Striking a fair balance between protection and access to information. *Intellectual Property Quarterly, 1*, 1–14.

Giannopoulou, A. (2020). Data Protection Compliance Challenges for Self-Sovereign Identity. Blockchain 2020, 91-100. doi:10.1007/978-3-030-52535-4_10

Guadamuz, A. (2019). Smart Contracts and Intellectual Property: Challenges and Reality. In *Intellectual property and the 4th industrial revolution*. Kluwer International Law. https://ssrn.com/abstract=3911121

Gürkaynak, G., Yilmaz, I., Yesilaltay, B., & Bengi, B. (2018). Intellectual property law and practice in the blockchain realm. *Computer Law & Security Review, 34*(4), 847–862. doi:10.1016/j.clsr.2018.05.027

Helberger, N., & Hugenholtz, P. B. (2007). No place like home for making a copy: Private copying in European copyright law and consumer law. *Berkeley Technology Law Journal, 22*, 1061–1098.

Jaszi, P. (1998). Intellectual property legislative update: Copyright, paracopyright, and pseudo-copyright [Paper presentation]. Association of Research Libraries conference: The Future Network: Transforming Learning and Scholarship, Eugene, OR, United States.

Kiemle, M. (2018). *Blockchain and Copyright Issues*. https://www.4ipcouncil.com/research/blockchain-and-copyright-issues

Lessig, L. (2006). *Code 2.0*. Basic Books.

Nakamoto, S. (2008). *Bitcoin: A Peer-to-Peer Electronic Cash System*. https://bitcoin.org/bitcoin.pdf

Orcutt, M. (2017). *Blockchains Use Massive Amounts of Energy - But There's a Plan to Fix That*. https://www.technologyreview.com/2017/11/16/147609/bitcoin-uses-massive-amounts-of-energybut-theres-a-plan-to-fix-it/

Pech, S. (2020). Copyright Unchained: How Blockchain Technology Can Change the Administration and Distribution of Copyright Protected Works. *Northwestern Journal of Technology and Intellectual Property*, (1). Advance online publication. doi:10.2139srn.3578311

Pina, P. (2011). Digital Copyright Enforcement: Between Piracy and Privacy. In C. Akrivopoulou & A. Psygkas (Eds.), *Personal Data Privacy and Protection in a Surveillance Era: Technologies and Practices* (pp. 241–254). IGI Global. doi:10.4018/978-1-60960-083-9.ch014

Rose, A. (2020). Blockchain: Transforming the registration of IP rights and strengthening the protection of unregistered IP rights. *WIPO Magazine*. https://www.wipo.int/wipo_magazine_digital/en/2020/article_0002.html

Savelyev, A. (2017). *Copyright in the blockchain era: Promises and challenges.* https://wp.hse.ru/data/2017/11/21/1160790875/77LAW2017.pdf

Shah, P., Forester, D., Berberich, M., Raspé, C., & Mueller, H. (2019). *Blockchain Technology: Data Privacy Issues and Potential Mitigation Strategies.* https://www.davispolk.com/publications/blockchain-technology-data-privacy-issues-and-potential-mitigation-strategies

Sunyaev, A. (2020). Distributed ledger technology. In A. Sunyaev (Ed.), *A. Internet Computing* (pp. 265–299). Springer. doi:10.1007/978-3-030-34957-8_9

Tresise, A., Goldenfein, J., & Hunter, D. (2018). *What blockchain can and can't do for copyright.* https://papers.ssrn.com/sol3/papers.cfm?abstract_id=3227381

Warren, S., & Brandeis, L. (1890). The Right to Privacy. *Harvard Law Review*, *4*(5), 193–220. doi:10.2307/1321160

Werra, J. (2001). Le régime juridique des mesures techniques de protection des oeuvres selon les Traités de l'OMPI, le Digital Millennium Copyright Act, les Directives Européennes et d'autres legislations (Japon, Australie). *Revue Internationale du Droit d'Auteur*, *189*, 66–213.

Zhao, H. (2018). *Bitcoin and Blockchain Consume an Exorbitant Amount of Energy. These Engineers Are Trying to Change That.* https://www.cnbc.com/2018/02/23/bitcoin-blockchain-consumes-a-lot-of-energy-engineers-changing-that.html

ZhaoZ. (2019). Fulfilling the Right to Follow: Using Blockchain to Enforce the Artist's Resale Right. *Cardozo Arts & Entertainment Law Journal*, *39*(1). https://ssrn.com/abstract=3871892

KEY TERMS AND DEFINITIONS

Digital Rights Management: A copyrighted work's management system based on digital technology that, amongst other powers, allows copyright holders to control access to works or to prevent unauthorized copies.

Distributed Ledger: A decentralized database managed by multiple members of a network across multiple nodes.

Limitations (on Copyright): A set of free uses of copyrighted works that escape rightholders' control, mainly because of public interests related to research, study, freedom of speech or the respect for privacy rights.

Permissioned Blockchain: A blockchain based in proprietary software, where permission from the administrator to a new user to become a node in the verification system is required.

Permissionless Blockchain: A blockchain which relies on open-source software, and where anyone can join the ledger simply by downloading and running the relevant software without the need for prior permission or approval to operate.

Private Ordering: The regulation, enforcement and dispute resolution by private actors potentially escaping the rules of the State of Law.

Smart Contracts: A computer program stored on a decentralized network that runs when predetermined conditions are met without the involvement of an intermediary.

Technological Protection Measures: Digital technology-based tools idealized to control third parties' access to copyrighted works or subsequent unauthorized uses.

Chapter 8
Internet of Things in Cyber Security Scope

Mazoon Hashil Alrubaiei
Modern College of Business and Science, Oman

Maiya Hamood Al-Saadi
Modern College of Business and Science, Oman

Hothefa Shaker
Modern College of Business and Science, Oman

Bara Sharef
Ahlia University, Bahrain

Shahnawaz Khan
ⓘ https://orcid.org/0000-0002-3675-4467
University College of Bahrain, Bahrain

ABSTRACT

IoT represents a technologically bright future where heterogeneously connected devices will be connected to the internet and make intelligent collaborations with other objects to extend the borders of the world with physical entities and virtual components. Despite rapid evolution, this environment is still facing new challenges and security issues that need to be addressed. This chapter will give a comprehensive view of IoT technologies. It will discuss the IoT security scope in detail. Furthermore, a deep analysis of the most recent proposed mechanisms is classified. This study will be a guide for future studies, which direct to three primary leading technologies—machine learning (ML), blockchain, and artificial intelligence (AI)—as intelligent solutions and future directions for IoT security issues.

DOI: 10.4018/978-1-7998-8382-1.ch008

INTRODUCTION

Internet of Thing (IoT) is an integration of a world-wide network of interconnected physical objects as sensors, actuators, machines, and smart devices which communicate based on standard protocols. This smart device impacts human daily life toward automation, intelligent, and smart transportation. Recently, the application of IoT such as health care, smart grid, smart home, online carted-items tracking, and environment monitoring are developing rapidly and such smart applications produce a huge amount of information which obtain vast computing facility, storage area, and communication data transfer capacity (Nižetić, Sandro, Petar Šolić, Diego López-de-Ipiña González-de, 2020). According to Cisco, in 2020, numerous of wearable devices, smart meters, wireless sensors, connected vehicles, and other smart devices will be 50 billion of them connected to the internet while by 2025 will be increased to 500 billion. Processing, sensing, heterogeneous access, services and applications, and additional components like privacy and security are the main mechanisms of IoT. Security is the most recent concern in this environment due to its extends the 'internet' via a traditional internet, sensor network mobile network and so on. Furthermore, everything will be connected to this internet. While the third is that these things will communicate with other. Therefore, the new privacy security issue will arise, and researcher must pay more care to these challenges related to authenticity, integrity and confidentiality of information in the IoT as well as there are many privacy and security concerns on different layer. As a solution to extend and improve the security and minimize the security weakness of IoT, many technologies have been used and blockchain is consider as one of the technologies used to mitigate the attacks as some researchers agreed that to strengthen security in IoT, four methods can be applied which are secure IoT communications using Blockchain technology, authenticate users, detect legal IoT and configure IoT. Blockchain has been a high demand technology since the initial advent of the bitcoin by Satoshi Nakamoto. At the first stages, this technology was used to prevent the duplicate ordain of transactions. Blockchain name is indicated to data structure, and it might cover network or system structure. It consists of a number of organized blocks where a transaction is stored each block and these blocks are directly attached to its previous block formatting a chain (Fakhri & Mutijarsa, 2018). Classification of access control management, protecting data in IoT and storing the public key and the private key in IoT objects are some of the main enchantments that blockchain provided to IoT security (Fakhri & Mutijarsa, 2018) (H. Yang et al., 2020). Additionally, Data records authorization, protecting data from being tampered in the data sharing stage, and managing access attributes are some of the powerful extends of blockchain technology in IoT (H. Yang et al., 2020).

The rest of this paper is divided into 2 main sections. Section 2 gives a full overview of IoT. While section 2 will explain the Security in IoT Scope.

OVERVIEW OF IOT TECHNOLOGIES

The concept of the internet of things started in 1998 and was introduced by Kevin Ashton in 1999 as it endeavors to take advantage of the smart technology by connecting anything anytime and anywhere and reduces the physical work by automation (Patra & Rao, 2016). As per The International Telecommunication Union definition, the Internet of Things is an international infrastructure for an information society that enables improved services to connect things physically or virtually based on communication technologies and interoperable data. PDA's, smartphones, tablets, laptops, and many other handheld devices(Viel, Silva, Valderi Leithardt, & Zeferino, 2019)(Chopra, Gupta, & Lambora, 2019). Like any technology, IoT has specific characteristics. In this section, IoT elements, architecture, applications, communications technologies, major constrains, security requirements and attacks, analysis of IoT security solutions and future direction and suggestion of security responses in IoT will be discussed.

IoT Components

IoT involves the number of sensors and smart interconnected devices that are often invisible nonintrusive, and transparent which are called elements. There are main components namely hardware, middleware and presentation which contains several elements. These elements are communicating along with related services which is expected to happen anywhere anytime, and it is frequently done in the wireless and autonomic manner. These components are described as following.

Hardware

The hardware is one of the basic elements of IoT which is consists of sensors, actuator, processor, storage unit, memory, power supply, etc. The sensor-actuator pair forms the backbone of an IoT implementation. The sensors connect to each other to form a sensor network. In IoT, sensors play a crucial part as they are considered as the interface of the IoT environment. They are responsible for information capture from the environment and perform any task offered by any IoT applications (Khursheed, Sami-Ud-Din, Sumra, & Safder, 2020). Moreover, they generate and implement a complex program code for accurate and proper data collection. According to the application domain, sensors may differ where some sensors and are devoted to some specific applications, whereas others can adapt to various fields. Yet, they categorized based on the data size, the number of connected nodes, sampling rate, and types of signals associated with the sensor. The IoT sensors are also specified as temperature sensors, pressure sensors, humidity sensors, touch sensors, and others. On the other side, the electrical signals are converted into functional and useful energy by the actuator. It basically establishes a motion or a mechanical behavior on energy supply. While the sensors gather the data, the actuator analyzes the collected data, and accordingly, it induces an appropriate action. The main reason to improve and design actuators is that the IoT actuators are the devices that convert smart and processed information into energy. Actuators are categorized on the energy source which they require and use to move. IoT actuators are known as hydraulic actuators, pneumatic actuators, thermal actuators, and electric actuators.

Middleware

The middleware is used for storing data, computing tools for data analytics, and context awareness (Patra & Rao, 2016). In contains both storage and computer tools for database analysis. The storage is one the main middleware component which stores data whether they are produced data, generated data, or processed data. Some applications like intelligent banking, real-time financial analysis, or smart health applications required massive storage and traditional storage is insufficient to store such data. Thus, cloud-based storage along with big data analytics is a suitable solutions to store the huge data. Cloud computing is the combination of several conventional technology just like hardware virtualization, service-based architecture and works split distributed computing, computer network and auto-sided computing. This resource-based computer model is operated as an internet service to earn (Khursheeed et al., 2020).

Presentation

The third element of IoT is the one who understands takes care of the interpretation and novel visualization tools that can be smoothly accessed from various platforms and can be used in an enormous range of IoT applications (Patra & Rao, 2016). The basic reason for these tools is the ability to adapt as they are achieved in different types of uses and available from any phase. From a system perspective and for the most part, the ability to access the huge data through the article labeled Internet perusing encouraged the Internet of things opportunity. In order to coordinate elements in the computer word and understand them using the internet address, some labeling advancements are provided like NFC, RFID, QR code, and others.

innovation, sensor innovation, insight RFID, and nanotechnology are initiating headways for the enhancement of it (Khursheeed et al., 2020).

IoT Architecture

There is no fix IoT architecture and many architectures have been planned in the earlier years, including generic architecture. All these architectures of IoT are multi-layer architectures, to each layer is well-defined via its roles and the devices used each layer. There are different ideas regarding the number of layers in IoT. Although, according to many academics the IoT mostly operates on five layers termed as perception, network, middleware, application and business layers. Figure 1 illustrates these layers and its components. Each layer of IoT has its own characteristics and functionality which will be explained below.

Figure 1. IoT architecture

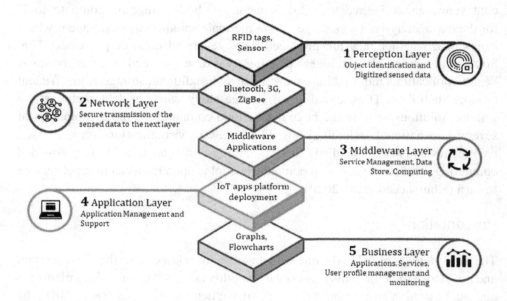

Perception Layer (PL)

PL is the first level of IoT which it is called also the Device Layer or the Sensing Layer that communicate with the physical devices and sensors concentrated on identifying and collecting the data via the sensor devices from several sources that contain the environmental conditions and object -thing- properties (Khursheeed et al., 2020). This layer consists of the real-world physical objects which can be RFID tags, infrared sensors, or even barcode based on the thing identification manner used. Based on the sensor type, collecting information might be related to humidity, temperature, location, motion, and others. The main function of this layer is identifying the developed object and digitized the sensed information by the object and send it to the next layer which is the network layer.

Transportation/Network Layer

In this layer, the information gathered from the sensor devices is transmitted securely to the processing unit of the system. It consists of smart devices, cloud computing, and the internet (Khursheeed et al., 2020). The main responsibility of this layer is connecting the network equipment and servers to the smart devices where the transmitted media of transferred information could be either wired or wireless like WiFi, Zigbee, Bluetooth, etc. depending on the device sensor. In other words, The concerned of this layer is the data routing and the transmission to the several IoT objects through internet gateways. Hence, simply, the main job of the transport layer is to carry the information from the perception layer to the middleware layer.

Middleware Layer

IoT objects are built for several kinds of services. Those devices can communicate and connect to other devices in a condition that they are providing the same service. This layer is mainly focused on managing the services. Moreover, this layer communicates with the databases in which it collects the information passed from the network layer and store them in the database (Chopra et al., 2019). Once the data stored, the layer performs information processing and ubiquitous computation as it is called the processing layer as well. Finally, by analyzing the outcomes of information processing, automatic decision making is taken. The produced decision is then transferred to the next layer (Khursheeed et al., 2020).

Application Layer

This layer relays on the pervious layer where the information of the device processed at the processing layer helps the application layer to provide entire application management (Chopra et al., 2019). It includes application support and real IoT application such as smart health, smart cities, smart home, etc. Additionally, it facilitates general management of the applications provides particular services to the users. In order to connect the intelligent application between the IoT with the end-user, Virtual Reality, Multimedia applications, Augmented Reality technologies are used.

Business Layer

Based on the application layer outcomes, the business layer manages the entire IoT systems including the application, services, profit model, and the privacy of the user. The business model, flowcharts, and graphs are created from the information extracted from the application layer in this layer. Besides, the business layer controls and monitors the whole previous four IoT layers. The importance of this layer leads to the success of IoT technology where the analysis of the results, future action, and business strategies are determined by this layer (Chopra et al., 2019).

IoT Enabling and Communication Technologies

Communication technology represents a major part of the successful IoT systems deployment. It is considered as one of the basic pillars that grant IoT existence. In addition, those communication technologies enable IoT objects to communicate with each other. To enable and support the evolving paradigm, some enabling technologies are needed and that also encompasses IoT (Viel et al., 2019) presents in figure 2. The following section discusses some of the available enabling and communication technologies that are involved in IoT.

Figure 2. IoT enabling and communication technologies

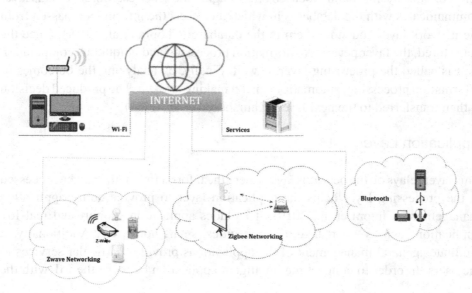

Radio Frequency Identification (RFID)

RFID plays a vital role in IoT development as it considers as a backbone of IoT architecture. It is a wireless communication technology that uses the radio frequency that allows the physical device to send the data for device tracking and object identification within some distance. RFID consists of a chip known as a tag that has a unique identification code and antenna so that the reader machine can detect and identify the chips in the environment. The tags can be either active or passive. While the active tags are embedded with their own power supply and do not rely on the reader, passive tags transmit their identification whenever the electromagnetic field spreads by the reader. Both tags are operated on UHF transmission band between 860 MHz and 960 MHz (Viel et al., 2019). This technology works in very limited data transmission as it cannot send a huge amount of data and it has very less power. Whenever there is a requirement to identify something in the environment, RFID technology can be used. At first, RFID was used for animal identifications and access control but currently, it is also used in many applications like Wal-Mart store and metro traveling cards and others.

Wireless Fidelity (WiFi)

WiFi is a wireless networking technology deployed by Vic Hayes that allows the computer and or other devices to start the communication using the signals. Currently, wifi provides high-speed data transmission to connect a high number of people in public locations like café, healthcare centers, airports, and other public organizations and private as houses. The wifi technology expanded to cover handheld devices like smartphones, a notebook, and others. It has two classifications which are Low power wifi called HaLow which is 802.11 ah and conventional 802.11 b, 802.11g, and 802.11n. The indoor range of the conventional technology is 70 meters, whereas the outdoor is 230 meters. Furthermore, the topology used in conventional technology is star topology and a bit rate of 1 mbps at 2.4 and 5 GHz and throughput between 2 to 50 mbps. conventional technology is not advised for ultra-low-power systems, but it is vastly applied in smart cities. On the other hand, the bit rate of HaLow is lower as it between 150 to 400 kbps and throughput reaches 100 kpbs. Its topology is also star topology and a rage covers 700 to 1000 meters (Viel et al., 2019)(Chopra et al., 2019).

Bluetooth

It is a non-wired technology that mostly present in mobile devices and covers a small network (personal Area Network). It has three classes which are Bluetooth Low

Energy (BLE), classic version, and Bluetooth 5.0 (BT v5). Bluetooth Low Energy is used for a limited distance approximately 100 meters. The supported topologies used in BTE are both star and scatternet and 1 mbps bit rate at 2.4 2.5 GHz. The main features of it are that it has low latency, low bandwidth, and low power consumption. In contrast, the classic version has high bandwidth and throughout covers 100 meters distance with a limited number of connected devices. It also used scatternet topology with a bit rate between 1 to 3 mbps at 2.4 and 2,5 GHz and a throughput reached 1.5 mbps. On the other hand, the third-class BT v5 has no specific topology where is provides more expanded rang reached to 300 meters with 1,5 mbps throughput for 2 mbps bit rate at 2.4 GHz (Viel et al., 2019).

ZigBee

ZigBee technology is founded in 2001 by ZigBee Alliance to improve the function of Wireless Sensor Network (WSN) that works on IEEE 80.15.4 with 2.4 GHz. It is implemented to cover approximately 20 meters area range with low cost, low battery consumptions, small size, and support several topologies such as a star, mesh, and cluster tree, but it is scalable and reliable. The protocol design of ZigBee is highly flexible and it operates within 2.40 frequency which is around 250 kbps. It is very similar to Bluetooth Low Energy and it is mainly applied to smart city and smart building applications (Chopra et al., 2019)(Khursheeed et al., 2020).

4G Long Term Evolution (LTE)

LTE is considered as one of the key data transmission technologies used in IoT. LTE is relays with VoIP (Voice over IP) support OFSMA (Orthogonal Frequency Division Multiplexing Access) as its radio technology along with advanced antenna technology. It is based on the earlier mobile network generation technology GSM (Global System for Mobile Communication) and HSPA (High-Speed Packet Access) as it provides high-speed data transmission in mobile communication.

Near Filed Communication (NFC)

NFC is a short-range wireless technology that operates on 20 cm distance, 13.65 MHz frequency, and a rate of 242 kbps to connect two devices. The topology used in this technology is peer to peer (P2P)(Viel et al., 2019). It is similar to RFID where it contains a tag that can be changed. There are two modes of NFC which are the active mode and the passive mode. In the active mode, communication is two ways whereas the passive mode is one-way communication. From the NFC tag perspective, the passive mode NFC tags have better replacement than the active mode. The NFC tags work as an electronic reader where it creates a magnetic field as it operates in inductive coupling coil method precept. whenever the NFC tag moves toward the induced electric domain, the changes in the field is detected by the reader from the NFC tag and record it and that allows the two dimensional communication between the devices at short distance.

Z-Wave

It is the low power process generated by Zensys (Khursheeed et al., 2020). It deems as one of the key wireless communication technologies for IoT that used to manage, monitor reading the status of smart IoT devices. it used for IoT interaction, mostly for the smart homes and little industrial field names. Generally, Z-wave technology used in small packets with a limited speed reached to 100 kbps and 30 meters. Therefore, it is optimum for small IoT communications programs such as power management, light management, healthcare management. This technology relays on two products which are servant and managing. the slave nodes are low-cost products where they are not able to establish communications. They just reply and apply the instruction received from the managing systems which start the communication.

IoT Application

The Internet of Things is applied in many fields. Traditionally, it has been applied in smart cities, smart buildings, healthcare, logistics, and industry 4.0. Later on, it expanded to agriculture, electricity grids, traffic, basic sanitation, and security-oriented surveillance (Viel et al., 2019). The applications of IoT provide real-time data delivery and dependable communication and they provide full functionality of the system to the user through several connected devices as IoT applications provide device-to-device and human-to device interactions. While visualization is deemed to be one of the main features which helps the user to smoothly interact with the environment and effectively present and understand the gathered information In the human-device applications, intelligence is usually implemented for enabling dynamic interactions in device-to-device applications, and that what makes the devices for automatically environment monitoring, problems identification, collaborating and making decisions properly without human involvement. Basically, IoT application divided into three main domains which are: *Industry* where the financial or commercial transaction activities between the organizations, companies, or other entities are involved, *Environment* in which the monitoring, protection, and development of natural resources activities are involved and the *Society* where it covers any activity related to the development and any inclusions of societies, cities, and population. Some real scenarios of IoT applications are explained.

Healthcare

IoT improved the quality of people's lives by monitoring the metrics associated with health. It helps to monitor the patients using Body Area Network (BAN) by using wearable devices embedded with sensors like accelerometer, gyroscope proximity sensors, etc. which are used to collect data like body temperature, blood pressure, heartbeats, etc. This collected information is sent to remote healthcare centers like hospitals in order to analyses the data and if there is any emergency and immediate action need to be taken. Moreover, using the wearable devices, the user can check the medical records and get diagnostic lab analysis conducted at the office or home and monitor the health patterns using a web-based application on the smart mobile devices(Nathani & Vijayvergia, 2018). Currently, Android has many applications that help sensor-enabled smartphones for daily activities tracking like monitoring jogging duration, workout, and the number of burns calories (Patra & Rao, 2016).

Smart Cities

They are also benefiting from IoT technology as it is used in observing and managing the air quality, reduce noise problems, smart water supply, advanced traffic control systems identifying the routes of emergency, and others. For the advanced traffic control systems, cars are treated as things or objects, and to avoid overcrowding, route guidelines can be provided with the help of IoT. Additionally, metro cities and highways traffic can be tracked, and route guidelines are provided to avoid traffic jamming. Moreover, using the data collected from the sensors and RFID, free parking can be found, and automated parking recommendations can be provided to the driver using a smart parking device system provided by IoT (Nathani & Vijayvergia, 2018). Apart from that, smart streetlights give service in a smart city in which that based on detecting the movement of cyclists, pedestrians, and cars it works. Once there is no movement, the traffic light is dim. A smart home or called home automation is another application of IoT. Managing energy consumption, spotting emergency, home appliances interactions. IoT provides ease of household activities. The smart of it allows it to sense our temperament thus music can be played and based on our activities, light visibility can be maintained. Once a person stands in front of the door, the user is able to see the person using the video doorbell anywhere on your smart mobile. Additionally, using the smartphone, a smart lock can be remotely managed from anywhere so that anyone can access remotely.

Agriculture Domain

IoT makes farming easier for the farmers where during the outbreak of contagious disease, the animals' movements and the health of herds can be detected and traced. Besides, the farmer can directly contact the consumer for crop delivery where this reduces the farmer time and cost and gives them more benefits (Nathani & Vijayvergia, 2018). Additionally, IoT agricultural machines can help in reducing grain losses and improving crop productivity. By using propping mapping and proper applying of global navigation satellite systems (GNSS) and Global Positioning System (GPS), machines can be operated in autopilot mode. The machines including vehicles, robots, and unmanned aerial vehicles can be remotely managed based on the available data gathered through the IoT system for efficient application of resources to the needed farm areas. The machines can also gather information and such data can help farmers in drawing the maps of their field for planning programs like irrigation, fertilizing, and nutrition.

Major IoT Constraints

The technology effectiveness is directly connected to the massiveness of linked challenges. In IoT, both solutions as well as challenges are existing. The challenges and their solutions are differed according to end-user type, various application types, and different IoT stakeholders types. Some of the key IoT challenges are illustrated in this section.

Standardizations and Interoperability

The IoT device suppliers and vendors introduce devices with their own underlying in-house technologies that are not familiar to everyone and might not be available with others which end up with a heterogeneous collection of devices. This makes identical devices from various manufacturers non-interoperable (Patra & Rao, 2016). Apart from that, IoT connect distributed, huge and heterogenous environments which increase the challenge of deploying it .In IoT, there is no standardized mechanism applied to ensure the interoperability of all IoT physical objects and sensors devices. Therefore, it is very important to standardize IoT devices and sensors in order to render interoperability between them (Chopra et al., 2019) including sensor technologies, RFID, communication protocols, and innovation of efficient middleware. Applying standardized communication protocols and middleware technologies helps the different IoT devices in the IoT framework to be intractable and can be operated with each other. Besides, that helps the IoT devices to communicate with the internet seamlessly (Patra & Rao, 2016).

Extensive Deployment

In order to extract reliable data from the surrounding environments, the smart IoT nodes with embedded intelligence must be extensively deployed. Applying that helps the network to obtain a fail-safe state so that if two nodes failed in the network does not highly affect the overall efficiency of the system. However, to deploy that, a huge financial overhead is required. The proper arrangement of the nodes so as to attain ideal network performance could be a challenge that must be addressed. The effective administration of the voluminous information gathered and its right interpretation i.e. data semantics for application purposes is a critical issue (Patra & Rao, 2016).

Identity Management

Internet of Things is a huge network that connects millions and billions of physical objects and devices. Each of those connected objects and devices required a proper identity management scheme on the internet. Therefore, a robust and efficient naming mechanism is needed to dynamically assign and observe each object's identity. the rapid depleting of IPv4 addressed might be no longer a suitable option in object addressing but using IPv6 which is 128 bit might reduce the issue by providing unique addresses to a whole large number of devices be included in the global IoT framework (Patra & Rao, 2016).

Energy Consumption

The high rates of data, a huge number of applications published on the internet, and the huge growth rate of edge-devices connected to the global network caused a rapid increase in the energy consumed by the network. With IoT, energy consumption will increase significantly in the future Additionally, the non-stop monitoring and data gathering by the physical nodes require a large amount of power which is a serious challenge for the low energy battery-powered objects. Besides, transmitting the collected data by these objects to the management point through the wireless medium needs more power compared to the wired medium transmission. Hence, green technologies that used to reduce the energy consumption is needed to be efficiently used in these network devices in which the nodes work on low power, and acquire the energy from wind, sun, etc. through the use of proper techniques so that the nodes lifetime can be prolonged without the need for frequent recharge (Patra & Rao, 2016)(Chopra et al., 2019).

SECURITY REQUIREMENT AND THREAT IN IOT SCOPE

Security requirements illustrate functional and non-functional attributes that need to be applied to achieve the required level of security. The three key principles of security attribute: Confidentiality, Integrity, and Availability (CIA) are applied to the IoT environment. However, due to IoT characteristics in terms of heterogeneity, resource limitation, and dynamic environment, further security concerns need to be handle. Therefore, traditional CIA-triad became insufficient in the context of security as new threats and challenges arise in a collaborative security environment. Hence, IAS-octave is proposed as an extension to CIA-triad. Figure 3 presents the security requirements of traditional CIA-triad and IAS-octave.

Figure 3. CIA security requirements vs. IAS-octave requirements

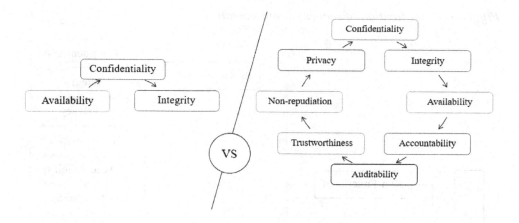

Security Requirements

The security requirement is a high-level specification on the tolerable performance of a system. These requirements are classified into functional and non-functional requirements which illustrates them in figure 4. The following sections present CIA, IAS-octave, and other required requirements each one under its category (Ahmad & Salah, 2018). Furthermore, how these attributes are expected to be met by the IoT environment.

Non-functional requirements encompass information and access level requirements which place constraints on how IoT object will do that. The first subcategory is Information Security (IS) requirements which include:

1. *Confidentiality:* prevent access by or disclosure to unauthorized of transmitting, process, and stored data.
2. *Integrity:* to ensure the authenticity of data has not been altered during transmission.
3. *Privacy:* ensuring system commitment of applying privacy policies and preserving the copyright of individuals' personal information.
4. *Non-repudiation:* is the assurance on occurrence and non-occurrence of an action cannot later be denying.
5. *Accountability:* the ability of the system to hold users responsible for their actions
6. *Anonymity:* the ability of the system to hide the source of the data.
7. *Freshness:* is the assurances that the data is very much recent and no outdated messages have been replayed.

Figure 4. Classification of security requirements

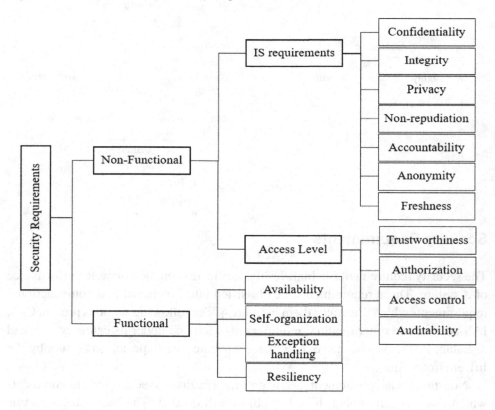

The second subcategory is Access level security requirements which contains:

1. *Trustworthiness/Authentication:* ensures identity is legitimate and establish trust in a third party (Dazine, Maizate, & Hassouni, 2018).
2. *Authorization*: ensure only authorized one get the right access.
3. *Access control*: a mechanism used to restrict and control authenticated object to access what it is authorized to.
4. *Auditability*: the ability of a system to operate constant monitoring of all actions.

While Functional requirement expresses what IoT objects should do. These requirements are listed as:

1. *Availability*: ensure services and data are reachable to authorized when needed.
2. *Self-organization:* the ability of the system object to be reorganized in case of fail or energy loss.
3. *Exception handling:* This confirms serving even in irregular situations occur (Ahmad & Salah, 2018).
4. *Resiliency:* if any of the interrelated objects are attacked the security structure must be safe and not affect as a whole and avoid a single of failure.

Integrity, trustworthiness, and confidentiality are required to protect sensor data due to short of computer power and storage capacity these sensors are unable to apply public-key encryption algorithm as it becomes a computationally expensive task of resources (Garg & Dave, 2019). Sensors do not disclose the collected data to neighboring nodes to ensure that the data is protected throughout the process. Hence, node authentication and trustworthiness are essential to prevent illegal node access and to protect the confidentiality of information transmission among the nodes. Likewise, confidentiality and integrity are very important at the communication level as it is a core of the network and can be compromised via a distributed denial-of-service attack (DDoS) and Man-in-the-Middle Attack (MIMA) as examples of attacks. Furthermore, a vulnerable node is an essential issue need to be handled, thus authentication mechanism is used to prevent the illegal nodes. Authentication will ensure that only valid objects in the IoT can get access to the IoT components as well as ensure the identity of the communicating parties for each interaction among IoT objects. While the availability of services and data should be reachable to authorized parties when required in a timely technique to achieve the expectations of IoT. Moreover, the ability to provide a minimum level of services in the occurrence of power loss or failures.

Security Challenges

Privacy and security issues are concerned with a scalable, distributed, resource constraint, and heterogeneous IoT environment especially in highly critical applications where commercial and personal privacy raised. Therefore, no lack of security should exist. The section below expresses some of the security challenges.

1. *Privacy:* is a serious challenge and the most sensitive area in the context of IoT. Due to the widely heterogeneous devices and that connected to the internet with a wide range of methods and protocols. Further, the ownership of heterogeneous devices is not specified this will result in a privacy issue. While the huge volume of generating data from IoT devices result in vulnerable confidential information and entry points for hackers.

2. *Scalability and Interoperability:* IoT environment contains an enormous number of devices that can be scale and extend however the proposed security mechanisms cannot be scale as a lot of power and memory required from connected devices. Besides, the functionality of interconnected heterogeneous devices in IoT system should not be prevented via a relevant security solution.

3. *Identity Management:* assign a unique identity to enormous numbers of objects that accessing and communicating with each other in the distributed nature of IoT this makes a challenge. Domain Name Servers (DNS) are used to assign an identity to these devices. However, DNS is vulnerable to many attacks as DNS cache positioning and MIMA. Hence, efficient and lightweight identity management schemes are required.

4. *Security Structure:* to build a security structure with the combination of control and information is the main challenge as to keep the IoT will remain stable-persisting all the time with the applying of all the security mechanism together in each logical layer can also arise challenge to implement it with defense-in-depth.

5. *Trust and End-to-End Security:* in a dynamic and collaborative IoT environment it is a challenge to define trust in an efficient way which will establish secure communication between IoT objects and apply it to varied IoT applications. While applying encryption and authentication codes to a packet in order to achieved end-to-end security is not sufficient for the resource-constrained IoT and the internet.

6. *Authentication, Authorization, and Access Control:* multiple devices and services require to be elasticity connect the network at any time. Authenticating themselves via using default passwords during processing results in increasing the security vulnerabilities. Thus communication between multiple devices and services should be secure. Furthermore, restricting the manipulating

reading/writing to data via authorization and controlling access to different resources are equally important as authentication. Interoperability and backward compatibility among the communicated number of devices are the two key challenges to be addressed.

7. *Attack Resistant Security Solution:* due to software vulnerabilities, backdoor analysis, and IoT constraints, IoT devices are vulnerable to enervation attacks. Hence, the attack resistant, dynamic analysis of the application, and lightweight cryptography security solutions should be configured as well as a mitigation plan should be followed to protect against this attack.

8. *Requirements for Growing Applications*: the key management in the real large-scale sensor network, policies, and regulations related to the IoT are also a challenge in growing applications with the development of Wireless Sensor Network (WSN), distributed real-time control theory, and pervasive computing technology.

9. *Resource constraint:* applying security with constraint resources is a big challenge resulting in insufficient processing of security algorithms. Furthermore, storage constraint is a challenge for embedding security features as well as restricted battery volume is an effect on the quantity of computation executed in the embedded processor (Garg & Dave, 2019).

10. *Implementation of security algorithms:* No "correct" solution, for each application there is a separate security solution used and it is different from application to application. Moreover, due to the device capabilities, the implementation of complex cryptographic algorithms is quite impossible.

Figure 5. IoT attacks based layer

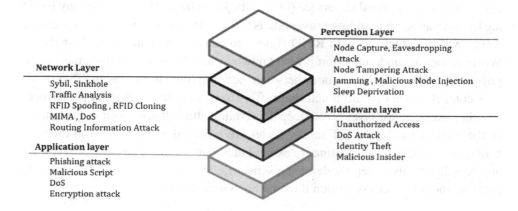

Security Threats and Major Attacks in IoT

IoT security is a field of protecting devices and networks on the Internet of things from the intruders. This section introduces the security threats with respect to each layer of the IoT architecture (Gulzar & Abbas, 2019). A summary diagram of several attacks in each layer is illustrated in figure 5.

Attack against Perception Layer

It is exposed to many threats at the node level due to its main functionality of sensing and digitizing the data. The attacker replaces the device software with a compromised one aiming to utilize sensors and manipulation the gathering sensed data from the physical and virtual objects. Common threats in this Layer are Node Capture Attacks is un unauthorized access aim to capturing and physically replacing the node or tampering data on Radio-frequency identification tags (RFID). This attack involves tag cloning where the attacker creates a compromised copy of the original tag hence the reader cannot distinguish between the real and the fake tag. Another attack is eavesdropping, it is an initial step for launching the other attacks where the attacker put malicious sensors close to the real sensors of the IoT devices, in order to acquire information from the device that communicating on unprotected wireless channels like the Internet. Furthermore, node tampering attack where the attacker attempts to damage the sensor of the node by either replacing the entire node or by replacing part of the node hardware. Also, the replacement can be done electronically to gain access and change the sensitive information of the node like shared cryptographic keys, affect the operation of the high-level communication layer or alter the routing tables if exist. Moreover, jamming as IoT used RFID for communication, a denial of service (DoS) attack can be implemented on any RFID tag by generating and sending noise signals through the radio signals. Thus, the sent signal will be interfered with RFID signals to cause communication obstruction. While malicious node injection is also known as MIMA in which the attacker can physically deploy a malicious node between the communicated nodes on IoT systems thus control of the operation and the traffic flow between the nods is performed. Another attack in this layer is the sleep deprivation attack that consumes the battery of the node. Usually, the IoT sensor nodes are powered by batteries and they are configured to be on sleep routines to expand their battery life. The sleep deprivation attack will stop the sleep mode of the sensor nodes and keep the nodes awake to increase the power consumption thus the node will shut down.

Attack against Network Layer

Most security threats affect the availability of resources due to the usage of the wireless communication links connection among IoT devices. This layer is responsible to transmit the sensed data hence the integrity and authentication attributes are vulnerable to security threats. This layer exposed to many threats that include Sybil Attack aims to compromise the system through creating redundancy of false information using a manipulated single node to present multiple identities. Another attack is a sinkhole attack where a compromised node advertises itself as the ideal node with the features of power, computation, and communication capabilities therefore neighboring nodes will select it as the optimal source node in the routing process of the data. Moreover, a traffic Analysis Attack is performed by sniffing the confidential information or any data flows confidential information because of their wireless characteristics. To perform the attack, attackers use sniffing tools like packet sniffer, port scanning, etc. Furthermore, RFID Spoofing attack where the attacker attempts to spoof the RFID signal to listen and record the data transferred from the RFID tag. Hence, the attacker sends his own data using the original tag ID, making it occurs as valid, thus, by pretending to be the original source, the attacker gains full access to the IoT system. While, RFID cloning, that done by copying the data from the node RFID tag and paste it onto another RFID tag. Although the two tags have the same data, this technique does not replicate the original ID tag so that it is difficult to differentiate the original tag and the compromised one. Another attack is MIMA in this the attacker is trying to interfere between the nodes, accessing confidential data, transgress the privacy of the nodes by observing, managing, and eavesdropping the communication between them. Additionally, Denial of Service (DoS) the attacker is trying to stop the service by flooding continuous traffic between the nodes making it unavailable to the legal entities. While routing information attack is done by spoofing and changing the routing information on the routing tables of the nodes (Deogirikar, 2017). This leads to complicating the network, creating loops, stopping traffic, sending wrong messages, and even segregating the IoT network. This attack is also known as the Blackhole attack and Hello attack.

Attack against Application Layer

It provides high-quality services requested by the users as healthcare, smart factory, etc. Hence software will be exploited to lunch the following threats like Phishing Attacks where the attacker gain access to the sensitive data by spoofing the authentication credentials of IoT user where that done usually by phishing web sites or phishing email. Additionally, the malicious script is one of the attacks that affect this layer due to the internet connection of IoT, the user who controls the gateway be fooled into running executable active-x scripts which might result in data theft or complete system shutdown. For example, modifying node-based applications via installing malicious rootkits. Likewise, trojan horses, worms, viruses, spyware, and aware where the system can be infected by malicious software resulting in many consequences like tampering data and obtaining confidential data or corrupts the IoT applications (Varshney, Sharma, Kaushik, & Bharat Bhushan, 2019). Moreover, DoS aiming to make the IoT application inaccessible which will affect the entire IoT network either by interruption of service or impacting all users that using the service via blocking the users to use the resources and give the attacker the full privilege to access the databases and the confidential data. For example, the un-ability to receive security patches for software bugs may result in terrible consequences. While encryption attack is mainly used to break the encryption scheme used in IoT system. One of these attacks is Side-channel Attacks. By using a specific method on the IoT encryption devices like power, timing and, Electromagnetic Analysis, the attacker can recapture the encryption key that used in the communication to decrypt the data (Gulzar & Abbas, 2019).

Attack against Middleware Layer

Gathering and transmitting data from sensor objects or end users are the main functionality of IoT middleware. The transmission occurs via different technologies of wireless communication. This wireless communication is considered more secure due to several encryption methods. However, the attack on this layer may take place in the following ways. Unauthorized Access is illegal to access through applications interfaces to the related services of IoT can cause damage to the system or deleting the existing data. Furthermore, DoS Attack in this layer aiming to create high levels of input traffic and congestion of channels results in the exhaustion of IoT resources using hello flood attacks and desynchronization attacks. While identity theft aims to obtain sensitive credential and authentication information as the password of IoT devices aiming to break the privacy and confidentiality of personal information. Finally, the malicious insider is an internally tampers and altering of data on purpose (Dazine et al., 2018).

Attack against Business Layer

One of the raised issues after deploying IoT devices to a network is the supervising of the nodes. Thus, creating a remotely signing device configuration and operational information becomes a challenge. Moreover, managing security information is a new problem that might split the trust relationship between network and service platform.

Analysis of IoT Security Solutions

Security mechanisms are required in each IoT layer to maintain confidentiality, authentication, and integrity or ensure secure transmission and routing of the data. *Encryption mechanism* is used to prevent data from been altered and disclosure when it is interrupted by attackers. The way of encryption processed either node to node which provides cipher text conversion on each node, or through end-to-end encryption that is performed in the application layer. Furthermore, *Confidentiality measurement* ensures that the sensor prevents the neighboring end devices to access the collected data by the unauthorized reader using an RFID electronic tag. Moreover, the *Authentication mechanism is* used to prevent Dos attacks when sensor nodes authenticate themselves initially. For example, OpenID is a standardized framework that its target is authentication based as it offers a method for a site to redirect the users somewhere else and return back with a certifiable declaration (Mahmoud, Yousuf, Aloul, & Zualkernan, 2015). While *Access Control measurement* is a way of proving the identity of both communication parties using Public Key Infrastructure to achieve strong authentication. It also prevents illegal access via effectively limit, control, and blocking access for IoT objects. For effective access control, the certification technology must be ensured. Figure 6 presents the categories of current mechanisms used to ensure IoT security into four grouping of mechanisms: Access Control and Privacy Protection, IoT Constraint Resources, Intrusion and Traffic Deduction, and Attacks-based Solution.

Figure 6. Classfication of IoT security mechanisms

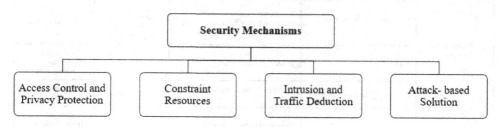

Table 1 summarizes the most recently proposed mechanisms. It is composed of five columns used to show: the Mechanism Category (Mechanism Category), the name of the proposed algorithm (The Proposed Mechanism), the aim of the mechanism (Aim), type of experimentations (Experimentation), and the related works taken from (Reference).

Table 1. Recent mechanisms used to ensure IoT security

Mechanism Category	The Proposed Mechanism	Aim	Experimental	Reference
Access Control and Privacy Protection	Identity Management Framework	Solves sensing authentication issue between IoT devices and Cloud	-	(Horrow, 2012)
	Secure Signature-Based Authenticated Key Establishment Scheme	Address authentication issue in IoT environment	NS2 simulator	(Challa et al., 2017)
	MORT algorithm and MBLP algorithm	Achieve the maximum total delivery for SMMS that insure the integrity	Waxman model	(Shi & Wang, 2018)
	A Trust-based Resilient Routing Mechanism	To manage the reputation of each node and support trust development in an IoT network	MATLAB	(Khan, Ullrich, & Herrmann, 2020)
	Embedding the MRC and SC Schemes into Trust Management Algorithm	To enhance the efficiency and solve the security problem of application layer	NS-3, and some Matlab@ codes	(Chen, 2017)
	Real-time intrusion detection and strong access control	To provide the security services of authentication, confidentiality, integrity, and availability at the system level	Cryptograph system and BLAKE 2	(Rathore et al., 2017)
	A hybrid CCC-CR-AODV	To discover and control data transmission within the CR	NS-2.31	(Anamalamudi, Sangi, Alkatheiri, & Ahmed, 2018)
	A user-centric approach	Towards a user privacy preservation system	-	(Tamani & Ghamri-Doudane, 2016)
Constraint Resources	A reputation model	To address the challenge of low memory and low energy constraints	TOSSIM simulator	(Sedjelmaci, Senouci, Taleb, & Saclay, 2017)
	CS optimization	To address the need for security and complexity of an encryption stage in every sensor node for a limited resource device	-	(Mangia, Pareschi, Rovatti, & Setti, 2017)
	Lightweight Enhanced-DLP	To obtain lower computational costs for the selection of a dummy location and it can resist side information attacks	Python 3.5 language	(Du, Cai, Zhang, Liu, & Jiang, 2019)
	Lightweight authentication protocol	To get secure access to confidential information from any private cloud server of the distributed system	BAN logic, AVSIPA tool, and informal cryptanalysis	(Amin, Kumar, Biswas, Iqbal, & Chang, 2018)
	E-LDAT	To identify DDoS attacks	EEM	(Bhuyan, Bhattacharyya, & Kalita, 2016)
	Lightweight biometric scheme	To enable secure access to the services	AVISPA tool	(Dhillon & Kalra, 2017)
	SNAuth	Aims to solve the issue of absent of the central control and management in PAC	PACNET	(NHU-NGOC DAO, YONGHUN KIM, SEOHYEON JEONG, MINHO PARK, 2017)
	LKA	To enhance the energy consumption and network lifetime of the IP-enabled WSN	NS-2	(Lavanya & Natarajan, 2017)
	IMLADS	Tor effective security monitoring of the IoT environment	-	(Qin, Wang, Chen, Qin, & Wang, 2019)

continues on following page

Table 1. Continued

Mechanism Category	The Proposed Mechanism	Aim	Experimental	Reference
Intrusion and Traffic Deduction	Automated evaluator of security analysis	To increase the IoT security level and mitigating the impact of attacks	-	(Ge, Hong, Guttmann, & Kim, 2020)
	HBST	To illustrate the statistical characteristics of sensory data in the aggregation-based communication mode	MICAz mote	(L. Yang, Ding, Wu, & Wang, 2017)
	Anomaly-based Intrusion Detection	To identifying anomalous sensor events using provenance graphs to intrusion detection of IoT devices	-	(Nwafor, Campbell, & Bloom, 2017)
	SFC and PCA algorithms	To improve the effectiveness and accuracy of the intrusion detection method	-	(L. Liu, Xu, Zhang, & Wu, 2018)
	A uniform Intrusion Detection System	Comparing the real-time action flows of the transmitting packets with the standard libraries	RADIUS	(Fu, Yan, Cao, Koné, & Cao, 2017)
	HIDS	used to settling the multi-class classification issue	-	(Saleh, Talaat, & Labib, 2017)
	COLIDE	To achieve efficient intrusion detection	Contiki and Cooja simulating	(Arshad, Azad, & Abdellatif, 2018)
	TDTC	to detect malicious activities U2R and R2L attacks	-	(Pajouh, Javidan, Khaymi, Dehghantanha, & Raymond, 2016)
	CBSigIDS	incrementally build a trusted signature database. Without the need of a trusted intermediary	CIDN environment	(Li, Tug, Meng, & Wang, 2019)
	An intrusion detection model	To generate an optimal network structure	MATLAB R2016a	(Y. Zhang, Li, & Wang, 2019)
	HADL	To detect malicious node packet dropping	Castalia 3.2	(Yahyaoui, Abdellatif, & Attia, 2019)
Attacks-based Solution	Detection System	To detect the Wormhole attack	Contiki OS and Cooja simulator	(Pontevedra & Sonavane, 2019)
	Intrusion detection systems	To detect and prevent the denial-of-service (DoS)	NS2	(Yazdankhah & Honarvar, 2017)
	S-LOT and M-SLOT	To solve the issue of new location spoofing attacks	Monte Carlo simulation	(P. Zhang, Nagarajan, & Nevat, 2017)
	SecRPL	To mitigate (DAO) attack	Contiki3.0	(Ghaleb et al., 2019)
	Masked AES Implementation	To prevent the stored secret key leaking from the substitution-box	-	(Yu & Köse, 2017)
	FourQ	Against side-channel attacks	ARM Cortex-M4	(Z. Liu, Longa, & Pereira, 2020)
	A hybrid countermeasure	To prevent link spoofing attacks in SDIoT controller	Mininet emulator tool	(Nguyen & Yoo, 2017)
	CDCA	Against volatile Jamming attacks	Cooja simulator	(Ayotunde, Othman, Abaker, Hashem, & Yaqoob, 2018)
	AAA	To detect the stealthy collision attack	OMNeT++	(Cs, Jung, & Min, 2017)
	GINI	To mitigate and detect Sybil Attack in RPL-Based IoT	OM-NeT++	(Pu, 2020)

Mechanisms on Access Control and Privacy Protection

S. Horrow et al. have proposed an identity management framework for cloud-based IoT that contains two main modules namely, Identity Manager and Service Manager. Identity manager modules are used to authenticate data and processes to the cloud while the service manager is used as an authorization module among sensor information and services. This framework solves the sensing authentication issue between the cloud and IoT devices. However, no protocols are implemented in the proposed architecture (Horrow, 2012).

S. Challa et al. have provided a new key Establishment scheme which is signature-based and authentication. This scheme is widely used Burrows-Abadi-Needham logic (BAN) for mutual authentication between a user and an accessed sensing device and broadly accepted Automated Validation of Internet Security Protocols and Applications (AVISPA) tool for the formal security verification. The result of testing reveals the practicability of the scheme as it can be safeguarded from different pupolar attacks by adversaries. Moreover, it is can be applied in different applications in IoT environment as it provides high security and efficient computational and communication costs (Challa et al., 2017).

L. Shi et al. have proposed two algorithms in order to achieve the maximum total delivery for multiple multicasts with multiple streams (SMMS) problem which refers to secure weighted throughput (SWT) in IoT using linear network coding (LNC). In a case of the sensor is connected with a fixed network device, a MORT algorithm is proposed to optimally solve the linear programming. While in the case of the sensor of each multicast can be selected from a set of nodes a near-optimal MBLP algorithm based on LP relaxation is proposed to solve the integer linear programming. The performance of the MORT algorithm is efficient when the network size is large and close to the upper bound while MBLP algorithm is effective when the available source node-set size is large and far away from the lower bound (Shi & Wang, 2018).

Z. A. Khan et al. have proposed a novel network-level framework of a trust-based approach for managing the reputation of each node and support trust development in an IoT network. This framework is based on the Routing Protocol for Low power and Lossy Networks (RPL). It evaluates the interaction with both positive as well as negative past experiences between nodes as packets are routed throughout the IoT network. Based on a computation that identify the dependence of a node on the information of its neighbor, a central node develops a rating for every single node of the network by merging the collected trust values for each node using Jøsang's Subjective Logic(Systems & Centre, 2001). Therefore, This will lead to detecting node ratings that placed below a pre-identified threshold and then detect nodes with doubtful attitude and attribute (Khan et al., 2020).

J. I. Chen has proposed a fusion diversity scheme that implements the Maximum Ratio Combining (MRC) and Selection Combining (SC) schemes with Trust Management (TM) security algorithm in order to enhance the efficiency as well as resolve the security issues related to layer of the application. With MRC stage, weighted of specified extracted parameters by one estimation value from each IoT layer and combined them with the control information at the same time. In addition, the decision-making phase will establish the outcome of QoS, according to the trust level acquired at the MRC output. The outcomes of some experimentations implemented with physical evaluation illustrate that the trust level could more dependability when the MRC scheme is integrated with the TM. Nevertheless, there is a need to find a correlation element between each two situations to come up with the final conclusion and decision for the control of information in IoT (Chen, 2017).

M. M. Rathore et al. have presented an effective access control and a real-time intrusion detection at Intelligent City Building (ICB). In addition, the real-time and safeguarded communication protocol guarantees no probability of a successful attack on data when transforming from Remote Smart System (RSS)/user to the ICB. This developed system provides Confidentiality, Availability, and Integrity (CIA) which are the security services of authentication at the system level. Evaluation of the system is performed to examine its trustworthiness in regard to both throughput and computation cost. Moreover, this system was evaluated and analysed against the current systems and the findings revealed that Rathore's system has more efficiency, more security and also has the capability to work in a real-time mode in high-speed Smart City environment (Rathore et al., 2017).

S. Anamalamudi et al. have developed a hybrid Control Channel-based Cognitive (CCC) Ad-hoc On-Demand Vector (AODV) routing protocol with directional antennas to discover and control data transmission within the Cognitive Radio Networks (CR) referred as CCC-CR-AODV. The CR-AODV routing protocol is utilized to transfer the IoT constrained data from IoT border node to CR destination that can act as entry to another IoT network. The Experimental findings illustrated that this approach is efficient when it compared to traditional Infrastructure based WS as it has decreased both the node and consumed energy in the network which leads to enhanced the system throughput (Anamalamudi et al., 2018).

N. Tamani et al . have designed a user-centric method for access control and users' privacy protection and in IoT environment. This approach involve on two principal blocks which are a habit-based approach for an anomaly-based intrusion detection system, and a semantic-based firewall for access control and communication security. The implantation is done, however, the accuracy and effectiveness of the testing should be hold in the dataset that are different adequate to establish real-world use-cases. Hence, KDD Cup, DARPA, and UNIXDS dataset are too ancient and cannot face new cybersecurity landscapes. This is one of the drawbacks of these datasets (Tamani & Ghamri-Doudane, 2016).

Mechanisms on Constraint Resources

H. Sedjelmaci et al. have come up with a reputation model related to a game-theoretic technique combining signature-based detection and lightweight anomaly-detection techniques used to address the challenge of low powered IoT devices that have constraints of energy and memory. Moreover, the anomaly detection technique works only if a new attack's signature is inticipated to happned by a malicious device. Hence, there is a balance between the consumption of energy, detection and rates of false-positive is established. This technique monitors and compares Signal Strength Intensity (SSI) and Packets Dropping Rate (PDR) if level of SSI and PDR surpass some pre-identified limits, the monitored node is authorized as an attacker regarding the signature-based detection. This technique proves that it has sufficient security for these high SSI attacks such as hello flood, wormhole, black hole, Sybil, sinkhole, spoofed, etc. However, false-negative may increase due to the varying of thresholds over time. Thus, updating these thresholds is required and develop the rule and analysis of every new attack's approach and pattern hence authors purpose a dynamic game for the anomaly detection technique (Sedjelmaci et al., 2017).

M. Mangia et al. have proposed Compressed Sensing (CS) optimization to address the need of security and complexity of an encryption stage in every sensor node for a limited resource device to generate low-cost compression and low-cost encryption resulting in reducing the volume of data to transfer and put them computationally protected. To increase compression performance by rakeness based design to ciphertext-only and known-plaintext attacks, an analyzing model is designed to expose the vulnerability of CS stages that are optimized. Rakeness-based CS presents a significant strength to classical attacks (Mangia et al., 2017).

Y. Du et al. have proposed a novel lightweight Enhanced Dummy-based Location Privacy-preserving (Enhanced-DLP). This Techinque that enhances from previous state-of-the-art schemes. Enhanced-DLP is used to address resource-constrained IoT devices challenges as it obtains reduced computational costs for the choice of a dummy location and it can also resist side information attacks. It involve with an enhanced greedy technique to better choose dummy locations to create a k-anonymous(Sweeney, 2002) set. Comparing Enhanced-DLP with existing DLP schemes, the generation time of the dummy location is reduced by 68.14%, and the likelihood of disclosing the real position of the users is decreased by 33.63% with similar attack situation. However, more research is required to solve the side information where the location data of the users cannot be completely concealed, and the adaption of furthermore attack schemes (Du et al., 2019).

R. Amin et al. have developed a lightweight authentication protocol for IoT-enabled devices in a distributed cloud computing environment. This technique uses to obtain secure access to restricted data from any private cloud server of the distributed system. Using BAN logic, AVSIPA tool and informal cryptanalysis the outcomes ensure security safety of the protocol and proof the mutual authentication. Furthermore, enhance other proposed work in term of communication cost, storage, as well as computation (Amin et al., 2018).

M. H. Bhuyan et al. have presented a lightweight extended-entropy metric (EEM-based) Distributed Denial of Service (DDoS) attack detection and Internet Protocol (IP) traceback system called E-LDAT with packet extreme computation on the sampled network traffic compare to time. Its target is to define DDos attacks through analyzing the metric difference between valid traffic and attack traffic. Also, IP traceback is created though applying the metric level for an attack sample that is discovered by the detection approach. The E-LDAT system is experimenting though numerous DDoS datasets from real-world and the evaluated results prove that this techinque has the ability to identify DDoS attacks in efficient and consistant way. In the other hand, the model of IP traceback is analyzed, as well, through NetFlow data in near real-time. It has been found that it work greatly, especially in huge-scale attack networks by zombies. However, this schema needs to be enhanced to towards the detection of newly introduced coremelt, crossfire, as well as distributed amplification attacks (Bhuyan et al., 2016).

P. K. Dhillon et al. have presented a lightweight biometric-based remote user authentication and key agreement scheme as multi-factor-based authentication to ensure security of access to the services. In this schema, lightweight hash and XOR operations are used. This method required a user first to register via an employed gateway node-based architecture for IoT environment, then the user will be able to immediately link to the needed sensor node by utilizing a smart device to have access to any service. While the AVISPA tool used to perform formal verification of this method that ensure its security in the presence of a possible intruder. However, the requirements of memory of the developed protocol are not found them out (Dhillon & Kalra, 2017).

S. C. Nhu-Ngoc Dao et al. have proposed a Social Networking-based Authentication (SNAuth) closely tied to the Peer-Aware Communication (PAC) to support authentication and key agreement procedures between lightweight IoT-enabled PAC device in a PAC network. Aims to address the problems of absence of the central control and management in PAC network where each PAC device (PD) act as an equal role in regard of communication. The analysis of security and performance measurement present that it defeated other existing applicants for PACNET security algorithms. Furthermore, it provides multiple layers of security. It also provide convenience and flexibility to the users with suitable consumption (NHU-NGOC DAO, YONGHUN KIM, SEOHYEON JEONG, MINHO PARK, 2017).

M. Lavanya et al. have proposed a lightweight key agreement (LKA) from the modified of the IKEv2. This algorithm is utilized to enhance the consumption of energy as well as network lifetime of the IP-enabled wireless sensor networks (WSN). It is a certificate-free implementation where elliptic curve digital signatures are used for authentication optionally and the hash value calculated for both authentication and public key verification. The processing of the LKA algorithm is analyzed in terms of, network lifetime as well as computation and communication (Lavanya & Natarajan, 2017).

T. Qin et al have developed an Intelligent Maintenance and Lightweight Anomaly Detection System (IMLADS) used as effective security monitoring of the IoT environment. This development includes designing a mobile agent for monitoring the security which enhances system stability and scalability and decreases the computational complexity. Furthermore, constructing a lightweight anomaly detection method with a little number of local processing resources that perform anomaly mining. Moreover, PCA is employed for node level security monitoring to achieve data dimensionality reduction as well as to mine the anomalies clustering and sliding time window model are used. Likewise, for system-level security monitoring the sketch method is used to calculate the statistical features instantly. While based on the anomaly mining results the system performs suitable response policies for controlling abnormal behavior and system maintenance. The findings confirm the effectiveness of these methods (Qin et al., 2019).

Mechanisms for Intrusion and Traffic Deduction

M. Ge et al. have proposed an automated evaluator for analysis of security in the IoT as a graphical security framework extended from on the Hierarchical Attack Representation Model (HARM). The aim of this evaluator is to increase the IoT security level and minimizing the effect of attacks. Using this framework, the authors able to capture all attack paths that is possible to occurred in the IoT, analyze the security degree by applying security factors, and measure the efficiency of defense strategy as attackers' actions are captured. However, heterogeneity, mobility, and verifying the correctness of the models are the limitations of this framework need to be resolved (Ge et al., 2020).

L. Yang et al. have adopted Hierarchical Bayesian Spatial-Temporal (HBST) technology to illustrate the statistical characteristics of sensory data in the aggregation-based communication mode. Furthermore, the authors proposed an anomaly detection based to overcome the False Data Iinjection (FDI) attack using state forecasting techniques that discover false aggregated data and sequential hypothesis testing to identify the nodes that are doubtful to inject false data. FDI deduction schema using the game-theoretic analysis to limit the attacker gain by the defenders even when worst-case exits and obtain the ideal strategies for adversaries and defenders. This model had been tested in terms of overhead parameters, efficiency, effectiveness, and the findings indicated that it has great rate of detection with low rate of false-positive (L. Yang et al., 2017).

E. Nwafor et al. have presented a method to identify anomalous sensor events using provenance graphs to intrusion detection of IoT devices. This approach is based on a comparison of observed source graphs and trends where origin graphs are created from an application's normal implemention to consider this provenance graph as either anomalous or benign. This approach has been evaluated and test the effectiveness via an offline set of data from a simulation of a climate control system. However, this approach does not cover real-time detection as well as identifying the false and true positive rates of this method is missing (Nwafor et al., 2017).

L. Liu et al. have presented the Principal Component Analysis (PCA) algorithm and a Suppressed Fuzzy Clustering (SFC) algorithm to improve the effectiveness and accuracy of intrusion detection method IoT. This method involve categorizing acquired data to either high-risk data and low-risk data. This is implement when the data is idenitify at either low frequency or high frequency depending on the data. The simulation experiment expresses better adaptability of these algorithms that other traditional methods like the Bayesian algorithm and Neural network algorithm. Nevertheless, these technologies are incomplete and inperfect because of its shortcomings such as inadequate efficiency in detection, high rates of wrong alarm and sometimes providing late alarms(L. Liu et al., 2018).

Y. Fu et al. have presented a uniform Intrusion Detection System (IDS) that is used in huge diverse IoT networks that are involving in an automata model. The idea behind this scheme is matching and analysing the real-time action flows of the transmitting packets with the standard libraries. This IDS can spot and reveal varouis kinds of security attacks such as false-attack, jam attack, and reply-attack that is automatically performed. Using RADIUS application this IDS system is verified and examine. However, this method can be enhanced to make the Normal Action Library to improve its efficiency as well as its accuracy(Fu et al., 2017).

A. I. Saleh et al. have designed a Hybrid IDS (HIDS) used to settle the multi-class classification issue. This approach is based on the data dimensionality reduction called a Naïve Base feature selection (NBFS) method. Furthermore, HIDS is suffering from outlier rejection issue which results in a high rate of misclassification. HIDS aims to maximize the intrusion detection rate and minimize the time of training. This mothed has three main contributions, which are: data dimensionality reduction using NBFS, Optimized Support Vector Machines (OSVM) used for outlier rejection, and Prioritized K-Nearest Neighbors (PKNN) used for detecting input attacks. These three algorithms have a great rates of detection especifically in case of rare attacks while PKNN is able to solve a multi-label classification problem. Experimental results verified the efficacy of HIDS via achieving maximum detection rates with minimal consequences (Saleh et al., 2017).

J. Arshad et al. have presented a framework for intrusion detection called COLIDE that integrate both of network-based detection and host in order to get appropriate and accurate intrusion recognition for IoT by applying 6LoWPAN. This approach controls collaboration of border nodes and sensors of resource-constrained. It is also utilized get appropriate and fast indentifications of intruders. Implementation had done using Contiki OS while the experimentation evaluating done via Contiki and Cooja simulating. Experimental results illustrate that COLIDE framework has great efficiency compared to the processing overheads as well as the consumed energy. However, no security evaluation such as detection speed and accurateness has been done on the proposed framework (Arshad et al., 2018).

H. H. Pajouh et al. has developed a unique technique of intrusion detection that involve Two-layer Dimension Reduction and Two-tier Classification (TDTC) model. This model aims to spot malicious and harmful actions such as Remote to Local (R2L) attacks and User to Root (U2R) attacks. To address high dimensionality issue authors had utilizing Principal Component Analysis (PCA) as well as Linear Discriminant Analysis (LDA) as unsupervised and supervised dimension reduction techniques, respectively. While identifying irregular behaviors Naïve Bayes and Certainty Factor are utilized. The experiment results using Network Security Laboratory and Knowledge Discovery in Databases (NSL-KDD) dataset indicate this model does better than other earlier approaches that are proposed to identify R2L and U2R attacks (Pajouh et al., 2016).

W. Li et al. have adopted blockchain technology to establish a strucure of collaborative blockchain signature-based IDSs referred to as CBSigIDS, which incrementally builds a trusted signature database. Without the need for a trusted intermediary, this framework uses a confirming method in distributed strucure. CBSigIDS had been evaluated in a real-time environment and simulated and the result showed the quality and efectiveness of signature-based detection under attack situations by distributing the signatures in a verifiable method (Li et al., 2019).

Y. Zhang et al. presented a technique of intrusion detection that depend on an enhanced genetic algorithm (GA) combined with a deep belief network (DBN). Where GA process several iterations to generate an ideal structure of network following by DBN that utilzes a produced ideal structure of network. The attacks then is categorized with an intrusion detection model. Hence, the issue of choosing a suitable neural network structure is resolved via deep learning techinques for intrusion recognition. The experimental result expresses that this mothed has ability to lessen the network structure complication and enhance classification generalization and accurateness for this method (Y. Zhang et al., 2019).

A. Yahyaoui et al. have proposed Hierarchical Anomaly Detection and Localization (HADL). This approach combined the deep learning technique for gateway intrusion detection and Support Vector Machines (SVM) for WSN intrusion detection. This new methodology permits identifying a trade-off among intrusion detection efficiency and resource overhead for WSN and gateway security. It able to detect malicious node packet dropping with high rates as well as when dropping with low rates using historical data. Moreover, it able to detect most critical IP attacks that might threaten the gateway using deep learning techniques. However, this method needs to be more simplify HADL for other types of security issue and attacks against IoT networks and WSN(Yahyaoui et al., 2019).

Attacks-Based Solution

V. Pontevedra et al. have implemented a Wormhole attack detection System using Contiki OS and Cooja simulator specifically for IoT environment. This attack occurs in 6LoWPAN layer of RPL network layer. This approach creates a Received Signal Strength Indicator (RSSI)for both the attack and the attacker node. The Experimental result illustrated that 90% of successful deduction rates with a network size of N=24. However, the positive deduction rate needs to be improved to deduct wormhole in a higher number of nodes (Pontevedra & Sonavane, 2019).

E. Yazdankhah et al. have proposed intrusion detection systems to detect and prevent the Denial of Service (DoS) attack based on game theory for a network of the IoT. Due to the expansion of IoT environment, unappropriate techinque of counteractions and weaknesses in the old intrusion detection systems. Thus, Smart solutions with the capability of speediness and effectiveness are required to handle the challenges of IoT. This method was implanted on NS2 simulator and evaluated with operational throughput, consumed energy and also latency. The experimental result shows differences between this method and other approaches in various ways like consumed energy (25-30%), operational throughput (10-15%) and better latency. This findings verify that this method is smart and has better performance (Yazdankhah & Honarvar, 2017).

P. Zhang et al. have developed a Secure Location of Things (SLOT) algorithm extend from state-of-the-art TW-TOA localization algorithms to address the issue of new location spoofing attacks that exist due to the rise of Geo-spatial location-based applications in (IoT). The location estimation problem has formulated using the audibility information as a stochastic censoring model and derives the Maximum Likelihood Estimator (MLE) for the tag's location thought two novels developed algorithms which are the Mixture (M-SLOT) model and Difference-Time-of-Arrival

(D-SLOT) model. The simulations result showed that the approach is effective over current state-of-the-art algorithms and is resistant to spoofing attacks. Furthermore, under the proposed framework the spatial Cram´er-Rao lower Bound of the source location estimate is obtained (P. Zhang et al., 2017).

B. Ghaleb et al. have proposed a mechanism named SecRPL to mitigate Destination Advertisement Object (DAO) attacks. DAO attack where malicious insider node exploited control messages between child nodes and their parents and transef false DAOs to its parents regularly then parents node move the false data streight to the root node. For this reason, this attack doesn't only impact the local scope but it can extend to the edge of the network. Furthermore, this type of attack could be set even without compromising security keys from genuine nodes. Moreover, DAOs harm the power consumption and reliability of the network. There are two options to applied restriction in this attack. The first option is to control all number of moved DAOs irrespectivete of the source node while the second option is to control the number of moved DAO based on the destination. Due to the effecting negatively of restricting some DAOs that derive from non-attacker nodes, the second approach is used when every parent node links a counter with each child node in its sub-DODAG. When it surpasses a the pre-defined limit, the parent rejects any DAO message. To enhance the quality of this approach the counter is retuned back to every two consecutive DIOs (Ghaleb et al., 2019).

W. Yu et al. have proposed a theory that is against Correlation Power Analysis CPA attacks to avoid the leaking of the stored secret key from the substitution-box. Both Wave Dynamic Differential Logic (WDDL)-based XOR gates and A false key helped AES method is used like a countermeasure. To decrease the correlation between the dynamic consumption of power and the real key, there have to be a false round key that added in every encryption round. In the other hand, to remove the mask at the final stage of the encryption process, the WDDL-based XOR gates are utilized in the reconstruction block. An attacker have to implement a CPA attack in two independent phases where the encryption process is consumed power is allied to the false key. Thus, MTD value becomes over 1.5×108 (Yu & Köse, 2017).

Z. Liu et al. have implemented FourQ on embedded devices with incorporating great and reliable countermeasures against side-channel attacks that target applications that consider a low-power like protocols for IoT. It deals with ECC and DH asymmetric key algorithms which offer effeciency in energy, adequate security and great speed. This approach works in three steps. First, set up a new speed record for ECC and DH at 128-bit security level with operations targeting 8-bit, 16-bit, and 32-bit microcontrollers. Then, getting benefits of FourQ's rich arithmetic countermeasures against side-channel attack is engineered. Finally, the experimental evaluation of this approach on an ARM Cortex-M4 illustrated that there was no leakage was found from over 10 million traces(Z. Liu et al., 2020).

T. Nguyen et al. have have proposed a hybrid countermeasure to prevent link spoofing attacks in a software-defined SDIoT controller using two schemes. Through performing the weakness analysis in the link service is found that the link service is vulnerable to the link spoofing attacks including Link Layer Discovery Protocol latency (LLDP) spoofing and LLDP Forwarding attacks. To guarantee the integrity of the LLDP packets the first schema is used which relies on adding the semi-dynamic signature of the controller to LLDP packets while the second scheme detects and blocks fake links by comparing the LLDP s2s time to a predefined threshold. The experiment result showed this framework is feasible and efficient and able to prevent all link spoofing attacks in a real-time environment (Nguyen & Yoo, 2017).

Ayotunde et al. have developed a different Countermeasure Detection and Consistency Algorithm (CDCA) against volatile Jamming attacks on IoT networks. CDCA utilized the variation of the limit value to identify and solve the attack. Additionally, it utilized the power of channel signal to verify the constancy of the packet and defining if the data transmission value does not match with pre-defined limit value. To determine if an attack has happened in the network periodically, the node that tranfers the limit value verified and matched with the present value after data transmission. The performance and evaluation of CDCA are done via using a Cooja simulator with varying parameters. The simulation results revealed this approach has a better performance than other contemporary methods. For example, better network throughput, better traffic delay, great consumped energy are all advantages of CDCA. The main value of CDCA is can work smoothly in case of an expansion in the number of jamming nodes in the network (Ayotunde et al., 2018).

D. Cs et al. have proposed the Adaptive Acknowledgment based Approach (AAA) to reveal the stealthy collision attack of several malicious and harmful nodes in energy harvesting motivated networks. A collision packet attack occurs when two malicious nodes synchronize their packet transmissions at the same time at a genuine node. In the AAA approach, the source node forwarding a data packet and then pauses as it waits for an obvious recogintion from the lower node, then and identifies the stealthy collision attack in a network. For performance assessment and analysis, OMNeT++ was used and the result reveals that AAA performs better in areas like ratio of packet delivery, latency of detection, and rate of detection than to MCC approach (Cs et al., 2017).

C. Pu has proposed a countermeasure to mitigate and detect Sybil Attack in RPL-Based IoT called a Gini Indexbased (GINI). GINI approach is proposed involve analysing the operations and possible vulnerabilities of RPL. The experimental simulation findings indicate that GINI efficiently can accurately spot and diminish Sybil attacks. Furthermore, it can improve implementation with better consumed energy, better latency of detection, and better rate of detection. However, this mechanism has not been tested yet in the real-time network as time radio propagation cannot clearly be seized by simulation (Pu, 2020).

FUTURE DIRECTION AND IMPROVEMENT SUGGESTION OF IOT

Although researches proposed several defense techniques, algorithms, and solution models to fill in the security gaps as expressed in the previous section. However, because of the prompt development and convergence of Internet information and processes that generate terabytes of data for everyday makes these solutions obsolete. Thus, realizing the need for enhanced problem-solving strategies are essential to be able to figure out the relevant security issue to this growth of IoT. Hence, three primary leading technologies have emerged which consider to be Intelligent solutions and future direction for IoT security issues like Machine Learning (ML), Blockchain, and Artificial Intelligent (AI). Recent studies have proved the incorporation of these technologies with IoT system are capable to address the IoT security issues (Patnaik, 2020).

ML-based IoT is an intelligent computational method of data exploration and providing performance optimization criteria to learn about regular and irregular performance according to the way of interaction of IoT components and devices as well as offers embedded intelligence in the IoT devices. ML investigation of input data to IoT system in the early stages allowing to identify basic trends of interaction and identifying suspicious and harmful behavior. Furthermore, smartly forecast the coming and unidentified threats though analying and reording current and previous attacks. Therefore, enabling ML methods in IoT systems to increase the security as well as effeciency of the systems. Several of ML methods have been used for securing IoT system namely Bayesian algorithms, Random Forest (RF), Decision Trees (DT), ensemble learning, K-Nearest Neighbor (KNN), k-means clustering, Association Rule (AR) algorithms, Support Vector Machines (SVM), and Principal Component Analysis (PCA). These Methods are enhanced based IoT authentication, secure offloading, malware detection schemes, and access control to safeguard the privacy of data that in turn will lead to safeguarding IoT. However, many constrains should be taken into consideration and resolve before developing the ML-based security methods in certain IoT systems (Al-garadi, Mohamed, Al-ali, Du, & Guizani, 2020).

Another intelligence technology utilized to secure IoT security is Blockchain. It is a decentralized storage system that records all transactions that rely on peer-to-peer network architecture regularly in an encrypted technique, to protect it from cybercriminals as it improves the ability of automatic response to a security incident.

In the blockchain, each IoT data operation is recorded as a transaction. Therefore, any unapproved actions that is not recorded as IoT data would be discovered. Furthermore, the identity credential for an IoT device as a transaction record help to retrieve later when the device is being used. Moreover, A blockchain also enables secure messaging exchanges among IoT devices as the message is to be treated like financial transactions in a Bitcoin network. Several requirements related to regulatoion and compliances of IoT systems are maintained via blockchain capabilities as a duly decentralized and trusted ledger, for example, Blockchain used to preserve data integrity and privacy as it provides access control rights and different policies and prevents unauthorized access and all of the nodes is having the same exact copy of records. Furthermore, it prevents abnormal behavior and ensures trusted accountability as every action is required to be saved in the blockchain network. Moreover, fault tolerance decentralized facility as blockchain is considered to be a point-to-point decentralizing network and avoided the single point of failure. In addition, trusted data origin as a one of kind ID is allocated to every IoT device where there will combining of the data extracted from such device with its specific ID. When the hash on the data is accounted, the data will be shared to the all network. No risk of the third party in blockchain technology where each operates without the intermediary. Blockchain allows sharing information of IoT network and prevents the illegal use of personal data. However, the implementation of blockchain in IoT strucure is a resource-constrained, and blockchain technology uses cryptography significantly. Hence, lightweight cryptographic algorithms are required for the effective development of blockchain-based security solutions.

While Artificial Intelligence (AI) is the ability of a machine to learn, analyze, and make a decision. AI-based IoT emerges when intelligence algorithms are required to collect and mined the volume of the explosive growth of data generated from IoT devices. AI techniques provide intelligent approaches for the IoT paradigm optimization, reliability, safety and risk management, real-time monitoring, succession planning, and improvements. The integration of IoT and AI improves the prediction analysis, enhance operational efficiency, and increase the accuracy rate. AI techniques categories are Machine Learning, Metaheuristic, Fuzzy Model, and Probabilistic Model. Swarm Intelligence (SI) is one of the Population-based methods under the Metaheuristic category which is currently widely been used (Osifeko & Hancke, 2020). In the following two sections, SI and SI based IoT will be studied in detail as one of the recommended intelligence solutions.

CONCLUSION

In the last few years, the emerging domain for IoT has been fascinating the significant attention and will continue for the years to come. Despite rapid evolution, this environment still facing new challenges and difficulties. The security and privacy implications of such development must be prudently considered to the promising technology. The protection of information and privacy of users has been identified as one of a key challenge in the IoT. To lessen the security issues of IoT, some technologies have been integrated with IoT and blockchain is one of these technologies due to its organized data structure which improves the security level. In this paper, a summarized a full view of IoT. Furthermore, a reviewed of different IoT security requirements and summarization of several challenges were given. Finally, some of countermeasures are explained. This research on the IoT will remain hot issue and lot of difficult challenges are waiting for researchers to handle. Thus, three primary leading technologies ML, Blockchain, and AI are ssuggested as Intelligent solutions and future direction for IoT security issues.

REFERENCES

Ahmad, M., & Salah, K. (2018). IoT security : Review, blockchain solutions, and open challenges. *Future Generation Computer Systems*, *82*, 395–411. doi:10.1016/j. future.2017.11.022

Al-garadi, M. A., Mohamed, A., Al-ali, A., Du, X., & Guizani, M. (2020). *A Survey of Machine and Deep Learning Methods for Internet of Things (IoT) Security*. Academic Press.

Amin, R., Kumar, N., Biswas, G. P., Iqbal, R., & Chang, V. (2018). A light weight authentication protocol for IoT-enabled devices in distributed Cloud Computing environment. *Future Generation Computer Systems*, *78*, 1005–1019. doi:10.1016/j. future.2016.12.028

Anamalamudi, S., Sangi, A. R., Alkatheiri, M., & Ahmed, A. M. (2018). AODV routing protocol for Cognitive radio access based Internet of Things (IoT). *Future Generation Computer Systems*, *83*, 228–238. Advance online publication. doi:10.1016/j.future.2017.12.060

Arshad, J., Azad, M. A., & Abdellatif, M. M. (2018). *COLIDE : A Collaborative Intrusion Detection Framework for Internet of Things*. Academic Press.

Ayotunde, F., Othman, M., Abaker, I., Hashem, T., & Yaqoob, I. (2018). A Novel Countermeasure Technique for Reactive Jamming Attack in Internet of Things. *Multimed Tools Appl*, 29899–29920.

Bhuyan, M. H., Bhattacharyya, D. K., & Kalita, J. K. (2016). E-LDAT : a lightweight system for DDoS flooding attack detection and IP traceback using extended entropy metric. doi:10.1002/sec

Challa, S., Wazid, M., Das, A. K., Kumar, N., Reddy, A. G., Yoon, E., & Yoo, K. (2017). Secure Signature-Based Authenticated Key Establishment Scheme for Future IoT Applications. doi:10.1109/ACCESS.2017.2676119

Chen, J. I. (2017). Embedding the MRC and SC Schemes into Trust Management Algorithm Applied to IoT Security Protection. *Wireless Personal Communications*. Advance online publication. doi:10.100711277-017-5120-4

Chopra, K., Gupta, K., & Lambora, A. (2019). Future Internet: The Internet of Things-A Literature Review. *Proceedings of the International Conference on Machine Learning, Big Data, Cloud and Parallel Computing: Trends, Prespectives and Prospects, COMITCon 2019*, 135–139. 10.1109/COMITCon.2019.8862269

Cs, D., Jung, B., & Min, M. (2017). Mitigating Stealthy Collision Attack in Energy Harvesting Motivated Networks. *Cyber Security and Trusted Computing Mitigating*, 539–544.

Dao, Kim, Jeong, & Park. (2017). Achievable Multi-Security Levels for Lightweight IoT-Enabled Devices in Infrastructureless Peer-Aware Communications. *IEEE Access: Practical Innovations, Open Solutions*, 26743–26753.

Dazine, J., Maizate, A., & Hassouni, L. (2018). Internet of things security. In *2018 IEEE International Conference on Technology Management, Operations and Decisions (ICTMOD)* (pp. 137–141). IEEE. 10.1109/ITMC.2018.8691239

Deogirikar, J. (2017). Security Attacks inIoT. *Survey (London, England)*, 32–37.

Dhillon, P. K., & Kalra, S. (2017). A lightweight biometrics based remote user authentication scheme for IoT services. *Journal of Information Security and Applications*, 1–16. doi:10.1016/j.jisa.2017.01.003

Du, Y., Cai, G., Zhang, X., Liu, T., & Jiang, J. (2019). *An Efficient Dummy-Based Location Privacy-Preserving Scheme for Internet of Things Services*. doi:10.3390/info10090278

Fakhri, D., & Mutijarsa, K. (2018). Secure IoT Communication using Blockchain Technology. *ISESD 2018 - International Symposium on Electronics and Smart Devices: Smart Devices for Big Data Analytic and Machine Learning*. 10.1109/ISESD.2018.8605485

Fu, Y., Yan, Z., Cao, J., Koné, O., & Cao, X. (2017). *An Automata Based Intrusion Detection Method for Internet of Things*. Academic Press.

Garg, H., & Dave, M. (2019). *Securing IoT Devices and Securely Connecting the Dots Using REST API and Middleware*. Academic Press.

Ge, M., Hong, J. B., Guttmann, W., & Kim, D. S. (2020). A framework for modeling and assessing security of the internet of things A framework for automating security analysis of the internet of things. *Journal of Network and Computer Applications, 83*(January), 12–27. doi:10.1016/j.jnca.2017.01.033

Ghaleb, B., Al-dubai, A., Ekonomou, E., Qasem, M., Romdhani, I., & Mackenzie, L. (2019). *Addressing the DAO Insider Attack in RPL's Internet of Things Networks*. Academic Press.

Gulzar, M., & Abbas, G. (2019). Internet of Things Security : A Survey and Taxonomy. In *2019 International Conference on Engineering and Emerging Technologies (ICEET)* (pp. 1–6). IEEE. 10.1109/CEET1.2019.8711834

Horrow, S. (2012). *Identity Management Framework for Cloud Based Internet of Things*. Academic Press.

Khan, Z. A., Ullrich, J., & Herrmann, P. (2020). *A Trust-based Resilient Routing Mechanism for the Internet of Things*. Academic Press.

Khursheeed, F., Sami-Ud-Din, M., Sumra, I. A., & Safder, M. (2020). A Review of Security Machanism in internet of Things(IoT). *3rd International Conference on Advancements in Computational Sciences, ICACS 2020*. 10.1109/ICACS47775.2020.9055949

Lavanya, M., & Natarajan, V. (2017). Lightweight key agreement protocol for IoT based on IKEv2 R. *Computers & Electrical Engineering, 64*, 580–594. doi:10.1016/j.compeleceng.2017.06.032

Li, W., Tug, S., Meng, W., & Wang, Y. (2019). Designing Collaborative Blockchained Signature-based Intrusion Detection in IoT environments. *Future Generation Computer Systems, 96*, 481–489. Advance online publication. doi:10.1016/j.future.2019.02.064

Liu, L., Xu, B., Zhang, X., & Wu, X. (2018). An intrusion detection method for internet of things based on suppressed fuzzy clustering. *EURASIP Journal on Wireless Communications and Networking, 2018*(1), 113. doi:10.118613638-018-1128-z

Liu, Z., Longa, P., & Pereira, G. C. C. F. (2020). Four Q on embedded devices with strong countermeasures against side-channel attacks. *IEEE Transactions on Dependable and Secure Computing, 17*(3), 1–21.

Mahmoud, R., Yousuf, T., Aloul, F., & Zualkernan, I. (2015). *Internet of Things (IoT) Security : Current Status, Challenges and Prospective Measures.* Academic Press.

Mangia, M., Pareschi, F., Rovatti, R., & Setti, G. (2017). Low-cost Security of IoT Sensor Nodes With Rakeness-Based Compressed Sensing : Statistical. *IEEE Transactions on Information Forensics and Security, 6013*(c), 1–14. doi:10.1109/TIFS.2017.2749982

Nathani, B., & Vijayvergia, R. (2018). The Internet of Intelligent things: An overview. *ICCT 2017 - International Conference on Intelligent Communication and Computational Techniques,* 119–122. 10.1109/INTELCCT.2017.8324031

Nguyen, T., & Yoo, M. (2017). A hybrid prevention method for eavesdropping attack by link spoofing in software-defined Internet of Things controllers. *Distributed Sensor Networks, 13*(11). Advance online publication. doi:10.1177/1550147717739157

Nižetić, S., Šolić, P., López-de-Ipiña González-de-Artaza, D., & Patrono, L. (2020). Internet of Things (IoT): Opportunities, issues and challenges towards a smart and sustainable future. *Journal of Cleaner Production, 274,* 122877. Advance online publication. doi:10.1016/j.jclepro.2020.122877 PMID:32834567

Nwafor, E., Campbell, A., & Bloom, G. (2017). *Anomaly-based Intrusion Detection of IoT Device Sensor Data using Provenance Graphs.* Academic Press.

Osifeko, M. O., & Hancke, G. P. (2020). *Artificial Intelligence Techniques for Cognitive Sensing in Future IoT : State-of-the-Art, Potentials, and Challenges.* Academic Press.

Pajouh, H. H., Javidan, R., Khaymi, R., Dehghantanha, A., & Raymond, K. (2016). A Two-layer Dimension Reduction and Two-tier Classification Model for Anomaly-Based Intrusion Detection in IoT Backbone Networks. *IEEE Transactions on Emerging Topics in Computing, 6750,* 1–11. doi:10.1109/TETC.2016.2633228

Patnaik, S. (2020). Survey on IoT Security : Challenges and Solution using Machine Learning. *Artificial Intelligence and Blockchain Technology.* Advance online publication. doi:10.1016/j.iot.2020.100227

Patra, L., & Rao, U. P. (2016). *Internet of Things- Architecture, applications, security and other major challenges*. Academic Press.

Pontevedra, V., & Sonavane, S. (2019). A Real-Time Intrusin Detection System for Wormhole Attack in in the RPL based Internet of Things. *Procedia Manufacturing*, *32*, 840–847. doi:10.1016/j.promfg.2019.02.292

Pu, C. (2020). Sybil Attack in RPL-Based Internet of Things : Analysis and Defenses. *IEEE Internet of Things Journal Sybil*, *4662*(c), 4937–4949. Advance online publication. doi:10.1109/JIOT.2020.2971463

Qin, T., Wang, B., Chen, R., Qin, Z., & Wang, L. (2019). *IMLADS : Intelligent Maintenance and Lightweight Anomaly Detection System for Internet of Things*. doi:10.3390/s19040958

Rathore, M. M., Paul, A., Ahmad, A., Chilamkurthi, N., Rathore, M. M., Paul, A., ... Seo, H. (2017). Real-Time Secure Communication for Smart City in High-Speed Big Data Environment. *Future Generation Computer Systems*. Advance online publication. doi:10.1016/j.future.2017.08.006

Saleh, A. I., Talaat, F. M., & Labib, L. M. (2017). A hybrid intrusion detection system (HIDS) based on prioritized k-nearest neighbors and optimized SVM classifiers. *Artificial Intelligence Review*. Advance online publication. doi:10.100710462-017-9567-1

Sedjelmaci, H., Senouci, S. M., Taleb, T., & Saclay, P. (2017). An Accurate Security Game for Low-Resource IoT Devices. *IEEE Transactions on Vehicular Technology*, *9545*(10), 2–15. doi:10.1109/TVT.2017.2701551

Shi, L., & Wang, Y. (2018). *Secure Data Delivery with Linear Network Coding for Multiple Multicasts with Multiple Streams in Internet of Things*. Academic Press.

Sweeney, L. (2002). *k-anonymity: A model for protecting privacy*. Academic Press.

Systems, D., & Centre, T. (2001). *A logic for uncertain probabilities*. Academic Press.

Tamani, N., & Ghamri-Doudane, Y. (2016). *Towards a User Privacy Preservation System for IoT Environments : a Habit-Based Approach*. Academic Press.

Varshney, T., Sharma, N., & Kaushik, I. (2019). Architectural Model of Security Threats & theirCountermeasures in IoT. In *2019 International Conference on Computing, Communication, and Intelligent Systems (ICCCIS)* (pp. 424–429). IEEE. 10.1109/ICCCIS48478.2019.8974544

Viel, F., Silva, L. A., Valderi Leithardt, R. Q., & Zeferino, C. A. (2019). Internet of things: Concepts, architectures and technologies. *2018 13th IEEE International Conference on Industry Applications, INDUSCON 2018 - Proceedings*, 909–916. 10.1109/INDUSCON.2018.8627298

Yahyaoui, A., Abdellatif, T., & Attia, R. (2019). Hierarchical anomaly based intrusion detection and localization in IoT. *2019 15th International Wireless Communications & Mobile Computing Conference (IWCMC)*, 108–113.

Yang, H., Bai, Y., Zou, Z., Zhang, Q., Wang, B., & Yang, R. (2020). Research on data security sharing mechanism of power internet of things based on blockchain. In *2020 IEEE 9th Joint International Information Technology and Artificial Intelligence Conference (ITAIC)* (Vol. 9, pp. 2029–2032). 10.1109/ITAIC49862.2020.9338843

Yang, L., Ding, C., Wu, M., & Wang, K. (2017). Robust Detection of False Data Injection Attacks for the Data Aggregation in Internet of Things based Environmental Surveillance. *Computer Networks*, *129*, 410–428. Advance online publication. doi:10.1016/j.comnet.2017.05.027

Yazdankhah, F., & Honarvar, A. R. (2017). An Intelligent Security Approach using Game Theory to Detect DoS Attacks in IoT. *Advanced Computer Science and Applications*, *8*(9). Advance online publication. doi:10.14569/IJACSA.2017.080944

Yu, W., & Köse, S. (2017). A Lightweight Masked AES Implementation for Securing IoT Against CPA Attacks. *IEEE Transactions on Circuits and Systems*, *64*(11), 2934–2944. doi:10.1109/TCSI.2017.2702098

Zhang, P., Nagarajan, S. G., & Nevat, I. (2017). Secure Location of Things (SLOT). *Mitigating Localization Spoofing Attacks in the Internet of Things*, *4*(September), 2199–2206. Advance online publication. doi:10.1109/JIOT.2017.2753579

Zhang, Y., Li, P., & Wang, X. (2019). Intrusion Detection for IoT Based on Improved Genetic Algorithm and Deep Belief Network. *IEEE Access: Practical Innovations, Open Solutions*, *7*, 31711–31722. doi:10.1109/ACCESS.2019.2903723

Section 3
Blockchain Emerging Trends and Applications

Chapter 9
Blockchain:
Emerging Trends, Applications, and Challenges

Taskeen Zaidi
Jain University (Deemed), India

ABSTRACT

A blockchain is a specific database stored in an electronic form. The databases stored in a block are put in a chain. When new data is added, it will be put in a new block. The blockchain may be created for storing different kind of information in which the most popular use of blockchain is ledger for transactions. Anything of value can be put in a blockchain, and this will reduce risk factors and cost. The blockchain is a chain of blocks used to store public databases. The blockchain can be a powerful tool in business applications for sharing and updating data. The blockchain may be used for the business process for handling transaction-related problems in an effective manner. The blockchain is also helpful in developing an ecosystem between various stakeholders. The policies, benefits, and cost are serious risk factors.

INTRODUCTION

The blockchain technology may be useful in insurance industry in various areas like sales, payments, assets transfer, claim processing and reassurance. The blockchain enabled applications may be helpful in government sectors also. The blockchain based governance may offer services used by state and its authorities in a decentralised manner. The blockchain based applications may be helpful in public services like patent management, income tax payment, marriage registration etc. Due to the increasing

DOI: 10.4018/978-1-7998-8382-1.ch009

attention of decentralised IoT platform, the block chain technology is playing crucial role in offering various services. The idea is to exchange data in a heterogeneous manner by interconnecting smart IoT devices, the blockchain technology is offering secure real-time payment services helping enhancement of ecommerce industry. The blockchain based IoT applications decrease maintenance cost of centralised servers. It also provides security to IoT and wireless sensors networks. The role of blockchain in energy sector with overview of key principles and detailed review of energy applications and use cases with benefits and limitations of blockchain is well explained (Merlinda Andoni, Valentin Robu, David Flynn, Simone Abram, Dale Geach, David Jenkins, Peter McCallum & Andrew Peacock,2019). The authors proposed law and policies for reducing energy consumption of Blockchain technologies (Jon Truby,2019). The authors discussed the role of Blockchain ecosystem for carbon markets including environmental assets, rights and liabilities in implementation (Galenovich, Lonshakov & Shadrin.2018). Different Blockchain schemes were analyzed by the authors (Tommy and Poll, 2018). The technical principles, role and policies for implementing Blockchain is studied. The author discussed the role of ethereum in secure transactions and smart contracts as well as scalability issues were also analyzed (Imran Bashir, 2018). A new distributed and tamper proof media transaction framework for blockchain model was proposed for securing transactions (Bhowmik, & Feng,2017). An article discussing the use of Blockchain to fight land ownership fraud was written(Browne, R. 2017). To provide security and privacy Blockchain technology based voting system is proposed (Hjalmarsson, Hreioarsson, Hamdaqa, & Hjalmtysson,2017). There are billions of devices to connect to IoT sensors and devices. But the current model of client server may have problem with synchronization. A new model using Blockchain is proposed by IoT system. This model is able to control and configure devices. An encryption algorithm is also proposed to secure the transactions (Huh, Cho, & Kim, 2017). It is not safe to put contracts, transactions and records information online butBlockchain technology can be solution to this kind of problem. The Blockchain provides open, distributed ledger which records the transactions safely and efficiently. The intermediaries like bankers and lawyers role can be slashed to transform economy (Iansiti, & Lakhani,2017). The authors have discussed the points related to Blockchain popularity and also issues like scalability, traffic monitoring is discussed (Imbrex & Sharding 2017). The use of Blockchain technology for IPR management with its operation and maintenance issue is discussed (Ito, Kensuke and O'Dair, 2019).

BACKGROUND

Banking

In banking industry blockchain technology is useful in reducing cost of transactions by eliminating the way of transaction in traditional way and increasing safety and efficiency in banking transaction. The vault OS has been developed which is running on cloud and provide a secure, fast and reliable way of end to end protected transaction. This operating system is capable of managing customers, account information, savings related information, mortgages and other financial related matters. The need of blockchain is studied (Wüst & Gervais, 2019). A new protocol for crypto-currency for securing bitcoin from attacks was proposed (Bentov, I., Lee, C., Mizrahi, A., & Rosenfeld, 2014).

Another application for banking system is corda which appears distributed ledger platform which is very useful for financial organizations. It is very useful in banking industry and participants can make transaction without central authorities with the involvement of blockchain technology in banking sector the cost is reduced and safety in improved. The money transaction in traditional way requires verification from central authority but this is very time consuming and complex process and with the emergence of blockchain technology there are many applications and services which provides payment settlements without bank accounts. Some of the blockchain applications are as follows:

1. Align Commerce: It is a payment service provider service that is used to send and receive payments.
2. Abra: This application is used for person to person money payment.
3. Rebit: This is money transfer service offers payment to immigrants.
4. Bitspark: This service is used for money transfer service covering different location worldwide.
5. CoinRip: This service offers quick money transfer facility at 2% flat rate.
6. Ethereum: It is a distributed public blockchain network which is reliable and allowed no third-party interference. The developers deploy decentralized applications using blockchain network which is not centrally controlled by any individual or organization. The Ehtereum Virtual Machine (EVM) is used to create any desired program in any programming language and users may create any application from the beginning and they can use in the build application also.

Some of other services offers by blockchain technology are as follows:

1.   Smart Bonds:

Smart bonds are automated as it uses blockchain technology for its registration services. The smart bonds are used for instant settlement of payments.

2.   Cross border transactions:

It uses decentralized ledger system in which verification and processing of cross border transactions will be done in seconds.

3.   Point of Sales System(PoS)

The blockchain technology may be helpful in PoS system as it provides mechanism to merchants and consumers to accept crypto-currency as payment.

4.   Money Borrowing:

The blockchain technology is helpful in banking and financial institutions for lending and borrowing money using decentralized distributed ledger system. This is very smart, efficient, reliable, secure and faster transaction approach.

5.   BCT in trading:

The BCT helps in reducing cost of trading in stock exchange and also offers exchange of assets in digital way without any intermediary.

6.   BCT in Payment Settlements:

The current payment settlement system is very complex and time consuming but due to emergence of Distributed Ledger Technology (DLT) the payment settlement process may be efficient, smooth and automated. The traditional approach may be removed by Blockchain technology.

7.   Role of BCT in Auditing:

The BCT may be helpful in verifying data of financial settlements and it is very useful in saving time and cost. The audits may be conducted in real time and it is a faster approach without any delay.

8.   Role of BCT in credit score reports:

The BCT provides application to save and store data and information related to credit score of an individual in a secure way. The information may not be leaked or modified due to immutable nature of distributed ledger.

9.   Role of BCT in Trade Finance:

The companies were implementing block chain technology for distributed ledger. Due to this the importers, exporters and banks share their personal information in a network which is helpful in trading deal without third party intervention.

10.   Role of BCT in KYC:

The KYC for every bank is mandatory. The KYC process is very time consuming and due to this sometime false entry and duplicate data will be added. But in BCT an organization may store data in central database and generates a reference number for sharing among all banks and financial institutions. So, the bank may access same data again and again for KYC. The data related to an individual may be store in secure form using some cryptographic approaches.

Role of Blockchain in Healthcare

The role of blockchain technology is emerging in health care sector. There are various blockchain applications which are useful in health care sector. The blockchain application may be helpful in collecting health record to patient history of illness, lab tests reports, and medical reports in a very secure and reliable way. The blockchain technology offers security and reliability to the data and it also protects the patient health related data from security breach. The blockchain technology is helpful in managing the integrity of medical drugs. The blockchain technology is helpful for collaboration between participants and researchers for improving quality of research in medical field. The blockchain provides real time transparency and consume time during payment by a customer. There are various services which are helpful in storing and accessing the information from E-Health care system in an efficient manner. A health care blockchain framework for secure and efficient access to medical records by preserving patient's sensitive data is proposed (Gaby G,Jordan Mohler, Matea & Praneeth Babu, 2018)

Role of Blockchain in Retail

The blockchain technology is emerging and useful in retail industry also. The open bazar is an online start-up based on blockchain services which is useful for person to person trade. The user has to run a simple application on the computer and start trading activity online. This service is decentralized and not under and administrative control and is free of cost.

The smart contract is playing an important role in transaction process. No intermediary is required in payment settlement using this technology. This is reducing the cost and improving the efficiency of transaction. The smart contract is used with IoT for sharing of resources, services and creating of marketplace using cryptographic approach. The services of blockchain technology may be useful in supply chain management as it doesnot involve intermediary which is helpful in developing trust between buyers and sellers. The companies like Walmart are working to use blockchain technology in business process.

Role of Blockchain in IoT and Cloud Computing

The blockchain technology is used in collaboration with IoT interconnecting the IoT devices in an efficient manner in homes and cities. The blockchain technology is a decentralized approach offers strong protection against data leakage and protects IoT devices at home, industry etc. from misleading information.

The cloud computing offers on demand computing and various companies like Amazon, Google and Microsoft web services were offering data storage facilities in online manner. The blockchain technology may offer storage services with lower to cloud services and securing data with encryption and decryption policy and also blockchain cloud storage is immutable means while modifying/updating any records the changes were automatically reflected on data.

Role of Blockchain in Certifications

The data and identities are certified by using blockchain technology. There are many areas where certification is applied using blockchain technology. Various universities were using blockchain distributed ledger technology for managing student certificates enrolled on various MOOC platforms. Many universities like university of Nicosia and Stanford University is offering various courses in blockchain technology and crypto-currencies.

Many students were rewarding students for learning. The online rewards were given to the teachers and students in form of digital currency. This reward will be auto-saved in blockchain wallet which may be helpful to pay fees and may be used for other purposes. The blockchain application may be helpful in reducing the fraud of degree. The student data may be maintained, checked, verified and validated using blockchain application. The Education Certificate Blockchain(ECBC) is also a standard for managing student certificates and all the information like student name, contact details, address stored in an encrypted form.The role of blockchain technology in education sector is well explained (Grech, Alexander; Camilleri & Anthony, 2017)

Role of Blockchain in Chemical and Gem Industry

The blockchain technology may be used in various industries for securing growth and improving cost, productivity and improving company growth by exposure. The supply chain management process will be tracked by blockchain technology. The blockchain technology may be useful in increasing the transparency of diamond, stones, and pearl in various industries. This technology will be helpful in mining of material in a transparent manner. An overview of blockchain role in gem industry is explained (Laurent, Saleem & Michael. (2018). The role and characteristics of Blockchain technology in mobility and logistics as well as challenges faced by blockchain technology is well explained (Hofman, & Brewster,2019).

CHALLENGES FACED BY BLOCKCHAIN

The implementation of blockchain technology may require change in existing system functioning and skilled persons were required to implement and integrate the technology.

The electricity consumption also required in huge amount. New technologies were required for blockchain implementation. There is need to reduce computation amount.

The virtual currency is also risky to keep it safe from fraudulent activity. There is technical problem in identifying bugs in the code. The scalability is also an issue in blockchain technology. There is requirement of innovative solution to solve the scalability issue. The blockchain technology may be helpful in analysing and discovering patterns in Artificial Intelligence. The blockchain technology may be helpful in areas like Autonomous vehicles, Smart contracts, IoT, Decentralized Autonomous Organizations (DAOs) and other areas. The block chain technology is very useful in government operations, they want to use it for reducing bureaucracy, improving efficiency of system, reducing pollution and resolving complexity of the system processes. The AI may be collaborating with Blockchain for Machine to Machine (M2M) transactions and payment settlements but the problem is lack of technical expertise in these fields.

There is lack of awareness about the technology in many sectors. The organisations have developed there self-blockchain and therefore all blockchains has different standards and this is impacting the performance of network and distributed ledgers blockchain. There is no common standard for creating blockchain. The organizations were not showing full support in creating blockchain technology. The organizations were not showing support for adaptation of this technology as they have to develop trust on decentralised system. Many organisations were working on centralised system module. The blockchain technology is related to business process modifications and newer technology implementation. So, the adoption is somehow slow. The cost for validating and sharing transaction is also huge due to inappropriate network range. The privacy and security is also an important concern. The customer concern about understanding of the blockchain is still not resolved in broader sense. So, it is difficult to engage customer in blockchain network due to lack of understanding and interest in adoption of newer technology. The cloud based framework is also dependent on block chain applications. The cloud service provider may have to upload data on cloud servers and the functionality of nodes is to maintain the integrity of blockchain and validation of blocks. So, it is necessary for the government to develop the rules which will protect the blockchain based cloud applications for uploading harmful contents or attackers in the system. The need of electricity in blockchain technology in data mining and transactions is discussed (P. Fairley, 2017)

Cloud service provider may also upload data on cloud systems and the functionality of nodes to maintain integrity of blockchain and validation of block. The government must develop the rules and regulations to protect the cloud system from uploading of any malicious contents on blockchain based applications. Due to the increase of transactions and validation issues, all the transactions may not be processed and validate in real time manner. The small blocks require high processing time and large block size process the transactions with slower propagation speed. Hence, scalability is a very serious issue. The bulk blockchain issue was proposed by crypto-currency. The bit coin Next Generation (NG) was proposed which divide the blocks into major and minor blocks. This approach is quite successful as all key blocks were counted and micro blocks have no weight. In this way network will be secure and attacks were countered.

ISSUES, CONTROVERSIES, PROBLEMS

Characteristics of Blockchain

1. Decentralised and Distributed: In blockchain technology each transaction may be performed without any authentication from central authority, so blockchain is reducing the unnecessary server cost and overall efficiency and performance is improved.
2. Persistency: As each transaction in blockchain network is confirmed and placed in the blocks, so it is difficult to tamper the transactions. The transaction is validated by the other nodes; any wrong input in the blocks may be checked and validated easily.
3. Reliability: There is no central entity to store private information of a user. A user may perform any transaction in blockchain with an address. A user may generate multiple addresses for multiple transactions for safety and non-exposure in the system. As there is no role of central authority so privacy on the transactions may be imposed strongly in blockchain.
4. Traceability and Auditability: As each transaction in blockchain is recorded with a timestamp value, so any transaction can be traced and previous transactions can be checked iteratively. The transparency and traceability is maintained in blockchain.

Security Issues Faced by Blockchain

The blockchain technology is the core technology used in finance industry and security is one of the major concerns. Various security issues were reported with blockchain based applications. The problem arises related to transactions security from third parties using blockchain is discussed (Nurzhan Zhumabekuly Aitzhan & D. Svetinovic,2018). The money in the form of digital currency is not as such secure; there are still certain issues to overcome for smooth adoption of the technology. Some of the key issues related to security of blockchain technology are listed below:

Double Spending of Money

In blockchain technology a single user may use digital currency multiple times for various online transactions and this will make correct transaction invalid. The digital currency will be stealing in this manner.

Timing Attack

The attacker may alter the network time counter of the nodes and in this manner the block will not be used in effective manner. This activity will be done by attacker by increasing or decreasing network counter time. The valid block will be lost without being used up and wastage of computational time also occurs.

Self-Mining

The self-mining is also an attack in which attackers misguide the honest miners. The hones miners exhaust their computing power in false direction. In this activity all the honest miners lost their resources and self-miners were benefited. The self-miners were adding blocks in private chain and private chain will became larger than public chain.

DDoS Attack

The DDoS attack is network intrusion attack in which illegitimate users were denied honest users access in the network and make them out of network. The resources will be utilized by illegitimate users and system will be crashed. The network activity will be denied in this manner.

Key Security Issues

In blockchain technology the private key is used as an identity during transaction processing. The user has privilege to create, generate and manage the key, but the private key may be hacked and used by the attacker.

Issues with Smart-Contracts

There may be certain issues with the smart contracts as it undergoes fault due to disorder, irregularity, type cast and bugs. The smart contracts were attacked by hackers. There is essential need to develop a secure system for blockchain bit-coin framework.

Block Chain in Quantum Computing

The blockchain is a distributed platform which allows decentralized computing and transactions are accountable and transparent and useful in variety of applications from smart contracts, finance, manufacturing and health care etc. The current practice of blockchain is vulnerable to attacks. The quantum computing follows quantum mechanics and used phenomenon like superposition and entanglement for preparing computations called as quantum computers. The blockchain rely on Elliptic Curve Digital Signature Algorithm (ECDSA) and create public and private keys. If the public key is known, the quantum computer is able to find out the private key. This would create a severe threat to blockchain. For handling this issue, new types of signature schemes were created by companies to protect the blockchain from the threat. Quantum computers are affecting the security of bitcoin blockchain at a greater extent. The post quantum cryptography is a solution for resisting quantum attacks.

BLOCKCHAIN IN STOCK EXCHANGE

The blockchain technology can be accelerator in stock trade, security traders, representative bankers require days to finish exchanges. Blockchain technology may be helpful to make stock trading more efficient through automation and decentralization. The blockchain can be helpful in fundraising and asset management as well as financing, trade settlements, securities and monitoring systemic risk. It eliminates the need for middleman. Equity token can also be taken which can be used as stock asset. An equity token can be used to record ownership on blockchain. Tokenization helps in converting right to an asset as stocks; bond etc. into digital token on a blockchain. The assets can be in form of stocks, real-estate, gold, oil etc. The tokenization connects assets into digital token on blockchain. The stock exchange smart contract has identities like CSD, FMA, broker, government etc. All of them play a specific role in stock exchange platform. Block chain make stock exchange more efficient as it allows automation and decentralization. It reduces huge costs on customers in terms of unnecessary commission and it speeds up the process of transactions easy.

The blockchain is helpful in clearing and settlement by automating the post trade process and legal ownership transfer of security. It eliminates third party regulator and financial institutions may settles dues with in few minutes instead of long process and it improves supply chain management and increased transparency and offering higher liquidity. A peer to peer stock market system with legal implications with current legislation and regulation is discussed (Larissa Lee,2016). A use case identification framework for blockchain and a use case canvas for identifying business models were analyzed. The use cases were designed to help practitioners to choose as per the usability of Blockchain technology (Gräther, Klein, Prinz,2018)

Issues with Blockchain

Blockchain requires more computing power and networking so this increases costing. Due to lack of regulator policy blockchain network may suffer from scams and market manipulation. The blockchain offers complexity as it was reciprocated that blockchain replaces middle man facilities in clearing payments and fraud detection but as far as knows the bank is also offering this service with lower cost to the end user. Due to increase in user the performance of the block chain network is degrading. The blockcahin protocols have designing issue due to lack of high scalability and power consumption and having a lot of security issues. Due to lack of policies and regulations the blockchain is not used on wider range. The blockchain used P2P network, communication overhead occurs.

FUTURE RESEARCH DIRECTIONS

As per the current trends the banking sector is investing in blockchain application. New crypto-currencies will be regulated in market based on monetary policy. The national crypto currencies will be introduced by many countries in 2022. The blockchain may be integrated with government agencies for effective management of decentralized data with an encryption approach. There will be huge demand of blockchain experts in various projects related to blockchain technology. The IoT companies were implementing blockchain technology based solutions as blockchain offers secure and scalable framework for communication and transactions. The blockchain technology may be used with smart contracts in future.

CONCLUSION

The blockchain technology is emerging and fast-growing trends in recent times. This technology is adopted by many industries and various applications were running in an easier and effective manner. The future of blockchain is very positive but there are certain challenges to overcome. In the current chapter the applications based on blockchain technologies, the adoption of blockchain technologies in various industries, challenges faced by blockchain technologies, characteristics of block chain technologies and security issues were discussed.

ACKNOWLEDGMENT

This research received no specific grant from any funding agency in the public, commercial, or not-for-profit sectors

REFERENCES

Aitzhan, N. Z., & Svetinovic, D. (2016). Security and privacy in decentralized energy trading through multi-signatures, blockchain and anonymous messaging streams. *IEEE Transactions on Dependable and Secure Computing, 15*(5), 840–852. doi:10.1109/TDSC.2016.2616861

Andoni, M., Robu, V., Flynn, D., Abram, S., Geach, D., Jenkins, D., McCallum, P., & Peacock, A. (2019). Blockchain technology in the energy sector: A systematic review of challenges and opportunities. *Renewable & Sustainable Energy Reviews, 100*, 143–174. doi:10.1016/j.rser.2018.10.014

Bashir, I. (2018). *Mastering Blockchain: Distributed ledger technology, decentralization, and smart contracts explained*. Packt Publishing Ltd.

Bentov, I., Lee, C., Mizrahi, A., & Rosenfeld, M. (2014). *Proof of Activity: Extending Bitcoin's Proof of Work via Proof of Stake*. IACR Cryptology ePrint Archive, 2014, 452.

Bhowmik, D., & Feng, T. (2017, August). The multimedia blockchain: A distributed and tamper-proof media transaction framework. In *22nd International Conference on Digital Signal Processing (DSP)* (pp. 1-5). IEEE. 10.1109/ICDSP.2017.8096051

Browne, R. (2017). *An Indian state wants to use blockchain to fight land ownership fraud*. Retrieved from https://www.cnbc.com/2017/10/10/this-indian-state-wantsto-use-blockchain-to-fight-land-ownership-fraud.html

Cartier, L. E., Ali, S. H., & Krzemnicki, M. S. (2018). Blockchain, Chain of Custody and Trace Elements: An Overview of Tracking and Traceability Opportunities in the Gem Industry. *The Journal of Geology, 36*(3).

Dagher, G. G., Mohler, J., Milojkovic, M., & Marella, P. B. (2018). Ancile: Privacy-preserving framework for access control and interoperability of electronic health records using blockchain technology. *Sustainable Cities and Society, 39*, 283–297. doi:10.1016/j.scs.2018.02.014

Fairley, P. (2017). Blockchain world-feeding the blockchain beast if bitcoin ever does go mainstream, the electricity needed to sustain it will be enormous. *IEEE Spectrum, 54*(10), 36–59. doi:10.1109/MSPEC.2017.8048837

Galenovich, A., Lonshakov, S., & Shadrin, A. (2018). *Blockchain ecosystem for carbon markets, environmental assets, rights, and liabilities. Concept Design and Implementation.* Elsevier.

Grech, A., & Camilleri, A. F. (2017). Blockchain in Education. Luxembourg: Publications Office of the European Union.

Hjalmarsson, F. P., Hreioarsson, G. K., Hamdaqa, M., & Hjalmtysson, G. (2018, July). Blockchain-Based E-Voting System. In *2018 IEEE 11th International Conference on Cloud Computing (CLOUD)* (pp. 983-986). IEEE. 10.1109/CLOUD.2018.00151

Hofman, W., & Brewster, C. (2019). The Applicability of Blockchain Technology in the Mobility and Logistics Domain. In *Towards User-Centric Transport in Europe* (pp. 185–201). Springer. doi:10.1007/978-3-319-99756-8_13

Huh, S., Cho, S., & Kim, S. (2017, February). Managing IoT devices using blockchain platform. *19th International Conference on Advanced Communication Technology (ICACT)* (pp. 464-467). IEEE. 10.23919/ICACT.2017.7890132

Iansiti, M., & Lakhani, K. R. (2017). The truth about blockchain. Harvard Business Review, 27(9).

Imbrex. (2017). *Sharding, Raiden, Plasma: The Scaling Solutions that Will Unchain Ethereum.* Retrieved from https://medium.com/imbrexblog/sharding-raiden-plasmathe-scaling-solutions-that-will-unchain-ethereum-c590e994523b

Ito, K., & O'Dair, M. (2018). A Critical Examination of the Application of Blockchain Technology to Intellectual Property Management. In *Business Transformation through Blockchain* (pp. 317–335). Palgrave Macmillan.

Klein, S., & Prinz, W. (2018). A Use Case Identification Framework and Use Case Canvas for Identifying and Exploring Relevant Blockchain Opportunities. *Proceedings of 1st ERCIM Blockchain Workshop 2018. European Society for Socially Embedded Technologies (EUSSET).*

Koens, T., & Poll, E. (2018). What Blockchain Alternative Do you Need? In T. Koens & E. Poll (Eds.), *Data Privacy Management, Cryptocurrencies and Blockchain Technology* (pp. 113–129). Springer. doi:10.1007/978-3-030-00305-0_9

Lee, L. (2015). New kids on the blockchain: How bitcoin's technology could reinvent the stock market. *Hastings Bus L J., 12*, 81. doi:10.2139srn.2656501

Truby, J. (2018). Decarbonizing Bitcoin: Law and policy choices for reducing the energy consumption of Blockchain technologies and digital currencies. *Energy Research & Social Science, 44*, 399–410. doi:10.1016/j.erss.2018.06.009

Wüst, K., & Gervais, A. (2018). Do you need a Blockchain? In *2018 Crypto Valley Conference on Blockchain Technology (CVCBT)* (pp. 45-54). IEEE. 10.1109/CVCBT.2018.00011

Chapter 10
Digital Economy:
The New Engine of Growth for Society 5.0

Bilyaminu Auwal Romo
University of East London, UK

ABSTRACT

Digital technology-enabled business processes are integrated into the digital economy. Such technologies also enable the internet to conduct digital commerce in a trustless network and decentralized environment. This chapter also draws attention to the new form of economy, which focuses on the development and functions of the digital economy as a new growth engine for Society 5.0 and sheds light on emerging technologies and how the disruptive element of blockchain technology challenges the status quo of the old economy and the underpinning digital disruption imposed by decentralize platformisation. The core components of the digital economy, including digital technologies that serve as the new engine of growth for Society 5.0, were identified. The chapter concluded by highlighting the implications of digital technologies, and how standardisation, upgrading curriculum, legislative frameworks, and policies remedy the impediment of growing the digital economy for Society 5.0.

INTRODUCTION

Digital disruptions led to huge wealth from small businesses and countries. Digitization has also led to fundamental challenges for policymakers in countries at all levels of development. The exploitation of its potential for the many, not just the few, requires

DOI: 10.4018/978-1-7998-8382-1.ch010

imaginative thinking to design and develop legislative frameworks and policies to exploit its full potential by the developing countries.

Due to the spread of new digital technologies, the world economy rapidly transforms societies and business practices, and digitization of economies and societies is crucial to creating new means of tackling global sustainable development. However, there are risks that digital disruptions will not favour underserved populations who do not have access to the digital economy, thereby affecting digital isolation due to insufficient access to knowledge and information in developing countries. Hence, digital disruption could favour those well-prepared to create and capture value in the digital era in developed countries, rather than contribute to more inclusive digital development globally.

The digital economy is progressing at a breakneck pace, driven by the ability to collect, use and analyse enormous amounts of machine-readable information. These huge amounts of machine-readable digital data stem from the digital footprints of companies, social and personal activities on various digital platforms. Accordingly, Global Internet Protocol (IP) traffic reported that a proxy for data flows increased in 1992 from 100 gigabytes per day to 45,000 GB per second in 2017. But only in the early days of a data-driven economy. Similar, IP traffic is expected to reach 150,700 GB per second by 2022.

Due to global lockdown during the COVID-19 pandemic, more businesses and people started coming online for the first time in developing countries. As such, a new "data value chain" evolved to support data collection, insights from data, storage, analysis and modelling, to enable companies and government to make informed decisions decisively. For example, the United Kingdom only depends on the COVID-19 data to lift the restriction on national lockdown. In this way, the value creation arises when the data could be transformed into digital intelligence and perhaps monetized through commercial usage by the businesses.

Over the last decade, a wealth of digital platforms have emerged worldwide, disrupting existing businesses with data-driven business models. Seven of the world's top eight companies by market capitalisation use digital platform-based business models. This reflects the power of digital platforms and centralised platformisation.

Digital platforms provide the mechanisms for bringing together businesses and societies in different geographical locations to interact and make transactions remotely. There are two distinctions between innovation and transaction platforms. Innovation platforms create environments for digital technologists to develop software applications and systems that enable users to operate and control machines, including operating systems (e.g. iOS, Android, Linux, Windows etc). In addition, this could be technology standards, like MPEG video or MP3 for content producers.

Notably, during the COVID-19 pandemic, a yawning gap considers the world between the under-connected and the hyper-digitalised countries. For example, in the least developed countries (LDCs), only one in five people use the Internet, compared to four in developed countries. This is only one aspect of the digital divide. Likewise, in other areas, including the ability to use digital data and frontier technologies, the gap is much larger. For instance, Africa and Latin America together account for less than 5% of the world's co-location data centres. If this is not addressed, these divisions will exacerbate existing income inequalities, especially in Africa, where the digital divide and isolation could be significant. It is therefore crucial to consider how developing countries can be affected by this (r) evolution in terms of value creation and capture, and what should be done to improve the status quo, improve the global digital economy, and sustainability in addressing the yawning gap and inequality between countries that are not connected.

In the digital economy, there is no geographical boundary, as in the old economy, where one has a traditional regional divide by geographical location, or in the North-South divide. It is therefore consistently led by one developed and one developing country: the United States and China. For example, the United States and China account for 75% of all patents related to blockchain technology. Most strikingly, they represent 90% of the market capitalization value of the world's 70 largest digital platforms. During Europe, its share is 4%, and Africa and Latin America combined are only 1%. Seven "frontier digital platform owners" - Microsoft, followed by Apple, Amazon, Google, Facebook, Tencent and Alibaba - account for two-thirds of total market value. As a result, the rest of the world, especially Africa and Latin America, is significantly behind the United States and China in many digital technological developments. Some current trade frictions reflect the quest for global dominance in frontier technology areas, where the United Kingdom mandated a cryptor market exchange platform to register in the UK to comply with the Financial Service Conduct Authority's new regulations.

This chapter re-examines the traditional approaches to investigating the digital divide, including access and use of digital technology, and also examines the evolution of the digital economy. The chapter also illustrates a concise new form of economy by first defining the digital economy as the new engine of growth for society 5.0. In addition, this chapter sheds some light on how blockchain technology, 5G broadband and Internet of Things' disruptive element challenge the status quo of the old economy and the underpinning digital disruption imposed by decentralised platformisation.

BACKGROUND

There is a growing body of literature that recognises the early stages of digitalisation, and the evolving digital economy terms lack broadly accepted definitions. Other renowned economists and digital technologists might offer different interpretations of the same term in the relevant literature. This reflects the high speed of technological progress, because in digital technology today, innovation could become tomorrow's museum piece. Hence, faulted the novelty and insufficient consensus, understanding or clarity regarding this phenomenon. In addition, the time required to agree on standard definitions often lags behind the velocity of technological advancement in this digital era.

In this chapter, it is essential not to fetter definitions in the midst of reaching a common understanding in a rapidly evolving situation. However, there is a need for a common ground on the meaning of the digital economy as a terminology to be widely and acceptable.

Digital economy is an imprecise term, since the definition varies in literature and there is terminological confusion. In this chapter, the author defines digital economy as digitalisation of business processes and society regardless of geographical location, to make a transaction either in centralise or decentralise network on a digital platform.

There are two notable key terms used in this definition, firstly, the businesses process and society. The digitalisation of business processes and society can support the potential to support the development of individuals, companies and countries in the digital economy. However, if individuals, companies and countries opted not to participate, it could adversely be affected indirectly. Countries with a large population of citizenry with limited digital skills and obsolete curriculum at primary, secondary and tertiary level will be at a disadvantage to those better equipped for the digital economy. In this digital era, various jobs and professions will be lost to automation and Artificial Intelligence. The net impact will depend on the level of development and digital readiness of individuals, companies and countries. It will also depend on the policies adopted and implemented at national, regional and international levels. Particularly in designing new curriculum to address the adverse skill shortage of digital technologies at primary and secondary level of education in developing countries.

Centralised digital platforms are increasingly important in the world economy. Though they became central authority and exhibited digital dictatorship by monetising individual, companies and society's data for commercial purpose. As such, the combined value of the centralised digital platform owners and market capitalisation reaches $100 million and estimated more than $7 trillion in 2017 – 67% higher in 2015 according to Dutch Transformation Forum, 2018.

Several factors contribute to the dominance of centralised digital platforms. The first is related to network effects, that is, the more users, the more the value of the platforms becomes in the eyes of investors and society. Secondly, once a centralised platform gains adhesion, offering different integrated services, users tend to opt for an alternative service provider, start to increase. This happened to Signal and BOTIM when WhatsApp started offering integrated services.

In the same vein, the platforms began to take steps to consolidate their competitive positions by acquiring potential competitors and expanding into complementary products or services. One notable acquisition by digital platform companies is Microsoft's acquisition of LinkedIn and Facebook's acquisition of WhatsApp. Other steps include strategically investing in research and development (R & D), Netflix, Google, and Facebook have offered funding to research institutions and individuals to conduct research and analyses to advance their digital platforms.

It's paramount for countries to put in place a legislative framework and policies needed to make the digital economy work for the mass population, not a fraction of the population. Digital technology is not deterministic. Rather, it creates both opportunities and challenges. Close dialogue with other stakeholders will shape the digital economy of a nation by defining the rules of the game in global race to digital economy for society 5.0. This in turn requires bold policy towards society with a reasonable sense of desirable digital future a country aspires. A country like Nigeria, the digital economy and its long-term repercussions remain untapped territory, and policies, regulations and curriculum have not been upgraded with the rapid digital transformations taking place in societies and economies.

The development of the digital economy merited eccentric economic thinking and political analysis, addressing the complications of enforcement of laws and regulations on cross-border trade in digital services and products. However, this could be addressed through national policies and strategies, as the digital economy requires consensus-building and policy-making at international level to reach consensus. Many more outstanding questions need to be answered, rather than definitive answers to how to deal with the digital economy. Until now, far too little attention has been paid, leading to the lack of relevant statistics and empirical evidence, as well as the rapid pace of digital technological progress, and policies must be constantly reassessed to make the digital economy work for the mass population.

EVOLUTION OF THE DIGITAL ECONOMY

This section of this chapter moves on to lay a concise detail evolution of the digital economy. Studies were mainly concerned with the adoption of the internet and early cogitating about its economic impacts in the late 1990s (Brynjolfsson and Kahin,

2002; Tapscott, 1996). As Internet use rapidly expanded, studies began to shift focused progressively on the conditions under which the Internet economy emerged and grow by mid-2000s onwards. In addition, definitions have evolved, including the studies of different policies and digital technologies. The growth of digital technologies oriented companies becomes the key actors (OECD, 2012a and 2014).

In recent years, the discussion has reoriented itself to more digital technologies, services, products, techniques and skills. These diffuse across economies and societies. In this way, the process is often called digitalisation, which was defined as the transition of companies through the use of digital technologies, products and services (Brennen and Kreiss, 2014). Digital products and services enable faster change in a wider range of sectors, rather than being confined to high-tech sectors that have been the focus in the past (Malecki and Moriset, 2007). Recent studies have focused on how digital products and services increasingly disrupt traditional sectors (OECD, 2016 and 2017; UNCTAD, 2017). Digitalization and digital transformation, for example, have begun to affect traditional sectors in most developing countries, including agriculture, tourism, transport, education, and health care. In fact, it is considered the most important economic transformations that may well occur through the digitization of traditional sectors, rather than through the emergence of new, digitally enabled sectors.

It is crucial to assess and analyse how investments and policies in digital technologies and infrastructure enable or serve as a limitation to the emergence of the digital economy. In this regard, it is essential to understand its development implications. To assess the digital economy, as highlighted by UNCTAD (2017), for example, the evolving digital economy can be associated with increased use of artificial intelligence, the Internet of Things (IoT), cloud computing, extensive data analytics, three-dimensional (3D) printing, and advanced robotics. In addition, interoperable systems and digital platforms are essential elements of the digital economy. However, there is always the risk of paying too much attention to the latest innovations that are most in the fashion, rather than to the technologies that are of the greatest relevance to developing countries. One way to overcome this limitation is to examine the main components of the digital economy. The following part of this chapter will focus on the digital technologies associated with the digital economy, which are of the greatest relevance to developing and industrialised countries.

COMPONENT OF THE DIGITAL ECONOMY

The author highlighted the core components that will serve as the new engine of growth for society 5.0. These components were also highlighted by (Bukht and Heeks, 2017; Malecki and Moriset, 2007; and UNCTAD, 2017a), the digital economy is becoming increasingly indivisible from the functioning of the global economy as a whole. Hence, the component of the digital economy was divided into three broad components:

1. Digital Transformation and Digitalisation. This includes, as already mentioned, digitally enabled sectors in which new business activities or models have emerged. Digital technologies are changing. Digital technologies are changing this business model. These sectors include finance, media, tourism, transport and education. It is vital to focus on digitally literate consumers, buyers and users of digital platforms. These are crucial for the growth and advancement of the digitalised economy for society 5.0.
2. Digital technology sectors that enable the production of key enablers, including products or services, which rely on core digital technologies and infrastructure, including digital platforms, mobile applications, and the new form application, also known as Decentralised Application (i.e., Dapp), which is currently on the rise in serving decentralised sectors including Decentralization Finance (DEFI) and services operating in a trusted network and environment. Innovation services affect the digital economy in these sectors, which are making a growing contribution to economies, and enable potential spillover effects to other sectors.
3. Fundamental innovations, core technologies and enabling infrastructures

These three components form the basis for measuring the extent and impact of the digital economy. Similar, those components can be applied in various ways starting at the most basic level. Studies have, however, measured the impact of digital sectors on an economy by using surveys and e-commerce data (Barefoot et al., 2018; Knickrehm et al., 2016). Others by studying the different geography of global data and knowledge (Manyika et al., 2014; Ojanperä et al., 2016).

In some literature, the definition of the digital economy tends to be closely linked to the three main components described above. Although an approach broadly in line with many other studies by Barefoot et al., 2018; OECD, 2012a; UNCTAD, 2017a. Furthermore, Bukht and Heeks (2017: 17) proposed the definition of the digital economy: "This part of economic output derived solely or primarily from digital technologies with a business model based on digital goods or services."

Another approach that covers all modes of transmission of digital technologies into the economy is the view of the digital economy by Brynjolfsson and Kahin, (2002), and Knichrehm et al. (2016: 2), in which the foundations of the digital economy are defined in a broader way, suggesting that it is the share of total economic output derived from many broad "digital" inputs. These digital inputs could include both hardware, software, and communication equipment, as well as the intermediate digital goods and services used in production. They reflect the foundations of the digital economy. Other digital inputs include digital skills, digital equipment or infrastructure.

In this chapter, the author emphasises the processes and changes in the digital economy. Conversely, there are implications for the types of policies needed regarding how the digital economy operates. Equally, it is necessary to focus on some aspects of digital technologies, specifically platformisation, digital data and e-commerce. This enables varying changes in the digital economy simultaneously, acknowledging the changes that might occur in different ways.

Turning on to this part of this chapter to touch on the digital technologies associated with the digital economy that are of the greatest relevance for developing countries and developed countries. These technologies are as follows:

Blockchain Technology

Blockchain technology is a form of distributed ledger technology that allows multiple parties to secure transactions without intermediaries. In this digital era, it is best known as the technology behind bitcoin, cryptocurrency and other digital currencies. These technologies are of crucial relevance to many other sectors that are important to developing countries. These include digital identification, property rights and palliative disbursements. There are open-source platforms that allow developers to develop decentralised applications that run on their blockchain network, including the Ethereum platform. However, some challenges that seemed demoralising, particularly in developing countries, on the adoption of this technology, are that it requires a substantial, stable electricity supply.10 Though some blockchain applications in decentralised applications are already in use in some developing countries, for instance in fintech, land management, transport, health and education in Africa (UNECA, 2017). The other limitation is also the amount of gas fees, in other words, it is too expensive to run a decentralise application deployed on the Ethereum network (i.e. the older version) due to the high transaction fees. Although significant improvements have been made by the release of the Ethereum version 2 platforms to address high transaction fees when migrated to run decentralised applications under the new Ethereum version 2.

Gartner's forecast of the value of blockchain business after the first phase of some high-profile successes in 2018-2021 is expected to be larger and widespread, particularly in various areas. Between 2022 and 2026, there would be many more successful models. And these are projected to explode in 2027–2030, to clinch at $3 trillion globally (WTO, 2018). As of 2021, China alone accounts for nearly 50% of all patent applications for blockchain technology, and with the United States, represents more than 75% of all blockchain technologies patent applications (ACS, 2018).

Internet of Things

The Internet of Things (IoT) refers to the increase in Internet-connected devices, including radio frequency identification chips, meters, sensors, and other devices embedded in various everyday objects. These Internet-connected devices can communicate and transfer various types of data autonomously. It is widely used in various areas, including energy for sending and receiving electricity consumption, RFID tagging of goods and their movement for manufacturing, livestock and logistics to monitor soil and weather conditions or temperature in agriculture. Accordingly, there were more devices (8.6 billion) connected to the Internet than people, based on 5.7 billion mobile broadband subscriptions recorded in 2018, and the number of IoT connections is expected to rise by 17% annually to exceed 22 billion by 2024 (Ericsson, 2018). Similarly, the seven most important countries are the United States, followed by China, then Japan, Germany, the Republic of Korea, France, and the United Kingdom, which account for nearly 75% of global IoT spending, with the first two countries nearly representing 50% of global spending. Furthermore, the global IoT market is expected to grow tenfold from $151 billion in 2018 to $1,567 billion by 2025 (IoT Analytics, 2018). IDC (2018) also estimates that by 2025, an average connected person in the world will interact with IoT devices to nearly 4,900 times a day.

5G Mobile Broadband

The role of mobile broadband technology of the fifth generation (5G) is considered critical for IoT due to its greater ability to process enormous amounts of data. 5G networks can process 1,000 times more data than today's systems (Afolabi et al., 2018). Specifically, it offers the possibility of connecting many other devices. It is expected that by 2025, the United States, followed by Europe and Asia Pacific, will be leaders in adoption of 5G. In some developing countries, significant investments in 5G infrastructure are urgently needed. The proportion of 5G in total connections is expected to rise to 59% in the Republic of Korea, compared with only 8% in Latin America and 3% in sub-Saharan Africa by 2025. However, the introduction of 5G could further increase the urban-rural digital divide due to lower demand for 5G networks in these areas. This poses some challenges to the wide adaptability and role of broadband companies in some places, particularly in developing countries with poor infrastructure (ITU, 2018).

The impact of the old economy, which could affect society 5.0 in the short run, as digital technologies speed up abruptly faster, makes the implementation of the above-mentioned digital technologies less relevant to compete and strive for developing countries. However, with legislative frameworks and policies that imposed standardisation in the application of digital technologies, periodic curriculum upgrades across different tiers of education, and of course to explore the main components of the digital economy highlighted in this chapter. Ultimately, will remedy the impediment of growing the digital economy for society 5.0 in developing countries.

CONCLUSION

The chapter will help broaden our understanding of traditional approaches to investigating the digital divide, including access and use of digital technology, and strengthen the growing work on the development of the digital economy. The new form of economy, as the new growth engine for society 5.0, could therefore be considered the digitization of business processes and society, regardless of the geographical location of the company, and society to make transactions in a centralised or decentralised network on a digital platform. The digital technologies associated with the digital economy, including blockchain technologies, IoT and 3G, were considered the greatest relevance to meeting the growing gap in the digital economy for developing countries.

REFERENCES

ACS. (2018). *Blockchain innovation. A patent analytics report*. IP Australia.

Afolabi. (2018). Evolution of wireless networks technologies, history and emerging technology of 5G wireless network: A review. *Journal of Telecommunications System & Management, 7*(3), 1–5.

Babbitt, T., Brynjolfsson, E., & Kahin, B. (2001). Understanding the Digital Economy: Data Tools, and Research. *Academy of Management Review, 26*(3), 463. doi:10.2307/259191

Barefoot, K., Curtis, D., Jolliff, W., Nicholson, J. R., & Omohundro, R. (2018). *Defining and measuring the digital economy. Working paper*. Bureau of Economic Analysis, United States Department of Commerce. Available at https://www.bea. gov/system/files/papers/WP2018-4.pdf

Brennen, S., & Kreiss, D. (2014). Digitalization and digitization. *Culture Digitally, 8*. Available at: https://culturedigitally.org/2014/09/digitalization-and-digitization/

Brynjolfsson, E., & Kahin, B. (Eds.). (2002). *Understanding the Digital Economy*. Massachusetts Institute of Technology.

Bukht, R., & Heeks, R. (2017). *Defining, conceptualising and measuring the digital economy.* GDI Development Informatics Working Papers, no. 68. University of Manchester.

Dutch Transformation Forum. (2018). *Unlocking the Value of the Platform Economy: Mastering the Good, the Bad and the Ugly.* The Hague: Dutch Transformation Forum. Retrieved from https://dutchitchannel.nl/612528/dutch-transformation-platform-economy-paper-kpmg.pdf

Ericsson. (2018). *Mobility report.* Available at: https://www.ericsson.com/assets/local/mobility-report/documents/2018/ericsson-mobility-report-november-2018.pdf

IDC. (2018). *Data Age 2025: The digitization of the world – From edge to core.* White paper. Available at: https://www.seagate.com/files/www-content/our-story/trends/files/idc-seagate-dataage-whitepaper.pdf

IoT Analytics. (2018). *State of the IoT 2018: Number of IoT devices now at 7B – Market accelerating.* Available at https://iot-analytics.com/state-of-the-iot-update-q1-q2-2018-number-of-iot-devices-now-7b/

ITU. (2018). Setting the Scene for 5G: Opportunities & Challenges. ITU.

Knickrehm, M., Berthon, B., & Daugherty, P. (2016). *Digital Disruption: The Growth Multiplier.* Accenture.

Malecki, E. J., & Moriset, B. (2007). *The Digital Economy: Business Organization, Production Processes and Regional Developments.* Routledge. doi:10.4324/9780203933633

Manyika, J., Bughin, J., Lund, S., Nottebaum, O., Poulter, D., Jauch, S., & Ramaswamy, S. (2014). *Global flows in a digital age: How trade, finance, people, and data connect the world economy.* McKinsey Global Institute.

OECD. (2012). *OECD Internet Economy Outlook 2012.* OECD Publishing.

OECD. (2014). *Measuring the Digital Economy: A New Perspective.* OECD Publishing.

OECD. (2016). *Ministerial Declaration on the Digital Economy ("Cancún Declaration") from the Meeting on The Digital Economy: Innovation, Growth and Social Prosperity.* Available at: https://www.oecd.org/internet/Digital-Economy-Ministerial-Declaration-2016.pdf

OECD. (2017). *OECD Digital Economy Outlook 2017.* OECD Publishing.

Ojanperä, S., Graham, M., & Zook, M. (2016). *Measuring the contours of the global knowledge economy with a digital index.* Paper presented at the Development Studies Association Conference 2016, Oxford, UK.

Tapscott, D. (1996). *The Digital Economy: Promise and Peril in the Age of Networked Intelligence.* McGraw-Hill.

UNCTAD. (2017). Information Economy Report 2017: Digitalization, Trade and Development. United Nations.

UNCTAD. (2019). Competition issues in the digital economy. TD/B/C.I/CLP/54. UNCTAD.

UNECA. (2017). *Blockchain Technology in Africa.* United Nations Economic Commission for Africa. Available at: https://www.uneca.org/sites/default/files/images/blockchain_technology_in_africa_draft_report_19-nov-2017-final_edited.pdf

WTO. (2018). *World Trade Report 2018: The Future of World Trade – How Digital Technologies are Transforming Global Commerce.* World Trade Organization.

Chapter 11

Applications of Blockchain Technology in the Finance and Banking Industry Beyond Digital Currencies

Sitara Karim

https://orcid.org/0000-0001-5086-6230
ILMA University, Pakistan

Mustafa Raza Rabbani

https://orcid.org/0000-0002-9263-5657
University of Bahrain, Bahrain

Hana Bawazir
University of Bahrain, Bahrain

ABSTRACT

Blockchain and cryptocurrency have almost become synonymous. Cryptocurrency is arguably one of the most sensational financial innovations of the 21st century. The current study claims that blockchain technology is not limited to the application of digital currencies in finance and banking; there are wide applications of blockchain technology in the given field. Blockchain uses the unique properties enabling decentralized, secured, transparent, and temper-proof financial transactions that have the potential to revolutionize the financial services industry. Given such a stance, the chapter outlines the application of blockchain technology in the finance arena beyond the digital currency. In this chapter, the authors provide the 10 applications of blockchain technology in the financial services industry implementing the blockchain technology and revolutionizing the finance and banking industry. The chapter also highlights the hurdles to application of blockchain technology in the finance and banking industry.

DOI: 10.4018/978-1-7998-8382-1.ch011

INTRODUCTION

Information technology, with all its miracles around the globe and its applications in several business areas, has astonishingly provided solutions to industry and other business sectors. On the other hand, the internet and other web sources have made the businesses quite easy. As a result of this ease, new businesses have emerged that were never existed before. The real application of information technology has made life of people comfortable where access to different resources have been at a tip of a finger of an individual by a single tap of a mobile screen or hand-held devices. Currently, the most important technology that has been deeply addressed and focused is the blockchain technology. This technology, beating the previous technologies, has enabled business to be conducted in most efficient ways where the payments of users have been shifted from unsecured mode to secured mode. In fact, blockchain is a safe, secured, and open ledger that relies on peer-to-peer (P2P) network systems that does not have a centralized system of controlling the transactions rather this system is maintained by several participants providing a decentralized approach (Vives, 2017). Due to its availability to all the participants involved in a transaction, the information recorded in the blockchain can never be tempered, retrieved, or misused by the irrelevant parties. For this reason, blockchain technology is considered as a trusted ledger which cannot be hacked by the hackers and other information systems (Rabbani et al., 2021a).

Although several studies addressed the blockchain technology in a different way, the consensus on the findings of the studies is still vague and unequivocal that opens door for further investigation and exploration. Similarly, the application of blockchain technology has been widely researched and scholars are still finding answers to their empirical investigations. In this stream, the study of (Geranio, 2017) investigated that how to reshape and redesign the patterns of securities trade and market exchange through blockchain technology. Moreover, by applying the blockchain technology, frauds and corruption in land registries and real estate matters can be completely avoided as this technology saves the transactions and leaves no chance of tempering.

Another study of (Cousins et al., 2019; Fosso Wamba et al., 2020) revealed that one of the significant applications of blockchain technology through smart contracts is able to replace several functions usually maintained by the post-trade organizations and firms. This fact must be accepted that technology will be reshaping the lives of every individual, every single business entity, and probably all the organizations around the globe not rapidly but gradually as the adoption of technological advancements in certain business aspects are quite slow and not yet emerged. However, (Ben & Xiaoqiong, 2019) is of the view that technology, just like internet two decades ago, will be eventually evolved and surrounded all the businesses with full boom in the near future. This revolution of technology will be so abrupt, rapid, and at quicker pace that without technological adoption, it will be difficult to run businesses, elevate the performance of firms (Karim et al., 2020a, 2021a), and maintain with the new technologies. Particularly, in the context of this chapter, it is interesting to note that financial and banking industry is also not spared from the revolutions of the blockchain technology, and this sector has wider applications of blockchain technology. It can be asserted that technologies will disrupt the nature of business in financial and banking industry as the main mechanisms handled in this industry are based on trust (Alam et al., 2021; S. Karim et al., 2021b).

Correspondingly, the financial sector slowly adopts the changes happening in the world related to different technologies. This is because financial sector is considered as highly conventional and much regulated industry by the regulatory authorities of states where they operate ((Karim et al., 2020b; Sitara Karim et al., 2020a). Notwithstanding, Price Waterhouse Coopers (PWC, 2016) an accounting firm, argued that banks are now rapidly adopting the technological changes that will benefit them both in short-run and long-run. Given the competitive business and work environment across the world, financial industry, one of the main industries of the world also needs to cope with the challenges and modify their processes in accordance with the current technological advancements. (Rabbani et al., 2021a) explained that in future, blockchain technology will revolutionize the financial sector to an extent that the conventional employment opportunities of brokers will be disappeared. At the same time, the adoption of blockchain technology will lead to several job openings. It is asserted by the scholars that in the coming era, the functions of banks will be minimized, and the adoption of technological innovation will make the function of banks unnecessary as the transactions will take place on online basis. But, the adoption of blockchain technology will not disappear the existence of banks rather it will elevate their strength (Radwan et al., 2020; Yussof & Al-Harthy, 2018; Zhang et al., 2020). Accordingly, this chapter focuses that the application of blockchain technology is not limited to cryptocurrencies and digital currency but there are other applications of this technology that will not even enhance the role of banks and financial intermediaries but will strengthen them to increase their profits.

This chapter, to elaborate the exceptional role of blockchain technology in finance and banking industry apart from digital currencies, tends to extend the scope and breadth of blockchain technology and provides ten applications of blockchain technology in finance and banking industry. Moreover, this chapter also presents some hurdles faced by the given industry to adopt the blockchain technology.

TEN APPLICATIONS OF BLOCKCHAIN TECHNOLOGY IN FINANCIAL AND BANKING INDUSTRY

As mentioned earlier, the application of blockchain technology is not limited to digital currencies and cryptocurrencies rather it has vast applications across finance and banking industry (Figure 1). The list below provides ten applications of blockchain technology and each of the items will be explained in detail afterwards.

1.   Digital Identity Verification
2.   Money Transfer
3.   Clearing and Settlements
4.   Trade Finance
5.   Credit Reporting
6.   Financial Inclusion
7.   Smart Contracts
8.   Initiating Data Ownership
9.   Accelerated Data Sharing
10. Blockchain Technology and Supply Chain Finance

Figure 1. Ten applications of blockchain technology in financial and banking industry

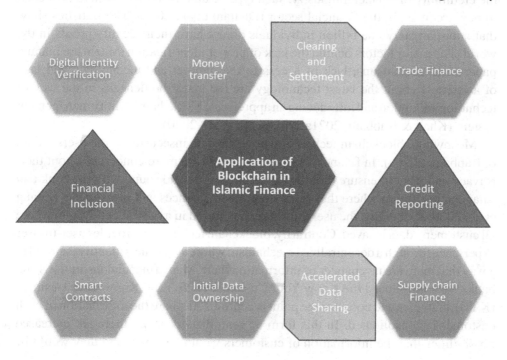

Digital Identity Verification

Digital identity verification is basically biometric system of identifying a person's fingerprints, facial prints, or thump impressions. In blockchain technology, digital identity works differently for companies, for IoT devices and for individuals. Companies use this technology to collect and store data of their customers to use them for different purposes. Firms gather the data and sensitive information of the individuals and store them in less sensitive business databases where there are greater possibilities of information hack and user privacy issues generating new risks for the businesses (Atif et al., 2021; Karim et al., 2021c). It is interesting to note that blockchain identity is necessary to be adopted through blockchain identity management system that can eliminate the information hacking risks, misuse of the users' information, user security risks, and privacy concerns (Dubey, 2019). Blockchain identity management system is helpful in resolving the problems of inaccessibility, data insecurity, and fraudulent identities (Lee et al., 2016).

Particularly, in finance and banking industry, it is stressed that blockchain identity management system needs to be adopted for ensuring the security of the users and creditors (Hassan et al., 2020; Shahnawaz Khan & Rabbani, 2020b). As finance and banking industry is most concerned with managing the financial resources and deposits of the investors, depositors, and lenders, so for maintaining and ensuring the credibility of financial industry, such type of unique identity system is needed to be introduced in the financial sector (Dharani et al., 2021). The statistics show that approximately one billion individuals do not have their identity proofs in the world. The major factors behind the lack of proper identification system are manual paperwork mechanisms, lack of access to the internet and technology, and lack of awareness about the latest technology are the major bottlenecks in the way of technology adoption and introducing an appropriate blockchain identity management system (Khan & Rabbani, 2021a; Moh'd Ali et al., 2020).

Meanwhile, blockchain technology prevents data insecurity of the users (Khan & Rabbani, 2020a). In financial sector, customers are more concerned about their privacy and want to ensure their investments are safe and sound with the bank and financial institution where they have stored their finances and investments (Zhang et al., 2020). Generally, the user information is stored in a centralized system where all customers' data is saved. Contrarily, blockchain technology provides user-to-user experience through a decentralized mechanism where everyone's identity is stored in a way that there are no chances of information theft. Many financial institutions and banks have introduced the Know Your Customer (KYC) and Know Your Business (KYB) strategies and core storage point is centralized where the information of each customer is consolidated. In this form of centralized system, there are increased possibilities that the information of customers would be stolen and they would be susceptible to hackers (Hassan et al., 2020b, 2021a). Thus, blockchain technology provides efficient mechanism of storing individual customer information that there is no information theft. As the number of fraudulent activities related to the user information and identities, blockchain technology that can be useful for this purpose is to build new identity management system, provide decentralized identifiers through digital identity frameworks and much sophisticated form is subset of decentralized identifies known as self-sovereign identity that potentially eradicates the chances of misinformation and tackle's identity frauds. So, finance and banking industry, using this unique technology management system, can reduce the risks associated with customers' identity and privacy.

Money Transfer

Money transfer is one of the significant applications of blockchain technology where financial intermediaries introduce a blockchain in their transactions. Every year, there are hundreds of transactions worth billion US dollars that are held across the globe by businesses and individuals because of cross-border money (Tapscott & Tapscott, 2017). The statistics by the World Bank revealed that total remittances in 2018 achieved a significant high trend where low- and middle-income countries had a growth of around $550 billion during 2018. Moreover, the growth in global remittances of high-income countries reached $689 billion in 2018. In this stance, the banks were marked as the most expensive channels of remittances with 11% fee charges in the 1st quarter of 2019 (Swan, 2017). The United Nation's 2030 Sustainable Development Goal also includes to reduce the international remittance charges from 7.1% to 3%. Since, the transactions are held in bulk and banks are the main channels through which international money is transferred, banks need to charge the transaction fee at a marginal rate. One of the conventional mechanisms of international money transfer is that the individual must have an account with the bank of his own country (Bank A) and that bank will have its subsidiaries in foreign countries (Bank B) and through proper documentation and processes, the international remittances are conducted (Achanta, 2018). This process takes an ample time and individuals, having their privacies at stake; need to wait for days and months to transfer the payment. In addition, the charges of banks for international money transfer are higher as there are several other banks associated in the whole mechanism. That is to say, the significant players involved in this process are the originating bank, the central or state bank, correspondent bank and finally the destination bank (Alam et al., 2021; S; Karim et al., 2021b). For a single transaction, each player charges its fee which accumulatively turns to be higher as compared to other transfer channels.

However, the blockchain technology namely mobile wallets have made the international transactions quite fast and easy without risk of information leakage. Mobile wallets usually work as installed mobile apps and offer significant varieties in their functions. The important question arises here that why and how payments are processed using the blockchain technology. The answer lies in the fact that blockchain provides users with most efficient, easier, transparent, and secure way based on distributed ledger technology (DLT) (Tapscott & Tapscott, 2017). This technology offers significant secure ways to process the payments of individuals within no time and without any security issues. Transactions taking place via DLT, once recorded, cannot be altered, reversed, and changed that makes the whole process highly safe and secured (Swan, 2017).

Figure 2 presents both conventional and modern ways of money transfer through banks A, B, C, and D. the conventional method adopts a long route and consumes much time and effort and charges a significant fee. On the contrary, the modern way of international payments using blockchain technology and DLT makes the whole process rapid and safe. The process is carried out by receiving information of payment which creates a digital block in the chain and distribute it to the network. There are multiple computers working to unscramble the block and share it with the network for verification. Verification is needed to confirm the availability of funds, user authenticity and authorizing the request. Once all are done, the transaction is posted to the ledger and both parties involved in the transaction get confirmation of their funds transfer and funds receipt. Earlier, such type of blockchain technology was only associated with cryptocurrencies but now the whole financial system including the regulators are embracing the use of this technology to make the financial transactions valuable within no time.

Figure 2. Conventional and modern routes of money transfer

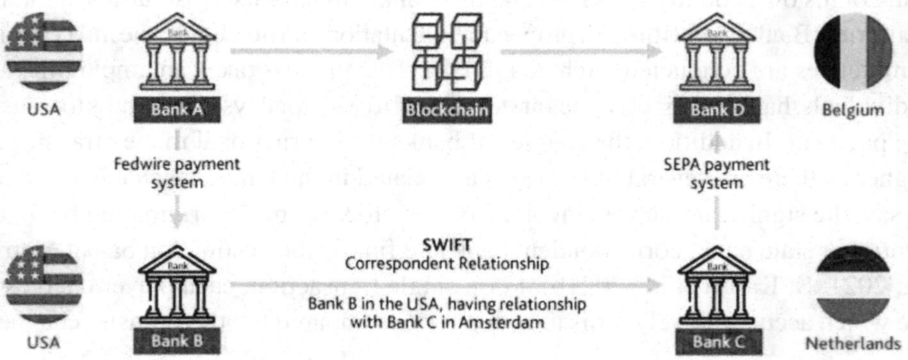

Clearing and Settlements

As mentioned earlier, the distributed ledger technology (DLT) offers significant new avenues for the international transactions and money transfer. Relating the similar with the clearing and settlements, it is asserted that DLT can transform the clearing mechanism too. For this purpose, blockchain works as a distributed database where different devices are connected to maintain and update the list of records that can hardly be altered. Similarly, when the same mechanism is linked with cryptography, the chances of tempering, changing the information, and unauthorizing the content become difficult. At first limited to cryptocurrency only, the blockchain technology has now a wider use in the clearing and settlement processes using DLT. Proponents of blockchain technology suggest that the use of blockchain technology employing the decentralized mechanism would save time, cost and counterparty risk in the clearing and settlement. Statistics show that the financial industry spends as much as around $80 billion annually on the clearing and settlement processes where most of the money goes depositories and various agents employed on the chain (Khan & Rabbani, 2021a; Sun et al., 2020a). But the use of blockchain technology would reduce this cost drastically as each party will interact directly along the chain.

Several practitioners are appraising this technology for managing the funds at a faster pace, but they are also arguing on the functional side of the use of blockchain technology where underlying assets are equities. Furthermore, there are several concerns that need to be maintained in terms of functionality such as reporting mechanism, connecting it to the market infrastructure, compliance with the regulations and legal issues and segregation of assets. The viewpoint of practitioners on the use of blockchain technology is that it is useful for those asset classes that do not require proper safekeeping of the assets (Hassan et. al., 2021b; Kosba et al., 2016; Zhang et al., 2020). However, for the class of assets which require collective safekeeping and appropriate handling, blockchain technology seems useless for it.

The debate continues and raises certain challenges for application of blockchain technology in financial industries across the globe as it has certain shortcomings in terms of regulations, decentralization and the classification of assets which needs to be understood by the scholars. However, for international clearing and settlement purposes, the use of DLT and blockchain technology plays significant role where it provides ease and reliability with no information theft and privacy leakage.

Trade Finance

Trade Finance usually refers to financial transactions involving exports and imports. It basically explains the mode of financing through international trade. Conventional mode of trade financing involves all the beneficiaries who directly and indirectly interact during the whole transaction. The common activities that surround the trade finance are lending, getting letters of credit, credit insurance and factoring. Trade finance includes several beneficiaries, for instance, importers, exporters, banks, financial intermediaries, and other credit agencies. Trade finance is of vital importance to the global economy, with the World Trade Organization estimating that 80 to 90% of global trade is reliant on this method of financing (Jessel & DiCaprio, 2018).

Trade finance aims to reduce the transaction costs and saves time in streamlining the trade processes. Apart from this facilitation, the biggest challenge faced by trade finance is to make the transactions and whole process secure and safe so that the deposits and investments of beneficiaries are risk-free. In doing so, the rapid processes of trade finance also bring different sort of risks such as seller's and buyer's risk, credit risk, and default risk. In this process, exporters consider any sale as a gift until payment is received. For this reason, exporter wants the payment whereas the importer, on the other side of the transaction, wants to receive the order as sooner as possible as they consider it as a donation from the seller until the actual goods are transferred (Zhang et al., 2020).

Figure 3 presents the conventional process of international trade where importer and exporter want to get involved in a particular business of handling good and commodities from one place of the world to another. Since both parties are located at different geographical locations, thus, the distance between the two parties makes it impossible of the physical handling of goods instantly. In this process, national and international banks act as intermediaries to ensure the creditworthiness of the seller and the buyer. The importer gets the letter of credit from his bank with a promise that he will pay for the goods received. Similarly, the exporter ships the goods and commodities to the country of importer through bill of lading. In this process, the vendor asks his bank to pay for the merchandise through a sight draft. The exporter's bank now obtains the title to get the payment from the importer's bank. When the goods are received by the importer, the importer provides funds and pays for the goods to his bank.

Applying the same mechanism in the blockchain technology, there is a great potential to change the business processes entirely and providing businesses with the opportunity to redefine their value chains, reduce the complexity of operations, and minimizing the transaction costs (Jessel & DiCaprio, 2018; Kowalski et al., 2021). As explained earlier, blockchain technology carries a distributed database that is decentralized, quick, and performs functions at a greater pace. In blockchain technology, every block is linked with the former block and combines several computer technologies which mainly include distributed data storage, point-to-point transmission, and encrypted algorithms. The conventional trade finance mechanism adopts a long route for conducting a business transaction. But, with blockchain technology, there are added advantages of time efficiency, speed of the transaction, and security concerns. Banks, playing the key role in trade finance, generate greater revenues from trade finance activities where the concern of companies is shifted from traditional ways of transactions to the advanced mode using the blockchain technology. It is claimed that blockchain technology has the capability to overcome the traditional methods of trade finance through digitization, optimization, reducing time elapse, and providing more transparency for a given transaction. Through digitization of documents, it would be unnecessary for banks and other financial intermediaries to collect, scan, and input the data into system which will ultimately provide efficiency to the complete process of trade finance.

Figure 3. The mechanism of trade finance

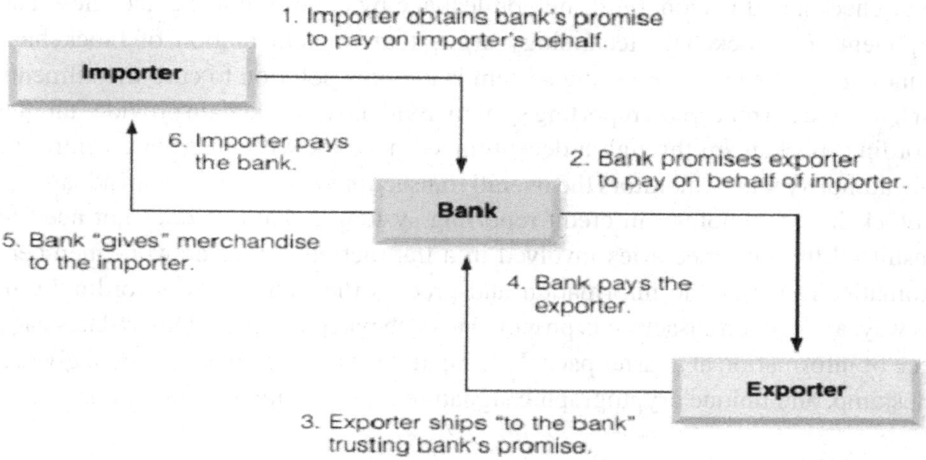

Credit Reporting

Credit reporting is the mechanism of posting the transactions into a daily ledger in a centralized database of a company. The credit reporting industry is suffering from several reporting criticisms in the current time due to plaguing the credit reporting process. It is expected by the practitioners that blockchain technology, by providing decentralized system to the reporting mechanisms of the firms will offer significant tackling of accounting and reporting frauds (Jessel & DiCaprio, 2018; Kowalski et al., 2021). Since credit reporting system mainly entails the recording of the transactions associated with deposits and investments of the customers, the cybersecurity issues are manifold in this industry. Large information hubs control the information and transactions of the firms. The statistics reveal that information theft, loss of data, inappropriate reporting mechanisms are the main bottlenecks that cause the firm to face losses. Most renowned firms such as TransUnion and Experian are an integral part of the USA credit reporting system where they collect the credit information of consumers and then sell it to the third party as credit reports. EquiFax, one of the Credit Reporting agencies in the USA, revealed to the Securities and Exchange Commission of USA that personal information and data of about 150 million natives was stolen and the most famous information thefts are related to the social security numbers of American natives, residential addresses, and digits of credit card (Zhu, 2020)

Currently, the conventional credit reporting mechanism provides imbalances in power between the lenders and customers. The consumers have no idea of information visibility, and they are not aware what is going behind in the name of credit scores, credit checks, and personal information leakage by credit reporting agencies. The proponents of blockchain technology argue that implementation of blockchain technology in the credit reporting system is the only solution to curb the ailments that haunt the current credit reporting system. Evidently, blockchain provides unique recording mechanism through a decentralized network without having central or main authority which monitors the overall transaction process. The main advantage of blockchain technology in credit reporting system is that one does not need to consult all the intermediaries involved in a transaction, rather network members automatically verify the information and process the transaction accordingly. In this way, a copy of transaction is provided to each party where system updates each piece of information at a faster pace. In the end, the transaction is recorded, given a timestamp, and unique cryptographic signature for each single transaction.

Financial Inclusion

Along with other uses of blockchain technology in financial and banking industry, it also welcomes the whole financial industry with its unique decentralized and user-friendly system. There are number of factors that address the issues of financial inclusion using the blockchain technology. Firstly, blockchain technology tackles the problem of high fees with its unique mechanisms of using blocks of information in the chain which encrypts the message in the chain and conducts a transaction (Baruri, 2016). It is arguing that processing the international payments using a national payment system is often expensive and takes ample time as there are different banks involved in the whole transaction. It is recommended that blockchain technology should be completely adopted to enjoy the real-time experience of quick money transfer (Muneeza et al., 2018). Blockchain reduces the costs and expenses associated with the money transfer as it will involve direct transfer of money from sender to receiver within less time and cost. Meanwhile, blockchain based banked and unbanked currencies would allow to send the payments around the world having the universal mode of exchange. This will allow individuals to send their funds without any costs paid to the banks, thus, reducing the expenses of international remittances.

Secondly, blockchain technology offers significant improvements in the account opening process (Rabbani et al., 2020c). Since there are around 2.4 billion individuals who do not have digital identity, blockchain technology, while overcoming the digital identity issue, can help in creating a decentralized system of identity management and can provide solutions in terms of social and financial titles (Schuetz & Venkatesh, 2020). In this way, blockchain technology, having its significant application in financial and banking industry, can help facilitate including all the beneficiaries simultaneously. These digital identities ensure that the individuals with their unique biometric characteristics have their deposits and investments secured in a blockchain.

Apart from these factors, blockchain technology reinforces mutual trust between the two parties involved in a financial transaction. Evidence suggests that blockchain technology provides secured system for its users through a decentralized network of computers to ensure that the payments are safely transferred from one party to another without involving any third or fourth party. This direct way of transactions fetches the trust of the individuals through which they can use this technology without losing privacy data and ethical concerns. The blockchain technology builds trust in a way that a comprehensive value proposition is developed by the parties involved in the transactions. Due to no involvement of any central authority or regulatory body, the only terms and conditions to comply with are the protocols of consensus where parties need to agree to these protocols. Consensus protocols are basically mathematical algorithms that require other computers on the network to build consensus on the terms; therefore, this technology is only dependent on the collaboration of its parties.

Smart Contracts

One of the most significant applications of blockchain technology is smart contracts that works on the decentralized mechanism as well as provides temper-proof algorithmic execution of a transaction. Smart contracts are basically series of digital contracts where two parties have to agree on the given terms and conditions before execution of the transaction or real-time transfer of funds (Bogucharskov et al., 2018). Smart contracts provide programming protocols through which the transaction is automated and executed. Principally, smart contracts provide the two unknown parties meet their level of trust without involving the third party such as bank. This mechanism is conducted to avoid unnecessary costs, international fund transfer charges and to access the speedy funds. The only thing in smart contract to be considered is to attain the level of trust of both parties that their transaction will be executed at a greater pace, without paying costs, and with high degree of trustworthiness.

Different scholars summed up the smart contracts as the way to reduce costs, to gather and process information, to draft and negotiate the contracts, to monitor and enforce the agreements, to manage relationships, and to allow for market-based governance systems under particular circumstances (Karim et al., 2021d; Naeem et al., 2022). Since smart contracts provide enhanced security through their storage systems, they guarantee the automation of processes without making any mistake and involvement of human being in executing the transactions. For these reasons, smart contracts enable trust among the parties through open account trading that eventually enhances transparency in the international payments. They also offer reliability of the data, reduce the risks of frauds and ensure exchange of funds. Figure 4 presents the mechanism how smart contracts work.

Figure 4. Smart contracts mechanism

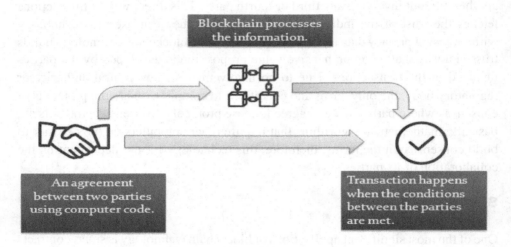

Initiating Data Ownership

Like previous applications, blockchain enables change in the data ownership while restoring the data control points of the users and empowering them to choose who can access their information on the online web systems and who cannot. The main element involved in the blockchain technology is of the trust and maintain the security of the information provided by the users (Liang et al., 2017). Meanwhile, the use of technology in the financial and banking industry inculcates that the customers with their digital identities need to protect their identities through their data ownership mechanism and they can control their data by themselves (Karafiloski & Mishev, 2017; Liang et al., 2017; Nawaz et al., 2020).

Quite often, consumers are not aware of the fact that they are providing permission to the companies to use their information and data with the use of different applications on smart phones and hand-held devices. In this way, they cannot control who can get their data and information and who cannot. Blockchain technology has the significant feature of user oriented controlling mechanism of data through which they are authorized to allow and provide permission to which their information is accessible Rabbani, Khan, & Atif, 2021; Rabbani, 2020; Mustafa Raza Rabbani et al., 2021d). The online applications of Facebook, Google, and Amazon have centralized systems and they mainly control the information of users raising the transparency and authenticity concerns (Liang et al., 2017; Nawaz et al., 2020). However, blockchain technology successfully caters such problems of privacy and information security where the user enjoys the rights of ownership on his/her own data. Blockchain technology contains several benefits for the users by providing ownership to the consumers. It also empowers the consumers that they can control and own their information and offers no chances of privacy hacks. One of the famous blockchain technologies for data ownership of individuals is blockstack that empowers consumers to control their data by using an add-on on their computers or devices. This decentralized system combines DNS with the blockchain technology to provide users with ownership of their data.

Accelerated Data Sharing

Blockchain technology is accelerating the data sharing across the chain through encrypted digital identities of customers. The process starts by automation of big data credit agencies and simultaneously storing the credit status information of customers among institutions (Sun et al., 2020b). Basically, banks need to store the information of the customers in their own databases and then encrypting the information a summarized profile can be generated and stored in a blockchain. When it is necessary to share the data, the main data provider is notified through a notification and a query is generated. By doing so, all parties can find, search, and explore the external big data by not distorting the information of their core businesses. Here, the significance of the whole process is dependent on the encrypting the information of the customers where it is necessary that the summary information of the profiles and original data must be consistent to avoid misleading results of the profiles. By providing consistent information, blockchain technology automatically realizes the encrypted information records the transaction. It ultimately helps banking and financial industry in reducing the extra work related to organizing the information (Dubovitskaya et al., 2020; Mamoshina et al., 2018; Zheng et al., 2018).

Blockchain Technology and Supply Chain Finance

Supply chain finance refers to the set of activities involved in receiving, recording, processing, and delivering the financial information across a supply chain. This process, similar to international money transfer, involves significant number of intermediaries to complete a single transaction. Alongside, there are many risks involved, for instance, regulatory risk, cybersecurity risk, default risk, and credit risk. The whole system also incurs high costs and provides lower efficiency. Blockchain technology, with its unique characteristics, tend to minimize the manual work involved in a supply chain at a faster pace as it offers the digitization of the processes (Rabbani, 2021). The application of blockchain technology in supply chain finance has several benefits where individuals, firms, vendors, and suppliers minimize the manual paperwork, improves the efficiency of the supply chain network and reduces the operational risk associated with it. Blockchain technology also ensures on-time delivery of processes and payments by combining the parties in a supply chain through automated messages once the transaction is set to be initiated.

As explained earlier, through its decentralized distributed ledger technology, every party involved in a transaction can rely on this mechanism, avoid unnecessary costs, ensure rapid execution of the transactions, and can transfer the international payments within no time. Based on statistics provided by McKinsey, banks are expected to reduce their operational cost by $13.5 to 15 billion annually and cost of risk to be minimized by $1.1 to 1.6 billion annually by employing the blockchain technology. Apart from that, blockchain technology also improves time elapse from sender of the payment to the receiver of the payment. This smooth workflow guarantees that processes are performed efficiently without information loss and temper-proof payments.

In sum, it can be argued that blockchain technology has significant applications in financial and banking industry where they mainly rely on the deposits and investments of the customers. Due to this sensitive nature of business, banks need to adopt blockchain technology to avoid extra costs, improve the speed of the processes and ensure on-time delivery of payments from one party to another. The various applications of blockchain technology indicate that financial industry needs to implement this unique technology for observing its real-time benefits and increase the profits. Besides, the application of blockchain technology and financial and banking industry is not without challenges and hurdles that are coming in its way to progress. The upcoming section describes these challenges and hurdles faced by financial industry to not implement blockchain technology in their organizational processes.

CHALLENGES TO IMPLEMENT BLOCKCHAIN TECHNOLOGY IN FINANCIAL AND BANKING INDUSTRY

There are certain challenges faced by financial and banking industry to implement the blockchain technology completely. They are given as follows:

1. Lack of awareness and knowledge of the blockchain technology is preventing the financial and banking industry to adopt this technology in their operations. There must be awareness workshops to identify the scope of the blockchain technology through which the organizations, particularly related to finance and banking industry, need to be aware of the potential benefits of blockchain. The passive approach of the firms towards blockchain technology can restrict them to enhance their profits and cut their costs.
2. Culture is also a significant challenge in the adoption and implementation of blockchain technology where it is, sometimes, difficult to build the required level of trust and authority in a given decentralized system instead of central authority that requires a more imaginative style to understand the potential of blockchain technology.
3. Environment is one of the key challenges of blockchain technology where main servers on the internet consume high levels of energy that hinders its adoption in many business sectors. Meanwhile, many cryptocurrencies that are backed by blockchain technology also need to embrace the challenges of wider scale financial inclusion.
4. Since blockchain technology is efficient in processing the transactions given the both parties maintain trust on the technology, it will need some more years to be implemented by the most of the business sectors. Before implementation, blockchain technology has to make clear its concept of providing efficient processes with temper-proof transactions and individuals need to understand it completely.
5. The other challenge in the face of blockchain technology adoption is organizations and firms where they are developing their own blockchains with their related parties. So a different orientation may not provide efficient mechanism as the single origin can provide which will ultimately reduce the network effects.
6. The most important challenge that is impeding the growth of blockchain technology in the financial and banking sector is regulation and governance. It is difficult to determine whether the blockchains can work and follow the

existing regulatory landscapes given that financial institutions work under a centralized authority to secure their interests. Blockchain technology, with its fast, decentralized approach would be able to work under such regulatory environment or not. So, it is recommended that the regulatory authorities of financial industry need to understand this technology and to implement it to reap its fruitful results.

Figure 5 presents six major challenges faced by the blockchain technology to be completely implemented in the organizations of each category whether they are service sector, finance and banking sector, manufacturing sector, or supply chain firms (Deloitte, 2019). The adoption of blockchain technology requires a significant time frame, understanding of the individuals, and regulatory barriers to cover. Since, many firms are reluctant in adopting the new technology, blockchain is also not spared from controversy of environment and its emissions in the environment. Many environmentalists would argue that with so much consumption of energy, the environmental resources may be depleted. At the same time, the wonders it creates in the lives of the beneficiaries are also not to be ignored.

Figure 5. Challenges faced by blockchain technology

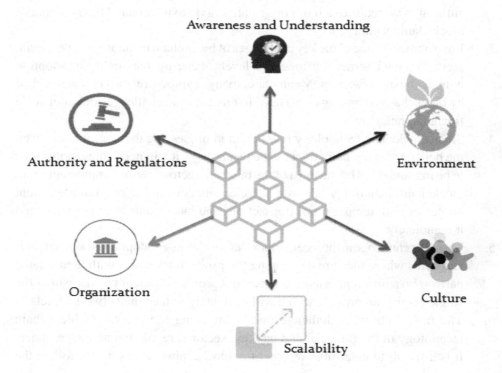

CONCLUSION

This chapter presented the ten applications of blockchain technology in the financial and banking industry beyond digital currencies. It is argued that blockchain technology is not limited to the use of digital currencies such as cryptocurrency rather it has wider scope. Ten applications explained that blockchain technology has its significant implementation in digital identities, money transfer, international trade payments, clearing and settlements, data ownership claims, data protection, financial inclusion, and supply chain finance. Due to its fast, temper-proof, and reliable mechanism of executing a transaction, blockchain technology has resolved the issues of time elapse, cost cutting, and quick delivery of funds from one party to another.

Apart from these benefits, blockchain technology is facing several hurdles in its way of growth where key challenges are given in figure 5. It is quite challenging to adopt this technology by the firms and individuals in terms of decentralized system where there is no regulatory authority is involved. Meanwhile, it requires an advanced level of understanding to be implemented. Given these arguments, it is concluded that blockchain is making international payments system quite easier and faster. And the use of blockchain technology is not only limited to digital currencies but it has its applications in different processes of organizations which provide real-time efficiency in transferring funds, ensuring data security and maintaining anonymity of both parties.

REFERENCES

Achanta, R. (2018). *Cross-border money transfer using blockchain-enabled by big data.* White Paper, External Document.

Alam, M., Rabbani, M. R., Tausif, M. R., & Abey, J. (2021). Banks' Performance and Economic Growth in India: A Panel Cointegration Analysis. *Economies*, *9*(1), 38. doi:10.3390/economies9010038

Atif, M., Hassan, M. K., Rabbani, M. R., & Khan, S. (2021). Islamic FinTech: The digital transformation bringing sustainability to Islamic finance. In *In COVID-19 and Islamic Social Finance* (pp. 94–106). Routledge. doi:10.4324/9781003121718-9

Baruri, P. (2016). Blockchain powered financial inclusion. Presentation at the *International Monetary Fund Global Symposium on Innovative Financial Inclusion: Harnessing Innovation for Inclusive Finance.*

Ben, S., & Xiaoqiong, W. (2019). Are Cryptocurrencies Good Investments? *Studies in Business and Economics*, *14*(2), 181–192. doi:10.2478be-2019-0033

Bogucharskov, A. V., Pokamestov, I. E., Adamova, K. R., & Tropina, Z. N. (2018). Adoption of blockchain technology in trade finance process. *Journal of Reviews on Global Economics*, *7*(Special Issue), 510–515. doi:10.6000/1929-7092.2018.07.47

Cousins, K., Subramanian, H., & Esmaeilzadeh, P. (2019). A value-sensitive design perspective of cryptocurrencies: A research agenda. *Communications of the Association for Information Systems*, *45*(1), 511–547. Advance online publication. doi:10.17705/1CAIS.04527

Dharani, M., Hassan, M. K., Rabbani, M. R., & Huq, T. (2021). Does the Covid-19 Pandemic Affect Faith-based Investments? Evidence from Global Sectoral Indices. *Research in International Business and Finance*, ●●●, 101537. PMID:34522060

Dubey, V. (2019). Fintech-Digital way of ID Verification and Biometric Verification in 2020. *International Journal of Innovation and Applied Studies*, *27*(4), 896–901.

Dubovitskaya, A., Novotny, P., Xu, Z., & Wang, F. (2020). Applications of blockchain technology for data-sharing in oncology: Results from a systematic literature review. *Oncology*, *98*(6, Suppl. 6), 403–411. doi:10.1159/000504325 PMID:31794967

Fosso Wamba, S., Kala Kamdjoug, J. R., Epie Bawack, R., & Keogh, J. G. (2020). Bitcoin, Blockchain and Fintech: A systematic review and case studies in the supply chain. *Production Planning and Control*, *31*(2–3), 115–142. doi:10.1080/095372 87.2019.1631460

Geranio, M. (2017). Fintech in the exchange industry: Potential for disruption? *Masaryk University Journal of Law and Technology*, *11*(2), 245–266. doi:10.5817/MUJLT2017-2-3

Hassan, M. K., Rabbani, M., & Daouia, C. (2021a). Integrating Islamic finance and Halal industry: Current landscape and future forward. *International Journal of Islamic Marketing and Branding*, *6*(1), 60. doi:10.1504/IJIMB.2021.117594

Hassan, M. K., Rabbani, M. R., & Abdullah, Y. (2021b). Socioeconomic Impact of COVID-19 in MENA region and the Role of Islamic Finance. *International Journal of Islamic Economics and Finance*, *4*(1), 51–78. doi:10.18196/ijief.v4i1.10466

Hassan, M. K., Rabbani, M. R., & Ali, M. A. (2020). Challenges for the Islamic Finance and banking in post COVID era and the role of Fintech. *Journal of Economic Cooperation and Development*, *43*(3), 93–116.

Jessel, B., & DiCaprio, A. (2018). Can blockchain make trade finance more inclusive? *Journal of Financial Transformation*, *47*, 35–50.

Karafiloski, E., & Mishev, A. (2017). Blockchain solutions for big data challenges: A literature review. *IEEE EUROCON 2017-17th International Conference on Smart Technologies*, 763–768.

Karim, S., Manab, N. A., & Ismail, R. (2020c). The Interaction Effect of Independent Boards on Corporate Governance-Corporate Social Responsibility (CG-CSR) and Performance Nexus. Asian Academy of Management Journal, 25(1).

Karim, S., Akhtar, M. U., Tashfeen, R., Raza Rabbani, M., Rahman, A. A. A., & AlAbbas, A. (2021c). Sustainable banking regulations pre and during coronavirus outbreak: the moderating role of financial stability. *Economic Research-Ekonomska Istraživanja*, 1–18.

Karim, S., Manab, N. A., & Ismail, R. B. (2020a). The dynamic impact of board composition on CSR practices and their mutual effect on organizational returns. *Journal of Asia Business Studies*, 14(4), 463–479. doi:10.1108/JABS-07-2019-0214

Karim, S., Manab, N. A., & Ismail, R. B. (2020b). Assessing the governance mechanisms, corporate social responsibility and performance: The moderating effect of board independence. *Global Business Review*. doi:10.1177/0972150920917773

Karim, S., Rabbani, M. R., & Bawazir, H. (2021a). Voluntary impacts of the risk management committee attributes on firm performance: Do board size matter? *Asian Academy of Management Journal*, 21(4), 608–625.

Karim, S., Rabbani, M. R., & Khan, M. A. (2021b). Determining the key factors of corporate leverage in Malaysian service sector firms using dynamic modeling. *Journal of Economic Cooperation and Development.*, 42(3).

Khan, S., & Rabbani, M. R. (2020b). Chatbot as Islamic Finance Expert (CaIFE): When finance meets Artificial Intelligence. *2020 International Conference on Computational Linguistics and Natural Language Processing (CLNLP 2020)*, 1–5. 10.1145/3440084.3441213

Khan, S., & Rabbani, M. R. (2020a). In Depth Analysis of Blockchain, Cryptocurrency and Sharia Compliance. *International Journal of Business Innovation and Research*, 1(1), 1. doi:10.1504/IJBIR.2020.10033066

Khan, S., & Rabbani, M. R. (2021). Artificial Intelligence and NLP based Chatbot as Islamic Banking and Finance Expert. *International Journal of Information Retrieval Research*, 11(3), 65–77. doi:10.4018/IJIRR.2021070105

Kosba, A., Miller, A., Shi, E., Wen, Z., & Papamanthou, C. (2016). Hawk: The blockchain model of cryptography and privacy-preserving smart contracts. *2016 IEEE Symposium on Security and Privacy (SP)*, 839–858. 10.1109/SP.2016.55

Kowalski, M., Lee, Z. W. Y., & Chan, T. K. H. (2021). Blockchain technology and trust relationships in trade finance. *Technological Forecasting and Social Change*, *166*, 120641. doi:10.1016/j.techfore.2021.120641

Lee, W. H., Chou, C. M., & Wang, S. W. (2016). An NFC Anti-Counterfeiting framework for ID verification and image protection. *Mobile Networks and Applications*, *21*(4), 646–655. doi:10.100711036-016-0721-9

Liang, X., Zhao, J., Shetty, S., Liu, J., & Li, D. (2017). Integrating blockchain for data sharing and collaboration in mobile healthcare applications. *2017 IEEE 28th Annual International Symposium on Personal, Indoor, and Mobile Radio Communications (PIMRC)*, 1–5.

Mamoshina, P., Ojomoko, L., Yanovich, Y., Ostrovski, A., Botezatu, A., Prikhodko, P., Izumchenko, E., Aliper, A., Romantsov, K., Zhebrak, A., Ogu, I. O., & Zhavoronkov, A. (2018). Converging blockchain and next-generation artificial intelligence technologies to decentralize and accelerate biomedical research and healthcare. *Oncotarget*, *9*(5), 5665–5690. doi:10.18632/oncotarget.22345 PMID:29464026

Moh'd Ali, M. A., Basahr, A., Rabbani, M. R., & Abdulla, Y. (2020). Transforming Business Decision Making with Internet of Things (IoT) and Machine Learning (ML). *2020 International Conference on Decision Aid Sciences and Application (DASA)*, 674–679. 10.1109/DASA51403.2020.9317174

Muneeza, A., Arshad, N. A., & Arifin, A. T. (2018). The application of blockchain technology in crowdfunding: Towards financial inclusion via technology. *International Journal of Management and Applied Research*, *5*(2), 82–98. doi:10.18646/2056.52.18-007

Naeem, M. A., Rabbani, M. R., Karim, S., & Billah, M. (2022). (in press). Religion vs Ethics: Hedge and haven properties of Sukuk and green bonds for stock markets pre- and during COVID-19. *International Journal of Islamic and Middle Eastern Finance and Management*.

Nawaz, A., Peña Queralta, J., Guan, J., Awais, M., Gia, T. N., Bashir, A. K., Kan, H., & Westerlund, T. (2020). Edge computing to secure iot data ownership and trade with the ethereum blockchain. *Sensors (Basel)*, *20*(14), 3965. doi:10.339020143965 PMID:32708807

PWC. (2016). Customers in the spotlight - How FinTech is reshaping banking. Global FinTech Survey 2016.

Rabbani, M. R. (2020a). The competitive structure and strategic positioning of commercial banks in Saudi Arabia. *International Journal on Emerging Technologies*, *11*(3), 43–46.

Rabbani, M. R., Abdulla, Y., Basahr, A., Khan, S., & Moh'd Ali, M. A. (2020b). Embracing of Fintech in Islamic Finance in the post COVID era. *2020 International Conference on Decision Aid Sciences and Application (DASA)*, 1230–1234. 10.1109/DASA51403.2020.9317196

Rabbani, M. R. (2021). COVID-19 and its impact on supply chain financing and the role of Islamic Fintech: Evidence from GCC countries. *International Journal of Agile Systems and Management*.

Rabbani, M. R., Ali, M. A. M., Rahiman, H. U., Atif, M., Zulfikar, Z., & Naseem, Y. (2021d). The Response of Islamic Financial Service to the COVID-19 Pandemic: The Open Social Innovation of the Financial System. *Journal of Open Innovation*, *7*(1), 1–18. doi:10.3390/joitmc7010085

Rabbani, M. R., Bashar, A., Nawaz, N., Karim, S., Ali, M. A. M., Khan, A., Rahiman, H., & Alam, S. (2021a). Exploring the role of Islamic Fintech in combating the after-shocks of COVID-19: The open social innovation of the Islamic financial system. *Journal of Open Innovation*, *7*(2), 136. doi:10.3390/joitmc7020136

Rabbani, M. R., Bashar, A., Nawaz, N., Karim, S., Ali, M. A. M., Rahiman, H. U., & Alam, M. S. (2021c). Exploring the role of islamic fintech in combating the aftershocks of covid-19: The open social innovation of the islamic financial system. *Journal of Open Innovation*, *7*(2), 136. Advance online publication. doi:10.3390/joitmc7020136

Rabbani, M. R., Khan, S., & Atif, M. (2021b). Machine Learning based P2P Lending Islamic FinTech Model for Small and Medium Enterprises (SMEs) in Bahrain. *International Journal of Business Innovation and Research*, *1*(1), 10040857. doi:10.1504/IJBIR.2021.10040857

Radwan, M., Calandra, D., & Koumbarakis, P. (2020). Takaful Industry and Blockchain : Challenges and Opportunities for Costs ' Reduction in Islamic Insurance Companies. *European Journal of Islamic Finance*, (October), 1–6. doi:10.13135/2421-2172/4926

Schuetz, S., & Venkatesh, V. (2020). Blockchain, adoption, and financial inclusion in India: Research opportunities. *International Journal of Information Management*, *52*, 101936. doi:10.1016/j.ijinfomgt.2019.04.009

Sun, H., Rabbani, M. R., Ahmad, N., Sial, M. S., Cheng, G., Zia-Ud-Din, M., & Fu, Q. (2020b). CSR, Co-Creation and Green Consumer Loyalty: Are Green Banking Initiatives Important? A Moderated Mediation Approach from an Emerging Economy. *Sustainability*, *12*(24), 10688. doi:10.3390u122410688

Sun, H., Rabbani, M. R., Sial, M. S., Yu, S., Filipe, J. A., & Cherian, J. (2020a). Identifying big data's opportunities, challenges, and implications in finance. *Mathematics*, *8*(10), 1738. Advance online publication. doi:10.3390/math8101738

Swan, M. (2017). Anticipating the economic benefits of blockchain. *Technology Innovation Management Review*, *7*(10), 6–13. doi:10.22215/timreview/1109

Tapscott, A., & Tapscott, D. (2017). How blockchain is changing finance. *Harvard Business Review*, *1*(9), 2–5.

Vives, X. (2017). The Impact of FinTech on the Banking Industry. *European Economy*, *2*, 97–105. https://www.fsb.org/what-we-do/policy-development/additional-policy-areas/monitoring-of-fintech/%0Ahttp://www.us.confirmation.com/blog/fintech-and-banking

Yussof, S. A., & Al-Harthy, A. (2018). Cryptocurrency as an Alternative Currency in Malaysia : Issues and Challenges. *Islam and Civilisational Renewal*, *9*(1), 48–65. doi:10.12816/0049515

Zhang, L., Xie, Y., Zheng, Y., Xue, W., Zheng, X., & Xu, X. (2020). The challenges and countermeasures of blockchain in finance and economics. *Systems Research and Behavioral Science*, *37*(4), 691–698. doi:10.1002res.2710

Zheng, X., Mukkamala, R. R., Vatrapu, R., & Ordieres-Mere, J. (2018). Blockchain-based personal health data sharing system using cloud storage. *2018 IEEE 20th International Conference on E-Health Networking, Applications and Services (Healthcom)*, 1–6.

Zhu, X. (2020). Blockchain-based identity authentication and intelligent Credit reporting. *Journal of Physics: Conference Series*, *1437*(1), 12086. doi:10.1088/1742-6596/1437/1/012086

Chapter 12
Application of Blockchain in E-Healthcare Systems

Aman Ahmad Ansari
The LNM Institute of Information Technology, India

Bharavi Mishra
The LNM Institute of Information Technology, India

Poonam Gera
The LNM Institute of Information Technology, India

ABSTRACT

The e-healthcare system maintains sensitive and private information about patients. In any e-healthcare system, exchanging health information is often required, making privacy and security a primary concern for e-healthcare systems. Another major issue is that existing e-healthcare systems use centralized servers. These centralized servers require high infrastructure and maintenance costs for day-to-day services. Along with that, server failure may affect the working of e-healthcare systems drastically and may create life-threatening situations for patients. Blockchain technology is a very useful way to provide decentralized, secure storage for healthcare information. A blockchain is a time-stamped series of immutable records of data that is managed by a cluster of computers not owned by any single entity. These blocks create a chain of immutable, tamper-proof blocks in a ledger. This chapter will discuss the different aspects of blockchain and its application in different fields of the e-healthcare system.

DOI: 10.4018/978-1-7998-8382-1.ch012

INTRODUCTION

Healthcare generates a large amount of health data regularly. Due to the sensitive nature of health data, storing and communicating such a vast amount of health data is critical and difficult (Griebel et al., 2015). In healthcare, safe, and secure health data sharing is vital for diagnosing and treating patients. Medical professionals should be able to communicate their patients' health data in a privacy-sensitive and timely fashion.

On the other hand, in e-healthcare, the patient data is transferred either by real-time monitoring or via store and forward technology (Bhatti et al., 2018; Houston et al., 1999). Patients can be diagnosed and treated remotely by experts using shared health data. Because of the sensitivity of health data, security and privacy are major challenges while sharing it. The capability to safely, securely, and scalably share health data helps in improving diagnostic accuracy and effective treatment (Berman & Fenaughty, 2005; Castaneda et al., 2015; Zhang et al., 2018).

Furthermore, various interoperability challenges are faced while sharing health data. The safe and secure communication of health data between healthcare providers or research institutes needs substantial, reliable, and healthy collaboration between them. Before sharing health data, involved entities need to be agreed upon a data-sharing agreement, nature of health data, sensitivity, procedures, ethical policies, and governing rules (Downing et al., 2017).

Recently, there has been unprecedented interest in using blockchains for store and share health data (Dubovitskaya et al., 2020; Hashim et al., 2021), real-time remote patient monitoring (Chelladurai et al., 2021; Ray et al., 2021), pharmaceutical supply chain (Bryatov & Borodinov, 2019; Jamil et al., 2019), health insurance claim (Loukil et al., 2021; Thenmozhi et al., 2021) and clinical research (Kim et al., 2021; Mamo et al., 2019).

BLOCKCHAIN

Blockchain is a growing list of records, known as blocks, and each block is linked to the previous block by including the hash of the previous block, with a timestamp and Markle tree. As each block contains information of the previous block, they form a chain (Figure 1). A server that installed a mining application and has sufficient computing resources to mine, called a full node, can generate a block. Developing a new block known as mining (Swanson, 2015). Complete blockchain will be loaded on the user's machine, which connects the blockchain with the full node to trace all transactions to the first block (Nakamoto, 2008). Presently, there exist four types of blockchain systems: public, private, hybrid, and consortium (Ray et al., 2021).

- Public Blockchains: It is a completely decentralized network where anyone with internet access can join and access the blockchain and participate in the consensus process.
- Private Blockchains: Private blockchains are permissioned blockchain that is every person require an invitation from a network administrator to join the blockchain. It is better suited for a single organization solution and stores and shares data inside the organization.
- Hybrid Blockchains: Hybrid blockchains are a combination of public and private blockchains. It allows organizations to set up a private system alongside a public system so they can control what data can be accessed by whom and what data will be made up public.
- Consortium Blockchains: A consortium blockchain, also known as a federated blockchain, is a semi-decentralized blockchain where multiple organizations govern the platform. This type of blockchain is best suitable to provide a common platform for multiple organizations to carry out transactions and share data.

Figure 1. Act of digital chains among the blocks in blockchain

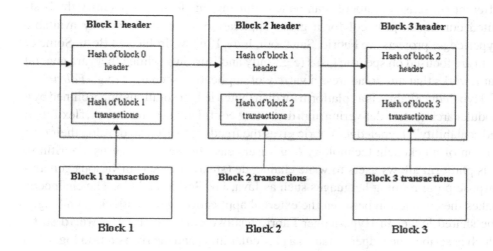

The ideation of blockchain technology was first demonstrated in the dissertation of David Chaum entitled "Computer Systems Established, Maintained, and Trusted by Mutually Suspicious Groups" (Sherman et al., 2019). In 1991, Haber and Stornetta proposed a cryptographically secured chain of blocks (Haber & Scott Stornetta, 1991; Narayanan et al., 2016). After that, Haber, Stornetta, and Bayer included the Markle tree in the design, allowing storage of several documents in one block, improving its efficiency (Bayer et al., 1993).

Satoshi Nakamoto introduced the first blockchain in the paper entitled "Bitcoin: A Peer-to-Peer Electronic Cash System". Nakamoto used a Hashcash-like method to timestamp block, eliminating trusted third parties' requirement to sign them. Nakamoto included a difficulty parameter to restrict the rate at which new blocks are added to the chain. Since bitcoin, many new cryptocurrencies have emerged, including Ether, which was founded by Vitalik Buterin in 2014. The Ether Platform, known as Ethereum, is an open blockchain platform that includes a programming language (Solidity) that enables smart contract development. Smart contracts are programs that perform some predetermined set of actions when particular condition(s) are met (*What Is Ethereum?*, 2016).

The Hyperledger Fabric, which is part of the Hyperledger project, is another major blockchain platform. The Linux Foundation started a project named Hyperledger in 2015 with the goal of advancing cross-industry collaboration by developing efficient and reliable blockchain to handle global transactions by major companies. Different companies have different requirements that a standard blockchain cannot fulfill. Hyperledger allows users to develop their own version of blockchain technology according to their needs by providing "greenhouse" architecture. For example, different consensus protocols can be tested using this feature to identify the best-suited consensus protocol for a given application scenario. Currently available Hyperledger projects are Fabric, Sawtooth, Indy, Burrow, Iroha, and Besu. Some of them are focused on specific tasks (e.g., Indy and Burrow), while others are general frameworks that aim to address a variety of application scenarios (e.g., *Fabric*).

Hypeledger Fabric is a "platform for distributed ledger solutions underpinned by a modular architecture delivering high degrees of confidentiality, resiliency, flexibility, and scalability". Hypeledger Fabric gives the freedom to users to develop their own version of blockchain technology (e.g., users can choose a consensus algorithm). This platform allows users to write chaincode (smart contract) in various general-purpose programming languages such as Java, JavaScript, and Go. The chaincode makes the connection between the external application and the blockchain ledger. The shared ledger in Hyperledger Fabric has two components: The **world state**, which describes the ledger's state at a particular time, and the **transaction log**, it is a record of all transactions that have contributed to the present world state. Hypeledger Fabric also offers the ability to create channels, which can allow a group of users to build their own private ledger, like a "sub-private" blockchain (*About Hyperledger*, 2017; *Hyperledger-Fabric Docs Main Documentation*, 2015).

ISSUES AND CHALLENGES FOR E-HEALTHCARE SYSTEM

In e-healthcare, we can use ICTs (Internet and Communication Technologies) to enhance the quality of care, to help in maintaining health records, enabling effective remote patient monitoring, etc. However, it still faces a lot of challenges in terms of security and privacy. Despite several improvements, inefficiency still exists in the healthcare system, sometimes causing severe threats to the life of the patients (Thakur et al., 2012). Since Healthcare providers collect highly sensitive patients' health information, it is a major target to cybercrimes (MailMyStatements, 2021). Health data stored in a centralized system are more prone to attack. The data breach leaks the patient health data and violates the organization's rules and regulations, causing a severe threat to patients and the organization.

- Sharing health data can help in providing effective collaborative treatment and care to the patient. It can improve diagnostic accuracy by obtaining confirmation and opinions from different specialists (Castaneda et al., 2015). We can also avoid inefficiencies and errors in treatment schedules and medication with its help (Kaushal et al., 2003; Schiff et al., 2009). Despite the importance of sharing health data, current systems need patients to collect and share their health data with medical practitioners using hard copies or electronic copies. As health data is highly sensitive, a secure and efficient way is required to share health data. In addition, patients must have a choice over when and with whom their health data is shared and should also be allowed to select to what extent they are willing to share their health data. Current healthcare systems lack such flexibility, and existing systems do not provide the facility to revert access to a particular healthcare provider. So, if a patient visits multiple healthcare providers in their lifetime, their sensitive health data are stored permanently at different locations. This raises the possibility of data leakage because it only causes a single provider with insufficient security.
- Health data is a collection of medical images, scan reports, X-rays, prescriptions, etc., that may be shared between stakeholders. Sharing this large amount of data on an electronics platform is difficult because of firewall settings or bandwidth restrictions. Loads of health data are generated daily, and it is scattered across various locations and parties like healthcare providers, patients, and medical practitioners. There is no single platform or infrastructure to retrieve, share and store health data from different locations. To safely share health data, the communicating parties should be able to trust each other before the exchange of health data. It can be between healthcare providers, patients, network providers, medical practitioners, and so on. The

delivery of fake medications can have a severe outcome on patients' health. To address this issue, the healthcare industry requires monitoring and evaluation of the overall process of manufacturing and supply chain of medical products (Plotnikov & Kuznetsova, 2018).

- Health insurance is practiced to safeguard personal assets from the disastrous toll of a grave accident, medical emergencies, or treatment of a chronic condition and guarantee that the care is available when it is required. Insurance claims of Partial or complete expenses of care are submitted to the insurer by a patient. The insurance company determines its financial responsibility for the payment and directly pays to the healthcare providers (Peterson et al., 1998). When an insurance company collects a claim, they start an investigation to decide whether to pay the claims in full, deny the claims, or reduce the amount based on the investigation report. It is called "claims adjudication" (*What Is Claims Adjudication?*, 2017). Most of the claims are now processed automatically, but claims adjudication remains complicated as claims become increasingly complex and afflicted with errors and fraud (*Insurance Fraud*, 2021; Mitic I, 2020).

- Clinical trials are an essential part of the healthcare industry. New medicines are therapies evaluated in clinical trials at various stages to identify ways to counteract new or existing diseases. These stages act as steps to test the effectiveness of a novel medication or treatment in a group of patients. The recorded data must be monitored continuously to make sure that the trials follow regulatory standards and maintain reliability. A study reported that 80% of medical studies are non-reproducible because of frauds, data misinterpretation, and trial misconduct (Benchoufi & Ravaud, 2017). Improving the quality of research ensures better reproducibility. Blockchain technology offers a decentralized approach for data tracking that enhances the trust of clinical trial participants. It also addresses the privacy and security issues of patients. Data traceability features may be useful during the clinical trial to increase medication safety. It may also facilitate active participation from healthcare industry participants, and the availability of a single platform does not leave any communication gap.

BLOCKCHAIN APPLICATIONS IN HEALTHCARE

This section explores the blockchain's applicability in the various areas of e-healthcare. The application of blockchain technology in healthcare data management, remote patient monitoring pharmaceutical supply chain, health insurance claims, and clinical trials are discussed below.

Blockchain in Healthcare Data Management

Azaria et al. presented "MedRec", a prototype for electronic health records (EHR) and medical research data. It uses blockchain to manage authentication, confidentiality, integrity, and sharing of data. MedRec stores the mark of health data on a blockchain and gives the control to the patients to choose where data can move. It enables the patient to take over the owner's responsibilities. MedRec offers patients detailed, unchangeable logs with their health data through multiple healthcare organizations. (Azaria et al., 2016).

Sharing health data often face critical limitations, like lack of authority on health data, data provenience, security, and privacy of health data. To overcome these limitations, Zhang et al. proposed FHIRChain (Fast Health Interoperability Records + Blockchain) (Zhang et al., 2018). FHIRChain is a blockchain-based application to share health data securely and scalably. It is implemented using Ethereum technology. Similarly, Xia et al. proposed MedShare (Xia et al., 2017), a trustless health data communication system to share health data among untrusted health service providers while maintaining privacy and security of health data. Medi-block (Singh et al., 2021) record proposed by Singh et al. integrates cloud and blockchain to provide a secure data sharing system. Chelladurai et al. proposed a patient-centric EHR-based system using blockchain. The proposed system offers secure health data sharing between blockchain participants (Chelladurai et al., 2021).

Health data is very sensitive and essential for patients, which is often communicated between medical professionals, health organizations, and research institutions for effective diagnosis and treatment. Patient treatment can be compromised during storage, transmission, and dissemination of sensitive health data that can cause critical threats to patients' wellbeing and maintain up-to-date patients' history. Keeping in view such limitations, Dubovitskaya et al. (Dubovitskaya et al., 2017) suggested a safe and trustworthy framework for health data using blockchain. They have used permissioned blockchain for access, management, and storage of encrypted health data. Benil and Jasper presented a cloud-based e-health system using blockchain. They use blockchain techniques for secure storage on the cloud (Benil & Jasper, 2020).

MedBlock was presented by Fan et al. (Fan et al., 2018), where they offer a mechanism for the record search. MedBlock stores the addresses of blocks holding a patient's health data associated with a healthcare provider. The inventory of the patient includes a link to the blockchain record that corresponds to it. Jiang et al. proposed BlocHIE (Jiang et al., 2018), which supports off-chain storage (data is kept in external hospitals' databases) with on-chain verification by storing the hash of external health data on a blockchain. Roehrs et al. proposed omniPHR (Roehrs et al., 2017), a distributed approach that maintains single-view interoperability of PHR. The suggested approach is built on a PHR data architecture that is flexible, interoperable, and scalable. In addition, omniPHR assessment might guarantee that PHR is divided into blocks and distributed throughout a routing overlay network.

Patients' health data is generally stored in different locations. It is not easy to access these data for patients or research institutions for biomedical research and new treatments. My Health My Data (MHMD) project uses blockchain to enable storage and communication of health data in a safe and secure manner and provide a dynamic consent interface that will enable the patients to decide who has access to their health data according to their preferences. SPchain is a blockchain-based, privacy-preserving health data exchange system. It suggested a novel chain structure for efficient retrieval of health data by combining RepuCoin and SNARKs-based hash algorithms to withstand blockchain attacks. (Zou et al., 2020).

Hashim et al. suggested a sharing technique in healthcare blockchain to resolve scalability issues known as "MedShard" (Hashim et al., 2021). It uses a transaction-based sharding technique to form shards depending on patients' previously visited entities. The proposed model improves the performance of healthcare blockchain by parallel processing of patients' appointments within shards. Preethi Harris (Harris, 2021) proposed a blockchain-based approach to store and view patient status and transaction log details related to their COVID-19 medical condition. It only provides secure data access to concerned government agencies and local authorities for monitoring and further action.

Misbhauddin et al. (Misbhauddin et al., 2020) suggested an architecture based on blockchain technology that can be used to develop scalable applications using an off-chain solution that will allow patients, lab technicians, and physicians to access the health data securely. However, only the patient has the private key, and so only the patient can share their health data with desired parties such as physicians or any medical practitioners. Deb et al. proposed CovChain (Deb et al., 2021) that provides identity preservation and anti-infodemics via a private blockchain-based internet of things solution. It maintains patient health data on a private blockchain that is secured via a distributed attribute-based encryption (d-ABE) method, allowing for restricted data access based on clearance level. A blockcahin assisted secure data management framework (BSDMF) presented by Abbas et al. (Abbas et al., 2021) to achieve secure communication of health data and improve the scalability and accessibility in the healthcare environment. It enables secure data transfer between implanted medical devices and personal servers, as well as between personal servers and cloud servers.

Dubovitskaya et al. implemented ACTION-EHR (Dubovitskaya et al., 2020), a blockchain-based patient-centric EHR data exchange and management system for patient care, particularly for cancer radiation treatment. It was implemented on Hyperledger Fabric using chaincode, a smart contract, for data exchange transactions. Wang et al. proposed GuardHealth (Z. Wang et al., 2020), a privacy-preserving blockchain-based system to provide secure storage and health data exchange. To ensure safe storage and exchange of health data. They used consortium blockchain and smart contract, which forbids data sharing without permission. A trust model is utilized to maintain trust, while a Graph Neural Network (GNN) is implemented to identify malicious nodes.

Because health data is so sensitive, different national rules place strict restrictions on what may be shared. Zhou et al. proposed BRUE (X. Zhou et al., 2020) as a solution to sharing health data across jurisdictions, allowing the secure exchange of health data with the data subject acting as a mediator at all times. They combined blockchain, user-managed access, OAuth (an authentication protocol enabling apps to obtain limited access without giving away user's password), and concept receipts in the development of BRUE.

A PHR system allows patients to control and share their health data. But in case of emergency, the patient may not be in condition to give access to his/her PHR to emergency staff. In this context, Rajput et al. presented a blockchain-based healthcare management framework that offers a tamper protection application by considering safe policies that include identifying access control, auditing, and tampering resistance in an emergency (Rajput et al., 2021).

The current healthcare systems are facing some issues regarding fragmentation, security, and privacy of health data. One of the proposed solutions to these issues has been the development of a blockchain-based e-healthcare system. However, most of them overlook the possibility of connectivity failures, such as those seen in many developing nations, which might lead to health data integrity issues. To address these issues, Gutiérrez et al. (Gutiérrez et al., 2020) proposed HealthyBlock as a blockchain-based architecture that enables the construction of unified electronic medical record systems amongst various healthcare providers with data integrity resilience in the event of connectivity failure.

Blockchain in Remote Patient Monitoring

Remote monitoring systems collect patients' health data using IOT devices, BAN sensors, and mobile devices to monitor patients' healthcare parameters. Blockchain technologies have the potential to revolutionize the storage, retrieval, and exchange of remotely gathered health data. In this context, Ichikawa et al. (Ichikawa et al., 2017) presented a tamper resistance mHealth application using blockchain that allows for trustworthy and auditable computations through the use of a decentralized network. Griggs et al. (Griggs et al., 2018) used Ethereum smart contracts to provide secure automated real-time patient monitoring. Ray et al. presented IoBHealth (Ray et al., 2021). It is a data-flow architecture that integrates the Internet of Things with blockchain to access, store, and manage e-health data.

During the COVID-19 situation, the requirement of remote patient monitoring increased significantly, as most of the patients now prefer to use online resources to obtain doctor's treatment and monitor their health state. The current remote patient monitoring systems are organization-centric, and the privacy and security of patients' health data are entirely at the discretion of healthcare providers. Wadud et al. (Wadud et al., 2020) suggested a remote patient monitoring system uses a private blockchain platform to maintain patients' privacy as well as improves system efficiency. It uses Proof of Validity (POV) and Proof of Integrity (POI) consensus algorithms to protect the privacy and integrity of health data.

Dr-MAPT is a mobile agent-based healthcare application proposed by Alruqi et al. to monitor the health status of the patient by providing health data to the doctor and patient and sending alerts in the event of an emergency. They utilized smart contracts to protect the mobile agents while mobile agents communicated with the stationary agent. Smart contracts govern the interaction of agents with the blockchains and with the mobile agents. Blockchain transactions help in the detection and prevention of malicious agents. Blockchain also keeps a blacklist to identify malicious agents and prevent future communication (Alruqi et al., 2020). Dr. Haoxiang Wang combined IoT, blockchain, and cloud technologies to provide remote monitoring of the health parameters of a patient. The suggested solution employs an Ethereum hybrid network certification mechanism, which provides a faster response time and lowers cost when compared to other techniques. It also provides a front-end web application that users can use to interact with the blockchain platform (H. Wang, 2020).

Blockchain in Pharmaceutical Supply Chain

The delivery of fake or deficient drugs can have severe outcomes on patients' wellbeing (Clauson et al., 2018). It has been recognized that blockchain technologies have the potential to overcome these issues. Bocek et al. (Bocek et al., 2017) present a blockchain-based startup that makes temperature records of pharmaceutical products available to the public during their transportation. (Bryatov & Borodinov, 2019; Haq & Esuka, 2018; Raj et al., 2019) used blockchain technology to prevent Counterfeit drugs by offering a pharmaceutical supply chain that is safe, immutable, and traceable. To address the issue of drug standardization and detect counterfeit drugs, Jamil et al. (Jamil et al., 2019) suggested a blockchain-based system. In the case of successful distribution of trustworthy and genuine medicines to patients, it is required to monitor, analyze, and assure all the steps of pharmaceutical product manufacture and supply process. In such a manner, a digital drug control system (DDCS) (Plotnikov & Kuznetsova, 2018) could be a solution to prevent fake medications. Sanofi, Pfizer, and Amgen pharmaceutical companies established a collaborative project to check and evaluate new medicines utilizing blockchain-based DDSC (Markov, 2018).

Sylim et al. (Sylim et al., 2018) developed a blockchain-based pharma surveillance system. The manufacture will initiate the supply chain process with recursive verification applied to every transaction. It will allow patients to review the drug history by scanning the code given in the receipt. Taylor (Taylor, 2016) used blockchain to achieve medicine traceability. Trujllo et al. used blockchain to ensure the security of the drug supply system (Guzman Trujllo, 2018).

Blockchain in Health Insurance Claims

Immutability, transparency, and auditability properties of blockchain can benefit the health insurance claims system (Gatteschi et al., 2018). However, implementations of such systems are minimal. Zhou et al. proposed MIStore (Zhou et al., 2018), a blockchain-based medical insurance storage system that immutably stores the encrypted insurance data to the health insurance company. Thenmozhi et al. developed a tampering-proof health insurance claim processing system using blockchain (Thenmozhi et al., 2021).

Leila Ismail and Sherali Zeadally proposed Block-HI (Ismail & Zeadally, 2021), a framework for healthcare insurance fraud detection based on a permissioned blockchain network. It uses the Practical Byzantine Fault Tolerance (PBFT) consensus algorithm. Loukil et al. proposed CioSy (Loukil et al., 2021), an insurance system built on blockchain technology for processing and monitoring insurance transactions. CioSy's goal is to use smart contracts to automate insurance policy processing, claim management, and payment. The authors have created an Ethereum blockchain-based prototype, demonstrating that the proposed technique is practical and cost-effective in terms of time and money.

Blockchains in Clinical Research

Clinical trials are facing many issues such as record keeping, data sharing, data integrity, data privacy and security, and so on. Researchers are focusing on solving these challenges utilizing blockchain technology. Soon, there will be many applications of blockchain with machine learning and artificial intelligence.

Nugent et al. presented a study to address the patient enrolment issue. It showed that the application of the Ethereum smart contract for data management system transparency in clinical trials. It showed the use of the Ethereum smart contract for transparency of the data management system in clinical trials (Nugent et al., 2016). Consent collecting is a continuous process that does not cease when consent is obtained prior to the start of a clinical study. There are several circumstances in which patient re-consent is needed. Minor trial issues, such as a change in the research process, new risks, and worsening of the medical condition, should be communicated to patients. In this context, Benchoufi et al. (Benchoufi et al., 2017) suggested a blockchain-based framework for obtaining informed permission from patients for tracking and maintaining a safe, publically verifiable, and unfalsifiable manner.

Kim et al. suggested DynamiChain (Kim et al., 2021), a medical blockchain based on a security management system and dynamic consent system for handling patients' health data. It supports dynamic consent algorithm-based modular design so that participants can choose functions like authentication function, consensus algorithm, etc. Mamo et al. presented Dwarna (Mamo et al., 2019), a web-based portal for dynamic consent. It uses blockchain to store the consent of research participants to create an immutable audit trail of consent changes. Dwarna's transparent structure will increase the trust in the biobanking process by providing research participants more control over research studies they are participated in by providing withdrawal of consent functionality. Withdrawing of consent will request the deletion of biospecimen and associated data related to the research participant.

Patients' health data can be utilized to improve healthcare delivery. Even so, indiscriminate processing of health data might compromise patients' security and privacy. To ensure the security and privacy of a patient's health data, the healthcare service providers require consent from the patient for any processing of their health data. Cornelius C. Agbo and Qusay H. Mahmoud (Agbo & Mahmoud, 2020) suggested an e-health consent management framework utilizing blockchain technologies for processing patients' health data.

Resolving the conflict between patients' privacy and research or commercial need for health data has become a difficult challenge. To address the problem, Huang et al. (Huang et al., 2020) presented a blockchain-based privacy-preserving scheme for sharing health data securely between patients, research institutions, cloud servers, and so on. Simultaneously, it provides data consistency and availability amongst patients and research institutions by using zero-knowledge proof to check if patients' health data fulfills the guidelines specified by research institutions without compromising the patient's privacy.

CHALLENGES TO APPLYING BLOCKCHAIN IN E-HEALTHCARE

Blockchain is a developing technology widely implemented in various sectors like cryptocurrency systems, healthcare, automobile industries, etc. (Alhadhrami et al., 2017; Shae & Tsai, 2017). But this technology brings its own collection of issues that must be tackled. This section discusses a few of these key issues.

Security and Privacy Risks

Implementation of an application using blockchain technology eliminates the requirement of a trusted third party to carry out transactions (Alhadhrami et al., 2017). Since the blockchain allows the entire community to carry out the verification process, the data becomes prone to security and privacy risks (Kuo & Ohno-Machado, 2018). As all the nodes in the network can access the data from one node, that will cause a considerable threat on data privacy. In the case of an emergency, one or more representatives can be selected by the patient to access the health data. The representative can choose more people and allow access to health data from the same patient. This may pose a security and privacy risk to health data. Using a high-security mechanism to secure health data may cause problems when moving the data between blocks. As a result, the recipients can retrieve limited or partial health data. furthermore, blockchain is vulnerable to 51% attack also known as Majority Consensus attack (Frankenfield, 2019). This can place when a group of miners have ownership of 50% or more blocks in the network. As a result, they gain power on the network and may be able to prevent future transactions by refusing to provide consent.

Storage Management Issues

Another challenge of using blockchain in healthcare is storage capacity management. Blockchain was initially intended to store limited size transactions, so it didn't require a large amount of storage (Esposito et al., 2018). The healthcare system typically has many users, including patients, medical professionals, billing agents, etc. When huge amounts of data such as patient records, health history, test reports, X-rays, MRI scans, and other medical images are stored on a blockchain, it may suffer enormous overhead. All data will be available to all network nodes that require large amounts of storage (Bennett, 2018; Pirtle & Ehrenfeld, 2018). In addition, blockchain is a transaction-based technology, so the datasets tend to grow rapidly. Due to the growing size of the datasets, searching and accessing health data becomes very slow, ill-suited for applications that need real-time or fast transactions. Therefore, scalable, and resilient blockchain solutions are required.

Interoperability Issues

Interoperability is also a problem for blockchain (Kuo & Ohno-Machado, 2018). The application developed on different blockchain platforms hardly complied with each other in terms of integrated functioning. Misbhauddin et al. (Misbhauddin et al., 2020) developed the application on the Ethereum platform, which is not operable with the application based on Hyperledger developed by Dubovitskaya et al. (Dubovitskaya et al., 2020). Many applications are implemented on the Ethereum platform (like MedRec, Ancile, etc.) and Hyperledger (like Healthclaims, medical chains, etc.). There is hardly any application that claims to be interoperable with integration support. Smart contracts that can enable sharing of data between different blockchain platforms will help to solve this issue of interoperable blockchain. Also, there isn't any standard format to exchange health data in blockchain-based healthcare applications. Sharing data between different applications will certainly face standardization challenges.

CONCLUSION

Blockchain technology has evolved since its introduction as an underlying technology for cryptocurrency bitcoin. Its scope has been expanded across different domains, including healthcare. Blockchain is expected to bring about a tremendous revolution in healthcare by offering decentralized, secure, and immutable health records. It will gradually decrease the need for human intervention and reduce the extra cost of third parties. In this chapter, we discussed the application of blockchain technology in different fields of e-healthcare systems. We started with blockchain technology then discussed the e-healthcare system and issues and challenges it faces. Then we highlighted the application of blockchain technology in the e-healthcare system. We also discussed the challenges faced by these blockchain applications in the e-healthcare system. Due to all of these challenges, we cannot find blockchain as a universal solution for the issues in e-healthcare yet. It is promising to use blockchain in e-healthcare, but more research is needed to overcome the challenges.

REFERENCES

Abbas, A., Alroobaea, R., Krichen, M., Rubaiee, S., Vimal, S., & Almansour, F. M. (2021). Blockchain-assisted secured data management framework for health information analysis based on Internet of Medical Things. *Personal and Ubiquitous Computing*, *2021*, 1–14. doi:10.100700779-021-01583-8

About Hyperledger. (2017). https://www.hyperledger.org/about

Agbo, C. C., & Mahmoud, Q. H. (2020). Design and Implementation of a Blockchain-Based E-Health Consent Management Framework. *IEEE Transactions on Systems, Man, and Cybernetics: Systems,* 812–817. doi:10.1109/SMC42975.2020.9283203

Alhadhrami, Z., Alghfeli, S., Alghfeli, M., Abedlla, J. A., & Shuaib, K. (2017). Introducing blockchains for healthcare. *2017 International Conference on Electrical and Computing Technologies and Applications, ICECTA 2017*, 1–4. 10.1109/ICECTA.2017.8252043

Alruqi, M., Hsairi, L., & Eshmawi, A. (2020). Secure mobile agents for patient status telemonitoring using blockchain. *ACM International Conference Proceeding Series*, 224–228. 10.1145/3428690.3429181

Azaria, A., Ekblaw, A., Vieira, T., & Lippman, A. (2016). MedRec: Using blockchain for medical data access and permission management. *Proceedings - 2016 2nd International Conference on Open and Big Data, OBD 2016*, 25–30. 10.1109/OBD.2016.11

Bayer, D., Haber, S., & Stornetta, W. S. (1993). Improving the Efficiency and Reliability of Digital Time-Stamping. In *Sequences II* (pp. 329–334). Springer. doi:10.1007/978-1-4613-9323-8_24

Benchoufi, M., Porcher, R., & Ravaud, P. (2017). Blockchain protocols in clinical trials: Transparency and traceability of consent. *F1000 Research*, 6, 66. Advance online publication. doi:10.12688/f1000research.10531.1 PMID:29167732

Benchoufi, M., & Ravaud, P. (2017). Blockchain technology for improving clinical research quality. *Trials 2017*, 18(1), 1–5. doi:10.1186/s13063-017-2035-z

Benil, T., & Jasper, J. (2020). Cloud based security on outsourcing using blockchain in E-health systems. *Computer Networks*, 178, 107344. doi:10.1016/j.comnet.2020.107344

Bennett, B. (2018). Blockchain HIE Overview: A Framework for Healthcare Interoperability. *Telehealth and Medicine Today*, 2(3). Advance online publication. doi:10.30953/tmt.v2.14

Berman, M., & Fenaughty, A. (2005). Technology and managed care: Patient benefits of telemedicine in a rural health care network. *Health Economics*, 14(6), 559–573. doi:10.1002/hec.952 PMID:15497196

Bhatti, A., Siyal, A. A., Mehdi, A., Shah, H., Kumar, H., & Bohyo, M. A. (2018). Development of cost-effective tele-monitoring system for remote area patients. *2018 International Conference on Engineering and Emerging Technologies, ICEET 2018*, 1–7. 10.1109/ICEET1.2018.8338646

Bocek, T., Rodrigues, B. B., Strasser, T., & Stiller, B. (2017). Blockchains everywhere - A use-case of blockchains in the pharma supply-chain. *Proceedings of the IM 2017 - 2017 IFIP/IEEE International Symposium on Integrated Network and Service Management*, 772–777. 10.23919/INM.2017.7987376

Bryatov, S. R., & Borodinov, A. A. (2019). Blockchain technology in the pharmaceutical supply chain: researching a business model based on Hyperledger Fabric. Information Technology and Nanotechnology. doi:10.18287/1613-0073-2019-2416-134-140

Castaneda, C., Nalley, K., Mannion, C., Bhattacharyya, P., Blake, P., Pecora, A., Goy, A., & Suh, K. S. (2015). Clinical decision support systems for improving diagnostic accuracy and achieving precision medicine. *Journal of Clinical Bioinformatics*, *5*(1), 4. doi:10.118613336-015-0019-3 PMID:25834725

Chelladurai, U., Pandian, D. S., & Ramasamy, D. K. (2021). A Blockchain based Patient Centric EHR Storage and Integrity Management for e-Health Systems. *Health Policy and Technology*, *100513*. Advance online publication. doi:10.1016/j.hlpt.2021.100513

Clauson, K. A., Breeden, E. A., Davidson, C., & Mackey, T. K. (2018). Leveraging Blockchain Technology to Enhance Supply Chain Management in Healthcare. *Blockchain in Healthcare Today*, *1*(0). Advance online publication. doi:10.30953/bhty.v1.20

Deb, P. K., Mukherjee, A., & Misra, S. (2021). CovChain: Blockchain-Enabled Identity Preservation and Anti-Infodemics for COVID-19. *IEEE Network*, *35*(3), 42–47. doi:10.1109/MNET.011.2000669

Downing, N. L., Adler-Milstein, J., Palma, J. P., Lane, S., Eisenberg, M., Sharp, C., & Longhurst, C. A. (2017). Health information exchange policies of 11 diverse health systems and the associated impact on volume of exchange. *Journal of the American Medical Informatics Association: JAMIA*, *24*(1), 113–122. doi:10.1093/jamia/ocw063 PMID:27301748

Dubovitskaya, A., Baig, F., Xu, Z., Shukla, R., Zambani, P. S., Swaminathan, A., Jahangir, M. M., Chowdhry, K., Lachhani, R., Idnani, N., Schumacher, M., Aberer, K., Stoller, S. D., Ryu, S., & Wang, F. (2020). ACTION-EHR: Patient-centric blockchain-based electronic health record data management for cancer care. *Journal of Medical Internet Research*, *22*(8), 1–15. doi:10.2196/13598 PMID:32821064

Dubovitskaya, A., Xu, Z., Ryu, S., Schumacher, M., & Wang, F. (2017). Secure and Trustable Electronic Medical Records Sharing using Blockchain. *AMIA Symposium*, 650–659.

Esposito, C., De Santis, A., Tortora, G., Chang, H., & Choo, K. K. R. (2018). Blockchain: A Panacea for Healthcare Cloud-Based Data Security and Privacy? *IEEE Cloud Computing, 5*(1), 31–37. doi:10.1109/MCC.2018.011791712

Fan, K., Wang, S., Ren, Y., Li, H., & Yang, Y. (2018). MedBlock: Efficient and Secure Medical Data Sharing Via Blockchain. *Journal of Medical Systems, 42*(8), 1–11. doi:10.100710916-018-0993-7 PMID:29931655

Frankenfield, J. (2019). *51% Attack.* https://www.investopedia.com/terms/1/51-attack.asp

Gatteschi, V., Lamberti, F., Demartini, C., Pranteda, C., & Santamaría, V. (2018). Blockchain and Smart Contracts for Insurance: Is the Technology Mature Enough? *Future Internet 2018, 10*(2), 20. doi:10.3390/fi10020020

Griebel, L., Prokosch, H. U., Köpcke, F., Toddenroth, D., Christoph, J., Leb, I., Engel, I., & Sedlmayr, M. (2015). A scoping review of cloud computing in healthcare. In BMC Medical Informatics and Decision Making (Vol. 15, Issue 1, pp. 1–16). BioMed Central Ltd. doi:10.118612911-015-0145-7

Griggs, K. N., Ossipova, O., Kohlios, C. P., Baccarini, A. N., Howson, E. A., & Hayajneh, T. (2018). Healthcare Blockchain System Using Smart Contracts for Secure Automated Remote Patient Monitoring. *Journal of Medical Systems, 42*(7), 130. doi:10.100710916-018-0982-x PMID:29876661

Gutiérrez, O., Romero, G., Pérez, L., Salazar, A., Charris, M., & Wightman, P. (2020). HealthyBlock: Blockchain-Based IT Architecture for Electronic Medical Records Resilient to Connectivity Failures. *International Journal of Environmental Research and Public Health 2020, 17*(19), 7132. doi:10.3390/ijerph17197132

Guzman Trujllo, C. G. (2018). *The role of blockchain in the pharmaceutical industry supply chain as a tool for reducing the flow of counterfeit drugs.* https://esource.dbs.ie/handle/10788/3556

Haber, S., & Scott Stornetta, W. (1991). How to time-stamp a digital document. Lecture Notes in Computer Science, 537, 437–455. doi:10.1007/3-540-38424-3_32

Haq, I., & Esuka, O. M. (2018). Blockchain Technology in Pharmaceutical Industry to Prevent Counterfeit Drugs Article in International Journal of Computer Applications · March. *International Journal of Computers and Applications, 180*(25), 975–8887. doi:10.5120/ijca2018916579

Harris, P. (2021). Blockchain for COVID-19 Patient Health Record. *Proceedings - 5th International Conference on Computing Methodologies and Communication, ICCMC 2021*, 534–538. 10.1109/ICCMC51019.2021.9418443

Hashim, F., Shuaib, K., & Sallabi, F. (2021). *MedShard: Electronic Health Record Sharing Using Blockchain Sharding*. doi:10.3390/su13115889

Houston, M. S., Myers, J. D., Levens, S. P., McEvoy, M. T., Smith, S. A., Khandheria, B. K., Shen, W. K., Torchia, M. E., & Berry, D. J. (1999). Clinical consultations using store-and-forward telemedicine technology. *Mayo Clinic Proceedings*, *74*(8), 764–769. doi:10.4065/74.8.764 PMID:10473351

Huang, H., Zhu, P., Xiao, F., Sun, X., & Huang, Q. (2020). A blockchain-based scheme for privacy-preserving and secure sharing of medical data. *Computers & Security*, *99*, 102010. doi:10.1016/j.cose.2020.102010 PMID:32895584

Hyperledger-fabric docs main documentation. (2015). https://hyperledger-fabric.readthedocs.io/en/latest/blockchain.html

Ichikawa, D., Kashiyama, M., & Ueno, T. (2017). Tamper-resistant mobile health using blockchain technology. *JMIR mHealth and uHealth*, *5*(7), e7938. https://doi.org/10.2196/mhealth.7938

Insurance Fraud. (2021). https://content.naic.org/cipr_topics/topic_insurance_fraud.htm

Ismail, L., & Zeadally, S. (2021). *Healthcare Insurance Frauds: Taxonomy and Blockchain-based Detection Framework (Block-HI) Energy Efficiency in Cloud Infrastructure View project Scheduling in Cloud Computing for Applications' Performance Optimization View project*. doi:10.1109/MITP.2021.3071534

Jamil, F., Hang, L., Kim, K. H., & Kim, D. H. (2019). A novel medical blockchain model for drug supply chain integrity management in a smart hospital. *Electronics, 8*(5), 505. doi:10.3390/electronics8050505

Jiang, S., Cao, J., Wu, H., Yang, Y., Ma, M., & He, J. (2018). Blochie: A blockchain-based platform for healthcare information exchange. *Proceedings - 2018 IEEE International Conference on Smart Computing, SMARTCOMP 2018*, 49–56. doi:10.1109/SMARTCOMP.2018.00073

Kaushal, R., Shojania, K. G., & Bates, D. W. (2003). Effects of Computerized Physician Order Entry and Clinical Decision Support Systems on Medication Safety: A Systematic Review. *Archives of Internal Medicine*, *163*(12), 1409–1416. https://doi.org/10.1001/ARCHINTE.163.12.1409

Kim, T. M., Lee, S.-J., Chang, D.-J., Koo, J., Kim, T., Yoon, K.-H., Choi, I.-Y., & DynamiChain, I. (2021). *DynamiChain: Development of Medical Blockchain Ecosystem Based on Dynamic Consent System Citation.* doi:10.3390/app11041612

Kuo, T.-T., & Ohno-Machado, L. (2018). *ModelChain: Decentralized Privacy-Preserving Healthcare Predictive Modeling Framework on Private Blockchain Networks.* https://arxiv.org/abs/1802.01746

Loukil, F., Boukadi, K., Hussain, R., & Abed, M. (2021). CioSy: A Collaborative Blockchain-Based Insurance System. *Electronics 2021, 10*(11), 1343. doi:10.3390/ELECTRONICS10111343

MailMyStatements. (2021). *7 Major Challenges Facing the Healthcare Industry in 2021.* https://mailmystatements.com/2020/10/27/2019challenges/

Mamo, N., Martin, G. M., Desira, M., Ellul, B., & Ebejer, J.-P. (2019). Dwarna: a blockchain solution for dynamic consent in biobanking. *European Journal of Human Genetics, 28*(5), 609–626. doi:10.1038/s41431-019-0560-9

Markov, A. (2018). *Use of blockchain in pharmaceuticals and medicine.* https://miningbitcoinguide.com/technology/blokchejn-v-meditsine

Misbhauddin, M., AlAbdulatheam, A., Aloufi, M., Al-Hajji, H., & AlGhuwainem, A. (2020). MedAccess: A Scalable Architecture for Blockchain-based Health Record Management. *2020 2nd International Conference on Computer and Information Sciences (ICCIS)*, 1–5. doi:10.1109/ICCIS49240.2020.9257720

Mitic, I. (2020). *The Fraudster Next Door: 30 Insurance Fraud Statistics - Fortunly.* https://fortunly.com/statistics/insurance-fraud-statistics/#gref

Nakamoto, S. (2008). *Bitcoin: A Peer-to-Peer Electronic Cash System.* https://www.bitcoinpaper.info/bitcoinpaper-html/

Narayanan, A., Bonneau, J., Felten, E., Miller, A., & Goldfeder, S. (2016). *Bitcoin and Cryptocurrency Technologies: A Comprehensive Introduction.* Princeton University Press. https://books.google.co.in/books?hl=en&lr=&id=LchFDAAAQBAJ&oi=fnd&pg=PP1&dq=Narayanan,+Arvind%3B+Bonneau,+Joseph%3B+Felten,+Edward%3B+Miller,+Andrew%3B+Goldfeder,+Steven+(2016).+Bitcoin+and+cryptocurrency+technologies:+a+comprehensive+introduction.+Prince

Nugent, T., Upton, D., & Cimpoesu, M. (2016). Improving data transparency in clinical trials using blockchain smart contracts. *F1000Research 2016, 5*, 2541. doi:10.12688/f1000research.9756.1

Peterson, B. E., Kwant, J. W., Cecil, V. C., & Provost, W. A. (1998). *Electronic creation, submission, adjudication, and payment of health insurance claims*. Academic Press.

Pirtle, C., & Ehrenfeld, J. (2018). Blockchain for Healthcare: The Next Generation of Medical Records? *Journal of Medical Systems, 42*(9), 1–3.

Plotnikov, V., & Kuznetsova, V. (2018). The Prospects for the Use of Digital Technology "blockchain" in the Pharmaceutical Market. *MATEC Web of Conferences, 193*. doi:10.1051/matecconf/201819302029

Raj, R., Rai, N., & Agarwal, S. (2019). Anticounterfeiting in Pharmaceutical Supply Chain by establishing Proof of Ownership. *IEEE Region 10 Annual International Conference, Proceedings/TENCON,* 1572–1577. doi:10.1109/TENCON.2019.8929271

Rajput, A. R., Li, Q., & Ahvanooey, M. T. (2021). A Blockchain-Based Secret-Data Sharing Framework for Personal Health Records in Emergency Condition. *Healthcare 2021, 9*(2), 206. doi:10.3390/HEALTHCARE9020206

Ray, P. P., Dash, Di., Salah, K., & Kumar, N. (2021). Blockchain for IoT-Based Healthcare: Background, Consensus, Platforms, and Use Cases. *IEEE Systems Journal, 15*(1), 85–94. https://doi.org/10.1109/JSYST.2020.2963840

Roehrs, A., da Costa, C. A., & da Rosa Righi, R. (2017). OmniPHR: A distributed architecture model to integrate personal health records. *Journal of Biomedical Informatics, 71*, 70–81. https://doi.org/10.1016/j.jbi.2017.05.012

Schiff, G. D., Hasan, O., Kim, S., Abrams, R., Cosby, K., Lambert, B. L., Elstein, A. S., Hasler, S., Kabongo, M. L., Krosnjar, N., Odwazny, R., Wisniewski, M. F., & McNutt, R. A. (2009). Diagnostic Error in Medicine: Analysis of 583 Physician-Reported Errors. *Archives of Internal Medicine, 169*(20), 1881–1887. https://doi.org/10.1001/ARCHINTERNMED.2009.333

Shae, Z., & Tsai, J. J. P. (2017). On the Design of a Blockchain Platform for Clinical Trial and Precision Medicine. *Proceedings - International Conference on Distributed Computing Systems*, 1972–1980. doi:10.1109/ICDCS.2017.61

Sherman, A. T., Javani, F., Zhang, H., & Golaszewski, E. (2019). On the Origins and Variations of Blockchain Technologies. *IEEE Security and Privacy, 17*(1), 72–77. https://doi.org/10.1109/MSEC.2019.2893730

Singh, C., Chauhan, D., Deshmukh, S. A., Vishnu, S. S., & Walia, R. (2021). Medi-Block record: Secure data sharing using block chain technology. *Informatics in Medicine Unlocked, 24*, 100624. doi:10.1016/j.imu.2021.100624

Swanson, T. (2015). *Consensus-as-a-service: a brief report on the emergence of permissioned, distributed ledger systems.* Academic Press.

Sylim, P., Liu, F., Marcelo, A., & Fontelo, P. (2018). Blockchain Technology for Detecting Falsified and Substandard Drugs in Distribution: Pharmaceutical Supply Chain Intervention. *JMIR Research Protocols, 7*(9). https://doi.org/10.2196/10163

Taylor, P. (2016). *Applying blockchain technology to medicine traceability.* https://www.securingindustry.com/pharmaceuticals/applying-blockchain-technology-to-medicine-traceability/s40/a2766/#.YN-ebNUzbIU

Thakur, R., Hsu, S. H. Y., & Fontenot, G. (2012). Innovation in healthcare: Issues and future trends. *Journal of Business Research, 65*(4), 562–569. https://doi.org/10.1016/J.JBUSRES.2011.02.022

Thenmozhi, M., Dhanalakshmi, R., Geetha, S., & Valli, R. (2021). Implementing blockchain technologies for health insurance claim processing in hospitals. *Materials Today: Proceedings.* doi:10.1016/j.matpr.2021.02.776

Wadud, M. A. H., Amir-Ul-Haque Bhuiyan, T. M., Uddin, M. A., & Rahman, M. M. (2020). A patient centric agent assisted private blockchain on hyperledger fabric for managing remote patient monitoring. *Proceedings of 2020 11th International Conference on Electrical and Computer Engineering, ICECE 2020,* 194–197. doi:10.1109/ICECE51571.2020.9393124

Wang, H. (2020). IoT based Clinical Sensor Data Management and Transfer using Blockchain Technology. *Journal of ISMAC, 02*(03), 154–159. https://doi.org/10.36548/jismac.2020.3.003

Wang, Z., Luo, N., & Zhou, P. (2020). GuardHealth: Blockchain empowered secure data management and Graph Convolutional Network enabled anomaly detection in smart healthcare. *Journal of Parallel and Distributed Computing, 142,* 1–12. https://doi.org/10.1016/J.JPDC.2020.03.004

What Is Claims Adjudication? (2017). https://apexedi.com/what-is-claims-adjudication/

What is Ethereum? (2016). https://ethdocs.org/en/latest/introduction/what-is-ethereum.html

Xia, Q., Sifah, E. B., Asamoah, K. O., Gao, J., Du, X., & Guizani, M. (2017). MeDShare: Trust-Less Medical Data Sharing among Cloud Service Providers via Blockchain. *IEEE Access: Practical Innovations, Open Solutions, 5,* 14757–14767. https://doi.org/10.1109/ACCESS.2017.2730843

Zhang, P., White, J., Schmidt, D. C., Lenz, G., & Rosenbloom, S. T. (2018). FHIRChain: Applying Blockchain to Securely and Scalably Share Clinical Data. *Computational and Structural Biotechnology Journal, 16*, 267–278. https://doi.org/10.1016/j.csbj.2018.07.004

Zhou, L., Wang, L., & Sun, Y. (2018). MIStore: A Blockchain-Based Medical Insurance Storage System. *Journal of Medical Systems, 42*(8), 149. https://doi.org/10.1007/s10916-018-0996-4

Zhou, X., Jesus, V., Wang, Y., & Josephs, M. (2020). User-controlled, auditable, cross-jurisdiction sharing of healthcare data mediated by a public blockchain. *Proceedings - 2020 IEEE 19th International Conference on Trust, Security and Privacy in Computing and Communications, TrustCom 2020*, 87–96. doi:10.1109/TRUSTCOM50675.2020.00025

Zou, R., Lv, X., & Zhao, J. (2020). SPChain: Blockchain-based Medical Data Sharing and Privacy-preserving eHealth System. *Information Processing & Management, 58*(4). https://doi.org/10.1016/j.ipm.2021.102604

Compilation of References

Abbas, A., Alroobaea, R., Krichen, M., Rubaiee, S., Vimal, S., & Almansour, F. M. (2021). Blockchain-assisted secured data management framework for health information analysis based on Internet of Medical Things. *Personal and Ubiquitous Computing, 2021*, 1–14. doi:10.100700779-021-01583-8

Abduvaliyev, A., Pathan, A. S. K., Zhou, J., Roman, R., & Wong, W. C. (2013). On the vital areas of intrusion detection systems in wireless sensor networks. *IEEE Communications Surveys and Tutorials, 15*(3), 1223–1237. doi:10.1109/SURV.2012.121912.00006

Aberer, K., Hauswirth, H., & Salehi, A. (2006). *Middleware Support for the Internet of Things.* Available: www.manfredhauswirth.org/research/papers/WSN2006.pdf

About Hyperledger. (2017). https://www.hyperledger.org/about

Abreu, P. W., Aparicio, M., & Costa, C. J. (2018). *Blockchain technology in the auditing environment.* Paper presented at the 2018 13th Iberian Conference on Information Systems and Technologies (CISTI). 10.23919/CISTI.2018.8399460

Achanta, R. (2018). *Cross-border money transfer using blockchain-enabled by big data.* White Paper, External Document.

ACS. (2018). *Blockchain innovation. A patent analytics report.* IP Australia.

Adat, V., & Gupta, B. B. (2017). A DDoS attack mitigation framework for Internet of things. *2017 International Conference on Communication and Signal Processing (ICCSP)*, 2036–2041. 10.1109/ICCSP.2017.8286761

Afolabi. (2018). Evolution of wireless networks technologies, history and emerging technology of 5G wireless network: A review. *Journal of Telecommunications System & Management, 7*(3), 1–5.

Agbo, C. C., & Mahmoud, Q. H. (2020). Design and Implementation of a Blockchain-Based E-Health Consent Management Framework. *IEEE Transactions on Systems, Man, and Cybernetics: Systems,* 812–817. doi:10.1109/SMC42975.2020.9283203

Ahemd, M. M., Shah, M. A., & Wahid, A. (2017). IoT security: a layered approach for attacks and defenses. *2017 International Conference on Communication Technologies (ComTech)*, 104–110. 10.1109/COMTECH.2017.8065757

Airehrour, D., Gutierrez, J. A., & Ray, S. K. (2019). Sectrust-rpl: A secure trust-aware rpl routing protocol for the Internet of things. *Future Generation Computer Systems*, *93*, 860–876. doi:10.1016/j.future.2018.03.021

Aitken, R. (2018). *Bitcoin & Beyond: Can Blockchain bring in "The Masses" to realize its full potential?* https://www.forbes.com/sites/rogeraitken/2018/06/30/bitcoin-beyond-can-blockchain-bring-in-the-masses-to-realize-its-full-potential

Aitzhan, N. Z., & Svetinovic, D. (2016). Security and privacy in decentralized energy trading through multi-signatures, blockchain and anonymous messaging streams. *IEEE Transactions on Dependable and Secure Computing*, *15*(5), 840–852. doi:10.1109/TDSC.2016.2616861

Alaba, F. A., Othman, M., Hashem, I. A. T., & Alotaibi, F. (2017). Internet of things security: A survey. *Journal of Network and Computer Applications*, *88*, 10–28. doi:10.1016/j.jnca.2017.04.002

Alam, M., Rabbani, M. R., Tausif, M. R., & Abey, J. (2021). Banks' Performance and Economic Growth in India: A Panel Cointegration Analysis. *Economies*, *9*(1), 38. doi:10.3390/economies9010038

Alccer, V., & Cruz-Machado, V. (2019). Scanning the industry 4.0: A literature review on technologies for manufacturing systems, Engineering Science and Technology. *International Journal (Toronto, Ont.)*, *22*(3), 899–919.

Al-garadi, M. A., Mohamed, A., Al-ali, A., Du, X., & Guizani, M. (2020). *A Survey of Machine and Deep Learning Methods for Internet of Things (IoT) Security*. Academic Press.

Alhadhrami, Z., Alghfeli, S., Alghfeli, M., Abedlla, J. A., & Shuaib, K. (2017). Introducing blockchains for healthcare. *2017 International Conference on Electrical and Computing Technologies and Applications, ICECTA 2017*, 1–4. 10.1109/ICECTA.2017.8252043

Alharby, M., & Van Moorsel, A. (2017). *Blockchain-based smart contracts: A systematic mapping study*. doi:10.5121/csit.2017.71011

Ali, M. S., Vecchio, M., Pincheira, M., Dolui, K., Antonelli, F., & Rehmani, M. H. (2019). *Applications of blockchains in the Internet of things: A comprehensive survey. IEEE Commun. Surv. Tutorials*.

Ali, M. S., Vecchio, M., Putra, G. D., Kanhere, S. S., & Antonelli, F. (2020). A Decentralized Peer-to-Peer Remote Health Monitoring System. *Sensors (Basel)*, *20*(6), 1656. doi:10.339020061656 PMID:32188135

Al-Kuwari, S., Davenport, J. H., & Bradford, R. J. (2011). Cryptographic Hash Functions: Recent Design Trends and Security Notions. Short Paper Proceedings of Inscrypt '10.

All, I. F. (2017). *The 5 Worst Examples of IoT Hacking and Vulnerabilities in Recorded History*. Academic Press.

Allison, I. (2017). Maersk and IBM want 10 million shipping containers on the global supply blockchain by year-end. *International Business Times, 8*.

Alruqi, M., Hsairi, L., & Eshmawi, A. (2020). Secure mobile agents for patient status telemonitoring using blockchain. *ACM International Conference Proceeding Series*, 224–228. 10.1145/3428690.3429181

Alsunaidi, S. J., & Alhaidari, F. A. (2019). A Survey of Consensus Algorithms for Blockchain Technology. *International Conference on Computer and Information Sciences (ICCIS)*, 1-6. 10.1109/ICCISci.2019.8716424

Al-Turjman, F., & Alturjman, S. (2018). Context-sensitive access in industrial Internet of things (iiot) healthcare applications. *IEEE Transactions on Industrial Informatics*, *14*(6), 2736–2744. doi:10.1109/TII.2018.2808190

Aman, M. N., Chua, K. C., & Sikdar, B. (2017). A lightweight mutual authentication protocol for IoT systems. *GLOBECOM 2017 - 2017 IEEE Global Communications Conference*, 1–6.

Amin, R., Kumar, N., Biswas, G. P., Iqbal, R., & Chang, V. (2018). A light weight authentication protocol for IoT-enabled devices in distributed Cloud Computing environment. *Future Generation Computer Systems*, *78*, 1005–1019. doi:10.1016/j.future.2016.12.028

Anamalamudi, S., Sangi, A. R., Alkatheiri, M., & Ahmed, A. M. (2018). AODV routing protocol for Cognitive radio access based Internet of Things (IoT). *Future Generation Computer Systems*, *83*, 228–238. Advance online publication. doi:10.1016/j.future.2017.12.060

Andoni, M., Robu, V., Flynn, D., Abram, S., Geach, D., Jenkins, D., McCallum, P., & Peacock, A. (2019). Blockchain technology in the energy sector: A systematic review of challenges and opportunities. *Renewable & Sustainable Energy Reviews*, *100*, 143–174. doi:10.1016/j.rser.2018.10.014

Andrea, I., Chrysostomou, C., & Hadjichristofi, G. (2015). Internet of things: security vulnerabilities and challenges. *2015 IEEE Symposium on Computers and Communication (ISCC)*, 180–187. 10.1109/ISCC.2015.7405513

Androulaki, E. (2018). Hyperledger Fabric: A Distributed Operating System for Permissioned Blockchains. *Proceedings of the 13th EuroSys Conference*. 10.1145/3190508.3190538

Araujo, J., Mazo, M., Anta, A. Jr, Tabuada, P., & Johansson, K. H. (2014, February). System Architecture, Protocols, and Algorithms for Aperiodic wireless control systems. *IEEE Transactions on Industrial Informatics*, *10*(1), 175–184. doi:10.1109/TII.2013.2262281

Arshad, J., Azad, M. A., & Abdellatif, M. M. (2018). *COLIDE : A Collaborative Intrusion Detection Framework for Internet of Things*. Academic Press.

Ashibani, Y., & Mahmoud, Q. H. (2017). An efficient and secure scheme for smart home communication using identity-based encryption. *2017 IEEE 36th International Performance Computing and Communications Conference (IPCCC)*, 1–7.

Atif, M., Hassan, M. K., Rabbani, M. R., & Khan, S. (2021). Islamic FinTech: The digital transformation bringing sustainability to Islamic finance. In *In COVID-19 and Islamic Social Finance* (pp. 94–106). Routledge. doi:10.4324/9781003121718-9

Atlam, H. F., Azad, M. A., Alzahrani, A. G., & Wills, G. (2020). A Review of Blockchain in Internet of Things and AI. *Journal of Big Data and Cognitive Computing*, 1-27.

Atlam, H. F., Alenezi, A., Alassafi, M. O., & Wills, G. B. (2018). Blockchain with Internet of things: Benefits, challenges, and future directions. *Int. J. Intell. Syst. Appl.*, *10*(6), 40–48. doi:10.5815/ijisa.2018.06.05

Atzei, N., Bartoletti, M., & Cimoli, T. (2017). *A survey of attacks on ethereum smart contracts (sok)*. Paper presented at the International conference on principles of security and trust. 10.1007/978-3-662-54455-6_8

Aumasson, J. P. (2021). *Crypto Dictionary: 500 Tasty Tidbits for the Curious Cryptographer.* No Starch Press.

Ayotunde, F., Othman, M., Abaker, I., Hashem, T., & Yaqoob, I. (2018). A Novel Countermeasure Technique for Reactive Jamming Attack in Internet of Things. *Multimed Tools Appl*, 29899–29920.

Azaria, A., Ekblaw, A., Vieira, T., & Lippman, A. (2016). MedRec: Using blockchain for medical data access and permission management. *Proceedings - 2016 2nd International Conference on Open and Big Data, OBD 2016*, 25–30. 10.1109/OBD.2016.11

Azbeg, K., Ouchetto, O., Andaloussi, S. J., & Fetjah, L. (2021). An Overview of Blockchain Consensus Algorithms: Comparison, Challenges and Future Directions. *Advances on Smart and Soft Computing*, 357-369.

Azzi, R., Chamoun, R. K., & Sokhn, M. (2019). The power of a blockchain-based supply chain. *Computers & Industrial Engineering*, *135*, 582–592. doi:10.1016/j.cie.2019.06.042

Babbitt, T., Brynjolfsson, E., & Kahin, B. (2001). Understanding the Digital Economy: Data Tools, and Research. *Academy of Management Review*, *26*(3), 463. doi:10.2307/259191

Bach, L. M., Mihaljevic, B., & Zagar, M. (2018, May). Comparative analysis of blockchain consensus algorithms. In *2018 41st International Convention on Information and Communication Technology, Electronics and Microelectronics (MIPRO)* (pp. 1545-1550). IEEE.

Baggetta. (n.d.). *Blockchain For Beginners: What Is Blockchain Technology? A Step-by-Step Guide*. Accessed on 4 July 2021 https://blockgeeks.com/guides/what-is-blockchain-technology

Baki, M. (2019). Auctioning Using Blockchain Advantage Analysis. *International Journal of New Technology and Research, 5*.

Bamakan, S. M. H., Motavali, A., & Bondarti, A. B. (2020). A survey of blockchain consensus algorithms performance evaluation criteria. *Expert Systems with Applications*, *154*, 113385. doi:10.1016/j.eswa.2020.113385

Barefoot, K., Curtis, D., Jolliff, W., Nicholson, J. R., & Omohundro, R. (2018). *Defining and measuring the digital economy. Working paper*. Bureau of Economic Analysis, United States Department of Commerce. Available at https://www.bea.gov/system/files/papers/WP2018-4.pdf

Barger, A., Manevich, Y., Meir, H., & Tock, Y. (2021). A Byzantine Fault-Tolerant Consensus Library for Hyperledger Fabric. In *2021 IEEE International Conference on Blockchain and Cryptocurrency (ICBC)* (pp. 1-9). IEEE. 10.1109/ICBC51069.2021.9461099

Barhanpure, A., Belandor, P., & Das, B. (2018, September). Proof of stack consensus for blockchain networks. In *International Symposium on Security in Computing and Communication* (pp. 104-116). Springer.

Baruri, P. (2016). Blockchain powered financial inclusion. Presentation at the *International Monetary Fund Global Symposium on Innovative Financial Inclusion: Harnessing Innovation for Inclusive Finance*.

Bashir, I. (2018). *Mastering Blockchain: Distributed ledger technology, decentralization, and smart contracts explained*. Packt Publishing Ltd.

Bayer, D., Haber, S., & Stornetta, W. S. (1993). Improving the Efficiency and Reliability of Digital Time-Stamping. In *Sequences II* (pp. 329–334). Springer. doi:10.1007/978-1-4613-9323-8_24

BEIS. (2020). *The use of distributed ledgers to verify the provenance of goods*. Final Report Department for Business, Energy & Industrial Strategy, Research Paper Number 2020/036.

Benchoufi, M., & Ravaud, P. (2017). Blockchain technology for improving clinical research quality. *Trials 2017, 18*(1), 1–5. doi:10.1186/s13063-017-2035-z

Benchoufi, M., Porcher, R., & Ravaud, P. (2017). Blockchain protocols in clinical trials: Transparency and traceability of consent. *F1000 Research*, *6*, 66. Advance online publication. doi:10.12688/f1000research.10531.1 PMID:29167732

Benil, T., & Jasper, J. (2020). Cloud based security on outsourcing using blockchain in E-health systems. *Computer Networks*, *178*, 107344. doi:10.1016/j.comnet.2020.107344

Bennett, B. (2018). Blockchain HIE Overview: A Framework for Healthcare Interoperability. *Telehealth and Medicine Today*, *2*(3). Advance online publication. doi:10.30953/tmt.v2.14

Ben, S., & Xiaoqiong, W. (2019). Are Cryptocurrencies Good Investments? *Studies in Business and Economics*, *14*(2), 181–192. doi:10.2478be-2019-0033

Bentov, I., Lee, C., Mizrahi, A., & Rosenfeld, M. (2014). *Proof of Activity: Extending Bitcoin's Proof of Work via Proof of Stake*. IACR Cryptology ePrint Archive, 2014, 452.

Bentov, I., Lee, C., Mizrahi, A., & Rosenfeld, M. (2014). Proof of activity: Extending bitcoin's proof of work via proof of stake [extended abstract]. *Performance Evaluation Review, 42*(3), 34–37.

Berman, M., & Fenaughty, A. (2005). Technology and managed care: Patient benefits of telemedicine in a rural health care network. *Health Economics*, *14*(6), 559–573. doi:10.1002/hec.952 PMID:15497196

Bernhard, K. (2018). *How Blockchain Technology could alter the real estate business*. https://www.bizjournals.com/houston/news/2018/08/15/how-blockchain-technology-could-alter-the-real.html

Bhargavan, K., Delignat-Lavaud, A., Fournet, C., Gollamudi, A., Gonthier, G., Kobeissi, N., ... Swamy, N. (2016). Formal verification of smart contracts: Short paper. *Proceedings of the 2016 ACM workshop on programming languages and analysis for security.* 10.1145/2993600.2993611

Bhatti, A., Siyal, A. A., Mehdi, A., Shah, H., Kumar, H., & Bohyo, M. A. (2018). Development of cost-effective tele-monitoring system for remote area patients. *2018 International Conference on Engineering and Emerging Technologies, ICEET 2018,* 1–7. 10.1109/ICEET1.2018.8338646

Bhowmik, D., & Feng, T. (2017, August). The multimedia blockchain: A distributed and tamper-proof media transaction framework. In *22nd International Conference on Digital Signal Processing (DSP)* (pp. 1-5). IEEE. 10.1109/ICDSP.2017.8096051

Bhuyan, M. H., Bhattacharyya, D. K., & Kalita, J. K. (2016). E-LDAT : a lightweight system for DDoS flooding attack detection and IP traceback using extended entropy metric. doi:10.1002/sec

Biswas, K., Muthukkumarasamy, V., & Tan, W. L. (2017). *Blockchain based wine supply chain traceability system.* Paper presented at the Future Technologies Conference (FTC) 2017.

BLAKE2. (2021). *Fast Secure Hashing.* https://www.blake2.net/

Bocek, T., Rodrigues, B. B., Strasser, T., & Stiller, B. (2017). Blockchains everywhere - A use-case of blockchains in the pharma supply-chain. *Proceedings of the IM 2017 - 2017 IFIP/IEEE International Symposium on Integrated Network and Service Management,* 772–777. 10.23919/INM.2017.7987376

Bodó, B., Brekke, J. K., & Hoepman, J.-H. (2021). Decentralisation: A multidisciplinary perspective. *Internet Policy Review, 10*(2). Advance online publication. doi:10.14763/2021.2.1563

Bodó, B., Gervais, D., & Quintais, J. P. (2018). Blockchain and Smart Contracts: The missing link in copyright licensing? *International Journal of Law and Information Technology, 26*(4), 311–336. doi:10.1093/ijlit/eay014

Bogucharskov, A. V., Pokamestov, I. E., Adamova, K. R., & Tropina, Z. N. (2018). Adoption of blockchain technology in trade finance process. *Journal of Reviews on Global Economics, 7*(Special Issue), 510–515. doi:10.6000/1929-7092.2018.07.47

Bower, J., & Christensen, C. (1995). *Disruptive technologies: Catching the wave.* Academic Press.

Bowman, M., Das, D., Mandal, A., & Montgomery, H. (2021). *On Elapsed Time Consensus Protocols.* IACR Cryptol. ePrint Arch., 2021, 86.

Boyes, H., Hallaq, B., Cunningham, J., & Watson, T. (2018). The industrial Internet of things (iiot): An analysis framework. *Computers in Industry, 101,* 1–12. doi:10.1016/j.compind.2018.04.015

Brennen, S., & Kreiss, D. (2014). Digitalization and digitization. *Culture Digitally, 8.* Available at: https://culturedigitally.org/2014/09/digitalization-and-digitization/

Brito, J., & Castillo, A. (2013). Bitcoin: A Primer for Policymakers (PDF). Fairfax, VA: Mercatus Center, George Mason University.

Browne, R. (2017). *An Indian state wants to use blockchain to fight land ownership fraud.* Retrieved from https://www.cnbc.com/2017/10/10/this-indian-state-wantsto-use-blockchain-to-fight-land-ownership-fraud.html

Bryatov, S. R., & Borodinov, A. A. (2019). Blockchain technology in the pharmaceutical supply chain: researching a business model based on Hyperledger Fabric. Information Technology and Nanotechnology. doi:10.18287/1613-0073-2019-2416-134-140

Brynjolfsson, E., & Kahin, B. (Eds.). (2002). *Understanding the Digital Economy.* Massachusetts Institute of Technology.

Bukht, R., & Heeks, R. (2017). *Defining, conceptualising and measuring the digital economy.* GDI Development Informatics Working Papers, no. 68. University of Manchester.

Burstiq. (2021). *Blockchain based healthcare data solutions.* https://www.burstiq.com/

Buterin, V. (2013). *A Next Generation Smart Contract & Decentralized Application Platform.* https://ethereum.org/whitepaper/

Buterin, V. (2014). A next-generation smart contract and decentralized application platform. *White Paper, 3*(37).

Buterin, V. (2015). *A next-generation smart contract and decentralized application platform.* Available: https://github.com/ethereum/wiki/wiki/White-Paper/

Buterin, V. (2020). *Combining GHOST and Casper.* Available: https://arxiv.org/abs/2003.03052

Butun, I., Morgera, S. D., & Sankar, R. (2014). A survey of intrusion detection systems in wireless sensor networks. *IEEE Communications Surveys and Tutorials, 16*(1), 266–282. doi:10.1109/SURV.2013.050113.00191

BuzuI. (2020). Blockchain, Smart Contracts and Copyright Management Disruption. doi:10.2139/ssrn.3759260

BVerfGE. (1983). *1BVerfGE 65, 1 – Volkszählung Urteil des Ersten Senats vom 15. Dezember 1983 auf die mündliche Verhandlung vom 18. und 19. Oktober 1983 - 1 BvR 209, 269, 362, 420, 440, 484/83 in den Verfahren über die Verfassungsbeschwerden.* https://www.servat.unibe.ch/dfr/bv065001.html

Cachin, C. (2016). *Architecture of the hyperledger blockchain fabric.* Paper presented at the Workshop on distributed cryptocurrencies and consensus ledgers.

Cachin, C., & Vukolić, M. (2017). *Blockchain consensus protocols in the wild.* arXiv preprint arXiv:1707.01873.

Cachin, C., (2017). Architecture of the Hyperledger Blockchain Fabric. *Leibniz Int. Proc. Informatics, 70*, 24.1-24.16.

Cartier, L. E., Ali, S. H., & Krzemnicki, M. S. (2018). Blockchain, Chain of Custody and Trace Elements: An Overview of Tracking and Traceability Opportunities in the Gem Industry. *The Journal of Geology*, *36*(3).

Casado-Vara, R., Prieto, J., De la Prieta, F., & Corchado, J. M. (2018). How blockchain improves the supply chain: Case study alimentary supply chain. *Procedia Computer Science*, *134*, 393–398. doi:10.1016/j.procs.2018.07.193

Castaneda, C., Nalley, K., Mannion, C., Bhattacharyya, P., Blake, P., Pecora, A., Goy, A., & Suh, K. S. (2015). Clinical decision support systems for improving diagnostic accuracy and achieving precision medicine. *Journal of Clinical Bioinformatics*, *5*(1), 4. doi:10.118613336-015-0019-3 PMID:25834725

CBInsights. (2021). *Banking Is Only The Beginning: 58 Big Industries Blockchain Could Transform.* https://www.cbinsights.com/research/industries-disrupted-blockchain

Cervantes, C., Poplade, D., Nogueira, M., & Santos, A. (2015). Detection of sinkhole attacks for supporting secure routing on 6lowpan for Internet of things. *2015 IFIP/IEEE International Symposium on Integrated Network Management (IM)*, 606–611. 10.1109/INM.2015.7140344

Challa, S., Wazid, M., Das, A. K., Kumar, N., Reddy, A. G., Yoon, E., & Yoo, K. (2017). Secure Signature-Based Authenticated Key Establishment Scheme for Future IoT Applications. doi:10.1109/ACCESS.2017.2676119

Chang, S. E., Luo, H. L., & Chen, Y. (2020). Blockchain-enabled trade finance innovation: A potential paradigm shift on using letter of credit. *Sustainability*, *12*(1), 188. doi:10.3390u12010188

Chan, M. (2017). *Why Cloud Computing Is the Foundation of the Internet of Things*. Academic Press.

Charalampidis, P., & Fragkiadakis, A. (2020). *When Distributed Ledger Technology meets Internet of Things - Benefits and Challenges*. https://arxiv.org/pdf/2008.12569.pdf

Cha, S., Chen, J., Su, C., & Yeh, K. (2018). A blockchain connected gateway for ble-based devices in the Internet of things. *IEEE Access: Practical Innovations, Open Solutions*, *6*, 24639–24649. doi:10.1109/ACCESS.2018.2799942

Chaudhary, R., Aujla, G. S., Garg, S., Kumar, N., & Rodrigues, J. J. P. C. (2018). Sdn-enabled multi-attribute-based secure communication for smart grid in riot environment. *IEEE Transactions on Industrial Informatics*, *14*(6), 2629–2640. doi:10.1109/TII.2018.2789442

Chaum, D., Rivest, R. L., & Sherman, A. T. (1998). *CRYPTO'82. In Advances in Cryptology 1981–1997*. Springer.

Chelladurai, U., Pandian, D. S., & Ramasamy, D. K. (2021). A Blockchain based Patient Centric EHR Storage and Integrity Management for e-Health Systems. *Health Policy and Technology*, *100513*. Advance online publication. doi:10.1016/j.hlpt.2021.100513

Chen, G., & Ng, W. S. (2017). An efficient authorization framework for securing industrial Internet of things. *TENCON 2017 - 2017 IEEE Region 10 Conference*, 1219–1224.

Chen, J. I. (2017). Embedding the MRC and SC Schemes into Trust Management Algorithm Applied to IoT Security Protection. *Wireless Personal Communications*. Advance online publication. doi:10.100711277-017-5120-4

Chen, J., & Micali, S. (2019). Algorand: A secure and efficient distributed ledger. *Theoretical Computer Science*, *777*, 155–183. doi:10.1016/j.tcs.2019.02.001

Chen, L., Lee, W.-K., Chang, C.-C., Choo, K.-K. R., & Zhang, N. (2019). Blockchain-based searchable encryption for electronic health record sharing. *Future Generation Computer Systems*, *95*, 420–429. doi:10.1016/j.future.2019.01.018

Chen, W., Zhou, K., Fang, W., Wang, K., & Bi, F. (2020). Review on blockchain technology and its application to the simple analysis of intellectual property protection. *International Journal on Computer Science and Engineering*, *22*(4), 437–444.

Choi, J., & Kim, Y. (2016). An improved lea block encryption algorithm to prevent side-channel attack in the IoT system. *2016 Asia-Pacific Signal and Information Processing Association Annual Summit and Conference (APSIPA)*, 1–4.

Chopra, K., Gupta, K., & Lambora, A. (2019). Future Internet: The Internet of Things-A Literature Review. *Proceedings of the International Conference on Machine Learning, Big Data, Cloud and Parallel Computing: Trends, Prespectives and Prospects, COMITCon 2019*, 135–139. 10.1109/COMITCon.2019.8862269

Christidis, K., & Devetsikiotis, M. (2016). Blockchains and smart contracts for the internet of things. *IEEE Access: Practical Innovations, Open Solutions*, *4*, 2292–2303. doi:10.1109/ACCESS.2016.2566339

Cieplak, J., & Leefatt, S. (2017). Smart contracts: A smart way to automate performance. *Georgetown Law Technology Review*, *1*(2), 417–427.

Cirani, S., Ferrari, G., & Veltri, L. (2013). Enforcing security mechanisms in the IP-based Internet of things: An algorithmic overview. *Algorithms*, *6*(2), 197–226. doi:10.3390/a6020197

Clark, C. (1996). The answer to the machine is in the machine. In P. Bernt Hugenholtz (Ed.), *The future of copyright in a digital environment*. Kluwer Law International.

Clauson, K. A., Breeden, E. A., Davidson, C., & Mackey, T. K. (2018). Leveraging Blockchain Technology to Enhance Supply Chain Management in Healthcare. *Blockchain in Healthcare Today*, *1*(0). Advance online publication. doi:10.30953/bhty.v1.20

Cohn, A., West, T., & Parker, C. (2017). Smart after all: Blockchain, smart contracts, parametric insurance, and smart energy grids. *Georgetown Law Technology Review*, *1*(2), 273–304.

Cousins, K., Subramanian, H., & Esmaeilzadeh, P. (2019). A value-sensitive design perspective of cryptocurrencies: A research agenda. *Communications of the Association for Information Systems*, *45*(1), 511–547. Advance online publication. doi:10.17705/1CAIS.04527

Croman, K., Decker, C., Eyal, I., Gencer, A. E., Juels, A., Kosba, A., Miller, A., Saxena, P., Shi, E., Sirer, E. G., Song, D., & Wattenhofer, R. (2016). *On Scaling Decentralized Blockchains (A Position Paper)*. https://www.comp.nus.edu.sg/~prateeks/papers/Bitcoin-scaling.pdf

Cs, D., Jung, B., & Min, M. (2017). Mitigating Stealthy Collision Attack in Energy Harvesting Motivated Networks. *Cyber Security and Trusted Computing Mitigating*, 539–544.

Dagher, G. G., Mohler, J., Milojkovic, M., & Marella, P. B. (2018). Ancile: Privacy-preserving framework for access control and interoperability of electronic health records using blockchain technology. *Sustainable Cities and Society*, *39*, 283–297. doi:10.1016/j.scs.2018.02.014

Daley, S. (2019). *9 Companies using Blockchain in Insurance to revolutionize possibilities*. https://builtin.com/blockchain/blockchain-insurance-companies

Daley, S. (2021). *How using Blockchain in healthcare is reviving the industry's capabilities*. https://builtin.com/blockchain/blockchain-healthcare-applications-companies

Dao, Kim, Jeong, & Park. (2017). Achievable Multi-Security Levels for Lightweight IoT-Enabled Devices in Infrastructureless Peer-Aware Communications. *IEEE Access: Practical Innovations, Open Solutions*, 26743–26753.

Dazine, J., Maizate, A., & Hassouni, L. (2018). Internet of things security. In *2018 IEEE International Conference on Technology Management, Operations and Decisions (ICTMOD)* (pp. 137–141). IEEE. 10.1109/ITMC.2018.8691239

De Angelis, S., Aniello, L., Baldoni, R., Lombardi, F., Margheri, A., & Sassone, V. (2018). PBFT vs proof-of-authority: Applying the CAP theorem to permissioned blockchain. *CEUR Workshop Proceedings*, *2058*. https://eprints.soton.ac.uk/415083

De Filippi, P., & Wright, A. (2018). *Blockchain and the Law: The Rule of Code*. Harvard University Press. doi:10.2307/j.ctv2867sp

Deb, P. K., Mukherjee, A., & Misra, S. (2021). CovChain: Blockchain-Enabled Identity Preservation and Anti-Infodemics for COVID-19. *IEEE Network*, *35*(3), 42–47. doi:10.1109/MNET.011.2000669

Deogirikar, J. (2017). Security Attacks inIoT. *Survey (London, England)*, 32–37.

De, S. J., & Ruj, S. (2017). *Efficient decentralized attribute-based access control for mobile clouds*. IEEE Transactions on Cloud Computing.

Deshpande, A., Stewart, K., Lepetit, L., & Gunashekar, S. (2017). Distributed Ledger Technologies/Blockchain: Challenges, opportunities and the prospects for standards. *Overview Report of BSI*.

Destefanis, G., Marchesi, M., Ortu, M., Tonelli, R., Bracciali, A., & Hierons, R. (2018). Smart contracts vulnerabilities: a call for blockchain software engineering? In *2018 International Workshop on Blockchain Oriented Software Engineering (IWBOSE)* (pp. 19-25). IEEE. 10.1109/IWBOSE.2018.8327567

Dharani, M., Hassan, M. K., Rabbani, M. R., & Huq, T. (2021). Does the Covid-19 Pandemic Affect Faith-based Investments? Evidence from Global Sectoral Indices. *Research in International Business and Finance*, •••, 101537. PMID:34522060

Dhillon, P. K., & Kalra, S. (2017). A lightweight biometrics based remote user authentication scheme for IoT services. *Journal of Information Security and Applications*, 1–16. doi:10.1016/j.jisa.2017.01.003

Dorri, A., Kanhere, S. S., Jurdak, R., & Gauravaram, P. (2019). *LSB: A Lightweight Scalable Blockchain for IoT Security and Privacy*. Academic Press.

Dorri, A., Kanhere, S. S., Jurdak, R., & Gauravaram, P. (2017). *Blockchain for IoT security and privacy: The case study of a smart home. In 2017 IEEE international conference on pervasive computing and communications workshops (PerCom workshops)*. IEEE.

Downing, N. L., Adler-Milstein, J., Palma, J. P., Lane, S., Eisenberg, M., Sharp, C., & Longhurst, C. A. (2017). Health information exchange policies of 11 diverse health systems and the associated impact on volume of exchange. *Journal of the American Medical Informatics Association: JAMIA*, *24*(1), 113–122. doi:10.1093/jamia/ocw063 PMID:27301748

Du, Y., Cai, G., Zhang, X., Liu, T., & Jiang, J. (2019). *An Efficient Dummy-Based Location Privacy-Preserving Scheme for Internet of Things Services*. doi:10.3390/info10090278

Dubey, V. (2019). Fintech-Digital way of ID Verification and Biometric Verification in 2020. *International Journal of Innovation and Applied Studies*, *27*(4), 896–901.

Dubovitskaya, A., Xu, Z., Ryu, S., Schumacher, M., & Wang, F. (2017). Secure and Trustable Electronic Medical Records Sharing using Blockchain. *AMIA Symposium,* 650–659.

Dubovitskaya, A., Baig, F., Xu, Z., Shukla, R., Zambani, P. S., Swaminathan, A., Jahangir, M. M., Chowdhry, K., Lachhani, R., Idnani, N., Schumacher, M., Aberer, K., Stoller, S. D., Ryu, S., & Wang, F. (2020). ACTION-EHR: Patient-centric blockchain-based electronic health record data management for cancer care. *Journal of Medical Internet Research*, *22*(8), 1–15. doi:10.2196/13598 PMID:32821064

Dubovitskaya, A., Novotny, P., Xu, Z., & Wang, F. (2020). Applications of blockchain technology for data-sharing in oncology: Results from a systematic literature review. *Oncology*, *98*(6, Suppl. 6), 403–411. doi:10.1159/000504325 PMID:31794967

Dutch Transformation Forum. (2018). *Unlocking the Value of the Platform Economy: Mastering the Good, the Bad and the Ugly*. The Hague: Dutch Transformation Forum. Retrieved from https://dutchitchannel.nl/612528/dutch-transformation-platform-economy-paper-kpmg.pdf

Ekblaw, A., Azaria, A., Halamka, J. D., & Lippman, A. (2016). A Case Study for Blockchain in Healthcare: "MedRec" prototype for electronic health records and medical research data. *Proceedings of IEEE open & big data conference.*

Ericsson. (2018). *Mobility report.* Available at: https://www.ericsson.com/assets/local/mobility-report/documents/2018/ericsson-mobility-report-november-2018.pdf

Esfahani, A., Mantas, G., Matischek, R., Saghezchi, F. B., Rodriguez, J., Bicaku, A., Maksuti, S., Tauber, M. G., Schmittner, C., & Bastos, J. (2019). A lightweight authentication mechanism for m2m communications in industrial IoT environment. *IEEE Internet of Things Journal*, 6(1), 288–296. doi:10.1109/JIOT.2017.2737630

Esposito, C., De Santis, A., Tortora, G., Chang, H., & Choo, K. K. R. (2018). Blockchain: A Panacea for Healthcare Cloud-Based Data Security and Privacy? *IEEE Cloud Computing*, 5(1), 31–37. doi:10.1109/MCC.2018.011791712

Ethereum. (2021). *What is Ethereum? The foundation for our digital future.* https://ethereum.org/en/what-is-ethereum

Everledger. (2021). *The Everledger Platform.* https://everledger.io/

Evernym. (2021). *The Self-Sovereign Identity Company.* Available: https://www.evernym.com/

Fairley, P. (2017). Blockchain world-feeding the blockchain beast if bitcoin ever does go mainstream, the electricity needed to sustain it will be enormous. *IEEE Spectrum*, 54(10), 36–59. doi:10.1109/MSPEC.2017.8048837

Fakhri, D., & Mutijarsa, K. (2018). Secure IoT Communication using Blockchain Technology. *ISESD 2018 - International Symposium on Electronics and Smart Devices: Smart Devices for Big Data Analytic and Machine Learning.* 10.1109/ISESD.2018.8605485

Fang, W., Chen, W., Zhang, W., Pei, J., Gao, W., & Wang, G. (2020). Digital signature scheme for information non-repudiation in blockchain: A state of the art review. *J Wireless Com Network*, 56(1), 56. Advance online publication. doi:10.118613638-020-01665-w

Fan, K., Wang, S., Ren, Y., Li, H., & Yang, Y. (2018). MedBlock: Efficient and Secure Medical Data Sharing Via Blockchain. *Journal of Medical Systems*, 42(8), 1–11. doi:10.100710916-018-0993-7 PMID:29931655

FCA. (2016). *Business Plan 2016/17.* https://www.fca.org.uk/publication/corporate/business-plan-2016-17.pdf

Fernndez-Carams, T. M., & Fraga-Lamas, P. (2018). A review on the use of blockchain for the Internet of things. *IEEE Access: Practical Innovations, Open Solutions*, 6, 32979–33001. doi:10.1109/ACCESS.2018.2842685

Ferrag, M. A., Derdour, M., Mukherjee, M., Derhab, A., Maglaras, L., & Janicke, H. (2019, April). Blockchain Technologies for the Internet of Things: Research Issues and Challenges. *IEEE Internet of Things Journal*, 6(2), 2188–2204. doi:10.1109/JIOT.2018.2882794

Ferran, M. A., Derdour, M., Mukherjee, M., Dahab, A., Maglaras, L., & Janicke, H. (2019). Blockchain technologies for the Internet of things: Research issues and challenges. *IEEE Internet of Things Journal.*

Ferrari, V. (2020). The regulation of crypto-assets in the EU – investment and payment tokens under the radar. *Maastricht Journal of European and Comparative Law, 27*(3), 325–342. doi:10.1177/1023263X20911538

Ferretti, S., D'Angelo, G., & Marzolla, M. (2018). *A Blockchain-based flight data.* Academic Press.

Finck, M. & Moscon, V. (2019). Copyright Law on Blockchains: Between New Forms of Rights Administration and Digital Rights Management 2.0. *IIC International Review of Intellectual Property and Competition Law, 50*(1), 77-108.

Forbes. (2019). Blockchain in healthcare: How it Could Make Digital Healthcare Safer and More Innovative. *Forbes.*

Fosso Wamba, S., Kala Kamdjoug, J. R., Epie Bawack, R., & Keogh, J. G. (2020). Bitcoin, Blockchain and Fintech: A systematic review and case studies in the supply chain. *Production Planning and Control, 31*(2–3), 115–142. doi:10.1080/09537287.2019.1631460

Frankenfield, J. (2019). *51% Attack.* https://www.investopedia.com/terms/1/51-attack.asp

Frustaci, M., Pace, P., Aloi, G., & Fortino, G. (2018). *Evaluating critical security issues of the IoT world: present and future challenges.* IEEE Internet Things.

Fu, Y., Yan, Z., Cao, J., Koné, O., & Cao, X. (2017). *An Automata Based Intrusion Detection Method for Internet of Things.* Academic Press.

Gai, J., Choo, K., Qiu, K. R., & Zhu, L. (2018). *Privacy-preserving content-oriented wireless.* Academic Press.

Galenovich, A., Lonshakov, S., & Shadrin, A. (2018). *Blockchain ecosystem for carbon markets, environmental assets, rights, and liabilities. Concept Design and Implementation.* Elsevier.

Gandino, F., Montrucchio, B., & Rebaudengo, M. (2014). *Key Management for Static Wireless Sensor Networks with Node Adding.* IEEE Transaction Industrial Informatics. doi:10.1109/TII.2013.2288063

Garg, H., & Dave, M. (2019). *Securing IoT Devices and Securely Connecting the Dots Using REST API and Middleware.* Academic Press.

Gatteschi, V., Lamberti, F., Demartini, C., Pranteda, C., & Santamaría, V. (2018). Blockchain and Smart Contracts for Insurance: Is the Technology Mature Enough? *Future Internet 2018, 10*(2), 20. doi:10.3390/fi10020020

Ge, M., Hong, J. B., Guttmann, W., & Kim, D. S. (2020). A framework for modeling and assessing security of the internet of things A framework for automating security analysis of the internet of things. *Journal of Network and Computer Applications, 83*(January), 12–27. doi:10.1016/j.jnca.2017.01.033

Geiger, C. (2010). The future of copyright in Europe: Striking a fair balance between protection and access to information. *Intellectual Property Quarterly, 1*, 1–14.

Geranio, M. (2017). Fintech in the exchange industry: Potential for disruption? *Masaryk University Journal of Law and Technology, 11*(2), 245–266. doi:10.5817/MUJLT2017-2-3

Ghaleb, B., Al-dubai, A., Ekonomou, E., Qasem, M., Romdhani, I., & Mackenzie, L. (2019). *Addressing the DAO Insider Attack in RPL's Internet of Things Networks*. Academic Press.

Giannopoulou, A. (2020). Data Protection Compliance Challenges for Self-Sovereign Identity. Blockchain 2020, 91-100. doi:10.1007/978-3-030-52535-4_10

Gibbon, J. (2018). *Introduction to Trusted Execution Environment: Arm's Trust zone*. Academic Press.

Glissa, G., Rachedi, A., & Meddeb, A. (2016). A secure routing protocol based on rpl for Internet of things. *IEEE Global Communications Conference (GLOBECOM)*, 1–7. 10.1109/GLOCOM.2016.7841543

Gomes, T., Salgado, F., Tavares, A., & Cabral, J. (2017). Cute mote, a customizable and trustable end-device for the Internet of things. *IEEE Sensors Journal, 17*(20), 6816–6824. doi:10.1109/JSEN.2017.2743460

Gope, P., & Sikdar, B. (2018). *Lightweight and privacy-preserving two-factor authentication scheme for IoT devices*. IEEE Internet Things.

Gramoli, V. (2020). From blockchain consensus back to Byzantine consensus. *Future Generation Computer Systems, 107*, 760–769. doi:10.1016/j.future.2017.09.023

Granja, J., Silva, R., Monteiro, E., Silva, J. S., & Boavida, F. (2008). Why is IPSec a viable option for wireless sensor networks. *2008 5th IEEE International Conference on Mobile Ad Hoc and Sensor Systems, 802–807*.

Granville, K. (2018). *Facebook and Cambridge Analytica: what You Need to Know as Fallout Widens*. Academic Press.

Grech, A., & Camilleri, A. F. (2017). Blockchain in Education. Luxembourg: Publications Office of the European Union.

Griebel, L., Prokosch, H. U., Köpcke, F., Toddenroth, D., Christoph, J., Leb, I., Engel, I., & Sedlmayr, M. (2015). A scoping review of cloud computing in healthcare. In BMC Medical Informatics and Decision Making (Vol. 15, Issue 1, pp. 1–16). BioMed Central Ltd. doi:10.118612911-015-0145-7

Griggs, K. N., Osipova, O., Kohlios, C. P., Baccarini, A. N., Howson, E. A., & Hayajneh, T. (2018). Healthcare blockchain system using smart contracts for secure automated remote patient monitoring. *Journal of Medical Systems, 42*(7), 1–7. doi:10.100710916-018-0982-x PMID:29876661

Groenfeldt, T. (2017). *IBM and Maersk apply blockchain to container shipping.* https://www.forbes.com/sites/tomgroenfeldt/2017/03/05/ibm-and-maersk-apply-blockchain-to-container-shipping

Guadamuz, A. (2019). Smart Contracts and Intellectual Property: Challenges and Reality. In *Intellectual property and the 4th industrial revolution.* Kluwer International Law. https://ssrn.com/abstract=3911121

Guan, Z., Si, G., Zhang, X., Wu, L., Guizani, N., Du, X., & Ma, Y. (2018). Privacy-preserving and efficient aggregation based on blockchain for power grid communications in smart communities. *IEEE Communications Magazine, 56*(7), 82–88. doi:10.1109/MCOM.2018.1700401

Guegan, D. (2017). *Public blockchain versus private blockchain.* Academic Press.

Guin, U., Singh, A., Alam, M., Caedo, J., & Skjellum, A. (2018). A secure low-cost edge device authentication scheme for the Internet of things. *31st International Conference on VLSI Design and 17th International Conference on Embedded Systems (VLSID)*, 85–90. 10.1109/VLSID.2018.42

Gulzar, M., & Abbas, G. (2019). Internet of Things Security : A Survey and Taxonomy. In *2019 International Conference on Engineering and Emerging Technologies (ICEET)* (pp. 1–6). IEEE. 10.1109/CEET1.2019.8711834

Gürkaynak, G., Yilmaz, I., Yesilaltay, B., & Bengi, B. (2018). Intellectual property law and practice in the blockchain realm. *Computer Law & Security Review, 34*(4), 847–862. doi:10.1016/j.clsr.2018.05.027

Gutiérrez, O., Romero, G., Pérez, L., Salazar, A., Charris, M., & Wightman, P. (2020). HealthyBlock: Blockchain-Based IT Architecture for Electronic Medical Records Resilient to Connectivity Failures. *International Journal of Environmental Research and Public Health 2020, 17*(19), 7132. doi:10.3390/ijerph17197132

Guzman Trujllo, C. G. (2018). *The role of blockchain in the pharmaceutical industry supply chain as a tool for reducing the flow of counterfeit drugs.* https://esource.dbs.ie/handle/10788/3556

Haber, S., & Scott Stornetta, W. (1991). How to time-stamp a digital document. Lecture Notes in Computer Science, 537, 437–455. doi:10.1007/3-540-38424-3_32

Hackius, N., & Petersen, M. (2017). Blockchain in logistics and supply chain: trick or treat? *Proceedings of the Hamburg International Conference of Logistics (HICL)*, 23.

Hammad, R., Odeh, M., & Khan, Z. (2015). Towards a model-based approach to evaluate the effectiveness of e-learning. *Proceeding of the 9th European Conference on IS Management and Evaluation ECIME*, 111-119.

Haq, I., & Esuka, O. M. (2018). Blockchain Technology in Pharmaceutical Industry to Prevent Counterfeit Drugs Article in International Journal of Computer Applications · March. *International Journal of Computers and Applications, 180*(25), 975–8887. doi:10.5120/ijca2018916579

Harris, P. (2021). Blockchain for COVID-19 Patient Health Record. *Proceedings - 5th International Conference on Computing Methodologies and Communication, ICCMC 2021*, 534–538. 10.1109/ICCMC51019.2021.9418443

Hashim, F., Shuaib, K., & Sallabi, F. (2021). *MedShard: Electronic Health Record Sharing Using Blockchain Sharding.* doi:10.3390/su13115889

Hassan, M. K., Rabbani, M. R., & Abdullah, Y. (2021b). Socioeconomic Impact of COVID-19 in MENA region and the Role of Islamic Finance. *International Journal of Islamic Economics and Finance, 4*(1), 51–78. doi:10.18196/ijief.v4i1.10466

Hassan, M. K., Rabbani, M. R., & Ali, M. A. (2020). Challenges for the Islamic Finance and banking in post COVID era and the role of Fintech. *Journal of Economic Cooperation and Development, 43*(3), 93–116.

Hassan, M. K., Rabbani, M., & Daouia, C. (2021a). Integrating Islamic finance and Halal industry: Current landscape and future forward. *International Journal of Islamic Marketing and Branding, 6*(1), 60. doi:10.1504/IJIMB.2021.117594

Hazari, S. S., & Mahmoud, Q. H. (2019). *A parallel proof of work to improve transaction speed and scalability in blockchain systems.* Paper presented at the 2019 IEEE 9th Annual Computing and Communication Workshop and Conference (CCWC). 10.1109/CCWC.2019.8666535

Hazari, S. S., & Mahmoud, Q. H. (2019). Comparative evaluation of consensus mechanisms in cryptocurrencies. *Internet Technol. Lett., 2*(3), e100. doi:10.1002/itl2.100

Hei, X., Du, X., Wu, J., & Hu, F. (2010). Defending resource depletion attacks on implantable medical devices. *2010 IEEE Global Telecommunications Conference GLOBECOM 2010*, 1–5. 10.1109/GLOCOM.2010.5685228

Helberger, N., & Hugenholtz, P. B. (2007). No place like home for making a copy: Private copying in European copyright law and consumer law. *Berkeley Technology Law Journal, 22*, 1061–1098.

Helliar, C. V., Crawford, L., Rocca, L., Teodori, C., & Veneziani, M. (2020, October). Permissionless and permissioned blockchain diffusion. *International Journal of Information Management, 54*, 102136. doi:10.1016/j.ijinfomgt.2020.102136

Heston, T. (2017). *A case study in blockchain healthcare innovation.* Academic Press.

Hewa, T. M., Hu, Y., Liyanage, M., Kanhare, S., & Ylianttila, M. (2021). Survey on blockchain based smart contracts: Technical aspects and future research. *IEEE Access: Practical Innovations, Open Solutions, 9*, 87643–87662. doi:10.1109/ACCESS.2021.3068178

Hjalmarsson, F. P., Hreioarsson, G. K., Hamdaqa, M., & Hjalmtysson, G. (2018, July). Blockchain-Based E-Voting System. In *2018 IEEE 11th International Conference on Cloud Computing (CLOUD)* (pp. 983-986). IEEE. 10.1109/CLOUD.2018.00151

Hofman, W., & Brewster, C. (2019). The Applicability of Blockchain Technology in the Mobility and Logistics Domain. In *Towards User-Centric Transport in Europe* (pp. 185–201). Springer. doi:10.1007/978-3-319-99756-8_13

Hölbl, M., Kompara, M., Kamišalić, A., & Nemec Zlatolas, L. (2018). A systematic review of the use of blockchain in healthcare. *Symmetry*, *10*(10), 470. doi:10.3390ym10100470

Horrow, S. (2012). *Identity Management Framework for Cloud Based Internet of Things.* Academic Press.

Houston, M. S., Myers, J. D., Levens, S. P., McEvov, M. T., Smith, S. A., Khandheria, B. K., Shen, W. K., Torchia, M. E., & Berry, D. J. (1999). Clinical consultations using store-and-forward telemedicine technology. *Mayo Clinic Proceedings*, *74*(8), 764–769. doi:10.4065/74.8.764 PMID:10473351

Huang, J., Kong, L., Chen, G., Wu, M., Liu, X., & Zeng, P. (2019b). Towards secure industrial IoT: blockchain system with credit-based consensus mechanism. IEEE Trans. Ind.

Huang, H., Zhu, P., Xiao, F., Sun, X., & Huang, Q. (2020). A blockchain-based scheme for privacy-preserving and secure sharing of medical data. *Computers & Security*, *99*, 102010. doi:10.1016/j.cose.2020.102010 PMID:32895584

Huang, X., Zhang, Y., Li, D., & Han, L. (2019a). An optimal scheduling algorithm for hybrid EV charging scenario using consortium blockchains. *Future Generation Computer Systems*, *91*, 555–562. doi:10.1016/j.future.2018.09.046

Huh, J.-H., & Seo, K. (2019). Blockchain-based mobile fingerprint verification and automatic log-in platform for future computing. *The Journal of Supercomputing*, *75*(6), 3123–3139. doi:10.100711227-018-2496-1

Huh, S., Cho, S., & Kim, S. (2017, February). Managing IoT devices using blockchain platform. *19th International Conference on Advanced Communication Technology (ICACT)* (pp. 464-467). IEEE. 10.23919/ICACT.2017.7890132

Huh, S.-K., & Kim, J.-H. (2019). The blockchain consensus algorithm for viable management of new and renewable energies. *Sustainability*, *11*(3184), 3184. doi:10.3390u11113184

Hunter, D. (1978). *Papermaking: The history and technique of an ancient craft.* Courier Corporation.

Hyperledger-fabric docs main documentation. (2015). https://hyperledger-fabric.readthedocs.io/en/latest/blockchain.html

Iansiti, M., & Lakhani, K. R. (2017). The truth about blockchain. Harvard Business Review, 27(9).

Iansiti, M., & Lakhani, K. (2017). The truth about Blockchain. *Harvard Business Review*, *95*(1), 118–127.

Ichikawa, D., Kashiyama, M., & Ueno, T. (2017). Tamper-resistant mobile health using blockchain technology. *JMIR mHealth and uHealth*, *5*(7), e7938. https://doi.org/10.2196/mhealth.7938

IDC. (2018). *Data Age 2025: The digitization of the world – From edge to core*. White paper. Available at: https://www.seagate.com/files/www-content/our-story/trends/files/idc-seagate-dataage-whitepaper.pdf

IEEE. (2012). *IEEE Standard for Local and metropolitan networks–Part 15.4: LowRate Wireless Personal Area Networks (LR-WPANs)*. IEEE.

Imbrex. (2017). *Sharding, Raiden, Plasma: The Scaling Solutions that Will Unchain Ethereum*. Retrieved from https://medium.com/imbrexblog/sharding-raiden-plasmathe-scaling-solutions-that-will-unchain-ethereum-c590e994523b

Insurance Fraud. (2021). https://content.naic.org/cipr_topics/topic_insurance_fraud.htm

IoT Analytics. (2018). *State of the IoT 2018: Number of IoT devices now at 7B – Market accelerating*. Available at https://iot-analytics.com/state-of-the-iot-update-q1-q2-2018-number-of-iot-devices-now-7b/

IoT-A. (2013). *Internet of Things–Architecture IoT-A Deliverable D1.5 –Final architectural reference model for the IoT v3.0*. https://iotforum.org/wpcontent/uploads/2014/09/D1.5-20130715-VERYFINAL.pdf

I-Scoop. (2021). *The future of Blockchain in organizations and business ecosystems*. https://www.i-scoop.eu/blockchain-distributed-ledger-technology/business-ecosystems-future-blockchain

Islam, S. H., Khan, M. K., & Al-Khouri, A. M. (2015). Anonymous and provably secure certificateless multireceiver encryption without bilinear pairing. *Security and Communication Networks*, *8*(13), 2214–2231. doi:10.1002ec.1165

Ismail, L., & Zeadally, S. (2021). *Healthcare Insurance Frauds: Taxonomy and Blockchain-based Detection Framework (Block-HI) Energy Efficiency in Cloud Infrastructure View project Scheduling in Cloud Computing for Applications' Performance Optimization View project*. doi:10.1109/MITP.2021.3071534

Ito, K., & O'Dair, M. (2018). A Critical Examination of the Application of Blockchain Technology to Intellectual Property Management. In *Business Transformation through Blockchain* (pp. 317–335). Palgrave Macmillan.

ITU. (2018). Setting the Scene for 5G: Opportunities & Challenges. ITU.

Jadhav, V. D., & Moosafintavida, D. S. (2020). Blockchain in Healthcare Industry and Its Application and Impact on Covid 19 Digital Technology Transformation. *Mukt Shabd Journal*, *9*, 479.

Jakobsson, M., Leighton, T., Micali, S., & Szydlo, M. (2003). *Fractal Merkle tree representation and traversal.* Paper presented at the Cryptographers' Track at the RSA Conference. 10.1007/3-540-36563-X_21

Jamil, F., Hang, L., Kim, K. H., & Kim, D. H. (2019). A novel medical blockchain model for drug supply chain integrity management in a smart hospital. *Electronics, 8*(5), 505. doi:10.3390/electronics8050505

Jamil, F., Iqbal, N., Imran, Ahmad, S., & Kim, D. (2021). Imran, Ahmad, S., and Kim, D. "Peer-to-Peer Energy Trading Mechanism Based on Blockchain and Machine Learning for Sustainable Electrical Power Supply in Smart Grid. *IEEE Access: Practical Innovations, Open Solutions, 9*, 39193–39217. doi:10.1109/ACCESS.2021.3060457

Jaszi, P. (1998). Intellectual property legislative update: Copyright, paracopyright, and pseudo-copyright [Paper presentation]. Association of Research Libraries conference: The Future Network: Transforming Learning and Scholarship, Eugene, OR, United States.

Jessel, B., & DiCaprio, A. (2018). Can blockchain make trade finance more inclusive? *Journal of Financial Transformation, 47*, 35–50.

Jiang, S., Cao, J., Wu, H., Yang, Y., Ma, M., & He, J. (2018). Blochie: A blockchain-based platform for healthcare information exchange. *Proceedings - 2018 IEEE International Conference on Smart Computing, SMARTCOMP 2018*, 49–56. doi:10.1109/SMARTCOMP.2018.00073

Kan, L., Wei, Y., Muhammad, A. H., Siyuan, W., Linchao, G., & Kai, H. (2018). *A multiple blockchains architecture on inter-blockchain communication.* Paper presented at the 2018 IEEE International Conference on Software Quality, Reliability and Security Companion (QRS-C). 10.1109/QRS-C.2018.00037

Kang, J., Xiong, Z., Niyato, D., Ye, D., Kim, D. I., & Zhao, J. (2019a). Toward secure blockchain-enabled Internet of vehicles: Optimizing consensus management using reputation and contract theory. *IEEE Transactions on Vehicular Technology, 68*(3), 2906–2920. doi:10.1109/TVT.2019.2894944

Kang, J., Yu, R., Huang, X., Maharjan, S., Zhang, Y., & Hossain, E. (2017). Enabling localized peer-to-peer electricity trading among plug-in hybrid electric vehicles using consortium blockchains. *IEEE Transactions on Industrial Informatics, 13*(6), 3154–3164. doi:10.1109/TII.2017.2709784

Kang, J., Yu, R., Huang, X., Wu, M., Maharjan, S., Xie, S., & Zhang, Y. (2019b). Blockchain for secure and efficient data sharing in vehicular edge computing and networks. *IEEE Internet of Things Journal, 6*(3), 4660–4670. doi:10.1109/JIOT.2018.2875542

Karafiloski, E., & Mishev, A. (2017). Blockchain solutions for big data challenges: A literature review. *IEEE EUROCON 2017-17th International Conference on Smart Technologies*, 763–768.

Karantias, K., Kiayias, A., & Zindros, D. (2020, February). *Proof-of-burn. In International Conference on Financial Cryptography and Data Security* (pp. 523-540). Springer.

Karati, A., Islam, S. H., & Karuppiah, M. (2018). Provably secure and lightweight certificateless signature scheme for iiot environments. *IEEE Transactions on Industrial Informatics*, *14*(8), 3701–3711. doi:10.1109/TII.2018.2794991

Karim, S., Akhtar, M. U., Tashfeen, R., Raza Rabbani, M., Rahman, A. A. A., & AlAbbas, A. (2021c). Sustainable banking regulations pre and during coronavirus outbreak: the moderating role of financial stability. *Economic Research-Ekonomska Istraživanja*, 1–18.

Karim, S., Manab, N. A., & Ismail, R. (2020c). The Interaction Effect of Independent Boards on Corporate Governance-Corporate Social Responsibility (CG-CSR) and Performance Nexus. Asian Academy of Management Journal, 25(1).

Karim, S., Manab, N. A., & Ismail, R. B. (2020a). The dynamic impact of board composition on CSR practices and their mutual effect on organizational returns. *Journal of Asia Business Studies*, *14*(4), 463–479. doi:10.1108/JABS-07-2019-0214

Karim, S., Manab, N. A., & Ismail, R. B. (2020b). Assessing the governance mechanisms, corporate social responsibility and performance: The moderating effect of board independence. *Global Business Review*. doi:10.1177/0972150920917773

Karim, S., Rabbani, M. R., & Bawazir, H. (2021a). Voluntary impacts of the risk management committee attributes on firm performance: Do board size matter? *Asian Academy of Management Journal*, *21*(4), 608–625.

Karim, S., Rabbani, M. R., & Khan, M. A. (2021b). Determining the key factors of corporate leverage in Malaysian service sector firms using dynamic modeling. *Journal of Economic Cooperation and Development.*, *42*(3).

Kaushal, R., Shojania, K. G., & Bates, D. W. (2003). Effects of Computerized Physician Order Entry and Clinical Decision Support Systems on Medication Safety: A Systematic Review. *Archives of Internal Medicine*, *163*(12), 1409–1416. https://doi.org/10.1001/ARCHINTE.163.12.1409

Kersten, W., Seiter, M., Von See, B., Hackius, N., & Maurer, T. (2017). Trends and strategies in logistics and supply chain management. In Digital Transformation Opportunities. DVV Media Group GmbH.

Kessler, G. C. (1998). *An Overview of Cryptography*. Available at: https://www.garykessler.net/library/crypto.html

Khan, F. I., & Hameed, S. (2019). Understanding security requirements and challenges in the Internet of things (iots): A review. *Journal of Computer Networks and Communications*.

Khan, Z. A., Ullrich, J., & Herrmann, P. (2020). *A Trust-based Resilient Routing Mechanism for the Internet of Things*. Academic Press.

Khan, M. A., & Salah, K. (2018). IoT security: Review, blockchain solutions, and open challenges. *Future Generation Computer Systems*, *82*, 395–411. doi:10.1016/j.future.2017.11.022

Khan, S., & Rabbani, M. R. (2020b). Chatbot as Islamic Finance Expert (CaIFE): When finance meets Artificial Intelligence. *2020 International Conference on Computational Linguistics and Natural Language Processing (CLNLP 2020)*, 1–5. 10.1145/3440084.3441213

Khan, S., & Rabbani, M. R. (2020a). In Depth Analysis of Blockchain, Cryptocurrency and Sharia Compliance. *International Journal of Business Innovation and Research*, *1*(1), 1. doi:10.1504/IJBIR.2020.10033066

Khan, S., & Rabbani, M. R. (2021). Artificial Intelligence and NLP based Chatbot as Islamic Banking and Finance Expert. *International Journal of Information Retrieval Research*, *11*(3), 65–77. doi:10.4018/IJIRR.2021070105

Khovratovich, D., Rechberger, C., & Savelieva, A. (2011). Bicliques for Preimages: Attacks on Skein-512 and the SHA-2 family. *IACR Cryptology Archive.*, *2011*, 286.

Khursheeed, F., Sami-Ud-Din, M., Sumra, I. A., & Safder, M. (2020). A Review of Security Machanism in internet of Things(IoT). *3rd International Conference on Advancements in Computational Sciences, ICACS 2020*. 10.1109/ICACS47775.2020.9055949

Kiemle, M. (2018). *Blockchain and Copyright Issues.* https://www.4ipcouncil.com/research/blockchain-and-copyright-issues

Kim, T. M., Lee, S.-J., Chang, D.-J., Koo, J., Kim, T., Yoon, K.-H., Choi, I.-Y., & DynamiChain, I. (2021). *DynamiChain: Development of Medical Blockchain Ecosystem Based on Dynamic Consent System Citation.* doi:10.3390/app11041612

Kim, J.-H., & Huh, S.-K. (1973). A study on the improvement of smart grid security performance and blockchain smart grid perspective. *Energies*, 11.

Kim, S.-K., Kim, U.-M., & Huh, H. J. (2017). A study on improvement of blockchain application to overcome vulnerability of IoT multiplatform security. *Energies*, *12*(402).

Klein, S., & Prinz, W. (2018). A Use Case Identification Framework and Use Case Canvas for Identifying and Exploring Relevant Blockchain Opportunities. *Proceedings of 1st ERCIM Blockchain Workshop 2018. European Society for Socially Embedded Technologies (EUSSET).*

Knickrehm, M., Berthon, B., & Daugherty, P. (2016). *Digital Disruption: The Growth Multiplier.* Accenture.

Koens, T., & Poll, E. (2018). What Blockchain Alternative Do you Need? In T. Koens & E. Poll (Eds.), *Data Privacy Management, Cryptocurrencies and Blockchain Technology* (pp. 113–129). Springer. doi:10.1007/978-3-030-00305-0_9

Koksal, I. (2019). *How Blockchain Technology can re-invent charity.* https://www.forbes.com/sites/ilkerkoksal/2019/07/12/how-blockchain-technology-can-re-invent-charity

Konigsmark, S. T. C., Chen, D., & Wong, M. D. F. (2016). Information dispersion for trojan defense through high-level synthesis. *ACM/EDAC/IEEE Design Automation Conference (DAC)*, 1–6. 10.1145/2897937.2898034

Kosba, A., Miller, A., Shi, E., Wen, Z., & Papamanthou, C. (2016). Hawk: The blockchain model of cryptography and privacy-preserving smart contracts. *2016 IEEE Symposium on Security and Privacy (SP)*, 839–858. 10.1109/SP.2016.55

Kouicem, D. E., Bouabdallah, A., & Lakhlef, H. (2018). Internet of things security: A top-down survey. *Computer Networks*, *141*, 199–221. doi:10.1016/j.comnet.2018.03.012

Koulu, R. (2016). Blockchains and online dispute resolution: Smart contracts as an alternative to enforcement. *Script-ed*, *13*(1), 40–69. doi:10.2966crip.130116.40

Kowalski, M., Lee, Z. W. Y., & Chan, T. K. H. (2021). Blockchain technology and trust relationships in trade finance. *Technological Forecasting and Social Change*, *166*, 120641. doi:10.1016/j.techfore.2021.120641

Kube, N. (2018). *Daniel Drescher: Blockchain basics: a non-technical introduction in 25 steps.* Springer. doi:10.100711408-018-0315-6

Kumar, R., & Tripathi, R. (2019). *Traceability of counterfeit medicine supply chain through Blockchain.* Paper presented at the 2019 11th International Conference on Communication Systems & Networks (COMSNETS). 10.1109/COMSNETS.2019.8711418

Kuo, T.-T., & Ohno-Machado, L. (2018). *ModelChain: Decentralized Privacy-Preserving Healthcare Predictive Modeling Framework on Private Blockchain Networks.* https://arxiv.org/abs/1802.01746

Lamport, L., Shostak, R., & Pease, M. (1982, July). The Byzantine Generals Problem. *ACM Transactions on Programming Languages and Systems*, *4*(3), 382–401. doi:10.1145/357172.357176

Larimer, D. (2017). *Delegated Proof-of-Stake (DPOS) 2014.* Academic Press.

Lavanya, M., & Natarajan, V. (2017). Lightweight key agreement protocol for IoT based on IKEv2 R. *Computers & Electrical Engineering*, *64*, 580–594. doi:10.1016/j.compeleceng.2017.06.032

Lee, L. (2015). New Kids on the Blockchain: How Bitcoin's Technology Could Reinvent the Stock Market. SSRN *Electron. J.*, *12*. doi:10.2139/ssrn.2656501

Lee, W. H., Chou, C. M., & Wang, S. W. (2016). An NFC Anti-Counterfeiting framework for ID verification and image protection. *Mobile Networks and Applications*, *21*(4), 646–655. doi:10.100711036-016-0721-9

Lessig, L. (2006). *Code 2.0.* Basic Books.

Liang, X., Zhao, J., Shetty, S., Liu, J., & Li, D. (2017). Integrating blockchain for data sharing and collaboration in mobile healthcare applications. *2017 IEEE 28th Annual International Symposium on Personal, Indoor, and Mobile Radio Communications (PIMRC)*, 1–5.

Li, C., & Palanisamy, B. (2019). Privacy in Internet of things: From principles to technologies. *IEEE Internet of Things Journal*, *6*(1), 488–505. doi:10.1109/JIOT.2018.2864168

Li, J., Jing, X., & Yang, H. (2019). Blockchain electronic counting scheme based on practical Byzantine fault tolerance algorithm. *Jisuanji Yingyong, 40*(4), 954–960.

Lin, C., He, D., Huang, X., Choo, K.-K. R., & Vasilakos, A. V. (2018). Basin: A blockchain-based secure mutual authentication with fine-grained access control system for industry 4.0. *Journal of Network and Computer Applications, 116*, 42–52. doi:10.1016/j.jnca.2018.05.005

Ling, Z., Liu, K., Xu, Y., Jin, Y., & Fu, X. (2017). An end-to-end view of IoT security and privacy. *IEEE Global Communications Conference*, 1–7. 10.1109/GLOCOM.2017.8254011

Lin, I., & Liao, T. (2017). A Survey of Blockchain Security Issues and Challenges. *International Journal of Network Security, 19*(5), 653–659.

Li, R., Song, T., Mei, B., Li, H., Cheng, X., & Sun, L. (2019). Blockchain for large-scale Internet of things data storage and protection. *IEEE Transactions on Services Computing, 12*(5), 762–771. doi:10.1109/TSC.2018.2853167

Liu, C., Cronin, P., & Yang, C. (2016). A mutual auditing framework to protect iot against hardware trojans. *2016 21st Asia and South Pacific Design Automation Conference (ASP-DAC)*, 69–74.

Liu, L., & Xu, B. (2018). *Research on information security technology based on blockchain.* Paper presented at the 2018 IEEE 3rd international conference on cloud computing and big data analysis (ICCCBDA). 10.1109/ICCCBDA.2018.8386546

Liu, X. (2019). MDP-based quantitative analysis framework for proof of authority. *Proceedings - 2019 International Conference on Cyber-Enabled Distributed Computing and Knowledge Discovery*, 227–236. 10.1109/CyberC.2019.00046

Liu, C. H., Lin, Q., & Wen, S. (2019b). *Blockchain-enabled data collection and sharing for industrial IoT with deep reinforcement learning.* IEEE Transaction Industrial Informatics. doi:10.1109/TII.2018.2890203

Liu, J., & Liu, Z. (2019, June 7). A survey on security verification of blockchain smart contracts. *IEEE Access: Practical Innovations, Open Solutions, 7*, 77894–77904. doi:10.1109/ACCESS.2019.2921624

Liu, J., Zhang, C., & Fang, Y. (2018). Epic: A differential privacy framework to defend smart homes against internet traffic analysis. *IEEE Internet of Things Journal, 5*(2), 1206–1217. doi:10.1109/JIOT.2018.2799820

Liu, L., Xu, B., Zhang, X., & Wu, X. (2018). An intrusion detection method for internet of things based on suppressed fuzzy clustering. *EURASIP Journal on Wireless Communications and Networking, 2018*(1), 113. doi:10.118613638-018-1128-z

Liu, Y., Guo, W., Fan, C., Chang, L., & Cheng, C. (2019a). A practical privacy-preserving data aggregation (3pda) scheme for smart grid. *IEEE Transactions on Industrial Informatics, 15*(3), 1767–1774. doi:10.1109/TII.2018.2809672

Liu, Z., Longa, P., & Pereira, G. C. C. F. (2020). Four Q on embedded devices with strong countermeasures against side-channel attacks. *IEEE Transactions on Dependable and Secure Computing, 17*(3), 1–21.

Li, W., Andreina, S., Bohli, J. M., & Karame, G. (2017). Securing proof-of-stake blockchain protocols. In *Lecture Notes in Computer Science, 2017* (Vol. 10436, pp. 297–315). LNCS. doi:10.1007/978-3-319-67816-0_17

Li, W., Tug, S., Meng, W., & Wang, Y. (2019). Designing Collaborative Blockchained Signature-based Intrusion Detection in IoT environments. *Future Generation Computer Systems, 96*, 481–489. Advance online publication. doi:10.1016/j.future.2019.02.064

Li, X., Niu, J., Bhuiyan, M. Z. A., Wu, F., Karuppiah, M., & Kumari, S. (2018a). A robust ECC-based provable secure authentication protocol with privacy-preserving for industrial Internet of things. *IEEE Transactions on Industrial Informatics, 14*(8), 3599–3609. doi:10.1109/TII.2017.2773666

Li, Z., Kang, J., Yu, R., Ye, D., Deng, Q., & Zhang, Y. (2018b). Consortium blockchain for secure energy trading in industrial Internet of things. *IEEE Transactions on Industrial Informatics, 14*(8), 3690–3700.

Longo, F., Nicoletti, L., Padovano, A., d'Atri, G., & Forte, M. (2019). Blockchain-enabled supply chain: An experimental study. *Computers & Industrial Engineering, 136*, 57–69. doi:10.1016/j.cie.2019.07.026

Loukil, F., Boukadi, K., Hussain, R., & Abed, M. (2021). CioSy: A Collaborative Blockchain-Based Insurance System. *Electronics 2021, 10*(11), 1343. doi:10.3390/ELECTRONICS10111343

Lukac, D. (2015). The fourth ICT-based industrial revolution "Industry 4.0"??? HMI and the case of CAE/CAD innovation with EPLAN. *23rd Telecommunications Forum Telfor (TELFOR)*, 835-838.

Lu, Q., & Xu, X. (2017). Adaptable blockchain-based systems: A case study for product traceability. *IEEE Software, 34*(6), 21–27. doi:10.1109/MS.2017.4121227

Luu, L., Chu, D.-H., Olickel, H., Saxena, P., & Hobor, A. (2016). Making smart contracts smarter. *Proceedings of the 2016 ACM SIGSAC conference on computer and communications security*. 10.1145/2976749.2978309

Lu, Y., & Li, J. (2016). A pairing-free certificate-based proxy re-encryption scheme for secure data sharing in public clouds. *Future Generation Computer Systems, 62*, 140–147. doi:10.1016/j.future.2015.11.012

Lyubashevsky, V., Micciancio, D., Peikert, C., & Rosen, A. (2008). SWIFFT: A Modest Proposal for FFT Hashing. Fast Software Encryption. *Lecture Notes in Computer Science, 5086*, 54–72. doi:10.1007/978-3-540-71039-4_4

Machado, C., & Frhlich, A. A. M. (2018). IoT data integrity verification for cyber-physical systems using blockchain. *2018 IEEE 21st International Symposium on Real-Time Distributed Computing (ISORC)*, 83–90.

Mahmoud, R., Yousuf, T., Aloul, F., & Zualkernan, I. (2015). *Internet of Things (IoT) Security : Current Status, Challenges and Prospective Measures*. Academic Press.

MailMyStatements. (2021). *7 Major Challenges Facing the Healthcare Industry in 2021*. https://mailmystatements.com/2020/10/27/2019challenges/

Makhdoom, I., Abolhasan, M., Abbas, H., & Ni, W. (2019). Blockchain's adoption in iot: The challenges, and a way forward. *Journal of Network and Computer Applications, 125*, 251–279. doi:10.1016/j.jnca.2018.10.019

Malecki, E. J., & Moriset, B. (2007). *The Digital Economy: Business Organization, Production Processes and Regional Developments*. Routledge. doi:10.4324/9780203933633

Mamo, N., Martin, G. M., Desira, M., Ellul, B., & Ebejer, J.-P. (2019). Dwarna: a blockchain solution for dynamic consent in biobanking. *European Journal of Human Genetics, 28*(5), 609–626. doi:10.1038/s41431-019-0560-9

Mamoshina, P., Ojomoko, L., Yanovich, Y., Ostrovski, A., Botezatu, A., Prikhodko, P., Izumchenko, E., Aliper, A., Romantsov, K., Zhebrak, A., Ogu, I. O., & Zhavoronkov, A. (2018). Converging blockchain and next-generation artificial intelligence technologies to decentralize and accelerate biomedical research and healthcare. *Oncotarget, 9*(5), 5665–5690. doi:10.18632/oncotarget.22345 PMID:29464026

Manditereza, K. (2017). *4 Key Differences between Scada and Industrial IoT*. Academic Press.

Mangia, M., Pareschi, F., Rovatti, R., & Setti, G. (2017). Low-cost Security of IoT Sensor Nodes With Rakeness-Based Compressed Sensing : Statistical. *IEEE Transactions on Information Forensics and Security, 6013*(c), 1–14. doi:10.1109/TIFS.2017.2749982

Manyika, J., Bughin, J., Lund, S., Nottebaum, O., Poulter, D., Jauch, S., & Ramaswamy, S. (2014). *Global flows in a digital age: How trade, finance, people, and data connect the world economy*. McKinsey Global Institute.

Manyika, J., Chui, M., Bughin, J., Dobbs, R., Bisson, P., & Mars, A. (2013). *Disruptive Technologies: Advances that will transform life, business and the global economy*. McKinsey Global Institute.

Manzoor, A., Liyanage, M., Braeken, A., Kanhere, S. S., & Ylianttila, M. (2019). Blockchain-Based Proxy Re-encryption Scheme for Secure IoT Data Sharing. *Clinical Orthopaedics and Related Research*.

Markov, A. (2018). *Use of blockchain in pharmaceuticals and medicine*. https://miningbitcoinguide.com/technology/blokchejn-v-meditsine

Marriam-Webster. (2021). *Definition of Cryptography*. Available: https://www.merriam-webster.com/dictionary/cryptography

Mayes, K., Jayasinghe, D., & Markantonakis, K. (2014). Optimistic Fair-Exchange with Anonymity for Bitcoin Users. *IEEE Computer Society, 11*, 44–51.

McGhin, T., Choo, K.-K. R., Liu, C. Z., & He, D. (2019). Blockchain in healthcare applications: Research challenges and opportunities. *Journal of Network and Computer Applications*, *135*, 62–75. doi:10.1016/j.jnca.2019.02.027

Mikroyannidis, A., Third, A., Chowdhury, N., Bachler, M., & Domingue, J. (2020). Supporting Lifelong Learning with Smart Blockchain Badges. *International Journal On Advances in Intelligent Systems*, *13*(3 & 4), 163–176.

Minoli, D., & Occhiogross, B. (2018). Blockchain mechanism for IoT security. *International Journal of Internet of Things*, 1-13.

Misbhauddin, M., AlAbdulatheam, A., Aloufi, M., Al-Hajji, H., & AlGhuwainem, A. (2020). MedAccess: A Scalable Architecture for Blockchain-based Health Record Management. *2020 2nd International Conference on Computer and Information Sciences (ICCIS)*, 1–5. doi:10.1109/ICCIS49240.2020.9257720

Mitchell, R., & Chen, I. R. (2014). Review: A survey of intrusion detection in wireless network applications. *Computer Communications*, *42*, 1–23. doi:10.1016/j.comcom.2014.01.012

Mitic, I. (2020). *The Fraudster Next Door: 30 Insurance Fraud Statistics - Fortunly*. https://fortunly.com/statistics/insurance-fraud-statistics/#gref

Moh'd Ali, M. A., Basahr, A., Rabbani, M. R., & Abdulla, Y. (2020). Transforming Business Decision Making with Internet of Things (IoT) and Machine Learning (ML). *2020 International Conference on Decision Aid Sciences and Application (DASA)*, 674–679. 10.1109/DASA51403.2020.9317174

Mohanta, B., Panda, S., & Debasish, J. (2018). An Overview of Smart Contract and Use Cases in Blockchain Technology. *International Conference on Computing Communication and Networking Technologies*. 10.1109/ICCCNT.2018.8494045

Mondal, S., Wijewardena, K. P., Karuppuswami, S., Kriti, N., Kumar, D., & Chahal, P. (2019). Blockchain inspired RFID-based information architecture for food supply chain. *IEEE Internet of Things Journal*, *6*(3), 5803–5813. doi:10.1109/JIOT.2019.2907658

Mosenia, A., & Jha, N. K. (2017). A comprehensive study of security of internet-of-things. *IEEE Transactions on Emerging Topics in Computing*, *5*(4), 586–602. doi:10.1109/TETC.2016.2606384

Muneeza, A., Arshad, N. A., & Arifin, A. T. (2018). The application of blockchain technology in crowdfunding: Towards financial inclusion via technology. *International Journal of Management and Applied Research*, *5*(2), 82–98. doi:10.18646/2056.52.18-007

Naeem, H., Guo, B., & Naeem, M. R. (2018). A lightweight malware static visual analysis for IoT infrastructure. *International Conference on Artificial Intelligence and Big Data (ICAIBD)*, 240–244.

Naeem, M. A., Rabbani, M. R., Karim, S., & Billah, M. (2022). (in press). Religion vs Ethics: Hedge and haven properties of Sukuk and green bonds for stock markets pre- and during COVID-19. *International Journal of Islamic and Middle Eastern Finance and Management*.

Nakamoto, S. (2008). *Bitcoin: A Peer-to-Peer Electronic Cash System.* Available: https://bitcoin. org/bitcoin.pdf

Nakamoto, S. (2008). Bitcoin: A peer-to-peer electronic cash system. *Decentralized Business Review.*

Nakamoto, S. (2008). *Bitcoin: A Peer-to-Peer Electronic Cash System.* https://bitcoin.org/bitcoin.pdf

Nakamoto, S. (2008). *Bitcoin: A Peer-to-Peer Electronic Cash System.* https://www.bitcoinpaper. info/bitcoinpaper-html/

Nakamoto, S. (2008a). *Bitcoin whitepaper.* https://bitcoin. org/bitcoin. pdf

Nakamoto, S. (2008b). Bitcoin: A peer-to-peer electronic cash system. *Decentralized Business Review.*

Nakamoto, S., & Bitcoin, A. (2008). *A peer-to-peer electronic cash system.* Bitcoin. https:// bitcoin. org/bitcoin. pdf

Narayanan, A., Bonneau, J., Felten, E., Miller, A., & Goldfeder, S. (2016). *Bitcoin and cryptocurrency technologies: a comprehensive introduction.* Princeton University Press.

Narayanan, A., Bonneau, J., Felten, E., Miller, A., & Goldfeder, S. (2016). *Bitcoin and Cryptocurrency Technologies: A Comprehensive Introduction.* Princeton University Press. https://books.google.co.in/books?hl=en&lr=&id=LchFDAAAQBAJ&oi=fnd&pg=PP1&dq= Narayanan,+Arvind%3B+Bonneau,+Joseph%3B+Felten,+Edward%3B+Miller,+Andrew%3 B+Goldfeder,+Steven+(2016).+Bitcoin+and+cryptocurrency+technologies:+a+comprehens ive+introduction.+Prince

Nathani, B., & Vijayvergia, R. (2018). The Internet of Intelligent things: An overview. *ICCT 2017 - International Conference on Intelligent Communication and Computational Techniques,* 119–122. 10.1109/INTELCCT.2017.8324031

Nawaz, A., Peña Queralta, J., Guan, J., Awais, M., Gia, T. N., Bashir, A. K., Kan, H., & Westerlund, T. (2020). Edge computing to secure iot data ownership and trade with the ethereum blockchain. *Sensors (Basel),* 20(14), 3965. doi:10.339020143965 PMID:32708807

Nguyen, T., & Yoo, M. (2017). A hybrid prevention method for eavesdropping attack by link spoofing in software-defined Internet of Things controllers. *Distributed Sensor Networks,* 13(11). Advance online publication. doi:10.1177/1550147717739157

Niranjanamurthy, M., Nithya, B., & Jagannatha, S. (2019). Analysis of Blockchain technology: Pros, cons and SWOT. *Cluster Computing,* 22(6), 14743–14757. doi:10.100710586-018-2387-5

Nižetić, S., Šolić, P., López-de-Ipiña González-de-Artaza, D., & Patrono, L. (2020). Internet of Things (IoT): Opportunities, issues and challenges towards a smart and sustainable future. *Journal of Cleaner Production,* 274, 122877. Advance online publication. doi:10.1016/j. jclepro.2020.122877 PMID:32834567

Nugent, T., Upton, D., & Cimpoesu, M. (2016). Improving data transparency in clinical trials using blockchain smart contracts. *F1000Research 2016, 5*, 2541. doi:10.12688/f1000research.9756.1

Nwafor, E., Campbell, A., & Bloom, G. (2017). *Anomaly-based Intrusion Detection of IoT Device Sensor Data using Provenance Graphs*. Academic Press.

Observe, I. T. (2018). *5 Examples of Insider Threat-Caused Breaches that Illustrate the Scope of the Problem*. Author.

OECD. (2012). *OECD Internet Economy Outlook 2012*. OECD Publishing.

OECD. (2014). *Measuring the Digital Economy: A New Perspective*. OECD Publishing.

OECD. (2016). *Ministerial Declaration on the Digital Economy ("Cancún Declaration") from the Meeting on The Digital Economy: Innovation, Growth and Social Prosperity*. Available at: https://www.oecd.org/internet/Digital-Economy-Ministerial-Declaration-2016.pdf

OECD. (2017). *OECD Digital Economy Outlook 2017*. OECD Publishing.

Oh, J., & Shong, I. (2017). *A case study on business model innovations using Blockchain: focusing on financial institutions. Asia Pacific Journal of Innovation and Entrepreneurship*.

Ojanperä, S., Graham, M., & Zook, M. (2016). *Measuring the contours of the global knowledge economy with a digital index*. Paper presented at the Development Studies Association Conference 2016, Oxford, UK.

Okorie, O., Turner, C., Charnley, F., Moreno, M., & Tiwari, A. (2017). A review of data-driven approaches for circular economy in manufacturing. *Proceedings of the 18th European Roundtable for Sustainable Consumption and Production*.

Oleshchuk, V. (2009). Internet of things and privacy-preserving technologies. *2009 1st International Conference on Wireless Communication, Vehicular Technology, Information Theory and Aerospace Electronic Systems Technology*, 336–340. 10.1109/WIRELESSVITAE.2009.5172470

Ølnes, S., & Jansen, A. (2017). Blockchain Technology as s Support Infrastructure in e-Government. *International Conference on Electronic Government*, 215-227. 10.1007/978-3-319-64677-0_18

Omar, A. A., Bhuiyan, M. Z. A., Basu, A., Kiyomoto, S., & Rahman, M. S. (2019). Privacy-friendly platform for healthcare data in cloud-based on blockchain environment. *Future Generation Computer Systems*, *95*, 511–521. doi:10.1016/j.future.2018.12.044

Orcutt, M. (2017). *Blockchains Use Massive Amounts of Energy - But There's a Plan to Fix That*. https://www.technologyreview.com/2017/11/16/147609/bitcoin-uses-massive-amounts-of-energybut-theres-a-plan-to-fix-it/

Osifeko, M. O., & Hancke, G. P. (2020). *Artificial Intelligence Techniques for Cognitive Sensing in Future IoT : State-of-the-Art, Potentials, and Challenges*. Academic Press.

Osmani, M., El-Haddadeh, R., Hindi, N., Janssen, M., & Weerakkody, V. (2020). Blockchain for next generation services in banking and finance: Cost, benefit, risk and opportunity analysis. *Journal of Enterprise Information Management*.

OWASP. (2016). *Top IoT Vulnerabilities*. https://www.owasp.org/index. php/Top_IoT_ Vulnerabilities

Oztemel, E., & Gusev, S. (2018). Literature review of industry 4.0 and related technologies. *Journal of Intelligent Manufacturing*.

Pahlajani, S., Kshirsagar, A., & Pachghare, V. (2019). Survey on private blockchain consensus algorithms. *2019 1st International Conference on Innovations in Information and Communication Technology (ICIICT)*, 1-6. 10.1109/ICIICT1.2019.8741353

Pajouh, H. H., Javidan, R., Khaymi, R., Dehghantanha, A., & Raymond, K. (2016). A Two-layer Dimension Reduction and Two-tier Classification Model for Anomaly-Based Intrusion Detection in IoT Backbone Networks. *IEEE Transactions on Emerging Topics in Computing, 6750*, 1–11. doi:10.1109/TETC.2016.2633228

Pal, K. (2017). *Building High Quality Big Data-Based Applications in Supply Chains*. IGI Global Publication.

Pal, K. (2018). *Ontology-Based Web Service Architecture for Retail Supply Chain Management*. The 9th International Conference on Ambient Systems, Networks and Technologies, Porto, Portugal. 10.1016/j.procs.2018.04.101

Pal, K. (2019). Algorithmic Solutions for RFID Tag Anti-Collision Problem in Supply Chain Management. *Procedia Computer Science, 151*, 929–934. doi:10.1016/j.procs.2019.04.129

Pal, K. (2020). Information sharing for manufacturing supply chain management based on blockchain technology. In I. Williams (Ed.), *Cross-Industry Use of Blockchain Technology and Opportunities for the Future* (pp. 1–17). IGI Global. doi:10.4018/978-1-7998-3632-2.ch001

Pal, K. (2021). Applications of Secured Blockchain Technology in Manufacturing Industry. In *Blockchain and AI Technology in the Industrial Internet of Things*. IGI Global Publication. doi:10.4018/978-1-7998-6694-7.ch010

Pal, K., & Yasar, A. (2020). Internet of Things and blockchain technology in apparel manufacturing supply chain data management. *Procedia Computer Science, 170*, 450–457. doi:10.1016/j. procs.2020.03.088

Park, N., & Kang, N. (2015). Mutual authentication scheme insecure Internet of things technology for comfortable lifestyle. *Sensors (Basel), 16*(1), 20. doi:10.339016010020 PMID:26712759

Patnaik, S. (2020). Survey on IoT Security : Challenges and Solution using Machine Learning. *Artificial Intelligence and Blockchain Technology*. Advance online publication. doi:10.1016/j. iot.2020.100227

Patra, L., & Rao, U. P. (2016). *Internet of Things- Architecture, applications, security and other major challenges*. Academic Press.

Pech, S. (2020). Copyright Unchained: How Blockchain Technology Can Change the Administration and Distribution of Copyright Protected Works. *Northwestern Journal of Technology and Intellectual Property*, (1). Advance online publication. doi:10.2139srn.3578311

Peterson, B. E., Kwant, J. W., Cecil, V. C., & Provost, W. A. (1998). *Electronic creation, submission, adjudication, and payment of health insurance claims*. Academic Press.

Pina, P. (2011). Digital Copyright Enforcement: Between Piracy and Privacy. In C. Akrivopoulou & A. Psygkas (Eds.), *Personal Data Privacy and Protection in a Surveillance Era: Technologies and Practices* (pp. 241–254). IGI Global. doi:10.4018/978-1-60960-083-9.ch014

Pirtle, C., & Ehrenfeld, J. (2018). Blockchain for Healthcare: The Next Generation of Medical Records? *Journal of Medical Systems*, *42*(9), 1–3.

Plotnikov, V., & Kuznetsova, V. (2018). The Prospects for the Use of Digital Technology "blockchain" in the Pharmaceutical Market. *MATEC Web of Conferences, 193*. doi:10.1051/matecconf/201819302029

Pontevedra, V., & Sonavane, S. (2019). A Real-Time Intrusin Detection System for Wormhole Attack in in the RPL based Internet of Things. *Procedia Manufacturing*, *32*, 840–847. doi:10.1016/j.promfg.2019.02.292

Popper, N., & Lohr, S. (2017). Blockchain: A better way to track pork chops, bonds, bad peanut butter. *New York Times, 4*, 4.

Porambage, P., Schmitt, C., Kumar, P., Gurtov, A., & Ylianttila, M. (2014). Pauthkey: A pervasive authentication protocol and key establishment scheme for wireless sensor networks in distributed IoT applications. *International Journal of Distributed Sensor Networks*, *10*(7), 357430. doi:10.1155/2014/357430

Propy. (2021). *Automating Real Estate Transactions*. Available: https://propy.com/

Pu, C., & Hajjar, S. (2018). Mitigating forwarding misbehaviors in rpl-based low power and lossy networks. *2018 15th IEEE Annual Consumer Communications Networking Conference (CCNC)*, 1–6.

Pu, C. (2020). Sybil Attack in RPL-Based Internet of Things : Analysis and Defenses. *IEEE Internet of Things Journal Sybil*, *4662*(c), 4937–4949. Advance online publication. doi:10.1109/JIOT.2020.2971463

PWC. (2016). Customers in the spotlight - How FinTech is reshaping banking. Global FinTech Survey 2016.

Qin, T., Wang, B., Chen, R., Qin, Z., & Wang, L. (2019). *IMLADS : Intelligent Maintenance and Lightweight Anomaly Detection System for Internet of Things*. doi:10.3390/s19040958

Rabbani, M. R., Abdulla, Y., Basahr, A., Khan, S., & Moh'd Ali, M. A. (2020b). Embracing of Fintech in Islamic Finance in the post COVID era. *2020 International Conference on Decision Aid Sciences and Application (DASA)*, 1230–1234. 10.1109/DASA51403.2020.9317196

Rabbani, M. R. (2020a). The competitive structure and strategic positioning of commercial banks in Saudi Arabia. *International Journal on Emerging Technologies*, *11*(3), 43–46.

Rabbani, M. R. (2021). COVID-19 and its impact on supply chain financing and the role of Islamic Fintech: Evidence from GCC countries. *International Journal of Agile Systems and Management*.

Rabbani, M. R., Ali, M. A. M., Rahiman, H. U., Atif, M., Zulfikar, Z., & Naseem, Y. (2021d). The Response of Islamic Financial Service to the COVID-19 Pandemic: The Open Social Innovation of the Financial System. *Journal of Open Innovation*, *7*(1), 1–18. doi:10.3390/joitmc7010085

Rabbani, M. R., Bashar, A., Nawaz, N., Karim, S., Ali, M. A. M., Khan, A., Rahiman, H., & Alam, S. (2021a). Exploring the role of Islamic Fintech in combating the after-shocks of COVID-19: The open social innovation of the Islamic financial system. *Journal of Open Innovation*, *7*(2), 136. doi:10.3390/joitmc7020136

Rabbani, M. R., Khan, S., & Atif, M. (2021b). Machine Learning based P2P Lending Islamic FinTech Model for Small and Medium Enterprises (SMEs) in Bahrain. *International Journal of Business Innovation and Research*, *1*(1), 10040857. doi:10.1504/IJBIR.2021.10040857

Radwan, M., Calandra, D., & Koumbarakis, P. (2020). Takaful Industry and Blockchain : Challenges and Opportunities for Costs ' Reduction in Islamic Insurance Companies. *European Journal of Islamic Finance*, (October), 1–6. doi:10.13135/2421-2172/4926

Rahulamathavan, Y., Phan, R. C., Rajarajan, M., Misra, S., & Kondoz, A. (2017). Privacy-preserving blockchain-based IoT ecosystem using attribute-based encryption. *IEEE International Conference on Advanced Networks and Telecommunications Systems (ANTS)*, 1–6. 10.1109/ANTS.2017.8384164

Raj, R., Rai, N., & Agarwal, S. (2019). Anticounterfeiting in Pharmaceutical Supply Chain by establishing Proof of Ownership. *IEEE Region 10 Annual International Conference, Proceedings/TENCON*, 1572–1577. doi:10.1109/TENCON.2019.8929271

Rajput, A. R., Li, Q., & Ahvanooey, M. T. (2021). A Blockchain-Based Secret-Data Sharing Framework for Personal Health Records in Emergency Condition. *Healthcare 2021, 9*(2), 206. doi:10.3390/HEALTHCARE9020206

Rambus. (n.d.). *Industrial IoT: Threats and countermeasures*. https://www.rambus.com/iot/industrial-IoT/

Rathore, M. M., Paul, A., Ahmad, A., Chilamkurthi, N., Rathore, M. M., Paul, A., ... Seo, H. (2017). Real-Time Secure Communication for Smart City in High-Speed Big Data Environment. *Future Generation Computer Systems*. Advance online publication. doi:10.1016/j.future.2017.08.006

Ray, P. P., Dash, Di., Salah, K., & Kumar, N. (2021). Blockchain for IoT-Based Healthcare: Background, Consensus, Platforms, and Use Cases. *IEEE Systems Journal*, *15*(1), 85–94. https://doi.org/10.1109/JSYST.2020.2963840

Reyna, A., Martn, C., Chen, J., Soler, E., & Daz, M. (2018). On blockchain and its integration with iot. challenges and opportunities. *Future Generation Computer Systems*, *88*, 173–190. doi:10.1016/j.future.2018.05.046

Rivest, R. L. (1990). Cryptography. In J. Van Leeuwen (Ed.), *Handbook of Theoretical Computer Science* (Vol. 1). Elsevier.

Roblek, V., Mesko, M., & Krapez, A. (2016). A complex view of Industry 4.0. *SAGE Open*, *6*(2). Advance online publication. doi:10.1177/2158244016653987

Roehrs, A., da Costa, C. A., & da Rosa Righi, R. (2017). OmniPHR: A distributed architecture model to integrate personal health records. *Journal of Biomedical Informatics*, *71*, 70–81. https://doi.org/10.1016/j.jbi.2017.05.012

Rogaway, P. (2004). *Nonce-based symmetric encryption.* Paper presented at the International workshop on fast software encryption. 10.1007/978-3-540-25937-4_22

Roman, R., Lopez, J., & Mambo, M. (2016). Mobile edge computing, Fog et al.: A survey and analysis of security threats and challenges. *Future Gener. Comput. Syst.*

Rose, A. (2020). Blockchain: Transforming the registration of IP rights and strengthening the protection of unregistered IP rights. *WIPO Magazine*. https://www.wipo.int/wipo_magazine_digital/en/2020/article_0002.html

Saleh, A. I., Talaat, F. M., & Labib, L. M. (2017). A hybrid intrusion detection system (HIDS) based on prioritized k-nearest neighbors and optimized SVM classifiers. *Artificial Intelligence Review*. Advance online publication. doi:10.100710462-017-9567-1

Savelyev, A. (2017). *Copyright in the blockchain era: Promises and challenges.* https://wp.hse.ru/data/2017/11/21/1160790875/77LAW2017.pdf

Schiff, G. D., Hasan, O., Kim, S., Abrams, R., Cosby, K., Lambert, B. L., Elstein, A. S., Hasler, S., Kabongo, M. L., Krosnjar, N., Odwazny, R., Wisniewski, M. F., & McNutt, R. A. (2009). Diagnostic Error in Medicine: Analysis of 583 Physician-Reported Errors. *Archives of Internal Medicine*, *169*(20), 1881–1887. https://doi.org/10.1001/ARCHINTERNMED.2009.333

Schuetz, S., & Venkatesh, V. (2020). Blockchain, adoption, and financial inclusion in India: Research opportunities. *International Journal of Information Management*, *52*, 101936. doi:10.1016/j.ijinfomgt.2019.04.009

Sedjelmaci, H., Senouci, S. M., Taleb, T., & Saclay, P. (2017). An Accurate Security Game for Low-Resource IoT Devices. *IEEE Transactions on Vehicular Technology*, *9545*(10), 2–15. doi:10.1109/TVT.2017.2701551

Sfar, A. R., Natalizio, E., Challal, Y., & Chtourou, Z. (2018). A roadmap for security challenges in the Internet of things. *Digital Communications and Networks.*, *4*(2), 118–137. doi:10.1016/j. dcan.2017.04.003

Shae, Z., & Tsai, J. J. P. (2017). On the Design of a Blockchain Platform for Clinical Trial and Precision Medicine. *Proceedings - International Conference on Distributed Computing Systems*, 1972–1980. doi:10.1109/ICDCS.2017.61

Shah, P., Forester, D., Berberich, M., Raspé, C., & Mueller, H. (2019). *Blockchain Technology: Data Privacy Issues and Potential Mitigation Strategies.* https://www.davispolk.com/publications/ blockchain-technology-data-privacy-issues-and-potential-mitigation-strategies

Sharma, K., & Jain, D. (2019, July). Consensus algorithms in blockchain technology: A survey. In *2019 10th International Conference on Computing, Communication and Networking Technologies (ICCCNT)* (pp. 1-7). IEEE.

Shen, M., Tang, X., Zhu, L., Du, X., & Guizani, M. (2019). Privacy-preserving support vector machine training over blockchain-based encrypted IoT data in smart cities. *IEEE Internet of Things Journal*, *6*(5), 7702–7712. doi:10.1109/JIOT.2019.2901840

Sherman, A. T., Javani, F., Zhang, H., & Golaszewski, E. (2019). On the origins and variations of blockchain technologies. *IEEE Security and Privacy*, *17*(1), 72–77. doi:10.1109/ MSEC.2019.2893730

Sherman, A. T., Javani, F., Zhang, H., & Golaszewski, E. (2019). On the Origins and Variations of Blockchain Technologies. *IEEE Security and Privacy*, *17*(1), 72–77. https://doi.org/10.1109/ MSEC.2019.2893730

Shi, L., & Wang, Y. (2018). *Secure Data Delivery with Linear Network Coding for Multiple Multicasts with Multiple Streams in Internet of Things*. Academic Press.

Shrestha, R., Bajracharya, R., Shrestha, A. P., & Nam, S. Y. (2019). *A new type of blockchain for secure message exchange in vanet*. Digital Communications and Networks.

Shukla, P. (2017). Ml-ids: A machine learning approach to detect wormhole attacks in the Internet of things. *Intelligent Systems Conference (IntelliSys)*, 234–240. 10.1109/IntelliSys.2017.8324298

Sicari, S., Rizzardi, A., Grieco, L., & Coen-Porisini, A. (2015). Security, privacy and trust in Internet of things: The road ahead. *Computer Networks*, *76*(Suppl. C), 146–164. doi:10.1016/j. comnet.2014.11.008

Sicari, S., Rizzardi, A., Miorandi, D., & Coen-Porisini, A. (2018). Reatoreacting to denial-of-service attacks in the Internet of things. *Computer Networks*, *137*, 37–48. doi:10.1016/j. comnet.2018.03.020

Singh, C., Chauhan, D., Deshmukh, S. A., Vishnu, S. S., & Walia, R. (2021). Medi-Block record: Secure data sharing using block chain technology. *Informatics in Medicine Unlocked*, *24*, 100624. doi:10.1016/j.imu.2021.100624

Singh, M., Rajan, M. A., Shivraj, V. L., & Balamuralidhar, P. (2015). Secure MQTT for the Internet of things (IoT). *5th International Conference on Communication Systems and Network Technologies*, 746–751. 10.1109/CSNT.2015.16

Song, T., Li, R., Mei, B., Yu, J., Xing, X., & Cheng, X. (2017). A privacy-preserving communication protocol for IoT applications in smart homes. *IEEE Internet of Things Journal*, *4*(6), 1844–1852. doi:10.1109/JIOT.2017.2707489

SOPHOS. (2015). *49 Busted in Europe for Man-In-The-Middle Bank Attacks*. https://nakedsecurity. sophos.com/2015/06/11/49-busted-in-europe-for-man-in-themiddle-bank-attacks/

Spatz, K. (2018). *Eight ways Blockchain will impact the world beyond Cryptocurrency*. https://www.forbes.com/sites/theyec/2018/03/09/eight-ways-blockchain-will-impact-the-world-beyond-cryptocurrency

Sreamr. (2017). *Streamr White Paper v2.0*. https://s3.amazonaws.com/streamr-public/ streamr-datacoin-whitepaper-2017-07-25-v1_0.pdf

Srinivas, J., Das, A. K., Wazid, M., & Kumar, N. (2018). *Anonymous lightweight chaotic map-based authenticated key agreement protocol for industrial Internet of things. IEEE Trans. Dependable Secure Comput.*

Stifter, N. (2021). What is Meant by Permissionless Blockchains? Cryptology ePrint Archive, Report 2021/023.

Su, J., Vasconcellos, V. D., Prasad, S., Daniele, S., Feng, Y., & Sakurai, K. (2018). Lightweight classification of IoT malware based on image recognition. *IEEE 42nd Annual Computer Software and Applications Conference (COMPSAC)*, *2*, 664–669.

Sukhwani, H., Martínez, J. M., Chang, X., Trivedi, K. S., & Rindos, A. (2017). Performance modeling of PBFT consensus process for permissioned blockchain network (hyperledger fabric). *Proceedings of the IEEE Symposium on Reliable Distributed Systems*, 253–255. 10.1109/SRDS.2017.36

Sun, H., Rabbani, M. R., Ahmad, N., Sial, M. S., Cheng, G., Zia-Ud-Din, M., & Fu, Q. (2020b). CSR, Co-Creation and Green Consumer Loyalty: Are Green Banking Initiatives Important? A Moderated Mediation Approach from an Emerging Economy. *Sustainability*, *12*(24), 10688. doi:10.3390u122410688

Sun, H., Rabbani, M. R., Sial, M. S., Yu, S., Filipe, J. A., & Cherian, J. (2020a). Identifying big data's opportunities, challenges, and implications in finance. *Mathematics*, *8*(10), 1738. Advance online publication. doi:10.3390/math8101738

Sun, Y., Yan, B., Yao, Y., & Yu, J. (2021). DT-DPoS: A Delegated Proof of Stake Consensus Algorithm with Dynamic Trust. *Procedia Computer Science*, *187*, 371–376. doi:10.1016/j.procs.2021.04.113

Sunyaev, A. (2020). Distributed ledger technology. In A. Sunyaev (Ed.), *A. Internet Computing* (pp. 265–299). Springer. doi:10.1007/978-3-030-34957-8_9

Swan, M. (2017). Anticipating the economic benefits of blockchain. *Technology Innovation Management Review, 7*(10), 6–13. doi:10.22215/timreview/1109

Swanson, T. (2015). *Consensus-as-a-service: a brief report on the emergence of permissioned, distributed ledger systems.* Academic Press.

Sweeney, L. (2002). *k-anonymity: A model for protecting privacy.* Academic Press.

Syeed, N. (2018). *Is Blockchain Technology the Future of Voting?* https://www.bloomberg.com/news/articles/2018-08-10/is-blockchain-technology-the-future-of-voting

Sylim, P., Liu, F., Marcelo, A., & Fontelo, P. (2018). Blockchain Technology for Detecting Falsified and Substandard Drugs in Distribution: Pharmaceutical Supply Chain Intervention. *JMIR Research Protocols, 7*(9). https://doi.org/10.2196/10163

Systems, D., & Centre, T. (2001). *A logic for uncertain probabilities.* Academic Press.

Szabo, N. (1994). *Smart contracts.* Unpublished manuscript.

Szabo, N. (1996). *Smart Contracts: Building Blocks for Digital Markets.* https://www.fon.hum.uva.nl/rob/Courses/InformationInSpeech/CDROM/Literature/LOTwinterschool2006/szabo.best.vwh.net/smart_contracts_2.html

Szabo, N. (1997). Formalizing and securing relationships on public networks. *First Monday, 2*(9). Advance online publication. doi:10.5210/fm.v2i9.548

Szydlo, M. (2004). *Merkle tree traversal in log space and time.* Paper presented at the International Conference on the Theory and Applications of Cryptographic Techniques. 10.1007/978-3-540-24676-3_32

Tamani, N., & Ghamri-Doudane, Y. (2016). *Towards a User Privacy Preservation System for IoT Environments : a Habit-Based Approach.* Academic Press.

Tapscott, D., & Tapscott, A. (2018). The Blockchain Revolution: How the Technology Behind Bitcoin is Changing Money, Business, and the World. Academic Press.

Tapscott, A., & Tapscott, D. (2017). How blockchain is changing finance. *Harvard Business Review, 1*(9), 2–5.

Tapscott, D. (1996). *The Digital Economy: Promise and Peril in the Age of Networked Intelligence.* McGraw-Hill.

Taylor, P. (2016). *Applying blockchain technology to medicine traceability.* https://www.securingindustry.com/pharmaceuticals/applying-blockchain-technology-to-medicine-traceability/s40/a2766/#.YN-ebNUzbIU

Thakur, R., Hsu, S. H. Y., & Fontenot, G. (2012). Innovation in healthcare: Issues and future trends. *Journal of Business Research, 65*(4), 562–569. https://doi.org/10.1016/J.JBUSRES.2011.02.022

Thenmozhi, M., Dhanalakshmi, R., Geetha, S., & Valli, R. (2021). Implementing blockchain technologies for health insurance claim processing in hospitals. *Materials Today: Proceedings*. doi:10.1016/j.matpr.2021.02.776

Toyoda, K., Mathiopoulos, P. T., Sasase, I., & Ohtsuki, T. (2017). A novel blockchain-based product ownership management system (POMS) for anti-counterfeits in the post supply chain. *IEEE Access: Practical Innovations, Open Solutions*, 5, 17465–17477. doi:10.1109/ACCESS.2017.2720760

Tresise, A., Goldenfein, J., & Hunter, D. (2018). *What blockchain can and can't do for copyright.* https://papers.ssrn.com/sol3/papers.cfm?abstract_id=3227381

Truby, J. (2018). Decarbonizing Bitcoin: Law and policy choices for reducing the energy consumption of Blockchain technologies and digital currencies. *Energy Research & Social Science*, 44, 399–410. doi:10.1016/j.erss.2018.06.009

UNCTAD. (2017). Information Economy Report 2017: Digitalization, Trade and Development. United Nations.

UNCTAD. (2019). Competition issues in the digital economy. TD/B/C.I/CLP/54. UNCTAD.

UNECA. (2017). *Blockchain Technology in Africa.* United Nations Economic Commission for Africa. Available at: https://www.uneca.org/sites/default/files/images/blockchain_technology_in_africa_draft_report_19-nov-2017-final_edited.pdf

Valduriez, P., & Ozsu, M. (2011). *Principles of distributed database systems.* Springer Science & Business Media.

Varga, P., Plosz, S., Soos, G., & Hegedus, C. (2017). Security Threats and Issues in Automation IoT. *2017 IEEE 13th International Workshop on Factory Communication Systems (WFCS)*, 1–6.

Varshney, T., Sharma, N., & Kaushik, I. (2019). Architectural Model of Security Threats & theirCountermeasures in IoT. In *2019 International Conference on Computing, Communication, and Intelligent Systems (ICCCIS)* (pp. 424–429). IEEE. 10.1109/ICCCIS48478.2019.8974544

Vechain Team. (2018). *Vechain White Paper.* https://cdn.vechain.com/vechain_ico_ideas_of_development_en.pdf

Viel, F., Silva, L. A., Valderi Leithardt, R. Q., & Zeferino, C. A. (2019). Internet of things: Concepts, architectures and technologies. *2018 13th IEEE International Conference on Industry Applications, INDUSCON 2018 - Proceedings*, 909–916. 10.1109/INDUSCON.2018.8627298

Vives, X. (2017). The Impact of FinTech on the Banking Industry. *European Economy, 2*, 97–105. https://www.fsb.org/what-we-do/policy-development/additional-policy-areas/monitoring-of-fintech/%0Ahttp://www.us.confirmation.com/blog/fintech-and-banking

Vogel-Heuser, B., & Hess, D. (2016). Guest editorial Industry 4.0 -prerequisites and vision. *IEEE Transactions on Automation Science and Engineering*, 13(2).

Wadud, M. A. H., Amir-Ul-Haque Bhuiyan, T. M., Uddin, M. A., & Rahman, M. M. (2020). A patient centric agent assisted private blockchain on hyperledger fabric for managing remote patient monitoring. *Proceedings of 2020 11th International Conference on Electrical and Computer Engineering, ICECE 2020*, 194–197. doi:10.1109/ICECE51571.2020.9393124

Wallac, B. (2011). *The Rise and Fall of Bitcoin*. https://www.wired.com/2011/11/mf-bitcoin/

Waltonchain. (2021). *Waltonchain white paper v2.0*. https://www.waltonchain.org/en/Waltonchain_White_Paper_2.0_EN.pdf

Wan, J., Li, J., Imran, M., Li, D., & e-Amin, F. (2019). A blockchain-based solution for enhancing security and privacy in smart factory. *IEEE Transaction.*

Wang, Y., Uehara, T., & Sasaki, R. (2015). Fog computing: Issues and challenges in security and forensics. *2015 IEEE 39th Annual Computer Software and Applications Conference, 3*, 53–59.

Wang, H. (2020). IoT based Clinical Sensor Data Management and Transfer using Blockchain Technology. *Journal of ISMAC, 02*(03), 154–159. https://doi.org/10.36548/jismac.2020.3.003

Wang, Q., Zhu, X., Ni, Y., Gu, L., & Zhu, H. (2019b). *Blockchain for the IoT and industrial IoT: a review*. Internet Things.

Wang, X., Zha, X., Ni, W., Liu, R. P., Guo, Y. J., Niu, X., & Zheng, K. (2019a). Survey on blockchain for Internet of things. *Computer Communications, 136*, 10–29.

Wang, Z., Luo, N., & Zhou, P. (2020). GuardHealth: Blockchain empowered secure data management and Graph Convolutional Network enabled anomaly detection in smart healthcare. *Journal of Parallel and Distributed Computing, 142*, 1–12. https://doi.org/10.1016/J.JPDC.2020.03.004

Wan, J., Tang, S., Shu, Z., Li, D., Wang, S., Imran, M., & Vasilakos, A. V. (2016). Software-defined industrial Internet of things in the context of industry 4.0. *IEEE Sensors Journal, 16*(20), 7373–7380.

Warren, S., & Brandeis, L. (1890). The Right to Privacy. *Harvard Law Review, 4*(5), 193–220. doi:10.2307/1321160

Werra, J. (2001). Le régime juridique des mesures techniques de protection des oeuvres selon les Traités de l'OMPI, le Digital Millennium Copyright Act, les Directives Européennes et d'autres legislations (Japon, Australie). *Revue Internationale du Droit d'Auteur, 189*, 66–213.

What Is Claims Adjudication? (2017). https://apexedi.com/what-is-claims-adjudication/

What is Ethereum? (2016). https://ethdocs.org/en/latest/introduction/what-is-ethereum.html

Why Proof-of-Capacity is the future. (n.d.). https://www.burst-coin.org/features/proof-of-capacity/

WrightA.De FilippiP. (2015). *Decentralized Blockchain technology and the rise of Lex Cryptographia*. doi:10.2139/ssrn.2580664

WTO. (2018). *World Trade Report 2018: The Future of World Trade – How Digital Technologies are Transforming Global Commerce*. World Trade Organization.

Wurm, J., Hoang, K., Arias, O., Sadeghi, A., & Jin, Y. (2016). Security analysis on consumer and industrial IoT devices. *21st Asia and South Pacific Design Automation Conference (ASP-DAC)*, 519–524.

Wüst, K., & Gervais, A. (2018). Do you need a Blockchain? In *2018 Crypto Valley Conference on Blockchain Technology (CVCBT)* (pp. 45-54). IEEE. 10.1109/CVCBT.2018.00011

Xia, Q., Sifah, E. B., Asamoah, K. O., Gao, J., Du, X., & Guizani, M. (2017). MeDShare: Trust-Less Medical Data Sharing among Cloud Service Providers via Blockchain. *IEEE Access: Practical Innovations, Open Solutions*, *5*, 14757–14767. https://doi.org/10.1109/ACCESS.2017.2730843

Xiong, Z., Zhang, Y., Niyato, D., Wang, P., & Han, Z. (2018). When mobile blockchain meets edge computing. *IEEE Communications Magazine*, *56*(8), 33–39.

Xu, L. D., He, W., & Li, S. (2014). Internet of things in industries: A survey. *IEEE Transactions on Industrial Informatics*, *10*(4), 2233–2243.

Xu, L. D., Xu, E. L., & Li, L. (2018). Industry 4.0: State of the art and future trends. *International Journal of Production Research*, *56*(8), 2941–2962. doi:10.1080/00207543.2018.1444806

Xu, Y., Ren, J., Wang, G., Zhang, C., Yang, J., & Zhang, Y. (2019). *A blockchain-based non-repudiation network computing service scheme for industrial IoT. IEEE Transaction Industrial Informatics*.

Yahyaoui, A., Abdellatif, T., & Attia, R. (2019). Hierarchical anomaly based intrusion detection and localization in IoT. *2019 15th International Wireless Communications & Mobile Computing Conference (IWCMC)*, 108–113.

Yang, H., Bai, Y., Zou, Z., Zhang, Q., Wang, B., & Yang, R. (2020). Research on data security sharing mechanism of power internet of things based on blockchain. In *2020 IEEE 9th Joint International Information Technology and Artificial Intelligence Conference (ITAIC)* (Vol. 9, pp. 2029–2032). 10.1109/ITAIC49862.2020.9338843

Yang, L., Ding, C., Wu, M., & Wang, K. (2017). Robust Detection of False Data Injection Attacks for the Data Aggregation in Internet of Things based Environmental Surveillance. *Computer Networks*, *129*, 410–428. Advance online publication. doi:10.1016/j.comnet.2017.05.027

Yang, W., Wang, S., Huang, X., & Mu, Y. (2019a). On the Security of an Efficient and Robust Certificateless Signature Scheme for IIoT Environments. *IEEE Access: Practical Innovations, Open Solutions*, *7*, 91074–91079.

Yang, Y., Wu, L., Yin, G., Li, L., & Zhao, H. (2017). A survey on security and privacy issues in internet-of-things. *IEEE Internet of Things Journal*, *4*(5), 1250–1258.

Yang, Z., Yang, K., Lei, L., Zheng, K., & Leung, V. C. M. (2019b). Blockchain-based decentralized trust management in vehicular networks. *IEEE Internet of Things Journal*, *6*(2), 1495–1505.

Yan, Q., Huang, W., Luo, X., Gong, Q., & Yu, F. R. (2018). A multi-level DDoS mitigation framework for the industrial Internet of things. *IEEE Communications Magazine, 56*(2), 30–36.

Yao, X., Kong, H., Liu, H., Qiu, T., & Ning, H. (2019). An attribute credential-based public-key scheme for fog computing in digital manufacturing. *IEEE Trans. Ind. Inf.*

Yazdankhah, F., & Honarvar, A. R. (2017). An Intelligent Security Approach using Game Theory to Detect DoS Attacks in IoT. *Advanced Computer Science and Applications, 8*(9). Advance online publication. doi:10.14569/IJACSA.2017.080944

Ye, C., Li, G., Cai, H., Gu, Y., & Fukuda, A. (2018, September). Analysis of security in blockchain: Case study in 51%-attack detecting. In *2018 5th International Conference on Dependable Systems and Their Applications (DSA)* (pp. 15-24). IEEE.

Yi, S., Qin, Z., & Li, Q. (2015). Security and privacy issues of fog computing: A survey. *Wireless Algorithms, Systems, and Applications the 10th International Conference on,* 1–10.

Yin, D., Zhang, L., & Yang, K. (2018). A DDoS attack detection and mitigation with software-defined Internet of things framework. *IEEE Access: Practical Innovations, Open Solutions, 6,* 24694–24705.

Yussof, S. A., & Al-Harthy, A. (2018). Cryptocurrency as an Alternative Currency in Malaysia : Issues and Challenges. *Islam and Civilisational Renewal, 9*(1), 48–65. doi:10.12816/0049515

Yu, W., & Köse, S. (2017). A Lightweight Masked AES Implementation for Securing IoT Against CPA Attacks. *IEEE Transactions on Circuits and Systems, 64*(11), 2934–2944. doi:10.1109/TCSI.2017.2702098

Zhang, H., Wang, J., & Ding, Y. (2019b). Blockchain-based decentralized and secure keyless signature scheme for smart grid. *Energy, 180,* 955–967. doi:10.1016/j.energy.2019.05.127

Zhang, L., Xie, Y., Zheng, Y., Xue, W., Zheng, X., & Xu, X. (2020). The challenges and countermeasures of blockchain in finance and economics. *Systems Research and Behavioral Science, 37*(4), 691–698. doi:10.1002res.2710

Zhang, N., Mi, X., Feng, X., Wang, X., Tian, Y., & Qian, F. (2018). *Understanding and Mitigating the Security Risks of Voice-Controlled Third-Party Skills on Amazon Alexa and Google Home.* Academic Press.

Zhang, P., Nagarajan, S. G., & Nevat, I. (2017). Secure Location of Things (SLOT). *Mitigating Localization Spoofing Attacks in the Internet of Things, 4*(September), 2199–2206. Advance online publication. doi:10.1109/JIOT.2017.2753579

Zhang, P., White, J., Schmidt, D. C., Lenz, G., & Rosenbloom, S. T. (2018). FHIRChain: Applying Blockchain to Securely and Scalably Share Clinical Data. *Computational and Structural Biotechnology Journal, 16,* 267–278. https://doi.org/10.1016/j.csbj.2018.07.004

Zhang, Y., Deng, R., Zheng, D., Li, J., Wu, P., & Cao, J. (2019a). *Efficient and Robust Certificateless Signature for Data Crowdsensing in Cloud-Assisted Industrial IoT.* IEEE Transaction Industry.

Zhang, Y., Li, P., & Wang, X. (2019). Intrusion Detection for IoT Based on Improved Genetic Algorithm and Deep Belief Network. *IEEE Access: Practical Innovations, Open Solutions*, 7, 31711–31722. doi:10.1109/ACCESS.2019.2903723

Zhang, Z. K., Cho, M. C. Y., Wang, C. W., Hsu, C. W., Chen, C. K., & Shieh, S. (2014). IoT security: Ongoing challenges and research opportunities. *2014 IEEE 7th International Conference on Service-Oriented Computer Applications*, 230–234.

Zhan, Y., Wang, B., Lu, R., & Yu, Y. (2021). DRBFT: Delegated randomization Byzantine fault tolerance consensus protocol for blockchains. *Information Sciences*, *559*, 8–21.

Zhao, H. (2018). *Bitcoin and Blockchain Consume an Exorbitant Amount of Energy. These Engineers Are Trying to Change That.* https://www.cnbc.com/2018/02/23/bitcoin-blockchain-consumes-a-lot-of-energy-engineers-changing-that.html

ZhaoZ. (2019). Fulfilling the Right to Follow: Using Blockchain to Enforce the Artist's Resale Right. *Cardozo Arts & Entertainment Law Journal, 39*(1). https://ssrn.com/abstract=3871892

Zheng, X., Mukkamala, R. R., Vatrapu, R., & Ordieres-Mere, J. (2018). Blockchain-based personal health data sharing system using cloud storage. *2018 IEEE 20th International Conference on E-Health Networking, Applications and Services (Healthcom)*, 1–6.

Zheng, Z., Xie, S., Dai, H., Chen, X., & Wang, H. (2017). An overview of blockchain technology: Architecture, consensus, and future trends. 2017 IEEE international congress on big data (BigData congress), 557-564.

Zheng, D., Wu, A., Zhang, Y., & Zhao, Q. (2018). Efficient and privacy-preserving medical data sharing in the Internet of things with limited computing power. *IEEE Access: Practical Innovations, Open Solutions*, *6*, 28019–28027.

Zheng, Z., Xie, S., Dai, H. N., Chen, W., Chen, X., Weng, J., & Imran, M. (2020). An overview on smart contracts: Challenges, advances and platforms. *Future Generation Computer Systems*, *105*, 475–491. doi:10.1016/j.future.2019.12.019

Zheng, Z., Xie, S., Dai, H., Chen, X., & Wang, H. (2017). An Overview of Blockchain Technology: Architecture, Consensus, and Future Trends. *IEEE International Congress on Big Data*. 10.1109/BigDataCongress.2017.85

Zheng, Z., Xie, S., Dai, H.-N., Chen, X., & Wang, H. (2018). Blockchain challenges and opportunities: A survey. *International Journal of Web and Grid Services*, *14*(4), 352–375. doi:10.1504/IJWGS.2018.095647

Zhou, X., Jesus, V., Wang, Y., & Josephs, M. (2020). User-controlled, auditable, cross-jurisdiction sharing of healthcare data mediated by a public blockchain. *Proceedings - 2020 IEEE 19th International Conference on Trust, Security and Privacy in Computing and Communications, TrustCom 2020*, 87–96. doi:10.1109/TRUSTCOM50675.2020.00025

Zhou, J., Cao, Z., Dong, X., & Vasilakos, A. V. (2017). Security and privacy for cloud-based IoT: Challenges. *IEEE Communications Magazine*, *55*(1), 26–33.

Zhou, L., Wang, L., & Sun, Y. (2018). MIStore: A Blockchain-Based Medical Insurance Storage System. *Journal of Medical Systems*, *42*(8), 149. https://doi.org/10.1007/s10916-018-0996-4

Zhou, R., Zhang, X., Du, X., Wang, X., Yang, G., & Guizani, M. (2018). File-centric multi-key aggregate keyword searchable encryption for industrial Internet of things. *IEEE Transactions on Industrial Informatics*, *14*(8), 3648–3658.

Zhu, Y., Guo, R., Gan, G., & Tsai, W. (2016). Interactive incontestable signature for transactions confirmation in Bitcoin Blockchain. *COMPSAC - IEEE 40th Annual*, *1*, 443–44.

Zhu, X. (2020). Blockchain-based identity authentication and intelligent Credit reporting. *Journal of Physics: Conference Series*, *1437*(1), 12086. doi:10.1088/1742-6596/1437/1/012086

Ziegeldorf, J. H., Morchon, O. G., & Wehrle, K. (2014). *Privacy in the Internet of Things: Threats and Challenges*. Academic Press.

Zilbert, M. (2018). *The Blockchain for Real Estate*. https://www.forbes.com/sites/forbesrealestatecouncil/2018/04/23/the-blockchain-for-real-estate-explained

Zou, R., Lv, X., & Zhao, J. (2020). SPChain: Blockchain-based Medical Data Sharing and Privacy-preserving eHealth System. *Information Processing & Management*, *58*(4). https://doi.org/10.1016/j.ipm.2021.102604

About the Contributors

Shahnawaz Khan received his PhD in Computer Science from Indian Institute of Technology (Banaras Hindu University), India. Currently, he is serving as Secretary General of Scientific Research Council and Assistant Professor in Department of Information Technology, University College of Bahrain, Bahrain. Prior to this, he has co-founded 2 IT companies and served as chief technical officer (CTO) and has been associated with multiple national and international universities as lecturer, course coordinator and program coordinator. He has always emphasized on bridging the gap between academics and industry keeping in mind the growing IT industry in terms of futuristic technologies. Under his leadership many modernized laboratories came into existence. He has been a key player during the accreditation process of the universities. He has more than 18 years of experience including 7+ years of industrial and 11+ years of teaching and research. He has delivered several invited/keynote talks at workshops/seminars in India & abroad. He has published 2 patents and more than 30 peer reviewed research articles. His areas of specialization are Machine learning, NLP, Blockchain and FinTech.

* * *

Maiya Al-Saadi is an IT-Networking Specialist holding IT Master's degree. Working as Officer-IT System Administrator and Acting Senior Officer - Applications & System Security at Oman Air since 2019 up to date. Worked as a Network Engineer for 3 years and acting as IT Head of Department for 9 months. A trainee at three powerful organizations and trained as a Network Administrator, Network Engineer, and IT technician.

Mazoon Alrubaiei is a system programmer at Muscat Municipality since 2011. She holds a Bachelor degree in Information Technology from Ibri College of Applied Science in Ibri, Oman and obtained a master degree in Information Technology from Modern College of Business and Science, Muscat, Oman in 2020. She has many papers published in reputable journals discussing several computer sciences areas especially security sector.

Bilyaminu Auwal Romo is a Lecturer in Computer Science & Digital Technology at the Department of Computing and Engineering at the University of East London (UEL). Bilyaminu attained a PhD in Computer Science (Software Engineering) from Brunel University London, with many years of experience in the industry and academia in empirical software engineering. His recent multidisciplinary research role at Exergy Global UK include a Software Development Consultant of €13M EU's Horizon 2020 ECOBulk.EU project to design and implement a circular economy digital platform; UEL Principal Investigator of £23K UCL Centre for Blockchain Technologies. Project titled "Circularity and Blockchain Technology for Food Redistribution and Community Well-being". His research interests include Open Source Software (OSS) projects, OSS-Component Re-use, software maintenance and evolution, digital economy and blockchain technology. In the past, his focus has been improving the quality of bug data in open-source software repositories. Bilyaminu is a Fellow of the Higher Education Academy (UK), Fellow of the Royal Society for the Encouragement of Arts, Manufacture and Commerce, Certified SAP Associate and Certified Microsoft Innovative Educator.

Mohammed Bahja is currently a Lecturer in computer science at the University of Birmingham. Before joining the University of Birmingham, he has served in the education sector at several universities in the U.K., including the University College London (UCL). His research interest includes data science for e-learning applications, including natural language processing for capturing user experience and engagement behavior. He has participated in a variety of multidisciplinary projects, including the EU-funded projects of Policy Compass, MINICHIP Decision Support System, and Green Datacentre. Apart from academia, he has strong connections within the ICT industry for both the public and private spheres. He provides robust data science solutions and software consulting services for both the public (including NHS) and the private sphere.

Sitara Karim is an Assistant Professor of Finance/ FinTech/ Business Analytics at ILMA University, Karachi, Pakistan. She is a Ph.D. in Finance & Banking from School of Economics, Finance, and Banking (SEFB), College of Business, Universiti Utara Malaysia. Her research interests include Financial Economics, Energy Economics, Financial Markets, Commodity Markets, Sustainable Corporate Governance, and Green Finance.

Mohammad Amin Kuhail received the M.Sc. degree in software engineering from the University of York, in 2006, and the Ph.D. degree in computer science from the IT University of Copenhagen, Denmark, in 2013. He has served as an Assistant Teaching Professor with the University of Missouri–Kansas City, USA, for six years. He joined Zayed University, United Arab Emirates, in 2019. He is currently a Computer Scientist and a Software Engineer with a diverse skillset that spans web development, object-oriented programming, algorithms, usability, and data science. He also serves as an Assistant Professor with Zayed University. His research interests include end-user development, usability analysis, and computer science education.

Sujith Samuel Mathew received the Ph.D. degree in computer science from The University of Adelaide, South Australia. He has over 18 years of experience working in both the IT Industry and in IT Academia. He has held positions as the Group Leader, a Technical Evangelist, and a Software Engineer within the IT industry. In academia, he has been teaching various IT related topics and pursuing his research interests in parallel. He is currently with the College of Technological Innovations, Zayed University, Abu Dhabi. His research interest includes ubiquitous and distributed computing, with focus on the Internet of Things.

Kamalendu Pal is with the Department of Computer Science, School of Mathematics, Computer Science and Engineering, City, University of London. Kamalendu received his BSc (Hons) degree in Physics from Calcutta University, India, Postgraduate Diploma in Computer Science from Pune, India, MSc degree in Software Systems Technology from Sheffield University, Postgraduate Diploma in Artificial Intelligence from Kingston University, MPhil degree in Computer Science from University College London, and MBA degree from the University of Hull, United Kingdom. He has published widely in the scientific community with research articles in the ACM SIGMIS Database, Expert Systems with Applications, Decision Support Systems, and conferences. His research interests include knowledge-based systems, decision support systems, blockchain technology, software engineering, and service-oriented computing. He is on the editorial board in an international computer science journal. Also, He is a member of the British Computer Society, the Institution of Engineering and Technology, and the IEEE Computer Society.

Pedro Pina is a lawyer and a law teacher in the Oliveira do Hospital School of Technology and Management (ESTGOH) at the Polytechnic Institute of Coimbra. He holds a law degree from the University of Coimbra Law School and a post-graduation in Territorial Development, Urbanism and Environmental Law from the Territorial Development, Urbanism and Environmental Law Studies Center (CEDOUA) at the University of Coimbra Law School. He holds a master degree in Procedural Law Studies from the University of Coimbra Law School.

Kanthavel R. has 22 years' experience in teaching and research in the field of information and Communication Engineering. He has the credit of more than 100 research articles in peer reviewed international Journals. His areas of interests are computer networking, Machine Learning and AI, Cooperative communication, computing and mobile networks.

Mustafa Raza Rabbani is holding Ph.D. in Commerce, Banking and Financial Services from the prestigious Jamia Millia Islamia, University, New Delhi, India. His areas of specialization are Financial Technology (FinTech), Artificial Intelligence and its application in Finance and banking, Blockchain and Cryptocurrency, Ethical issues in FinTech application etc. Dr. Rabbani specialized in SPPSS in other data analysis tools. He has conducted many workshops/Seminars in India & abroad. He has published more than 15 papers in peer reviewed international/national journals and conferences. He is a fellow at HIGHER EDUCATION ACADEMY (HEA), UK. He also a life member of Indian Commerce Association. His research interest includes Financial Technology (FinTech), Artificial Intelligence and its application in Finance and Banking, Blockchain and Cryptocurrency, Ethical issues in FinTech application etc.

Mohammad Khalid Imam Rahmani (Senior Member, IEEE) was born in Patherghatti, Kishanganj, Bihar, India, in 1975. He received the B.Sc. (Engg.) degree in computer engineering from Aligarh Muslim University, India, in 1998, the M.Tech. degree in computer engineering from Maharshi Dayanand University, Rohtak, in 2010, and the Ph.D. degree in computer science engineering from Mewar University, India, in 2015. From 1999 to 2006, he was a Lecturer with the Maulana Azad College of Engineering and Technology, Patna. From 2006 to 2008, he was a Lecturer and a Senior Lecturer with the Galgotias College of Engineering and Technology, Greater Noida. From 2010 to 2011, he was Assistant Professor with GSMVNIET, Palwal. Since 2017, he has been an Assistant Professor with the Department of Computer Science, College of Computing and Informatics, Saudi Electronic University, Riyadh, Saudi Arabia. He has published more than 35 research papers in journals and conferences of international repute, three book chapters, and holds one patent of innovation. His research interests include algorithms, the IoT, cryptography, image retrieval, pattern recognition, machine learning, and deep learning.

Dhaya Ramakrishnan has 16 years-experience in teaching and research in the field of Computer Science and Engineering. She published more than 80 research papers in peer reviewed international Journals. She was the recipient of IEI Young women Engineer award. Her areas of interests are wireless sensor networks, embedded systems, Machine Learning, Communication Systems.

Sidhu Sharma received her PhD in Mathematics from Shri Venkateshwara University UP, India. She has been associated with national and international universities as lecturer and course quality coordinator. She has worked as faculty in MGM's College of Engineering and Technology and Saudi Electronic University in the department of Applied and Theoretical Sciences, Kingdom of Saudi Arabia. She has more than 18 years of experience years of teaching and research. She has many papers in conferences and Journal of repute. His areas of specialization are Machine learning, NLP, Blockchain.

Arish Siddiqui is the Program Leader for MSc Blockchain and Financial Technologies and BSc (Hons) Computing for Business at the University of East London. He joined as a Lecturer at the School of Architecture, Computing and Engineering in 2001. He received his BSc (Hons) in Computer Science from Aligarh Muslim University, India and an MSc in Technology Management from the University of East London. He has also received a Postgraduate Certificate in Teaching and Learning in Higher Education from the University of East London. He was also honoured with an Honorary Professorship at the Hangzhou Dianzi University in Hangzhou, China in the year 2019. He also played a key role in establishing collaboration between Hangzhou Dianzi University, China and University of East London, United Kingdom where he also served as a visiting professor from 2013 to 2019. He was also part of collaboration team in establishing the partnership between Ain Shams University (ASU), Egypt and University of East London, United Kingdom. His main research interest spans the area of Ubiquitous Computing, mostly around interdisciplinary topics covering Blockchain Technology, Cyber Security, Digital Forensics, Social Engineering, Artificial Intelligence, Application Development, Internet of Things, Satellite Communication and GPS, Project Management, E-business, ERP systems. His multi-disciplinary nature of work also emphasises the challenges of solving security and privacy issues regarding Sociotechnical systems. In the domain of rapidly emerging Blockchain Technology, his research focuses on Smart Contracts, Decentralised Applications, Cryptocurrencies, Digital Asset Management and Consensus Mechanism. He teaches various Computer Science and Informatics courses at both Postgraduate and Undergraduate levels. He has contributed towards establishing a University collaboration programme with Hangzhou Dianzi University in China where he was sent on behalf of the University of East London to deliver Information Systems and Mobile Communication Modules. He has co-developed an effective framework for enhancing student engagement and performance in final year projects. He has also demonstrated his knowledge and expertise in the industry as an E-Business Developer and Business Consultant.

Kazi Jubaer Tansen is a PhD Researcher in the School of Architecture, Computing and Engineering at the University of East London. He also received MSc Information Security & Digital Forensics and BSc (Hons) Computer Science degrees from the same institution. His main research interest spans the area of Ubiquitous Computing, mostly around interdisciplinary topics covering Cyber Security, Blockchain Technology, Digital Forensics, Artificial Intelligence and Machine Learning, Data Science and Genomics Data Analysis, Software Engineering, IoT, Satellite Communication and GPS. He has a deep interest in socio-technical security, particularly in the comprehension of risks from the cyber-enabled system and the application of AI and Machine Learning to confront problems related to cyber-crime. In the Blockchain Technology domain, his research focuses on Smart Contract, Consensus Mechanism, Cryptography, Decentralised Application, Digital Asset Management and Cryptocurrencies. He is currently working on a Blockchain-based anti-corruption system.

Taskeen Zaidi is currently working in the School of CS & IT at Jain Deemed to be University. She has 10 years of experience in teaching and research in areas like cloud computing, distributed computing, AdHoc Networks, etc.

Index

5G IoT 75

B

banking 14, 19-20, 54, 57, 68, 126, 149, 191-192, 200, 216, 218-221, 226-235, 237-238
BCT 189, 192-193
Bitcoin 1-3, 5, 9-11, 14, 17-20, 23-24, 26, 29, 34, 37, 42-46, 48, 54, 56, 58, 61-64, 66-69, 74-75, 98-101, 104-105, 108, 110, 126, 134, 143-144, 147, 181, 191, 199, 201-203, 211, 234, 242, 252, 257
blockchain 1-21, 23-39, 41-46, 48-58, 60-81, 85, 89, 94, 98-109, 111-123, 125-128, 130-134, 138, 140-147, 176, 180-182, 184-185, 187, 189-204, 206, 211, 213, 215-242, 244-260
blockchain network 4, 6-7, 16-18, 33-34, 46, 53, 63, 99, 101-104, 181, 191, 196-197, 200, 211, 249
blockchain technology 1-8, 12, 14, 16-19, 21, 25-30, 36-38, 41-42, 48-49, 51-52, 54-58, 60, 62, 70, 75-78, 80-81, 85, 89, 98-99, 102-104, 106-107, 109, 111-112, 120, 126-127, 130-132, 141-142, 144, 147, 176, 181, 184-185, 189-204, 206, 211, 215-234, 236, 239, 241-242, 244, 246, 248-249, 251-256, 259

C

cloud computing 14, 60, 72, 76, 81, 88, 90, 110, 113-114, 149, 151, 173, 182, 189, 194, 202, 209, 255-256

consensus algorithm 18, 20, 22, 24, 27-28, 30, 32-36, 41, 46, 101-102, 107, 116, 242, 249-250
countermeasures 120, 178, 182, 185, 238
cryptocurrency 4, 9-11, 21-23, 34-35, 42, 45-46, 48, 54, 56, 58, 99, 108, 211, 216, 223, 233, 235, 238, 250, 252, 257
cryptography 26, 28, 30-32, 41, 44-47, 71, 100, 102, 129, 163, 181, 199, 223, 236

D

decentralized 2, 14, 16, 18-20, 23-26, 30, 33, 41, 43, 48, 58, 61-62, 64, 69-71, 75, 85, 94, 98-99, 102, 104, 106-107, 109-110, 114, 123, 126-127, 131-132, 138, 142, 145, 180-181, 191-192, 194-195, 198, 200-201, 204, 216-217, 220-221, 223-227, 229-233, 239, 241, 244, 247, 252, 257
decryption 31, 47, 194
digital economy 3, 204-211, 213-215
Digital Rights Management 125-126, 129, 143, 145
digital technology 44, 125, 128-129, 132, 145, 204, 206-208, 210, 213, 258
digital transformation 14, 81-82, 204, 209-210, 233
disruptive technology 29, 48, 50, 53-56, 133, 141
distributed ledger 2, 24, 43, 48-49, 54, 57, 72, 98-100, 102, 106, 109, 125-126, 142, 144-145, 190-194, 201, 211, 222-223, 230, 242, 259
distributed system 1, 4, 127, 173

DLT 72, 98-100, 102, 189, 192, 222-223

E

edge computing 60, 72, 78, 90, 116, 121, 123, 236
e-healthcare 239-240, 243-244, 247, 250, 252
encryption 15, 31, 45, 47, 72-73, 75, 93-94, 100, 112-114, 116, 120, 124, 137, 161-162, 166-167, 172, 178, 190, 194, 200, 246

F

financial services 8, 48, 76, 216
Fintech 211, 233-234, 237-238
foundations 28-29, 64, 132, 210-211

H

hash function 20, 32, 34, 49, 133
hashing 32, 41-43, 45, 47, 100, 126
Health information exchange 254
Health Information Management 239
healthcare 7, 13-14, 20, 28-29, 38, 42-44, 48, 54-55, 57, 80-85, 88, 95, 110-112, 114-115, 119, 126, 153, 155-156, 165, 193, 236, 239-240, 243-260
healthcare industry 44, 80-81, 83-85, 110-111, 244, 257

I

innovation 12, 44-45, 50, 62-65, 68-71, 73-75, 81-82, 118, 139, 150, 157, 205, 207, 210, 213-214, 218, 233-235, 237-238, 259
insurance 7-8, 13, 20, 54-55, 57, 61, 65, 69, 75, 189, 224, 237, 240, 244, 249, 255-260
Intelligent Networks 60, 62, 76-77
Internet of Things 12, 37, 44, 61, 64, 74, 77, 80-81, 84-85, 87, 94, 111-124, 142, 146, 148-149, 155, 158, 164, 182-187, 206, 209, 212, 236, 246-247

K

KYC 189, 193, 220

M

MOOC 189, 194

P

peer-to-peer network 2, 16, 41, 49, 100, 132, 138, 180
permissioned blockchain 30, 43-44, 46, 127, 133, 145, 241, 245, 249
permissionless blockchain 30, 103, 145
platformisation 204-206, 211
PMS 189
private ordering 125-126, 129, 133, 141, 145
proof of authority 35, 45
Proof of Work 13, 17, 20, 26, 34, 38, 40-41, 47, 107-109, 201
Python 28, 31, 38

S

security and privacy 27, 43, 95, 105, 114, 117, 122-124, 138, 182, 190, 201, 236, 240, 243, 250-251, 255, 258, 260
security challenges 91, 121, 162
security requirement 146, 159
smart contracts 12-15, 20, 28, 30-31, 36-38, 42-46, 50, 53-54, 102, 108, 110-111, 115, 125-126, 128, 131-133, 140-143, 145, 190, 195, 198, 200-201, 217, 219, 227-228, 236, 242, 247-249, 252, 255, 257

T

technological protection measures 126, 129-130, 145
trade finance 8, 12, 193, 219, 223-225, 234, 236
Tutorial 28

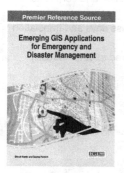
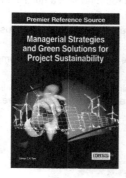

IGI Global Author Services

Providing a high-quality, affordable, and expeditious service, IGI Global's Author Services enable authors to streamline their publishing process, increase chance of acceptance, and adhere to IGI Global's publication standards.

Benefits of Author Services:

- **Professional Service:** All our editors, designers, and translators are experts in their field with years of experience and professional certifications.
- **Quality Guarantee & Certificate:** Each order is returned with a quality guarantee and certificate of professional completion.
- **Timeliness:** All editorial orders have a guaranteed return timeframe of 3-5 business days and translation orders are guaranteed in 7-10 business days.
- **Affordable Pricing:** IGI Global Author Services are competitively priced compared to other industry service providers.
- **APC Reimbursement:** IGI Global authors publishing Open Access (OA) will be able to deduct the cost of editing and other IGI Global author services from their OA APC publishing fee.

Author Services Offered:

English Language Copy Editing
Professional, native English language copy editors improve your manuscript's grammar, spelling, punctuation, terminology, semantics, consistency, flow, formatting, and more.

Scientific & Scholarly Editing
A Ph.D. level review for qualities such as originality and significance, interest to researchers, level of methodology and analysis, coverage of literature, organization, quality of writing, and strengths and weaknesses.

Figure, Table, Chart & Equation Conversions
Work with IGI Global's graphic designers before submission to enhance and design all figures and charts to IGI Global's specific standards for clarity.

Translation
Providing 70 language options, including Simplified and Traditional Chinese, Spanish, Arabic, German, French, and more.

Hear What the Experts Are Saying About IGI Global's Author Services

"Publishing with IGI Global has been an amazing experience for me for sharing my research. The strong academic production support ensures quality and timely completion." – **Prof. Margaret Niess, Oregon State University, USA**

"The service was very fast, very thorough, and very helpful in ensuring our chapter meets the criteria and requirements of the book's editors. I was quite impressed and happy with your service." – **Prof. Tom Brinthaupt, Middle Tennessee State University, USA**

Learn More or Get Started Here: For Questions, Contact IGI Global's Customer Service Team at cust@igi-global.com or 717-533-8845

Publisher of Peer-Reviewed, Timely, and
Innovative Academic Research Since 1988

www.igi-global.com

IGI Global's Transformative Open Access (OA) Model:
How to Turn Your University Library's Database Acquisitions Into a Source of OA Funding

Well in advance of Plan S, IGI Global unveiled their OA Fee Waiver (Read & Publish) Initiative. Under this initiative, librarians who invest in IGI Global's InfoSci-Books and/or InfoSci-Journals databases will be able to subsidize their patrons' OA article processing charges (APCs) when their work is submitted and accepted (after the peer review process) into an IGI Global journal.

How Does it Work?

Step 1: **Library Invests in the InfoSci-Databases:** A library perpetually purchases or subscribes to the InfoSci-Books, InfoSci-Journals, or discipline/subject databases.

Step 2: **IGI Global Matches the Library Investment with OA Subsidies Fund:** IGI Global provides a fund to go towards subsidizing the OA APCs for the library's patrons.

Step 3: **Patron of the Library is Accepted into IGI Global Journal (After Peer Review):** When a patron's paper is accepted into an IGI Global journal, they option to have their paper published under a traditional publishing model or as OA.

Step 4: **IGI Global Will Deduct APC Cost from OA Subsidies Fund:** If the author decides to publish under OA, the OA APC fee will be deducted from the OA subsidies fund.

Step 5: **Author's Work Becomes Freely Available:** The patron's work will be freely available under CC BY copyright license, enabling them to share it freely with the academic community.

Note: This fund will be offered on an annual basis and will renew as the subscription is renewed for each year thereafter. IGI Global will manage the fund and award the APC waivers unless the librarian has a preference as to how the funds should be managed.

Hear From the Experts on This Initiative:

"I'm very happy to have been able to make one of my recent research contributions *freely available* along with having access to the *valuable resources* found within IGI Global's InfoSci-Journals database."

— **Prof. Stuart Palmer,**
Deakin University, Australia

"Receiving the support from IGI Global's OA Fee Waiver Initiative *encourages me to continue my research work without any hesitation.*"

— **Prof. Wenlong Liu,** College of Economics and Management at Nanjing University of Aeronautics & Astronautics, China

For More Information, Scan the QR Code or Contact:
IGI Global's Digital Resources Team at eresources@igi-global.com.

Printed in the United States
by Baker & Taylor Publisher Services